Oracle8 on Windows NT

Oracle8 on Windows NT

Lilian Hobbs

with Ramu V. Sunkara

Foreword by

Ken Jacobs

of Oracle Corporation

Digital Press

Boston • Oxford • Johannesburg • Melbourne • New Delhi • Singapore

 Butterworth-Heinemann suports the efforts of American Forests and the Global ReLeaf program in its campaign for the betterment of trees, forests, and our environment.

Library of Congress Cataloging-in-Publication Data

Hobbs, Lilian, 1959–
    Oracle8 on Windows NT/ Lilian Hobbs.
        p. cm.
    Includes index.
    ISBN 1-55558-190-0 (alk. paper)
    1. Relational databases. 2. Oracle (Computer file) 3. Microsoft Windows NT. I. Title
QA76.9.D3H5867   1998
005.75'85 — dc21   97–46516
                                                                        CIP

British Library Cataloguing-in-Publication Data

A catalogue record for this book is available from the British Library

The publisher offers discounts on bulk orders of this book.
For information, please write:

Manager of Special Sales
Butterworth–Heinemann
225 Wildwood Avenue
Woburn, MA 01801–2041
Tel: 781-904-2500
Fax: 781-904-2620

For information on all Digital Press publications available, contact our World Wide Web home pages at: http://www.bh.com/digitalpress

Order number: EY–W935E–DP

10 9 8 7 6 5 4 3 2 1

Printed in the United States of America

Contents

Foreword

The Windows NT operating system from Microsoft Corporation and the Oracle8 data server from Oracle Corporation represent two of the most important software products of our time. Both are fast-selling products and are popular with small, medium and large organizations.

Microsoft, the world's largest independent software vendor, has been very successful in recent years leveraging its considerable expertise and dominant position in client software and end-user office applications. The company has built on its market success with the MS-DOS and Windows desktop operating systems to enter the multi-user work-group and departmental marketplace with Windows NT. However, the Unix operating system remains very popular for mid-range and high-end environments and complex applications, and many large-scale systems still run successfully on proprietary operating systems like IBM's MVS and Digital's OpenVMS. Many information technology (IT) managers anticipate that the expected release of Windows NT Version 5 will begin to offer the reliability, availability and scalability required by their larger and more important applications.

Oracle is the dominant database system in the industry, with the largest market share for both NT and Unix-based databases. Based on industry standards and an open-systems architecture, Oracle was the first commercially available relational database system and the first that implemented the SQL database language. Unlike Microsoft, which originally focused on client and end-user computing considerations, Oracle Corporation has historically concentrated on data management, servers and enterprise-class applications and services. Oracle Corporation has grown to a $6 billion company, exploiting its core competence of managing large amounts of information and delivering it to large numbers of users across a network, reliably, securely and economically. The Oracle database system has become an important platform for third party developers and independent software vendors (ISVs) who want to offer their services and products to the widest possible market. Today, Oracle Corporation is the second largest independent software vendor in the industry. The Oracle database system has become the standard in many enterprises, which rely on it for some of their most mission-critical applications.

Oracle was the first database management system ported to Windows NT, beginning Oracle Corporation's long-standing and significant commitment to the Windows NT environment. The Oracle database system is developed and released simultaneously on Unix and Windows NT. The Oracle database system is well integrated with Windows NT, using operating system threads and other NT-specific services. Although the command line interfaces common in the Unix environment are provided with the Windows NT implementation, Oracle also provides an extensive set of graphical user interfaces (GUIs) comfortable for the NT user and administrator. Oracle is the leader in exploiting clusters of NT systems to provide high performance and availability. In addition, Oracle offers a comprehensive set of application development tools, application servers and business applications for the NT environment. Oracle Corporation's focus and investment on the NT environment has helped Oracle become the best-selling database for Windows NT, surpassing Microsoft's own SQL Server.

Oracle8 includes features not present in other database systems available for Windows NT. For example, only Oracle employs unrestricted row-level locking and eliminates contention between database readers and writers, maximizing performance and simplifying application design. Oracle Failsafe uses Microsoft Cluster Services to provide fail-over capability from one node to another to provide higher availability, while the Oracle Parallel Server provides concurrent access to a single database from two or more nodes of a cluster of NT systems. Oracle is unique in its ability to provide scalability, availability and performance for database management on NT. Features such as table and index partitioning and incremental online backup and recovery make Oracle8 suitable for mission-critical applications, which employ large databases and require minimal downtime.

Oracle Corporation has long been a leader of the SQL standardization process. Oracle8 has the industry's most robust implementation of the SQL language, with many features that enhance application development and make complex tasks simple. Oracle8 introduces the ability to define and manipulate complex objects, as SQL has been extended with object-relational features such as object IDs, nested tables and methods. New "data cartridges" further extend Oracle's ability to handle such important application data types as text, images, spatial and time series data.

The power of Oracle is complemented with easy-to-use tools for system administration, including remote monitoring and job scheduling. Oracle on NT also supports popular programmatic interfaces for application development such as ODBC, JDBC (for Java) and the high-performance Oracle Call Interface and Oracle precompilers.

The combination of the Oracle database system and the Windows NT operating system represents the best choice for many organizations today. Oracle on NT can reliably support online transaction processing (OLTP) applications that must be used by large numbers of users. Published benchmarks demonstrate that Oracle on NT can provide industry-leading performance for data warehouse applications with databases ranging into hundreds of gigabytes. Even if initial system requirements are more modest, many IT managers choose Oracle (whether on NT or on Unix) for the scalability it can provide to meet growing needs. Some organizations choose the Oracle database system for Windows NT because of Oracle's portability, assuring that applications can be ported to and from Unix-based systems. Organizations that standardize on Oracle can best utilize the skills of their database administrators and application developers by minimizing the number of database management systems they have because Oracle runs on so many hardware and software environments.

This book introduces Oracle as implemented on Windows NT, and is targeted at experienced Windows NT administrators learning about Oracle for the first time, as well as DBAs familiar with Oracle studying the Windows NT implementation. In a simple way, Lillian Hobbs describes the important features of Oracle8 and the responsibilities of the database administrator (DBA), while leaving complexity and exhaustive detail for other sources. The text provides a good overview of essential DBA roles such as creating and configuring a database, managing security, and performing backup and recovery. You will find special value in the author's hints, tips and recommendations offered along the way. Lillian maintains her focus on the NT environment throughout the book. Liberal use of sample dialogues from the graphical user interface give the reader a hands-on sense for the "look and feel" of database administration of an Oracle8 database on Windows NT.

Armed with the information in this book, you'll maximize your own value in the marketplace, as well as the value to your organization of the power of Oracle8 as implemented on Windows NT.

Ken Jacobs

Vice President of Data Server Marketing, Oracle Corporation

Preface

Recently the very popular Oracle database was released on the Windows NT platform. The number of new systems running on NT is growing at an amazing rate and the Oracle database is proving a very popular choice as the database on this platform. Many books have been written about the Oracle database, but usually their focus is on the UNIX platform. This book is different because it is aimed specifically at the user of the Oracle database on NT. All of the examples are form an NT system and extensive use is made in the examples of all the GUI tools that are available on NT.

The chapters are written to follow one another in a logical fashion, building on some of the topics introduced in previous chapters. The structure of the chapters is as follows:

- Chapter 1 introduces the components of Oracle, such as the architecture, the components within the Oracle8 server and how the product is packaged.

- Chapter 2 describes the basic components, what an instance is and how to create and delete a database.

- Chapter 3 introduces the detail of the Oracle database describing the physical and logical components such as tablespaces and datafiles.

- Chapter 4 describes all the components that are used to define the actual database, such as tables, views, indexes and clusters.

- Chapter 5 introduces the SQL language, the powerful PL/SQL procedural language and details about the optimizer.

- Chapter 6 discusses how to manage the database using tools like Enterprise Manager and the routine tasks that must be performed.

- Chapter 7 covers database security which involves defining users, roles and using database privileges.

- Chapter 8 introduces the very important subject of backing up and recovering the database. Here we learn some of the various ways that this important task can be performed.

- Chapter 9 discusses the techniques that can be used to tune the database. Here we can see how to use tools like the Performance Manager, Oracle Trace and Oracle Expert.

- Chapter 10 describes how an Oracle database can be used on a network and how to use it in a distributed environment, replicate it and when snapshots are very useful.

- Chapter 11 discusses is one of the hottest topics, that is how to query and update your database from the Internet or Intranet.

- Chapter 12 informs us about the Oracle Fail Safe product and Oracle Parallel Server.

- Chapter 13 illustrates how the Oracle8 database can become an object database using the objects option.

- Chapter 14 discusses the Oracle database and where it can be used.

Readers who are familiar with the Oracle product could probably skip over chapters three, four and five. However, unless the reader is experienced using the GUI tool Oracle Enterprise Manager, it is suggested that these chapters are not omitted.

8
Oracle

This book has been based on Oracle 8.0.3 release, but it is still relevant to Oracle7 NT users. To help you identify features that are only available in Oracle8, I have marked them as shown to the left of this paragraph.

ACKNOWLEDGMENTS

When one is writing a book, the assistance given by people is very much appreciated, because without them, this book would not have been possible.

For the author the most important people are those who conduct the technical review. This book is lucky to have three excellent technical reviewers, Mark Large, Robert Farringdon and Paul Gaffer.

Mark Large joined Oracle UK in January 1995 as a consultant in Technical Consulting Services and is now a Principal Consultant and Practice Manager of Enterprise Scalable Solutions. He manages a team of 30 people in Oracle who specialise in architecting RAMP systems – Reliable, Available, Maintainable and Performance systems. His practice comprises of four groups – System Performance Group, VLDB/Warehousing, Server Design and TP Systems. Mark has, in his time with Oracle, been involved in a variety of situations from short 'cure my system performance' visits to long term design of VLDB systems where RAMP factor is crucial. He has operated on the international scene both within Oracle and previously with Rdb system tuning, a marketplace where he was well known.

Robert Farringdon is a senior consultant with Oracle Worldwide Customer Support Services in the UK where he provides support to Oracle customers using the database on Windows NT and UNIX. Training courses he has developed in these areas have been delivered to support analysts in Oracle's Global Support Centres in the United Kingdom and United States.

Paul Gaffer is a very experienced DBA with many years service in the industry. Almost since the introduction of Oracle7 on NT, Paul has been building and designing Oracle systems on NT.

When it comes to Chapter 12, the author is extremely grateful to Ramu V. Sunkara for very kindly writing this chapter.

Ramu V. Sunkara is the Director of Fail Safe Solutions product line in the Server Technologies division of Oracle working in the New England Development Centre. He has been working on the Oracle Solutions for NT Clusters for the last 2 years and led the development team that built an early prototype of Oracle Parallel Server for Windows NT that scales for N-Node clusters. Ramu is a frequent speaker at conferences, tradeshows and customer events promoting Oracle solutions. He has worked on distributed database integration, relational query processors, query optimizers, non-relational data access using SQL and access methods during his career at Oracle and Digital Equipment Corporation. He holds an MBA from Boston Univerity, Boston, USA, MS from University of Wisconsin, Madison, USA and a B.Tech from Indian Institute of Technology, Madras, India.

A big thank you also goes to **Steve Hagan,** Vice President of the New England Development Centre and **Susan Hillson** a Senior Director also at the NEDC for giving me with the opportunity to work with the Oracle server.

Everyone at Butterworth-Heinemann has been marvelous in making this book happen. Mike Cash in the UK, Liz McCarthy from the US and everyone on the production team who made this book possible. Finally, a big thank you also to MacBride who does a fantastic job finishing off the layout of the book.

1   Oracle on NT

1.1   WHY USE NT

There was a time when nobody had heard of the Windows NT operating system from Microsoft. Today, it is one of the hottest topics in the computer industry and everyone seems to be developing systems using NT. So what makes NT so special?

Windows NT from Microsoft can be considered an operating system for the 1990s. Unlike other operating systems that were developed many years ago and have matured during that time, NT was not conceived until 1989, when the first specifications of the NT operating system were reviewed. We now live in an age where advances in the computer industry occur very rapidly. Therefore Microsoft wanted to develop an operating system that was:

- portable, so that it can easily move from one processor architecture to another;
- scalable and supported multiprocessing;
- ready to provide distributed computing, by providing services such as file and print servers;
- POSIX compliant;
- class C2 level for security;
- reliable and robust, and applications should not be able to corrupt the operating system;
- fast and provides good performance.

Today Windows NT systems can be found in a very high percentage of IT departments. At some sites, NT systems are being used to replace desktop systems that were running Windows for Workgroup or Windows 95. But increasingly, it is being used as the platform on which new systems are being developed. NT has really proved itself as an ideal platform for desktop and departmental computing. Now with the rapid developments in computer speeds, NT systems are starting to scale and move into supporting enterprise wide systems.

Windows NT (which stands for new technology) is a 32 bit operating system, available in two versions:

- NT Workstation
- NT Server

NT *Workstation* is ideal for people who are developing software and running client applications in a client/server environment. *NT Server* is the version that offers high performance and a secure and scalable environment. Therefore, most Oracle databases will be run on NT Server, but small scale ones could run on NT Workstation. All the examples in this book were run on Oracle8 on NT Workstation.

At the time of writing, the latest version of Windows NT, 4.0 is a reliable and robust platform. Its GUI interface at first makes it very hard for the end user to tell whether the system is running Windows 95 or Windows NT. But it is the ease with which NT systems can be managed and used via their GUI interfaces that helps to make NT systems so popular. Oh, another good reason for using NT is that costs are reduced and the finance department always like to keep the costs down!

1.2   ORACLE DATABASE EVOLUTION

Until recently, anyone wanting to buy a relational database had quite a few to choose from. But now the situation has changed, and in the world of databases only a few product names spring to mind, and Oracle is one of them.

The Oracle relational database is used extensively across a wide variety of applications around the world. Available on many different hardware platforms and operating systems, it is considered a portable database system. Along with its maturity and rich functionality, it is a database that is equally at home supporting thousands of users, a few users or holding the contents of a massive data warehouse or a data mart.

Recently, the Oracle database was made available on the NT platform and NT users now have the ability to use a very comprehensive database system. An important point to remember is that Oracle is Oracle, no matter what the platform. Occasionally there will be features that are not supported on a platform, but these instances are rare. Consequently, anyone using Oracle on NT has access to virtually all the features that for example a UNIX Oracle developer can use. As a result, Oracle on NT offers a rich set of features and provides advanced features like partitioning, sophisticated security and distribution and replication. Oracle8 on NT provides a reliable, scalable, efficient and secure environment, which comes with a comprehensive range of tools for managing the database and is ready to be Web enabled for Internet access.

1.3 ORACLE ARCHITECTURE

The architecture of the Oracle database is shown in Figure 1.1. At first glance it may seem incredibly complex, but one of the nice aspects of running the Oracle8 database on Windows NT is that most of the components are hidden and therefore transparent to the user.

Essentially an Oracle database comprises the actual data files and the System Global Area, which is usually referred to as the SGA, and a number of background processes. There are a number of background processes that perform specific tasks like checkpointing and writing records back to the database. On

Figure 1.1 Oracle Architecture

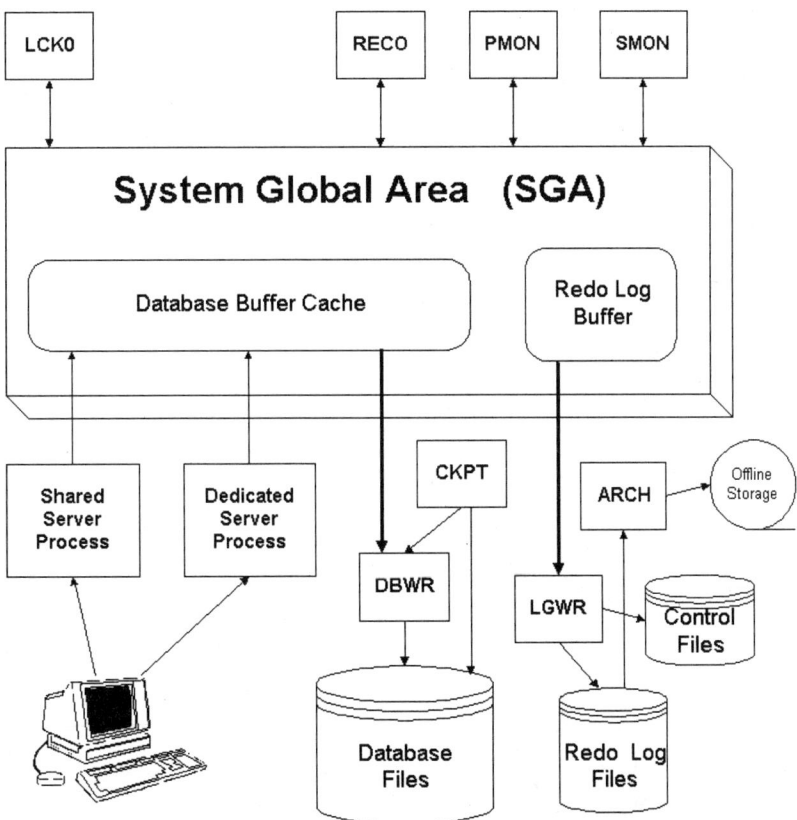

NT, the background processes like DBWR are hidden from the user inside NT threads. Therefore, system managers on NT have to be concerned with monitoring the NT services and the threads that carry out the tasks like DBWR.

However, the description of all these behind-the-scene processes and components is described here to enable the reader to better understand what the Oracle8 database encompasses.

As we will see in Chapter 2, an Oracle database physically comprises three different types of files: the actual database files, redo log files, which are used to reapply changes made to the database, and the control files, which contain specific internal information. Optionally, the contents of the redo log files can be archived to external storage via the ARCH process.

Oracle Instance

Throughout this book, the reader will see references to the Oracle instance. Terms will be used like starting and stopping the instance, so why is the instance a kernel part of the Oracle database? The instance, as illustrated in Figure 1.2 is composed of the SGA, the memory part of the database and the background processes. Therefore, when someone states that the instance has been started, what they mean is that the memory has been allocated and the background processes started. An important part of the database is the initialisation file, which holds parameters that are used to configure the database. It is described in more detail in Chapter 2, but references are made to it in this text.

The *System Global Area* (SGA) includes a group of shared memory buffers, which are the *shared pool*, the *database buffer cache* and the *redo log buffer*. In the *shared pool* you will find the SQL statements that have been applied against the database, their execution plans and the data dictionary. The size of this pool is determined by the initialization parameter SHARED_POOL_SIZE. When data is retrieved or written to the database, it is first placed in the *database buffer cache* the size of which is determined by the initialisation parameters DB_BLOCK_SIZE and DB_BLOCK_BUFFERS. The *redo log buffer* is where all changes made to the database are held before they are written to the physical redo log files. The size of the redo log buffer is determined by the parameter LOG_BUFFER.

Background Processes

Part of the Oracle instance is the background processes shown in Figure 1.1. On an NT system, these tasks are carried out by NT threads. Although they

Figure 1.2 Oracle Instance

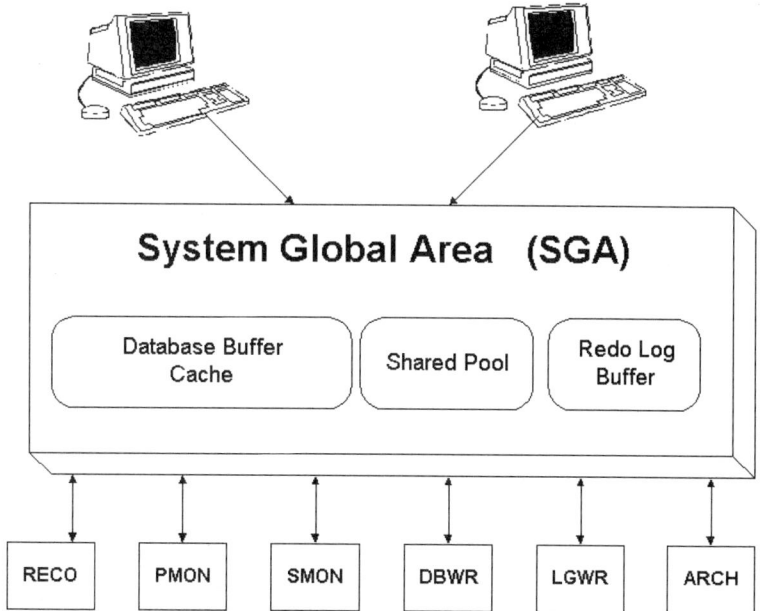

cannot be easily identified, nevertheless, a brief description of each of these threads follows, to help the reader better understand the work being done by the database on the user's behalf.

DBWR, database writer is responsible for writing back to the database records that are contained in the database buffer cache.

LGWR, log writer takes the entries in the redo log buffer and writes them to the redo log.

CKPT, is the checkpoint background process, which at the specified time, updates all the data and control files with the new log file control number.

SMON, stands for system monitor. If the database ever has to be recovered when the instance is first started, then this task is completed by SMON. It is also responsible for reclaiming the space used by temporary segments that are no longer in use and it also merges contiguous areas of free space in the datafiles.

ARCH, the archive log process is responsible for archiving records in the redo log to another file on disk or tape.

RECO, is a recovery process which resolves failures in a distributed transaction.

Three other processes are also worth a mention, however, you are only likely to see them if you are using specific features in the Oracle database.

LCKn is only used when there are multiple instances in a parallel server environment.

Qnnn is a parallel query process which provides parallel operations such as parallel index creation, query and data loading.

SNPn is a snapshot process, used for refreshing snapshots.

1.4   KEY FEATURES

When selecting a database to use on Windows NT, why is the Oracle database a serious contender? Here are some of the key features with respect to using Oracle8 on Windows NT.

- Oracle8 is "The Database for Network Computing"
- Oracle8 Server can be run on Windows NT Server or Workstation
- Only the Oracle8 Client software can be run on Windows 95
- Optimized to take advantage of Windows NT multitasking
- Achieves maximum performance and scalability by using Windows NT multithreaded architecture
- Very rich set of features available
- Many clients can share a few server threads
- Easy to use GUI interface through Enterprise Manager
- Assistants for creating databases and configuring the network
- Integration with the Windows NT Performance Manager, Event Viewer and Registry
- Wizard for creating HTML pages containing information from the database
- Easy to use, GUI based installation
- Distributed and replication support
- Enterprise Manager can schedule and execute jobs, including database administration tasks like backup

Anyone selecting the Oracle database to use on NT should not be disappointed with the wide range of features and the easy to use interfaces available for managing the database. So much of the complexity of the database is hidden from the user that anyone should be able to install the Oracle database and have it up and running very quickly.

1.5   **COMPONENTS OF THE ORACLE8 DATABASE**

The Oracle database is recognized as one of the industry leaders, so why has it become so popular? The Oracle database architecture provides a reliable environment, offering high availability and performance. Listed here is an overview of some of the key features by area.

Performance

- shared database buffer cache
- record level locking
- sequence generator for numeric unique keys
- async I/O for high-performance data access
- multithreaded server architecture
- shared dictionary cache
- fast and group commits
- deferred writes
- extensive stored procedure capability

Data Warehouse

- optimizer enhancements to support data warehouse type queries
- star query support
- query parallelization
- fast data loader
- bitmapped indexes
- hash joins
- data partitioning

Parallel

- parallel execution of table scans, sorts, joins and aggregates
- parallel direct database reads and direct database writes
- parallel CREATE INDEX and CREATE TABLE AS SELECT
- parallel usage is transparent to the application

General

- clustered tables, hash-clusters, and application-specific hash functions
- cost-based optimizer

- web integration
- ANSI/ISO SQL92 entry-level compliant SQL
- server-based business rules
- precompilers
- national language support
- integrity Constraints
- stored procedures
- database triggers

Database Administration

- online backup
- online, parallel recovery
- read-only tablespaces
- mirrored, multisegment logs
- redo logs
- standby database
- Oracle Enterprise Manager GUI for administration
- parallel recovery
- parallel backup/restore utility
- profiles limit user resource consumption
- job queues for automatic scheduling of PL/SQL stored procedure
- table truncate
- enable/disable constraints and triggers

Distributed Database

- a single SQL statement can query data from multiple databases
- transparent two-phase commit mechanism
- access to non-Oracle data
- transparent remote and distributed query
- location transparency, network transparency

Data Replication

- multiple, read-only snapshots (basic primary site replication)
- incremental refresh of snapshot copies
- symmetric replication

- updatable snapshots
- synchronous and asynchronous replication support

Security

- user authentication
- database privileges
- security roles
- auditing
- encrypted passwords

Hopefully, after reading this list, you will now appreciate what the Oracle database has to offer the user.

1.6 WHAT IS NEW FOR ORACLE8

8
Oracle

Oracle8 is a significant new release of the popular Oracle relational database. There are many new features, some significant, other minor. Shown here is a list of some of the new features, but it is by no means a definitive list.

- Partitioned tables and indexes
- Parallel insert, delete and update on partitions
- Ability to enable/disable parallel operations
- Direct load insert
- Backup and restore utility, including an incremental backup
- Parallel recovery
- Recovery Manager
- More hint options
- Import/export by partition
- Deferred constraint checking
- Descending or reverse key index
- Object support
- Image cartridge for storing and retrieving images via an object datatype
- Spatial cartridge for manipulating spatial data
- Account lockout
- Password checking, expiration, history and verification
- Oracle8 advanced queuing

1.7   ORACLE8 PACKAGING

8

Oracle

Oracle8 is available in two forms

- Oracle8 Server
- Oracle8 Server Enterprise Edition

When selecting which product to use, your decision will be influenced by your environment (e.g., a transaction processing system for hundreds of users or a few users, the functionality needed in your system and whether any of the Oracle8 options are required).

The majority of the features described in this book are provided as standard, however some functionality is only available by purchasing special options.

So which product should you use? Well, Oracle8 server is aimed at workgroup and departmental computing, whereas the Enterprise Edition is ideally suited

Table 1.1 Oracle8 Product Differences

Feature	Oracle8 Server	Oracle8 Server Enterprise Edition
Enterprise Manager	Y	Y
Enterprise Manager Performance Pack	N	Y
Fail Safe	Y	Y
Client Failover	N	Y
Server Managed Backup and Recovery	Y	Y
Recovery Catalog for Online Backup	Y	Y
Online Recovery	Y	Y
Incremental Backup and Recovery	N	Y
Parallel Backup and Recovery	N	Y
Point-in-time Tablespace Recovery	N	Y
Advanced Queuing	N	Y
Bit-mapped Indexes	N	Y
Star Queries	Y	Y
Parallel Query, DML, Index Scans, Index Build	N	Y
Basic Replication	Y	Y
Advanced Replication	N	Y

for high volume transaction processing environments and data warehousing. Of course, the Enterprise edition can be used in any environment. An important difference between the Enterprise and Server editions of Oracle8 is the features that are available and the ability with the Enterprise Edition to purchase additional options and select data cartridges.

For anyone who is familiar with Oracle7, Oracle8 Server is the new name for the Oracle7 Workgroup Server and Oracle8 Server Enterprise Edition, is the new name for Oracle7 Server.

To help you decide which version of the Oracle8 server is required, Table 1.1 identifies which features are available in each version.

There are some features that are available in both versions, such as the OCI interface, objects for OLE, the ODBC driver, the ability to execute distributed queries and distributed transactions using two-phase commit protocols, Net8, the security server, reverse indexes and index-only tables.

1.7.1   Options

Even if the Enterprise Edition is used, there are still several options which can be purchased separately and these are shown in Table 1.2 and described in a little more detail here.

Objects Option

8
Oracle

This option is new for Oracle8 and it allows the definition of object types and all the features that use object types, including object tables, object views, the object cache, extended OCI and extended SQL and PL/SQL support of objects.

Parallel Server Option

The parallel server option allows multiple nodes in a loosely coupled system to share access to a single database.

Time Series

8
Oracle

The time series cartridge provides a means of storing time based data easily and efficiently in the database. It provides a comprehensive set of functions, time series and time scaling which can be used via both the relational and object interfaces. It also includes an interface which allows developers to add functions to the cartridge.

Spatial

The image cartridge is used to manage two-dimensional images. It provides compression schemes and the ability to convert images between different formats. The image cartridge can be used by both the relational and the object interface.

Table 1.2 Options

Option	Oracle8 Server	Oracle8 Server Enterprise Edition
Objects Option	N	Y
Partitioning Option	N	Y
Advanced Networking Option	N	Y
Enterprise Manager Performance Pack	N	Y
Parallel Server Option	N	Y

Partitioning Option

The partitioning option is an exciting new feature in Oracle8 that allows indexes and tables to be partitioned. This feature is especially of interest to people building data warehouses and high-end transaction processing systems. By placing data in partitions, I/O can be distributed across the partitions, management can be performed on individual partitions and the optimizer can limit searching to specific partitions. For certain types of applications, significant benefits can accrue from using partitions.

Advanced Networking Option

The advanced networking option provides client/server and server/server network security using encryption and data integrity checking as well as supporting enhanced user authentication services.

Oracle Enterprise Manager Performance Pack

Oracle Enterprise Manager is provided as part of the Oracle8 database. The performance pack is an option which includes six applications for advanced diagnostics, monitoring and tuning of Oracle databases. We will see in Chapter 6 how to use some of the tools.

1.7.2 Cartridges

8
Oracle

Table 1.3 also includes a list of the cartridges available with Oracle8. Which cartridges you want to use will influence your choice of which version of Oracle8 to purchase.

Table 1.3 Cartridges

Data Cartridge	Oracle8 Server	Oracle8 Server Enterprise Edition
ConText Cartridge	Y	Y
Video Cartridge	Y	Y
Image Cartridge	N	Y
Time Series Cartridge	N	Y
Spatial Data Cartridge	N	Y

ConText

Allows text queries to be performed through SQL and PL/SQL. Therefore, client tools such as SQL*Plus, Oracle Forms and Pro*C can retrieve and manipulate text in an Oracle database.

Video

Allows the user to store video files and run videos on clients at their request.

Image

Is a cartridge that allows one to store, retrieve and process two-dimensional bitmapped images.

Time Series

The time series cartridge is for anyone who has to store temporal or time based data. It also contains a comprehensive set of functions for performing tasks relating to calendars and time series.

Spatial

The spatial cartridge is for storing, retrieving and manipulating spatial data.

1.8   INSTALLATION REQUIREMENTS

The Oracle database is very easy to install. On the server it is recommended that you have at least 48mb memory. With memory being so cheap, the more memory that is available, the better the performance will be. Today, it seems that all software requires a lot of disk space and database products are no exception to that rule.

When the product CD is inserted into the CDROM drive, the window shown in Figure 1.3 is displayed. To install the product click on *Begin Installation* and the Oracle Installer will start. The Oracle Installer is very easy to use and it is worth getting to know this tool because from within it you can both install and remove products.

The Oracle Installer can be invoked at any time from the Oracle for Windows NT folder. It is a self-explanatory tool and the reader should find it easy to follow, however, here are a few tips. Referring to Figure 1.4, if we were installing products, then the list of available products would show in the left window. In this example, all we can see is the products that are installed on this computer in the right window.

Figure 1.3 Product Installation

If you click on any of those products, the space used by the product is displayed in the Space Requirements section. To deinstall a product, simply click on the remove button in the center of the window.

Figure 1.4 Oracle Installer

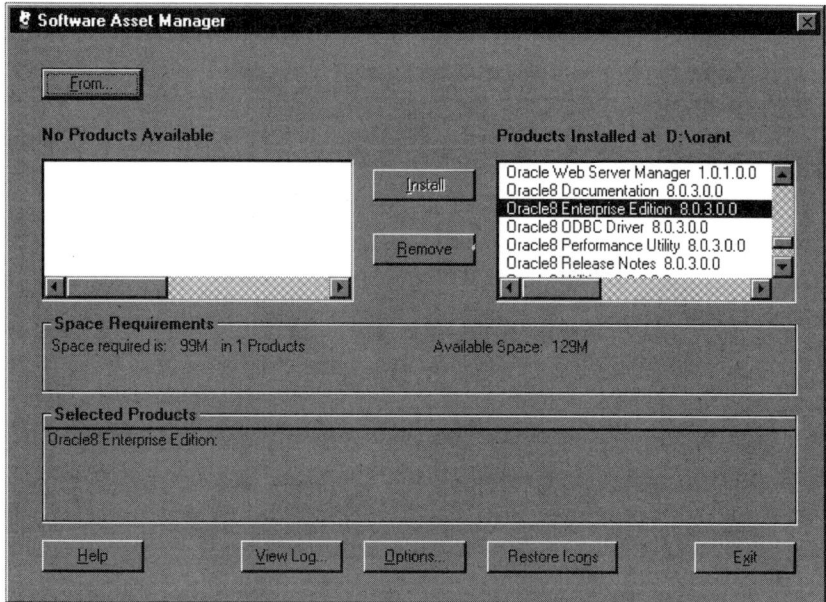

If a product relies on other products, which is quite common in the Oracle environment, then you will be prompted as to whether it is to be deleted. As a rule of thumb, if you are not sure, leave the software there. Generally, dependent software uses minimal disk space and it is best to keep it, rather than delete it and then have to reinstall it again.

1.9 SUMMARY

This has been a brief introduction to the Oracle database product. One can see that it is a very comprehensive database system with a vast number of features and options. Anyone using it on the NT platform should not be disappointed, because it is easy to install and use and requires minimal maintenance. In the following chapters, we acquire more of an appreciation of what the product can do for us.

2   Basic Concepts

Now it is time to start using Oracle8. In this chapter we will learn how to verify that the Oracle8 server is ready to use, then look at how to create a database and which tools to use when working with the database.

2.1   GETTING STARTED

When Oracle8 is installed, it can be configured so that when the computer is started, the Oracle database is automatically available. If at any time the Oracle database is unavailable you are likely to receive the message shown in Figure 2.1 if you are using the GUI tools, or error ORA-1034, Oracle not available on a new connection attempt.

Figure 2.1 Database Not Available

So what does all this mean? When this happens there are two simple checks to make:

1. The Oracle NT Services are running;
2. Oracle Instance has been started.

2.1.1   Oracle Services

A service in NT is a process that performs a specific task and when Oracle is installed it adds its own services to the ones already supplied with the operating system.

The Oracle8 server makes use of NT services which are used by many software products running on NT. For the Oracle database, there are a minimum of three NT services that must be started and there are others which we will see later in this book. For now we will only concern ourselves with the two services which control the Oracle instance and the one controlling the network.

To see which services are running and available on this computer, clicking on the icon in the Control Panel will result in Figure 2.2 being displayed.

Figure 2.2 NT Services

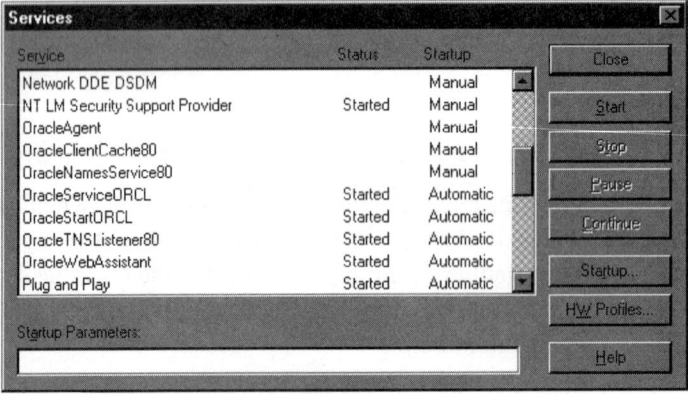

The Oracle Services are easy to identify because they always begin with the word *Oracle.* Referring to Figure 2.2, we can see that there are seven Oracle services. However, we are only concerned for the moment with three of them.

Every Oracle database has a name and an *SID* (system identifier) which is a maximum of four characters. The database services are easy to identify as the SID is included in the service name. The SID for the default database is ORCL, therefore two of the services that belong to this database are called *OracleServiceORCL* and *OracleStartORCL.* The *OracleServiceORCL* service for the database must have a status of *Started* for us to access the database. If the *OracleStartORCL* service is also started, then the database will be opened automatically when NT is started.

Another service that we must also check is *OracleTNSlistener80*, which is part of Oracle networking and must also have been started if we want to use the database.

It is possible to create a new database and change the SID from the default name. If you are new to working with Oracle on NT then it is recommended that you use the default database before progressing on to the advanced technique of using different SIDs. All the examples in this book will use the default database; however, we will customize it to contain our own data.

Once the Oracle services have been started, the Oracle instance must be started using the Instance Manager, Enterprise Manager or via the command line tool server Manager. The database should be open and ready for use. If for any reason it hasn't been opened, then refer to Section 2.5 for details on starting and stopping the Oracle instance.

2.1.2   Logging into the default database

You cannot do anything against an Oracle8 database without a username and password to login to the database. These usernames are different to the ones used to logon on to the NT system and are used exclusively by the database server. By default, several usernames and passwords are supplied, the useful ones to remember are:

Username	Password
internal	oracle
system	manager
sys	change_on_install

Anyone responsible for managing an Oracle8 database should remember these passwords, especially the one called internal. However, don't forget to change them using the Security Manager, otherwise security on your database could be compromised.

Hint: If the default database is created using the Database Assistant custom option, then the password for the internal username will not be oracle and will be whatever was specified by the user

When Oracle8 is installed all the applications are available from the button in the folders.

Figure 2.3 Oracle Folders on the Start Menu

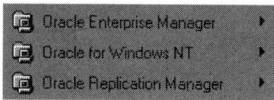

A good test to check that everything is working is to run the application *SQL Worksheet*, which can be found in the Enterprise Manager folder, shown in Figure 2.4, to connect to the default database.

Figure 2.4 Applications available from the Start Menu

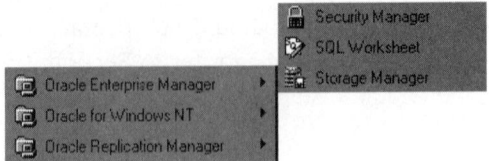

When the SQL Worksheet logon screen, as shown in Figure 2.5 is displayed, enter a valid *username* and *password*, leave the *service name* blank so that it will use the default database and don't change the contents of the *Connect As* box.

Figure 2.5 SQL Worksheet Logon Screen

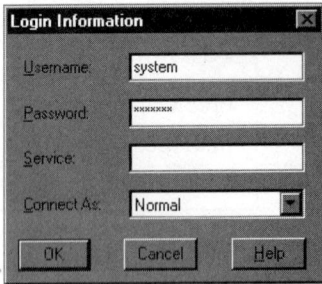

If everything works the SQL Worksheet application will start and you will be connected to the database. Once we know that everything is working, we can start to discover the power of the Oracle8 server. To close the SQL Worksheet, select *Exit* from the *File* menu drop down list.

2.2   THE DEFAULT ORACLE8 DATABASE

When Oracle8 is installed, a default database can be created. It is usually located in *oracle_home\database* and consists of some of the files shown in Figure 2.6. The database is actually only the files with an extension of .ORA. Figure 2.6 does include some extra files plus the archive directory for the redo logs which we will meet later.

There are a number of different types of files that comprise the database which will be described in the next chapter. For the moment all we need to be concerned with is that the actual files containing the data have an extension of .ORA and usually include the SID somewhere in the name (e.g. the SID for the default database is ORCL, therefore the file containing the redo log information is held in LOGORCL1).

Database files don't have to include the SID, but it is a good naming convention to use because it helps easily identify all the files for the database and hopefully avoid accidental deletions.

Figure 2.6 Default Database Files

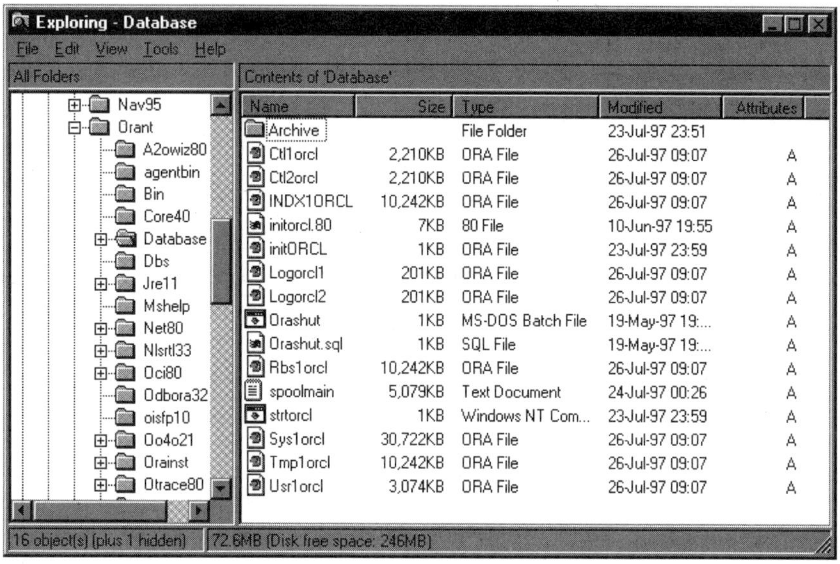

2.2.1 Init.Ora Parameter File

Just because a file has an extension of .ORA, doesn't mean that it is only a database file. Oracle8 requires parameter files and these are also created with an extension of .ORA.

The most important parameter file is the database initialization file, which is often referred to as the init.ora. This parameter file contains all the parameters that are used to start the database. For the default database it can easily be identified as the small file initORCL.ORA. This file is very important, because whenever the database is started, it is used to tell the Oracle8 server how certain features and options are to be used for this database.

2.3   **MANAGING THE ORACLE8 SERVER**

People reading this book who are familiar with Windows based software will probably wonder why this section exists, because the world of Windows usually relies on GUI based tools to interact with the user. However, any reader who has used a database on a typical commercial system will know that often the DBA uses command-line based tools to manage the database.

The Oracle server is a very mature product that is available on a wide variety of platforms and operating systems. Initially its interaction with the user was typically via command-line based tools and it is only recently that GUI based tools have been available. There are three main tools that the DBA can use to manage and access the database:

- Server Manager   command line
- SQL*Plus   command line and GUI
- Oracle Enterprise Manager   a GUI based tool

When the Oracle server was ported to the NT platform, the command line tools were also converted. DBAs who have worked with the Oracle server on UNIX platforms will probably feel far more comfortable using tools like Server Manager and character based SQL*Plus. Throughout this book emphasis will be placed on the GUI based tools because this is the traditional user interface mechanism for the NT platform. However, sometimes we will use tools like Server Manager because it is much faster.

Which tool you use is a matter of personal choice and don't be afraid to use a command-line tool if it is the most appropriate for the job you are doing. GUI tools sometimes feel as if they are slower, especially when you are waiting. But when you consider the benefits of never having to remember the syntax and always completing the task first time, then they are probably faster.

2.3.1   **Server Manager**

This is a command-line tool that is well known to DBAs prior to Oracle8. From within Server Manager you can perform the important database management tasks as shown in Figure 2.7.

It shouldn't really be necessary to use the Server Manager because all these tasks can be performed from within the GUI based Oracle Enterprise Manager. However, if for any reason there is a problem and the GUI tools can't be run, then Figure 2.8 illustrates how to start Server Manager from an MS-DOS window using the SVRMGR30 command.

Figure 2.7 Oracle Server Manager Commands

```
Command Prompt - svrmgr30                                        _ □ ×
SVRMGR> help
The following are SIMPLIFIED syntax descriptions. For complete syntax
descriptions, please refer to the Oracle Server Manager User's Guide.

STARTUP        [DBA] [FORCE] [PFILE=filespec] [EXCLUSIVE : SHARED]
               [MOUNT dbname : OPEN dbname] [NOMOUNT]

SHUTDOWN       [NORMAL : IMMEDIATE : ABORT]

MONITOR        For graphical modes only, bring up a monitor

ARCHIVE LOG    [START] [STOP] [LIST] [NEXT] [<n>] [ALL] ['destination']

RECOVER        { [DATABASE [MANUAL] ] : [TABLESPACE ts-name [,tsname]] }

CONNECT        [username [/password] ] [INTERNAL] ['@'instance-spec]
DISCONNECT

SET            options: INSTANCE, ECHO, TERMOUT, TIMING, NUMWIDTH, CHARWIDTH
SHOW           LONGWIDTH, DATEWIDTH, AUTOPRINT and for SHOW: ALL, SPOOL

EXIT
REM
               SQL statements can also be executed.
SVRMGR> _
```

Hint: Keep the Oracle8 Documentation CD in your CDROM drive and then HELP will always be quickly available.

Figure 2.8   Starting Oracle Server Manager

```
D:\ORANT\BIN>SVRMGR30

Oracle Server Manager Release 3.0.3.0.0 - Production

(c) Copyright 1997, Oracle Corporation.  All Rights Reserved.

Oracle8 Enterprise Edition Release 8.0.3.0.0 - Production
With the Partitioning and Objects options
PL/SQL Release 8.0.3.0.0 - Production

SVRMGR> _
```

Hint: If you are reading the Oracle8 documentation you may see lots of references to the Server Manager tool. This is because the documentation is written for all platforms on which Oracle8 can be used, not just NT, and Server Manager is often the only tool available.

2.3.2   SQL*Plus

Before the introduction of SQL Worksheet in Oracle Enterprise Manager, the application SQL*Plus was the tool a user would use to write SQL commands to apply against the database. SQL*Plus is a typical command line application and for many DBAs this is still the preferred method of writing SQL. From within SQL*Plus, you can issue all your favorite SQL commands that are described in the Oracle documentation.

The alternative to using SQL*Plus is the SQL Worksheet tool which is part of Oracle Enterprise Manager. Which one you use is up to you. This author prefers to use SQL Worksheet because it is a GUI, although you still have to type the SQL statement. To be honest, SQL*Plus and SQL Worksheet behave almost identically. The biggest difference is that SQL Worksheet has two windows, one for the SQL statements and another for the results. On very rare occasions you may find a command that can be used only in SQL*Plus, otherwise the tool to use is your decision. The GUI version of SQL*Plus is started by selecting it from the *Oracle for Windows NT* folder as shown in Figure 2.9.

Figure 2.9 Starting SQL*Plus

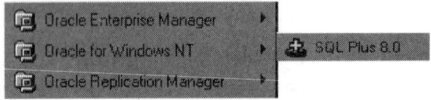

Figure 2.10 Typical SQL*Plus Session (GUI mode)

```
Oracle SQL*Plus
File  Edit  Search  Options  Help

SQL*Plus: Release 8.0.3.0.0 - Production on Sat Jul 26 15:18:39 1997

(c) Copyright 1997 Oracle Corporation.  All rights reserved.

Connected to:
Oracle8 Enterprise Edition Release 8.0.3.0.0 - Production
With the Partitioning and Objects options
PL/SQL Release 8.0.3.0.0 - Production

SQL> create table lilian
  2  (field1 number,
  3   field2 number );

Table created.

SQL> insert into lilian values (1,1);

1 row created.

SQL> select * from lilian;

   FIELD1    FIELD2
--------- ---------
        1         1
SQL>
```

When invoked, SQL*Plus runs in a window and a typical session is shown in Figure 2.10. One important point to bear in mind is that no online help is available. Therefore, if you do not know the syntax for the SQL command you must refer to the documentation.

2.3.3   Oracle Enterprise Manager

Anyone familiar with NT software will expect to use a GUI based tool to interact with the system and the database. So far we have only seen command line based tools such as SQL*Plus. The GUI based tools used to administer the Oracle8 server can be found as part of Oracle Enterprise Manager.

Oracle Enterprise Manager is a very powerful environment and in a later chapter we will learn about the advanced facilities available to the DBA. But first let's see what Oracle Enterprise Manager has to offer. It comprises the main console, shown in Figure 2.11 which is used to administer the databases, and a number of tools for performing database management tasks as shown in Figure 2.12.

Figure 2.11 Oracle Enterprise Manager Console

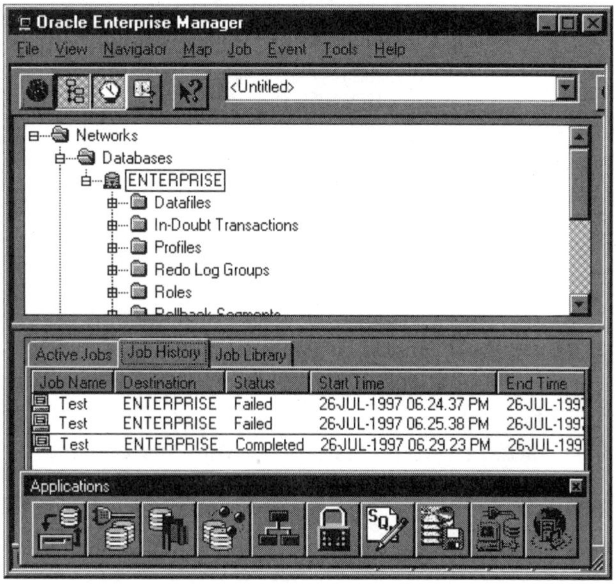

The console, shown in Figure 2.11 comprises a number of windows. In this example there are two, but there can be more. The first window, known as the *navigator pane,* contains every node that can be accessed from Enterprise Manager and the databases that may be monitored.

In Figure 2.11 we can see that in the database section, the computer called ENTERPRISE has been identified as having a database. If we select the database and then click on the icon representing one of the tools listed in Figure 2.12 we will automatically be attached to this database using the selected tool, provided of course, that the username and password defined as part of our credentials, pass the database security checks. Oracle Enterprise

Manager is more than just a launching tool to start a GUI; other facilities include the ability to schedule jobs. In Figure 2.11 we can see the job history for a job called *test* which eventually runs successfuly after two failed attempts.

In order to use Oracle Enterprise Manager it is very important to follow the setup instructions following installation. This involves checking that the NT service *OracleAgent* is running, a suitable NT user has been created and a suitable database user is created.

Hint: If the Discovery process doesn't detect your database, don't continue to use Enterprise Manager until the problem is resolved.

Figure 2.12   Oracle Enterprise Manager GUI Tools

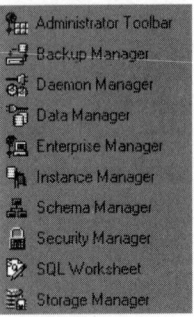

Some of the tools shown in Figure 2.12 can be started directly without the need to have the Oracle Enterprise Manager console running, such as SQL Worksheet, Storage and Schema Manager. Others like the Backup Manager must be started from the Enterprise Manager console.

2.3.4   Administrator Toolbar

One part of Oracle Enterprise Manager that is worth configuring when you first start using the Oracle8 Server on NT is the Administrator Toolbar, shown in Figure 2.13. By default it appears at the top of the screen, but it can be moved to any of the sides of the desktop.

The toolbar can be customized to:

● launch any application;
● logon to the database using a specific username and password.

Figure 2.13 Administrator Toolbar

It really is worth customizing the toolbar because then database applications can be quickly started without you having to specify a username and a password. If you are right handed, simply click the right mouse button anywhere on the toolbar and select the customize option.

Figure 2.14 Customize the Toolbar

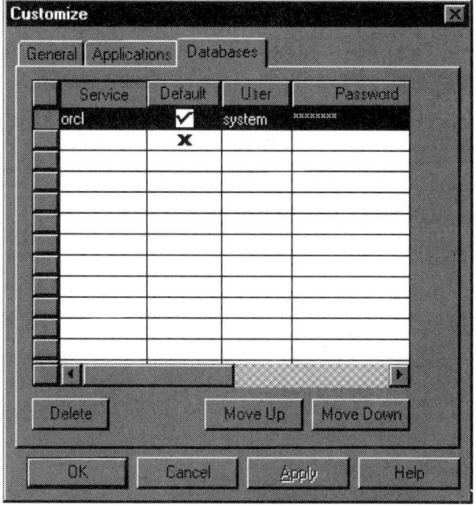

From the *General* tab you can specify where the toolbar should be located on the desktop. The *Applications* tab allows you to specify which applications can be launched from the toolbar and in what order they are displayed. You can add any application to the toolbar; it doesn't have to be a database one and could even be something entirely unrelated to managing the Oracle8 server.

Figure 2.14 shows you how to specify which *database* to connect to. Simply enter the service name; the default service is called ORCL. Then enter the username and the password. Finally, don't forget to click on the default column and change it from the cross to a checkmark. Then this database will be the one that you will automatically be logged on to.

2.4   CREATING A DATABASE

Now that we know how to logon to Oracle, probably the first task you will want to complete is creating a database and several options are available.

- Extend the default database.
- Create a database using the Oracle Database Assistant.
- Create a database using Server Manager.

Many of us will probably want to create a new database, but there is nothing wrong with extending the default database. One important point to bear in mind is that, unlike other database systems that you may have used which result in the creation of multiple databases, it is not uncommon for an Oracle system to use only one database.

As we saw earlier, each database has its own NT services which must be started to use the database. Every time the NT service is created it consumes valuable system resources, therefore it is wise to keep the number of Oracle services running to a minimum.

We will learn in the following chapter how we can easily divide the database internally so that different systems or users' data can be kept apart. This is why throughout the book all the examples will use only the default database although we will see now how to create a database.

OFA Standard

Oracle suggests that systems are constructed using the OFA (Optimal Flexible Architecture) standard. There is an excellent document, written by Cary Millsap of Oracle, called *The OFA Standard – Oracle7 for Open Systems*, which is a set of configuration guidelines for creating an Oracle database. Although written for the Unix and VMS platform, it nevertheless contains some very useful guidelines on how to build high performance Oracle systems, that require low maintenance in an environment that is changing.

2.4.1   Extending the Default Database

If the chosen method is to extend the default database, then you can proceed directly to the next chapter to learn about how to create the various components inside the database.

2.4.2 Using the Oracle Database Assistant

8
Oracle

This is the best method to use to create a database and is an option new to Oracle8. It is a GUI wizard that takes the pain out of creating a database. If you don't use this tool, then you have to follow all the steps described in Section 2.4.3 and use the Server Manager. Why go through all that hassle when this tool does it for you? No more do you have to find a skeleton init.ora file and edit it, then start an MS-DOS session to run Server Manager, then run another application to create the NT services and finally run the Oracle scripts to add the necessary metadata to the database.

Figure 2.15 Running the Oracle Database Assistant

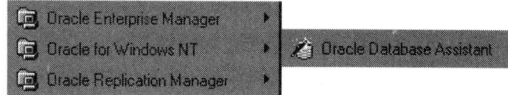

Using Database Assistant you can:

- Create a Database;
- Delete a Database.

When creating a database you can ask for a typical database to be created but it is probably better to select the *custom* option which will give you more control over what is created.

Figure 2.16 shows us some of the simple questions that have to be answered. Every database must have a name which is different from the SID which we met earlier. The *database name* is only used in the initialization file, therefore you don't have to be too careful as to what you choose because you won't refer to it very often.

The *SID*, however, is very important because it is used extensively. Therefore choose a four-character description for your database that you will easily remember. The SID is used in the NT service name and optionally in the database files, which is why it is important to get it right. Once specified it can only be changed by recreating the database, so there has never been a better reason to choose the name wisely.

The *initialization filename* must contain the path and name for the initialization file. By default it will be named init<sid>.ora but you can change it to whatever you like. The initialization file contains configuration parameters that determine how the database instance is started. Since it is read every time the database is started, don't lose this file.

Figure 2.16 Creating a Database Using Oracle Database Assistant

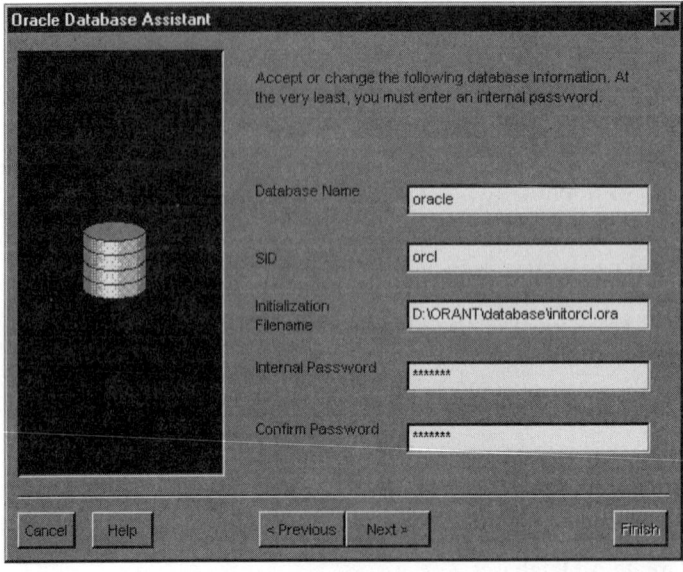

Change for security reason.

Figure 2.16 is where you must specify the *internal* password. This is probably the most important password in the database because it is the one that is needed to start and shutdown the database.

Figure 2.17 Creating a Database Using Oracle Database Assistant

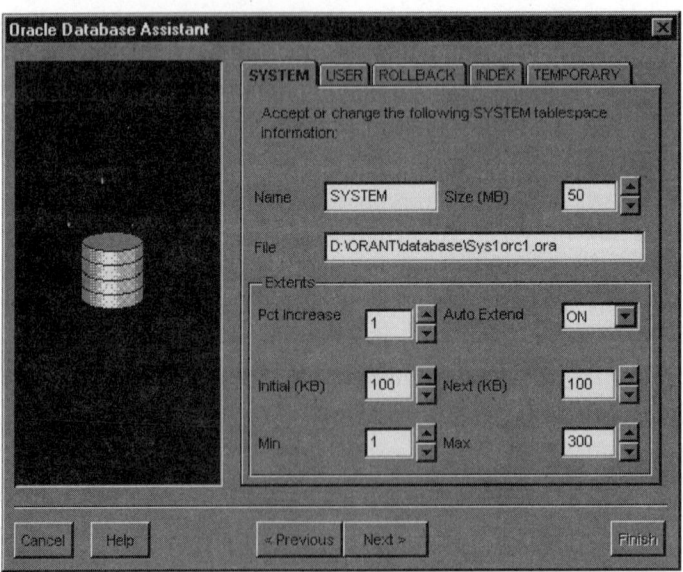

The next screen that the wizard presents asks you to specify the location of the control files. That is followed by Figure 2.17 which contains one of the most important screens. There are five important areas that all require separate areas in the database. Each of these can be customized for location, size and extension options by clicking on the tab and then filling in the appropriate information.

The five key areas that are created using this wizard all result in the creation of actual physical files in the NT system. The first area is the *system* information which should be reserved for Oracle8 server specific information.

The *user* area is created for users' data; however, you will probably want to create additional user data areas, which we will see how to do in the next chapter. It is therefore probably a good idea to make this a small area and keep it for, say, small test tables.

The *rollback* area is used to hold rollback segments, which we will also learn about in the next chapter. Creating this first rollback area is a good start, but you will probably want to create additional rollback areas.

Creating an area specifically for indexes is to encourage good physical database design. Once again you will want to create additional index areas but this is a good starting point.

Finally, there is the *temporary* area that is used by the Oracle8 server when it needs to perform complex operations such as joins, group bys, sorts and creating indexes. If you are going to perform lots of these types of operations it is a good idea to create a large temporary area, which is always at least one block larger than the space required for a sort, for example.

The next screen presented by the wizard asks you where to locate the redo log files and what size to create them. These are very important files because they contain all the changes that have been made to the database.

The following three screens presented to you by the wizard will contain various parameters which you can change. Unless you understand them, take the system recommendations. However, ones that may require modification are the shared pool size, block buffers and database block size because they are fundamental to the overall performance of the database.

Finally, the wizard will ask you whether to create the database or provide a script for you to create it later. If you choose this option then you could create the database later using Oracle Server Manager. Otherwise the database will be created and you can monitor its progress. Depending on the options selected and the hardware available it can take quite a few minutes. This can be a good time to take a break, but don't tell your manager that I suggested it.

2.4.3   Using Oracle Server Manager

Anyone who has used the Oracle server prior to Oracle8, most likely used Server Manager to create their database. There are a number of steps to follow if this method is used. Before the database can be created an initialization file is required. A default one is provided in *oracle_home\database* which must be edited and renamed to the new database. Next, Server Manager is started and the CREATE DATABASE statement is used to create the database. Then the utility ORADIM80 must be run to create the NT services for the database. Finally, the scripts *catalog.sql* and *catproc.sql* must be run to create some special views that are required by the Oracle Server. Now the database is ready for use. With all these steps to remember, it is easier to use the Database Assistant and let it be responsible for doing everything in the correct order.

2.4.3.1   Initialization File

The database cannot be created without an initialization file. A simple one is located in *oracle_home\database*, which can be edited, renamed and used to create the database. A typical initialization file is shown in Figure 2.18 with the names in bold being the ones that you will want to customize to your own environment. As we proceed through this book we will learn about the impact that most of these parameters have on the database.

Figure 2.18 Typical Oracle Initialization File

```
background_dump_dest = d:\orant\rdbms80\trace
compatible = 8.0.3.0.0
control_files = (d:\orant\database\ctl1orc2.ora,
d:\orant\database\ctl2orc2.ora)
db_block_buffers = 200
db_block_size =2048
db_files = 100
db_file_multiblock_read_count = 8
db_name = oracle
dml_locks = 100
log_buffer = 8192
log_checkpoint_interval = 8000
log_checkpoint_timeout = 0
max_dump_file_size = 10240
remote_login_passwordfile = shared
shared_pool_size = 6500000
sort_area_size = 65536
user_dump_dest = d:\orant\rdbms80\trace
```

Good values to set for *db_file_multiblock_read_count* are 8, 16 and 24, depending on the quantity of data that must be read by the application. The *log_buffer* parameter can take any value that is a factor of 2 up to 32k. The *log_checkpoint_interval* should be set as large as possible to prevent the system checkpointing too frequently. If your application will be doing a lot of sorting, then increase the size of the parameter *sort_area_size*.

Hint: Don't make the shared_pool_size and db_block_buffers too large or it will consume all of the available memory and your system will run slowly.

2.4.3.1 Create the Oracle NT Services

Before the database is created the Services required by NT which run the database must first be created using the *oradim80* command. Below is a typical script to create it for a database called ORC2.

```
ORADIM80 -new -sid orc2 -intpwd password -startmode auto
-pfile d:\orant\database\initorc2.ora
ORADIM80 -startup -sid ORC2 -starttype srvc,inst -usrpwd
password -pfile d:\orant\database\initorc2.ora
```

If you are replacing a database and the NT services already exist then this step can be omitted.

2.4.3.2 Create the Database

Now the moment has arrived to create a database. Figure 2.19 contains a typical script which could be used to create a basic database to which datafiles can be added. Of course, if the Database Assistant is used to create the database then script files like this do not have to be created and tested. The Database Assistant will create the database successfully first time; anyone creating a script file such as that shown in Figure 2.19 will probably fail the first time due to a syntax error.

In this example we connect to the Oracle8 server using the internal username and password. The NT instance is started in *nomount* database mode because we don't yet have a database, using the initialisation file that we just created. Then the database can be created using two log files and some datafiles.

Figure 2.19 Script to Create a Database

```
SPOOL  d:\orant\database\spoolmain
set echo on
CONNECT      internal/password
STARTUP NOMOUNT pfile=d:\orant\database\initorc2.ora
CREATE DATABASE orc2
LOGFILE 'd:\orant\database\Log1orc2.ora' size 200K,
   'd:\orant\database\Log2orc2.ora' size 200K
MAXLOGFILES 32
MAXLOGMEMBERS 2
MAXLOGHISTORY 1
DATAFILE 'd:\orant\database\Sys1orc2.ora' SIZE 50M
MAXDATAFILES 254
MAXINSTANCES 1
CHARACTER SET WE8ISO8859P1
NATIONAL CHARACTER SET WE8ISO8859P1;
SPOOL OFF
```

2.4.3.3   Creating Tablespaces and Rollback Segments

We now have a basic database, and the next step is to add tablespaces for the Oracle8 server and some rollback segments.

Figure 2.20 Script to add Tablespaces and Rollback Segments

```
CREATE TABLESPACE TEMPORARY DATAFILE
'd:\orant\database\tmp1orc2.ora' SIZE 10M
STORAGE     ( INITIAL 1M  NEXT 1M ) ;
ALTER DATABASE DATAFILE
   'd:\orant\database\tmp1ORC2.ora'   AUTOEXTEND ON;

CREATE ROLLBACK SEGMENT rb1 TABLESPACE 'rbs'
STORAGE ( INITIAL 50K NEXT 50K
      MINEXTENTS 2 MAXEXTENTS 121 );
ALTER ROLLBACK SEGMENT 'rb1' ONLINE;
```

Tablespaces are the place in the Oracle8 database where information is stored and we will learn more about them in the following chapter. Rollback segments are used to return the database to its original state if we decide to back-out the changes we have just applied. We need these database structures to enable us to finish creating the database. Don't worry if they seem a bit confusing at the moment, all will become clear very soon.

2.4.3.4   Database Scripts

As you work with Oracle8 databases you quickly learn that you frequently have to run database scripts containing SQL against the database. The purpose of these scripts is to populate the system metadata with views and tables and stored procedures. They can be run from any application that supports SQL, such as SQL*Plus, SQL Worksheet and Server Manager.

The scripts reside in various locations, but the ones we are interested in to finish creating the database are in *oracle_home\rdms80\admin*. These scripts should be run when the user is connected as internal and not as the user system.

catalog.sql	creates the data dictionary views
catproc.sql	enables PL/SQL use for this database
utlxplan.sql	to use the explain plan feature

Running the scripts are the final step. The database is now ready for use.

2.5   STARTING AND STOPPING THE INSTANCE

Every Oracle8 database runs in what is known as the *instance*. Therefore, before any work can be done against the database, the instance must be started and then stopped when it is no longer required.

Within Oracle Enterprise Manager there is a tool called the Oracle Instance Manager which should be used to start and stop the Oracle8 instance. In order to use it, you must first login using, for example, the internal username and password that has the privileges required to manage the database.

Figure 2.21 Login to Oracle Instance Manager

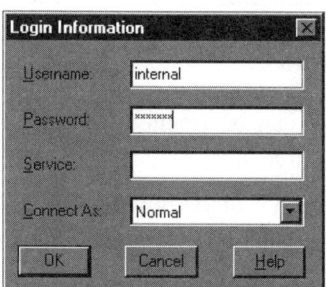

Hint: If you get the message ORA-1031, insufficent privileges, then you may have entered the wrong password.

Figure 2.22 shows us the Oracle Instance Manager, which can do a lot more than just start and stop the instance. The traffic light tells us instantly what state the database is in; green means open and ready for users.

From here we can also manage different startup configurations, change the initialization parameters and monitor who is accessing the database.

Figure 2.22   Oracle Instance Manager

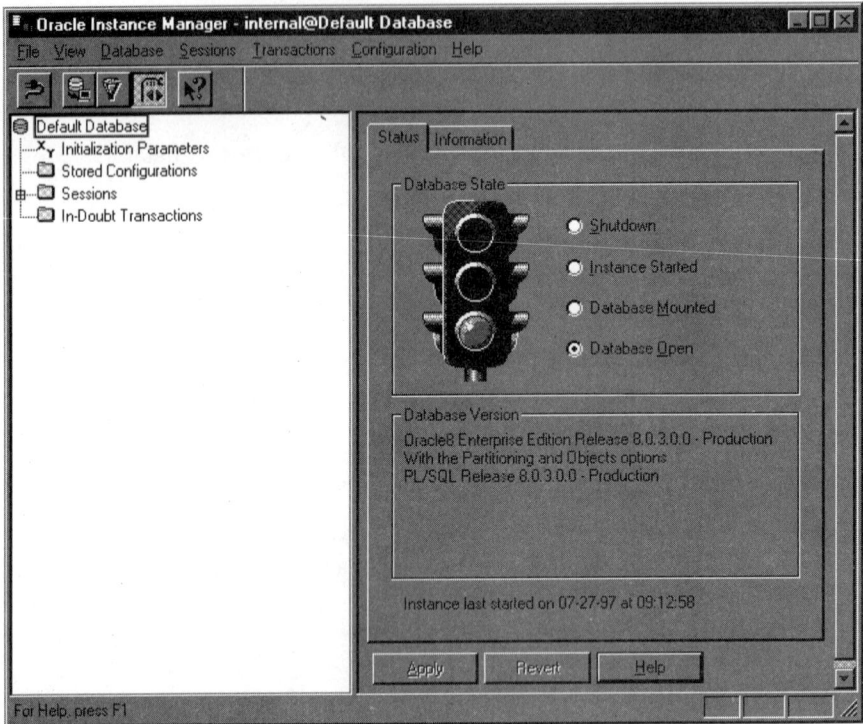

2.5.1   Instance Start Modes

Before the database can be opened, the appropriate startup mode must be selected. There are three start modes.

Instance Started, which is also known as NOMOUNT, is used when you want to create a database. It has the effect of starting the Oracle instance but not opening a database.

Database Mounted, which is also known as MOUNT, is used when recovery of the database or maintenance on the database or control files must be performed.

Database Open, which is also known as OPEN, is the mode most frequently used because it allows everyone to access the database.

To open the database, simply click on the appropriate option and click on the *Apply* button. You will then be prompted for the initialization file, as shown in Figure 2.23, which can either be a previously stored configuration or you can point to an actual file on one of your disks.

Figure 2.23 Start the Instance

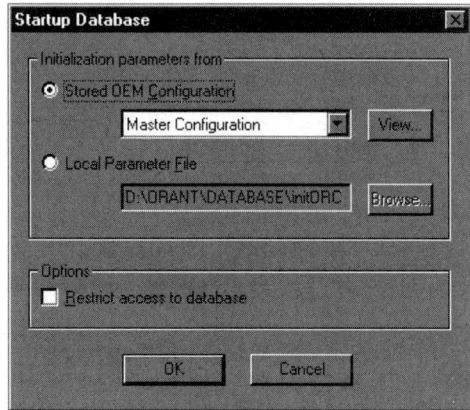

Starting the instance is normally a very quick operation for small to medium-sized databases. If you will be starting the instance using different parameter values then it is a good idea to build up a library of stored configurations as described in Section 2.5.3.

2.5.2   Stopping the Instance

To stop the instance select *Shutdown* and then click on the button marked *Apply*. Then choose how you want to close the database.

Normal should be selected when you want to prevent any new users from accessing the database, but allow existing users to finish what they are doing. The database will only shutdown when all existing users have disconnected. Although this is a very friendly mode, it does rely on existing users disconnecting from the database when they have finished, and we all know that users cannot always be relied upon to do this!

Immediate mode closes the database immediately. All open transactions are rolled back and all users are disconnected. This is a very safe method to use to close the database, but unfortunately, it doesn't give any of the users a chance to finish what they were doing. Therefore if you use this method, be prepared to suffer the wrath of the users if you stop them in the middle of something very important.

Figure 2.24 Shutting down the Instance

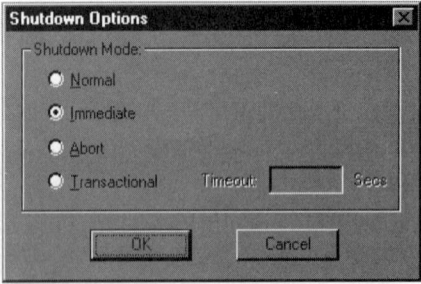

Abort mode should be used with extreme caution because it shuts down the instance immediately, terminating all user connections and not rolling back open transactions. Therefore when the instance is started again, database recovery must be performed before the database is available for use. Be extremely careful about using this option and use it only as a last resort.

2.5.3   Changing Instance Values

We saw earlier how important the initialization file is as an integral part of the database. From the Instance Manager we can see what values are actually being used. Referring to Figure 2.22 the first window contains a hierarchy, and if we click on *Initialization Parameters* we can see the values being used by the instance, as illustrated in Figure 2.25.

Hint: Click on View and then Advanced to see additional instance parameters.

To change any of the values simply click on them, edit the value, and then save them to a configuration file. Not all of the parameters can be changed immediately, therefore you may be asked if the instance can be shutdown and restarted. Answering yes will do this automatically, so your only concern is affecting any users currently accessing the database.

Every time you change these parameters you will be prompted to save the configuration. Therefore it is a good idea to give them a sensible name and they will appear in the left window in the *Stored Configurations* section. When the database is opened, each of these saved configurations will appear in the drop down list, and it's easy to choose the right one.

Figure 2.25 Changing the Instance Values

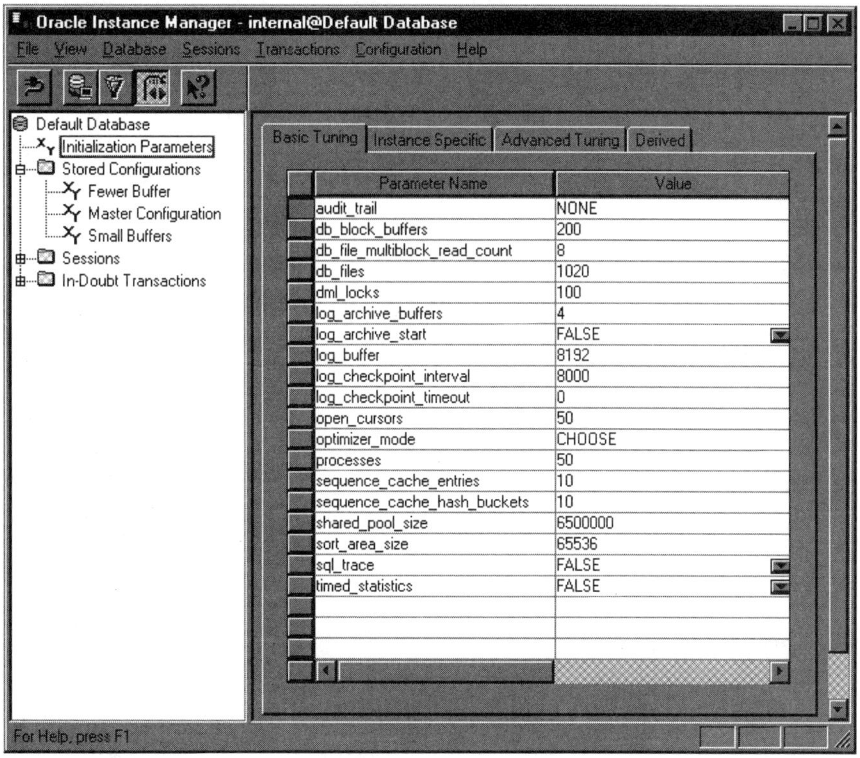

2.6   DELETING THE DATABASE

If a database must be deleted then use the Database Assistant, which we met earlier, which will remove the database and its NT services, thereby removing all reference to the database.

Prior to Oracle8, the only way a database could be deleted was to manually remove all its files, because there was no equivalent delete database command. Therefore the preferred and safest method is to use the Database Assistant. An important reason for not manually deleting the database is that the NT service for the database will not be removed. To remove the NT service use the application ORADIM80.

2.7   HOUSEKEEPING

Have you noticed how when you click on the Oracle for Windows NT folder from the  　 button a very long list of programs and documents appear?

If, like me, you find this untidy and hard to locate the application of interest, take a few minutes to structure this into a more meaningful grouping.

Using the right mouse button, or the left one if you are left-handed, click over the *Start* button and select *Open All Users*. Then double click on *Programs* and then double click on *Oracle for Windows NT*. Now click on *File*, then *New*, then *Folder* to create the categories you require. You will probably want to create around three or four new categories. Now select the icon and drag it to the folders that you have just created. Repeat this process for all the icons that you would like grouped together. Finally, close all the windows for the Start menu and Programs that you have just entered. Now click on the Start button and select Oracle for Windows NT to see the final result. Hopefully, you will agree that this has been a few minutes wisely invested.

2.8   USING ORACLE HELP

Unless hardcopy documentation was ordered, your Oracle8 kit will come with the documentation on a CDROM. To many people this may take some getting used to, especially if you are used to thumbing through a book. However, I think that you will soon find that having the documentation on a CDROM has distinct advantages, and think of all that shelf space you will save!

The documentation is available in HTML format and when viewed through a frames-enabled browser you can search it very quickly. Help is started by opening the welcome document, which will result in two windows being displayed, the main browser window and the Oracle Information Navigator, as shown in Figure 2.26.

Figure 2.26 Oracle Information Navigator

The Information Navigator displays all the books that are available. By click-ing on the search icon, you can quickly find any reference to the topic you are interested in. In Figure 2.27 we see where there are references to the word "partitioning," and by clicking on the reference we can go to precisely that page in the book. No more does one have to search through lots of books trying to find information.

One of the nice features of having the documentation in HTML is making use of the hypertext links. Now, when you are reading a page, and it makes a reference to another book or page you can instantly go to that page. There has never been a better reason to upgrade to a browser that supports frames.

Figure 2.27 Searching the Documentation

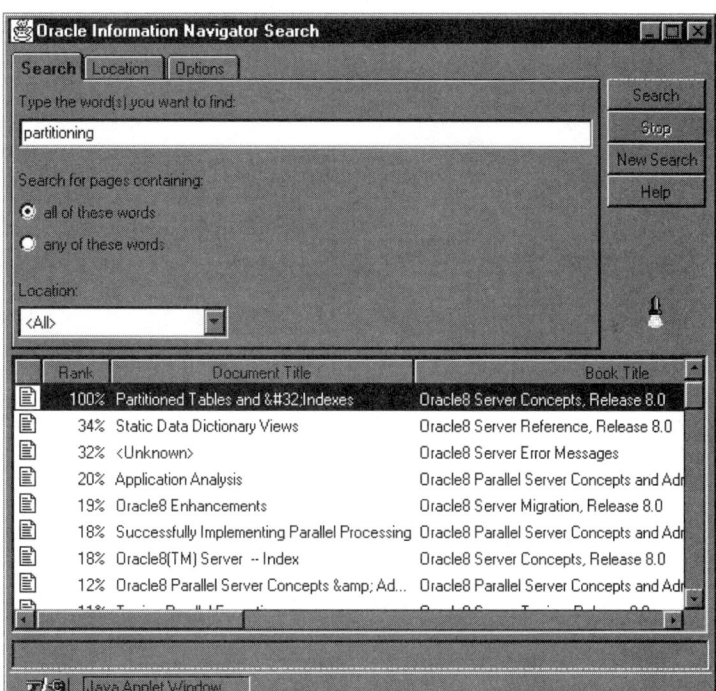

2.9   SUMMARY

By now you should have a basic understanding of what is involved in creating an Oracle8 database, how to start and stop the database and the tools that are available to access and manage it. Now it is time to move on and learn about the components of the database.

3   What Is an Oracle Database?

This chapter describes the parts that make up an Oracle database. We will learn about components such as the control files, datafiles, tablespaces and redo logs.

3.1   ORACLE DATABASE PHYSICAL OVERVIEW

An Oracle database comprises a number of physical files, as illustrated in Figure 3.1 which will be one of four different types:

- Control files;
- Datafiles;
- Redo Log files;
- Parameter.

All of these files can be located on different disks on your system; in fact, it is recommended that they are not all located on the same disk, if at all possible.

Figure 3.1 Physical Components of an Oracle8 Database

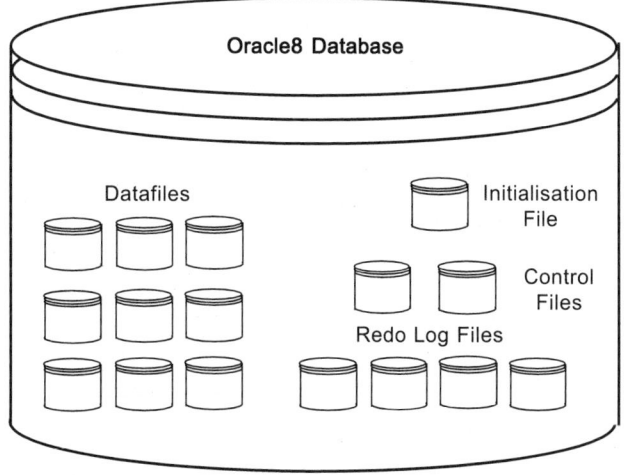

Of course, if you are building a small test database then this is not so important, but for a production system it is wise to try and minimize the number of files to recover in the unlikely event of a disk failure. Some of the files such as the control and redo logs, can have multiple copies which are automatically kept up to date by the database server. For a production system, it is wise to take advantage of this feature.

When the physical files are created they can have a file extension of whatever you like; however, it is probably a good idea to name them all .ORA so that you know they belong to the database server.

3.2   CONTROL FILES

When we created our database in the previous chapter, in the initialization parameter file we specified the location and name of the control files. These are a very important part of the Oracle8 database because they hold:

- details of the files that comprise the database

- name of the database

- information needed to recover the database

They are tiny files, typically less than 3K each, but lose them and the database is unusable because they are needed to start the Oracle instance.

Therefore it is wise to have several control files, at least three, and locate them on different disks. The Oracle8 server will ensure that all the control files are kept up to date.

The location and name of the control files is determined by the initialization parameter CONTROL_FILES. No routine maintenance is required on these files; just ensure that they are backed up along with all the other database files. There is a CREATE CONTROLFILE command available for use in emergencies, but only use this after carefully reading all the advice and instructions in the documentation.

Whenever changes are made to the database, the control files can be backed up before and after using the ALTER DATABASE BACKUP command which is illustrated below.

```
ALTER DATABASE BACKUP CONTROLFILE TO
    'd:\orant\database\bkp_control';
```

Another important step which is often omitted, is ensuring that SQL script files are updated so that the changes can be reproduced. A script file, containing the initialization parameters and the SQL to create the database can be obtained by adding the clause TRACE to the previous command.

```
ALTER DATABASE BACKUP CONTROLFILE TO TRACE;
```

This statement writes all this information into the database trace files, which can be found in the folder specified by the initialization parameter user_dump_dest.

3.3   INITIALIZATION OR PARAMETER FILE

We have already seen that some of the information used to describe the database is held in the control files, but most of it is held in a parameter file, which is known as the initialization file or init.ora, which we saw in Section 2.4.3.1.

Unlike the control files, which are held in a special Oracle format, the parameter file is a simple text file that is designed to be edited using your favorite text editor.

It is an extremely important file, because without one containing the correct values, it will not be possible to access the database. Therefore, once again, multiple copies of this file should be retained on different disks and a hard copy of the parameters. The initialization file is important because it contains:

- parameters that determine the size of the SGA;
- location of files such as control and dump;
- database block size;
- parameters for tuning the database;
- database limits, e.g. number of users.

The initialization file is only read when the instance is first started, so any modifications made to it will not take effect until the instance is restarted.

There is a large number of parameters that can be defined and a list of them can be found in the Oracle8 Server Reference Guide. Throughout this book references will be made to parameters that can be included in this file.

Comments can be placed in the parameter file, as shown in Figure 3.2, by starting the line with a #. This is a good practice to maintain because then anyone looking at your parameter file will understand why these values have been chosen.

Hint: It is a good idea to define your parameters in alphabetic order, then they will be easy to find.

Figure 3.2 Sample Initialization File with Comments

```
# Parameter File for Lilian's Test Database
#
control_files =
(d:\orant\database\ctl1orc2.ora,
d:\orant\database\ctl2orc2.ora)
# Using only 50 buffers since this is a configuration
for a small database
db_block_buffers = 50
db_files = 25
db_name = oracle
```

If you are likely to want to start the database using different configurations, such as a smaller number of buffers, this can be achieved in several different ways. One method is to create parameter files for each set of values and select which one to use when the instance is started. Alternatively, consider using the *Stored Configurations* option, part of the Oracle Enterprise Manager Instance Manager GUI, which was described in Section 2.5.3. Using this approach many different configurations can be created which are then held with the database. When the instance is started using Instance Manager, you can then select which configuration you want to use, as shown in Figure 3.3.

Figure 3.3 Using Multiple Configurations

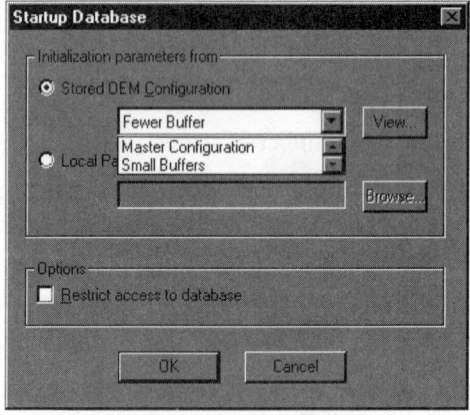

However, don't rely only on keeping the different configurations here. As a safety measure use the *Export to File* option, which can be found on the *Configuration* menu, to save a copy of the parameters in an ordinary file.

Hint: If the initialization file is not subject to change, consider storing a copy on a floppy disk and store it with other essential disks, such as the emergency repair disk and disk configuration disk.

3.4   REDO LOGS

One of the reasons that you are using a database is likely to be the ability to recover all the completed transactions in the event of a failure. Suppose some hardware failure occurs and the fastest way to restore the system to normal operation is to restore the database from the last backup. But that only restores the database to the state it was in at the last backup. To bring the database to the state it was in at the time it failed, the archived redo log files and current redo log files are used to recover the database and apply all the changes made to the database since the last backup was taken. Therefore the redo log files are another very important part of the database because they hold a copy of all the changes that have been applied to the database.

It is essential that the database is run in archivelog mode, which keeps copies of the redo logs before they are overwritten.

There must be at least two redo log files, which are written to in a circular fashion. Since the contents of these files are so valuable, the redo log files can be multiplexed. That is, each set of redo log files is grouped together and whenever anything is written to the redo log, each group is written to simultaneously. Therefore the Oracle8 server is responsible for ensuring that every redo log contains exactly the same information. If each group is located on different disks, then if one disk containing the redo logs was to fail, their contents would still be available on another disk.

One very important thing to remember with the redo log files, is that they are written to in a circular fashion. That is, when one log is full, the next redo log is selected, as shown in Figure 3.4. If the contents of the full redo log are not archived to another file, they will eventually be overwritten when it is time to start writing to this redo log again. To ensure against data loss, what is known as archivelog mode must be enabled.

Figure 3.4 Redo Log Files

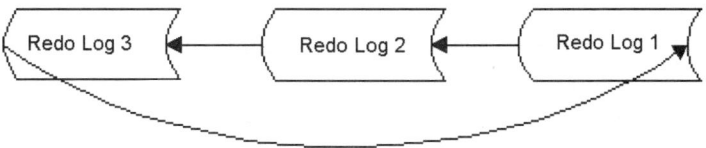

In Figure 2.17 we saw the syntax for creating a database and defining the redo log files using the LOGFILE clause. Alternatively, the Database Assistant prompts for their name. Once the database has been created, additional logfiles can be created using the ALTER DATABASE command.

3.5   ARCHIVELOG MODE

When the archivelog mode is enabled, once a redo log file fills up, the switch is made to the new redo log file, and the contents of the previous redo log file are archived to another file. Since the redo log files are written to in a circular fashion, we could only restore the database to the last backup instead of to the current position. If archivelog mode was enabled, then using the archived log file and the current redo logs, we could restore to the latest position.

Archivelog mode is not enabled by default and is turned on by setting the following initialization parameters:

```
LOG_ARCHIVE_START = TRUE
LOG_ARCHIVE_DEST        = pathname for storing the file
LOG_ARCHIVE_FORMAT      = filename
```

It can also be started from the Instance Manager, but this doesn't permanently set the mode to run every time the instance is started. Therefore, the initialization file must still be modified with these parameter settings.

If a sensible naming convention is used for the filename, then if several archived redo logs are needed for recovery, it will be easy to identify which ones are needed and in which order to apply them. The name of the file can include any literals and the following variables:

```
%s      log sequence number
%t      thread number
```

The file could be named LOG_ARCHIVE_FORMAT = "LOG%s_%t.ARC", which would result in the redo log being archived to a file called *log1_1.arc*

We will learn how to recover a database using the archive logs in Chapter 8.

When deciding where to store the archive log, it is important to make sure that a location is chosen that has plenty of disk space and that sufficient redo logs are available. If the archive process cannot write the redo records into its area, the database will be suspended until space becomes available. A strategy should be put in place for moving the archived files from this area to another location.

In the folder pointed to by the initialization parameter *user_dump_dest*, a number of trace files are created. These can be used to determine if the process is working efficiently and not impacting upon system performance.

Hint: Periodically check the trace file called <instance>ALRT to see if archiving has been suspended.

3.6 DATAFILES

An Oracle8 database comprises mainly of datafiles which contain all the tables and indexes. These datafiles can be located on any disk and can vary in size. They are maintained using the Oracle Storage Manager which is shown in Figure 3.5. The Storage Manager is a very useful tool because it enables you to see at a glance, where the files are located, their size and how much free space is available.

Figure 3.5 Oracle Storage Manager

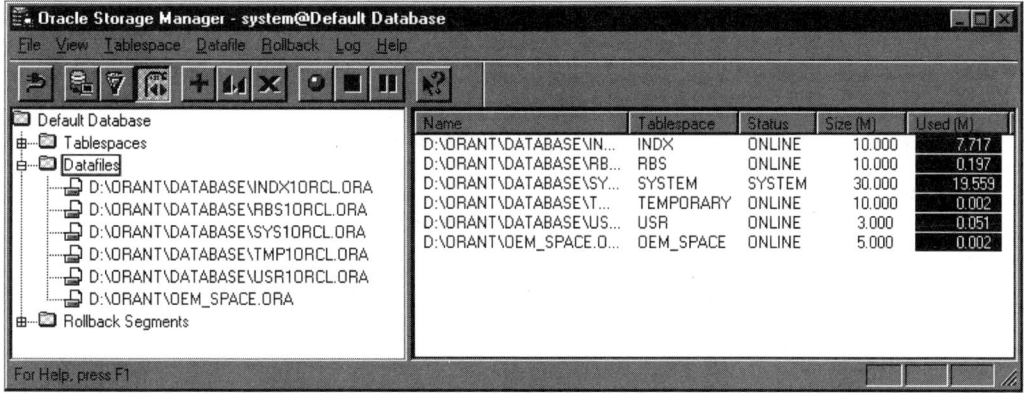

New datafiles can be created using the Storage Manager by selecting *Datafile* from the strip menu and then *Create*. To create a datafile the two boxes shown in Figures 3.6 and 3.7 must be completed. First give the datafile a name, specifying the disk, folder and filename, for example,

e.g. D:\ORANT\DATABASE\INDX1ORCL.ORA

The naming conventions for datafiles are entirely a personal decision, but OFA suggests that database files should be named so that:

- database files are easily distinguishable from other files;
- files of one database are easily distinguishable from files of another;

- control files, redo log files, and data files are easily distinguishable from one another;

- the association of data file to tablespace is easily identifiable.

Next specify which tablespace will use the datafile, and whether the datafile is to be online or offline; choose offline and no one can access the database. Then specify the size of the datafile and click on the M or K button.

All the datafiles are created fixed in size. If you try to store data in the files and there is insufficient room, an error will be returned. In some cases this may be acceptable, but often it can be very annoying because usually it means that you have to repeat the job that just failed. To avoid this situation, at any time, click on the name on the datafile in the navigator window on the left, and Figure 3.6 is displayed, which contains the attributes of the datafile.

Figure 3.6 Datafile Attributes

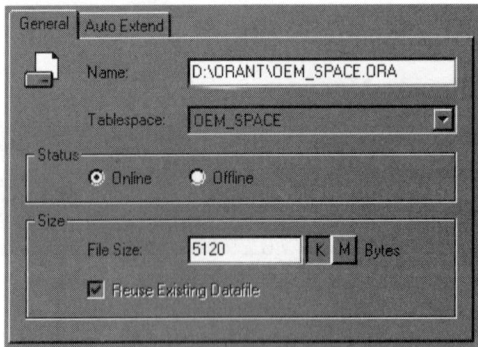

Figure 3.7 Auto Extend

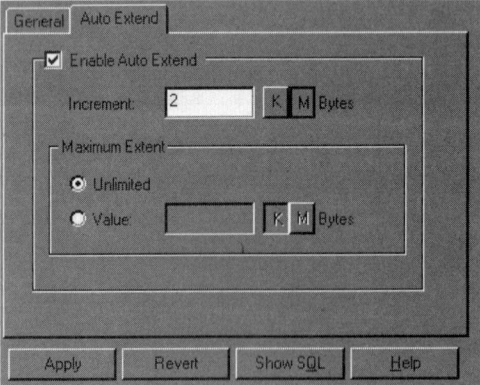

By changing the size of the file in Figure 3.6 and then clicking on the *Apply* button, the datafile will be automatically resized. Alternatively, click on *Enable*

Auto Extend as shown in Figure 3.7 to have the datafile automatically increase in size if it needs to grow.

Hint: Don't forget to click on the M button to state that the increment is megabytes, otherwise you will find your file growing in very small kilobyte increments.

One of the nice aspects of using a GUI is that you don't have to write and remember the SQL instructions to complete the task. However, if you click on the *Show SQL* button, a box containing the SQL, as shown in Figure 3.8, is displayed. The contents of this box can then be selected, cut and pasted into any tool such as SQL Worksheet.

Figure 3.8 SQL Text Box

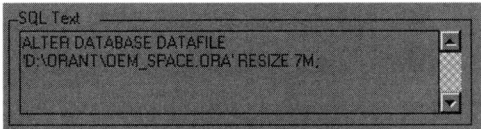

3.7 LOGICAL DATABASE COMPONENTS

So far we have learned about the physical components of the Oracle8 database, such as the data and parameter files. Referring to Figure 3.9, we will discover how data is actually stored inside the database and the relationship between a datafile, tablespaces, extents and blocks.

Figure 3.9 Database Components

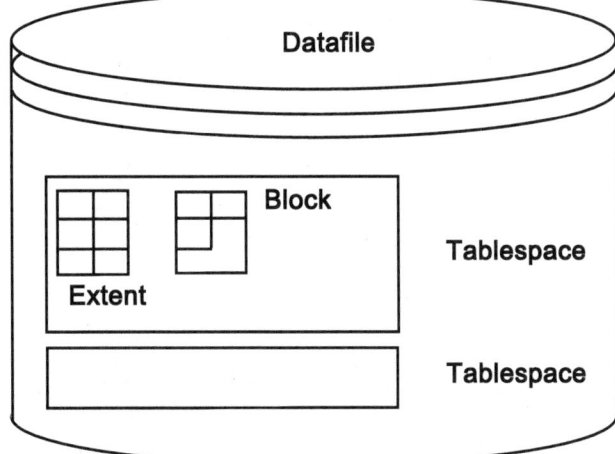

3.8   TABLESPACES

Information in the database is logically held in tablespaces. These are very important structures, because when a table or index is created you have to specify in which tablespace it is to be placed. There are several types of tablespaces:

- System
- Data

The *system* tablespace must always be available, otherwise the database cannot be opened. It contains the Oracle8 data dictionary, stored procedures, packages, triggers and the system rollback segment. It can also contain ordinary data, but this is not recommended; user data should be held in its own tablespace. If user data resides in the system tablespace, it could cause the system data to fragment, which could have a serious impact on system performance.

The *data* tablespaces do not all have to be online at the same time and usually contain a number of tables and indexes. A tablespace can be very large because it can consist of one or more datafiles.

Tablespaces are managed and created using the Storage Manager. As per the datafiles, we can see in Figure 3.10 an overview of our tablespace and the space they are using (e.g., the INDX tablespace is using 7.717 Mb out of the 12 Mb available).

Figure 3.10 Tablespaces in the Database

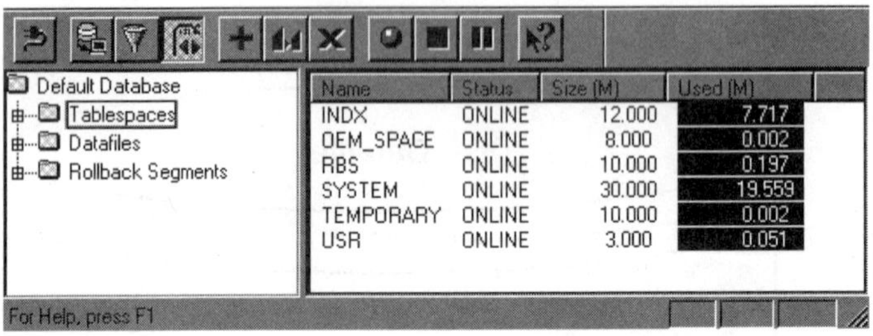

The easiest way to create a tablespace is to use the Storage Manager and select *Tablespace* and then *Create* from the menu. This will result in the window shown in Figure 3.11 being displayed.

First give the tablespace a name and then click on the *Add* button to specify the location and size of each of the datafiles that will be used by this tablespace. Remember that spreading the tablespace over several disks may help improve performance.

Figure 3.11 Creating a Tablespace

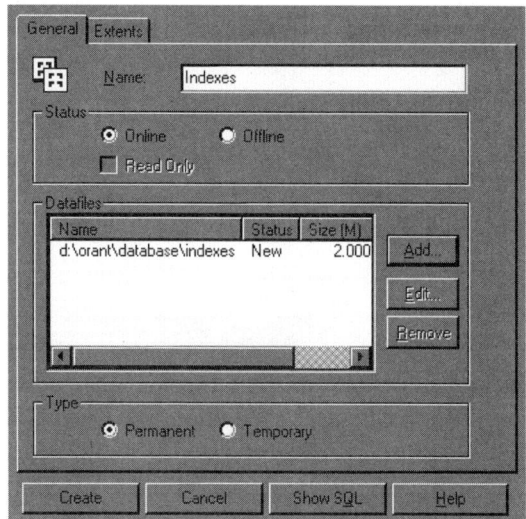

Scripts – recommended

If you have a number of tablespaces to create, you may find that the GUI is a rather slow tool for completing the task, because you can only define one tablespace at a time. One solution to this problem is to click on the *Show SQL* button to extract the SQL for the first tablespace that you defined. Then paste that SQL into the SQL Worksheet tool. Now edit the SQL to create the other tablespaces and create a script in SQL Worksheet to create all of your tablespaces. One advantage of using this approach is that the script can be saved and reused if you ever have to create the database again.

The definition of the tablespace is not complete until the Extents tab has been selected.

3.9 EXTENTS

In Figure 3.9 we saw how information inside a tablespace is held in an extent, where an extent consists of one of more segments, which themselves are made up of a number of blocks.

Everything stored in the database, such as a table or an index, lives in its own extent. Therefore if five tables and six indexes were going to use a tablespace, a minimum of eleven extents would be needed to store the data. We will see in the next chapter how to define the size of the extent specifically for a table or index. But for now, we will assume that everything being stored in the tablespace is exactly the same size and create default values for the tablespace.

An extent is sized in kilobytes or megabytes and describes the amount of space that will be used to store an object, for example a table. Figure 3.12 shows us the information that is required to create the extent. We must specify:

- size of the first extent;
- size of all subsequent extents;
- amount to increase the size of future extents;
- maximum number of extents that may be created.

Figure 3.12 Specify the Extents

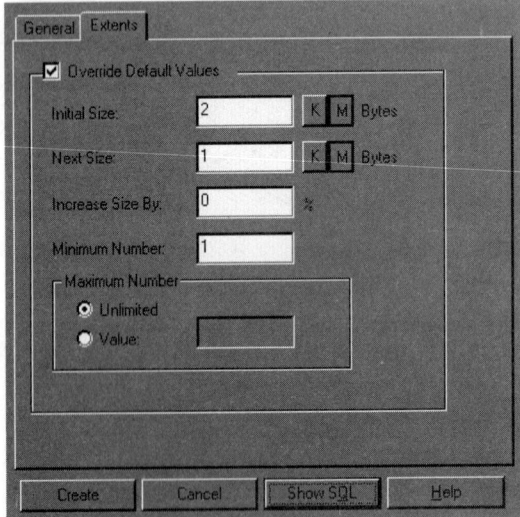

To achieve good performance it is wise to create your extents so that only full blocks will fit into the extent. This tip is really relevant when defining the size of the first extent for a specific object such as a table. If you know the volume of data that, say, a table will hold, especially if it is a nonvolatile object, then create the first extent to be the same size as the volume of data to be stored.

It is not important to hold all the data in the first extent and it is quite normal to have a table that consists of many extents. When calculating the size of the next extent, consider how much data will fit in there, and if you make it too large, how much space could be wasted.

When defining the size of the extents, you have the ability to specify a percentage growth factor for each subsequent extent (e.g., you could specify that each extent grows by 5% over the previous extent). Sometimes this may be useful, but generally it is best to set the *Increase Size By* to zero. Then you will always know how much space will be used by each extent.

3.10 BLOCKS

An extent in the database actually consists of one or more blocks, where the size of the block is determined by the initialization parameter DB_BLOCK_SIZE. The block size is the same for all datafiles and cannot be changed once it has been defined, so choose a value wisely. A typical block size is 2 or 4K, which would result in an initialization parameter of DB_BLOCK_SIZE=2048 for a 2K block or DB_BLOCK_SIZE=4096 for a 4K block. The factors to consider when trying to determine a suitable block size are:

- type of access retrieval (e.g., small discrete pieces of information such as customer account details, or searching a whole table);
- the impact the size will have on the number of buffers that can be held in the SGA.

For example, a data warehouse or data mart is likely to use a large block size such as 16K, because queries will require access to a lot of the data so it makes sense to bring in as much data as possible per I/O. Whereas a system involved in taking orders may prefer a smaller block size of 2K, which is large enough to hold all of the customer details. In this example, the small block size would mean that more buffers could be defined in the SGA to support the hundreds of users querying the system. The number of buffers used to hold information is determined by the initialization parameter DB_BLOCK_BUFFERS.

3.11 SEGMENTS

So far we have seen that information is held in tablespaces, in an area called an extent, which itself consists of a number of blocks. To help identify what is being stored in the database, there are four types of segments used in the database, where a segment comprises one or more extents.

- Data   holds tables and clusters
- Index   contains indexes
- Rollback   used to roll back a transaction, recovery and provide read consistency
- Temporary where temporary objects are held

3.12   TABLESPACES, SEGMENTS AND EXTENTS

To summarize what we have just learned, from the perspective of managing the database, the DBA needs to consider the following:

- how many *datafiles* to store data in;
- the names of the *tablespaces* to hold the various database objects;
- the size of the *initial extent* used to hold the data;
- the size of all *subsequent* extents;
- maximum number of *extents* that will be allowed.

3.13   ROLLBACK SEGMENTS

The rollback segment is the only one of the five segment types that must be defined when the database is created. The purpose of the rollback segment is to keep a copy of data before it was changed. Today we take for granted the ability to undo changes that we have made to the data if we decide that we don't want to keep them. How is this achieved? By using the rollback segments.

When a transaction is started, it is given a unique identifier and assigned to a rollback segment. Every time a change is made to anything in the database, such as changing a column value or adding entries to an index, the previous version of the database structure is written to the rollback segment. One important point to bear in mind is that the rollback segment must be large enough to hold all the changes for the largest transaction. No maintenance of the rollback segments is required because since they are used in a circular fashion, they are automatically reused by the system when they are no longer required.

Figure 3.13 Managing Rollback Segments

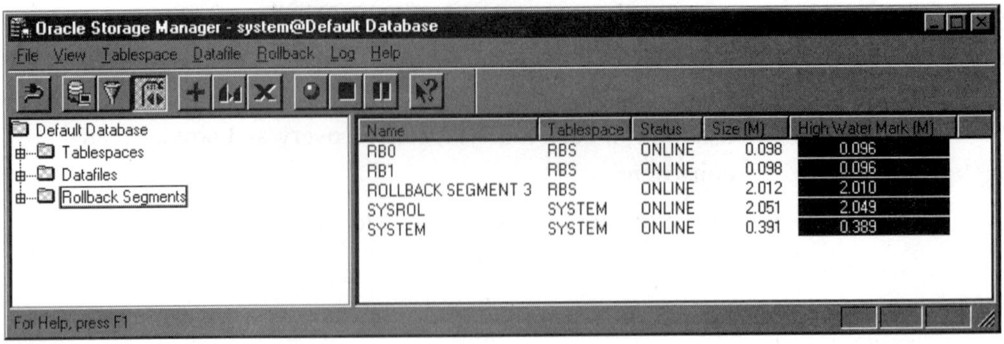

Since a rollback segment can only be used by users of the system if it is online, the Storage Manager (as shown in Figure 3.13) is very useful because it provides an instant, quick display of all the segments, their size and whether they are available.

Hint: If the rollback segment is online it will always display its high watermark as the size of the file. Do not be alarmed into thinking that the rollback segment is full. It merely tells the system that all this space is available for use.

Using the Storage Manager, rollback segments can be created, taken on- or offline and shrunk if they have used too much space. Simply click on *Rollback* in the strip menu to get a list of the available options.

To add a new rollback segment, simply complete the box shown in Figure 3.14. First give the rollback segment a name and then say in which tablespace the rollback segment is to be created. It is a good idea to place the rollback segments in their own tablespaces, away from the actual production data.

Don't forget to click the online box so that the rollback segment is available for everyone to use. In Figure 3.12 we saw how to define the size of the extents for a tablespace. The same information is required for a rollback segment and the technique for filling in the boxes is as described previously.

In Figure 3.14, one of the options is whether the rollback segment is classified as private or public. If it is a public rollback segment then it will automatically be placed online when the instance is started. Private rollback segments must

Figure 3.14 Creating a Rollback Segment

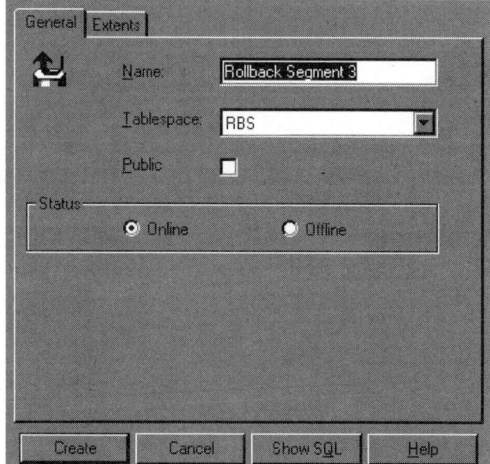

be brought online manually using the Storage Manager or by specifying the rollback segments in the initialization file using the parameter ROLLBACK_SEGMENTS=( )

One final tip when naming rollback segments, in Figure 3.14 the rollback segment was given a typical Windows NT name containing spaces. Names such as Rollback Segment 3 cannot be placed in the initialization file. Therefore, if you want to use NT style names, the rollback segment will have to be of type public so that it is brought online automatically. If it is defined as a private rollback segment, then with an NT style name it can only be brought online manually, using the Storage Manager. However, the use of names that contain spaces is not normally recommended.

Hint: To quickly change the status of a rollback segment, click the right mouse button while over the name of the rollback segment to obtain a list of actions.

3.14   SUMMARY

You should now have an understanding of the physical and logical composition of an Oracle8 database. It is important to have a basic understanding of its makeup because it has a significant bearing on how it will perform in the real world. Also, when performing management tasks like backups, it is nice to know all the files that need to be backed up.

4   Designing the Database

Now that we have learned how to create a database, it is time to learn how to create all the different types of objects that exist inside an Oracle8 database, such as tables, indexes, clusters, constraints and triggers. At the end of this chapter we should have a database that is ready to accept data.

4.1   SCHEMAS

Before we define any tables in our database, we must first understand the concept of schemas in the database. A schema is a logical construct which describes a collection of objects. Schemas are a nice way of grouping together the various components of the database. For example, suppose our database holds customer and order information. One approach would be to create two schemas, one for customers and the other for orders. In the customer schema, we would find the customer table and index. In the order schema, there might be tables and indexes for the order, order lines, products and warehouse tables.

How many schemas the DBA defines is a design decision. If your database is only going to contain information pertaining to one area of the company, then a single schema would suffice. But if you are going to hold data from various areas, then it is wise to consider how many schemas would be needed.

> **Hint: It is very important to make the decision at the outset of the design because the schema name plays an integral part in retrieving and storing data in the database.**

Whenever an object is described, it is identified by:

schema name. object name

For example, the fully qualified name for the customer table in the orders schema would be:

orders.customer

Therefore applications will include the schema name in their SQL statements. Consequently, if this name changes, the applications must be modified as well. Hopefully this situation will never arise, but if you have never met the concept of a schema before, this could surprise you later in the development cycle.

4.1.1   Creating a Schema

The process for creating a schema may seem a little strange, but since it is done once and then forgotten, what may seem like a time consuming process is not really.

The first step is to create an Oracle user as described in Chapter 7 using the *Security Manager*. Then you logon to the database using the Oracle username you have just created. For our Ordering system we created a username of Orders. Now create a database object such as a table and the schema will be automatically created. If we look at the example in Figure 4.1, we can see that for tables we have four schemas being used; oem, orders, sys and system.

Figure 4.1 Available Schemas

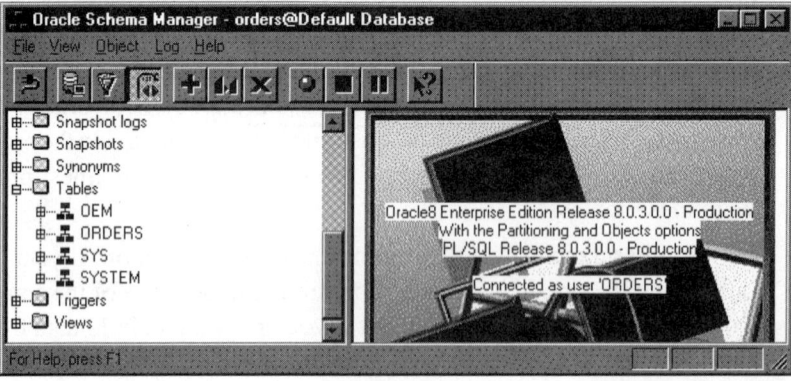

By default, the username we have used to login to the database will define the schema where all objects like tables and indexes will be placed. This username need only be used by the DBA for managing the metadata. The actual users of the database can use any Oracle username to retrieve data because they have to specify in which schema the object can be found. Therefore provided they know the schema name and have sufficient privileges to access the data, the information is made available to them.

When creating objects such as tables, it is not necessary to keep logging in under the schema username. Provided the schema exists, you can specify into which schema the object is to be included.

Hint: Before creating any object in the database, always check the username used to logon to the database. In Schema Manager it can be seen by clicking on Schema Objects – it is then displayed in the navigator box – or look at the top line of the window in Schema Manager.

4.2 TABLES

A table is the place in the database where all our information is held. Tables can be created using one of several methods:

- SQL CREATE TABLE statement;
- Schema Manager Table Wizard;
- Schema Manager GUI.

Before we can define the table we need to know what its name will be, in which tablespace it is to be stored and how much space it is likely to occupy. It is a good idea to try and use a meaningful name for the table, such as Customers or Orders; a name like CUSYS01 is too cryptic. This may seem obvious, but you won't believe how many people use names like this for their tables. In the past it was never really a problem how objects were named in the database. But now with the propensity for allowing endusers with few computer skills direct access to the database using PC query tools, they see the object names that were used to create the database. To avoid constant queries to the help desk of what does this table or column contain, sensible naming conventions go a long way to resolving this problem.

This section will primarily cover creating a table using the Schema Manager. However, I am sure there are readers of this book that will feel much more comfortable using the SQL CREATE TABLE command. There is nothing wrong with this approach and if you have a lot of tables to create, then a script containing all the SQL statements may be quicker. Just remember that a GUI tool never gets the syntax wrong and it always works first time, provided you have filled in the boxes correctly. Therefore by the time you have found the manual or searched through the online documentation, using the GUI tool could very well have been quicker.

The *Schema Manager* is a very easy to use tool for managing all the objects in the database because it enables you to see at a glance what is available. Without *Schema Manager*; the alternative is *SQL Worksheet* or *SQL*Plus*, where you have to know each objects name and explicitly request its description. This is fine if you know the database, but how many of us can precisely name all of the objects in our database? Maybe the tables, the author would be very surprised if you could name all of your indexes.

To create any object in Schema Manager, not just a table, click on *Object* from the strip menu at the top, then click on *Create* and the box shown in Figure 4.2 appears.

Figure 4.2 Creating an Object Using Schema Manager

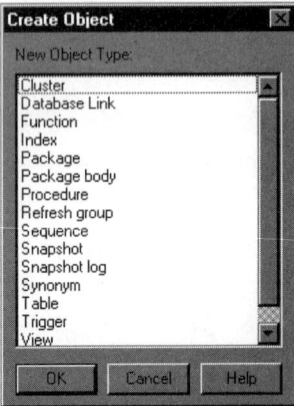

Choose the object to be created from the list and either double click on it or select the object and click on OK.

If you are creating a table then Figure 4.3 will appear asking you whether you want to use the wizard or create it manually. If you have never created a table before then select the wizard route because it will ask you all the important questions and make table creation look so easy. If you are familiar with tables, then choose the manual option which will still provide you with a GUI environment where you can manage the database. Please don't think that manual means writing SQL; all it means is that you must remember which tabs to click to define the table.

Figure 4.3 Selecting the Table Creation Method

8
Oracle

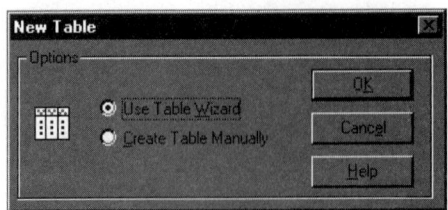

4.2.1   Columns and Datatypes

A table in the database consists of a number of columns. Every column has a name and a datatype which tells the database what type of information is being held in this column. Oracle8 offers a wide variety of datatypes which should satisfy all your data needs, as shown in Table 4.1.

When defining numeric data use the datatype *Number* and for dates, of course, use the *Date* datatype. The format of dates in the database is determined by the initialisation parameter NLS_DATE_FORMAT which offers a comprehensive range of formats. One of the big advantages of using the date datatype is that it allows you to present the date in a number of formats. For example, the NLS_DATE_FORMAT parameter could be set to "DD-MON-YY", but in your application you could change the presentation of the date format using

```
ALTER SESSION SET NLS_DATE_FORMAT = 'YYYYMMDD'
```

In this application, dates would appear as 19970801 instead of 01-Aug-97.

For textual data, the *Char* datatype appears to be the obvious choice but it is not. Usually *Varchar2* is chosen because it is a variable size field. If you use a datatype of Char(50) for example, you will always use 50 bytes to store the column, because the char datatype is of fixed length, whereas the Varchar2 datatype is a variable length column and only occupies the space required to store the column. Therefore you could define a column as Varchar2(50), but if you only used 15 characters out of the 50 available, then you would only use a little over 15 bytes to hold the column details.

Table 4.1 Oracle8 Datatypes

Datatype	Description
Char	Fixed length character, maximum size is 255
Date	Any date from 4712 BC to 4712 AD
Long	Variable length character up to 2 gigabytes
Long Raw	Raw binary data up to 2 gigabytes
Number(a,b)	A number where a can range from 1 to 38 and b from -84 to 127
Raw(*size*)	Raw binary data of length *size* bytes
Rowid	Unique address within the database
Varchar2(*size*)	Variable length string of maximum length *size*

If there is a requirement to store very long text strings, then consider using the *Long* datatype.

If you have any binary type data such as images to store, then use one of the *Raw* datatypes.

4.2.2   Table Wizard

8

Oracle

If you have never created a table before, or it has been a while since you last defined one, then use the table wizard to create your first table. Once you are familiar with the questions that have to be answered, you can always use the GUI next time.

The wizard will present a number of screens. The first is shown in Figure 4.4, where it will ask you for the name of the table, the schema in which the table is to be placed and the tablespace where the table is to be stored. We can see in Figure 4.4 that it has already chosen the schema as ORDERS, but we could change this. In Section 3.8 we learned how information in the database is held in tablespaces. We have the ability to specify, when we create a table, into which tablespace the data will be stored. If we don't specify the tablespace, then the contents of this table will be stored in the default tablespace for the user. Therefore, it is good design practice and sensible database management to specify for each table, which tablespace should be used to hold its contents.

Figure 4.4 Table Wizard – Step 1

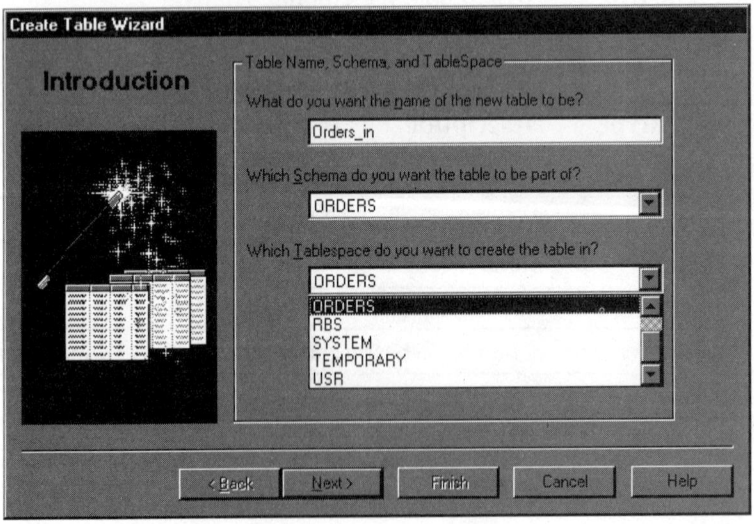

It is not uncommon to reach this step and realize that the tablespace you require has not been created. If this is the case, simply start the *Storage Manager* and create a tablespace as described in Section 3.8. Then press the *Cancel* button in the *Create Table Wizard*, start it again and the tablespace you just created will now appear in the list as illustrated in Figure 4.4.

In the example shown here we are creating a table called *Orders_in*, which will be held in the *Orders* schema and the contents of the table will be stored in the *Orders* tablespace.

By clicking on *Next*, we can define the columns in the table using the screen shown in Figure 4.5.

Figure 4.5 Table Wizard – Step 2

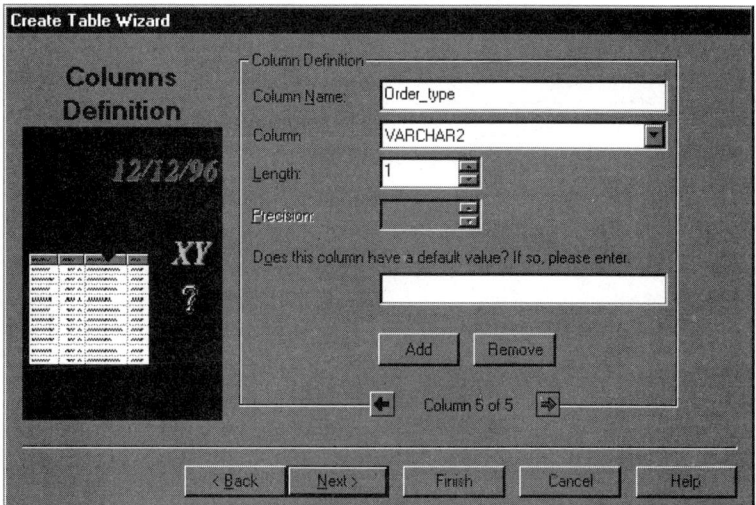

For every column in the table simply give it a name, state its datatype and then press *Add*. Don't press the *Next* button until you have defined all of the columns.

Once all the columns have been defined, you may think that is the end of the table definition and if you think it is then press the *Finish* button. However, the wizard will also allow you to create constraints on the table. We will learn more about constraints in Section 4.3, but for now all we have to say is which, if any, of the columns in the table must be unique. By clicking on the *Yes, I want to create a primary key button*, shown in Figure 4.6, the list of columns in the table is displayed, and by clicking on the gray square to the left of the column name, you can specify which of these columns is the primary key.

Figure 4.6 Table Wizard – Step 3

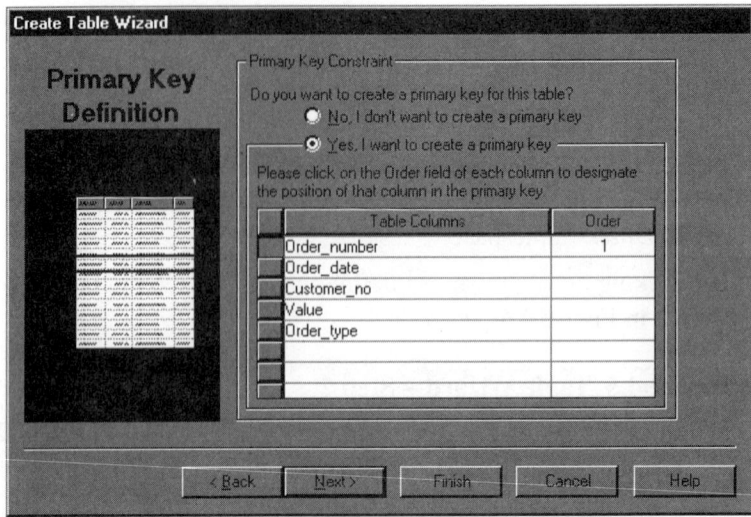

Figure 4.7 Table Wizard – Step 4

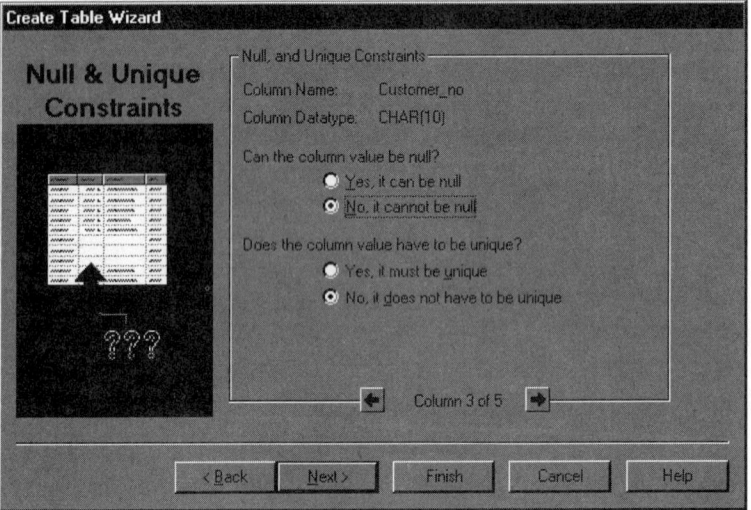

Then for each column that has been defined you will be asked whether the column can be null and if it has to be unique. Each column is displayed as in Figure 4.7; simply click on the appropriate box and then press one of the arrows to proceed to the next column.

One of the big benefits of using a database is the integrity that can be enforced. The wizard always asks if any foreign key constraints are needed, as shown in Figure 4.8. A foreign key is when the contents of a column in one table match a value in a column in another table (e.g., in our orders table there is a column called customer_no). When a foreign key is defined, the contents of the customer_no in the orders table must match a customer_no held in the customer table.

Figure 4.8 Table Wizard – Step 5

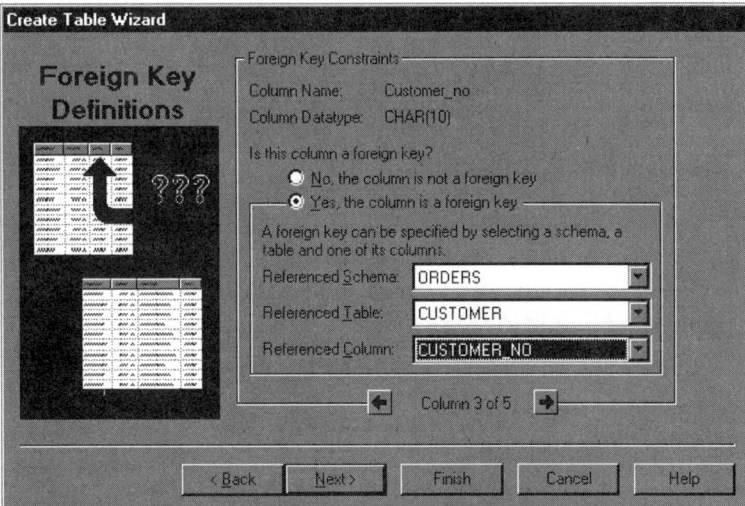

Other validations can also be applied to the columns in the database. One very useful one is the check condition shown in Figure 4.9. A check clause ensures

Figure 4.9 Table Wizard – Step 6

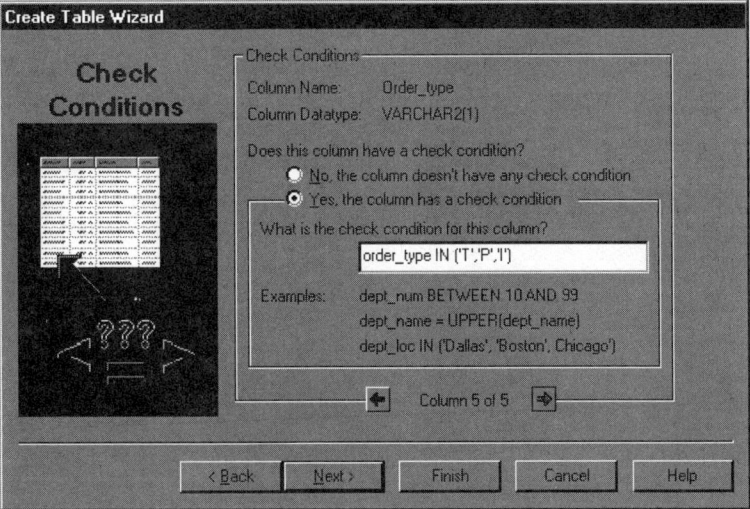

that the contents of a column match the criteria specified. But the check clause can only be a simple one; in Figure 4.9, we see how the contents of the column order_type must be T, P or I.

When defining a check condition, the column name must be included in the check clause.

The definition of the table is almost complete. The final piece of information that is required is how much data is likely to be stored in this table. This is where the wizard makes this task very easy because all you have to know is how many rows are likely to be in the table and whether the table will grow, as shown in Figure 4.10. The wizard then interprets that information into the appropriate Oracle storage parameters.

Pressing the *Next* button will display the last window, the final review which is shown in Figure 4.11. This is your last chance to review the table definition before it is created. Should you spot anything that is incorrect, simply click on the *Back* button to return to that screen and amend the information supplied. Once you are happy with the definition, press the *Finish* button and the table is created.

Figure 4.10 Table Wizard – Step 7

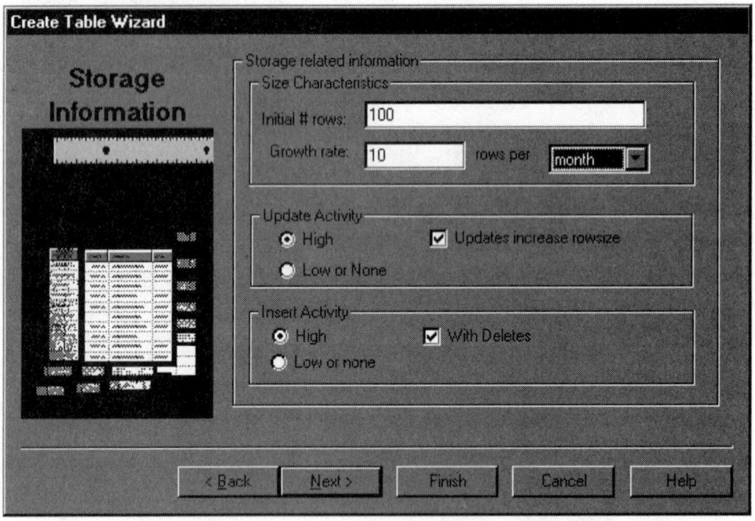

Now we can see the table that we have defined and review it before creating it in the database.

Figure 4.11 Table Wizard – Step 8

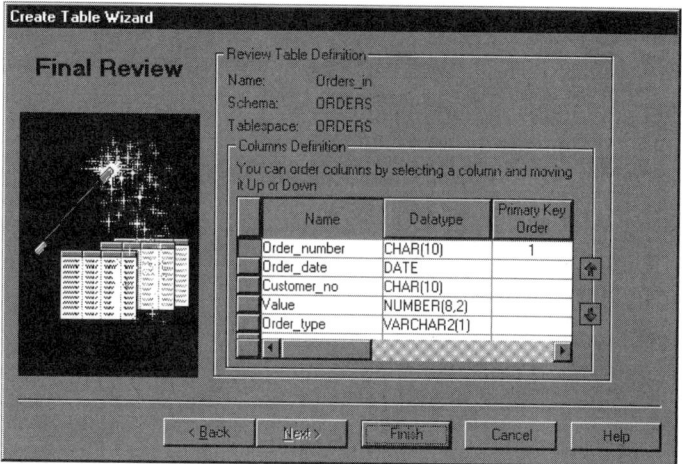

Figure 4.12 Schema Manager Tables

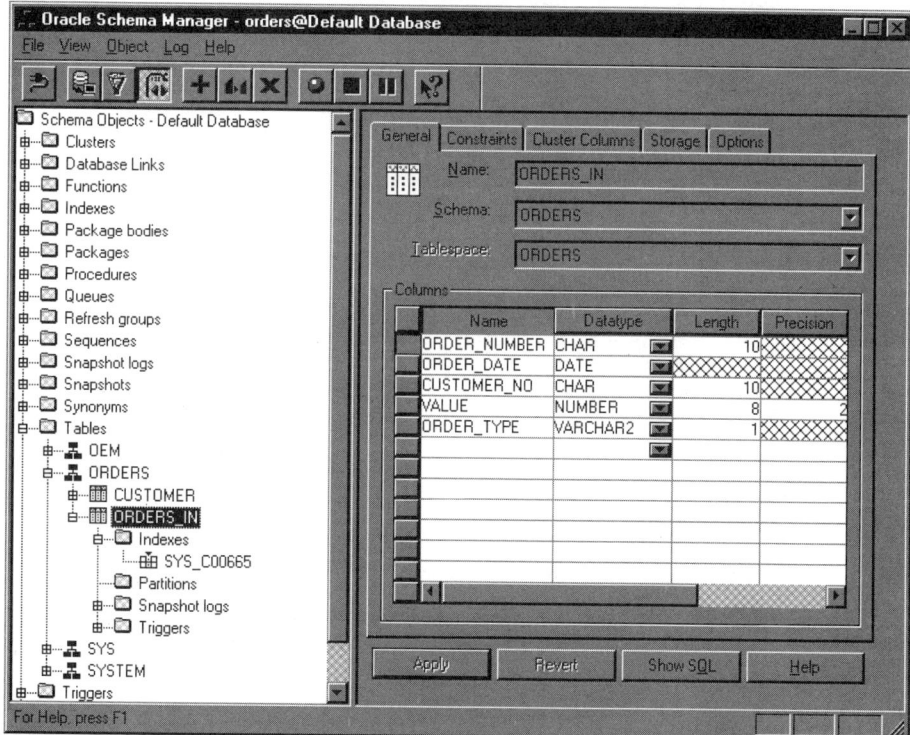

Hint: Some of the windows are quite small, so don't forget to use the scrollbars to see all of the table definition.

4.2.3   Table GUI

The wizard is fine to use if you are only creating a table, but most of the time you will want to review and edit the table definition, which is where the *Schema Manager* table GUI is required. We saw in Figure 4.1 how the Schema Manager GUI starts with a list of all the object types. If we select one of them, such as tables, then we can expand it to see the available schemas and tables.

In Figure 4.12, by expanding the schema *Orders* and then clicking on the table *Orders_in* in the left-hand navigator window, the definition of the table is shown in the right window.

The table details are broken down into five categories, each of which can be selected by pressing on the appropriate tab. Any box that is grayed out, such as Tablespace in Figure 4.12, is an attribute that cannot be changed but is displayed because it is useful information to the DBA.

The alternative to using the table wizard is to create the table manually by completing the various table dialog boxes.

Figure 4.13 Create a Table

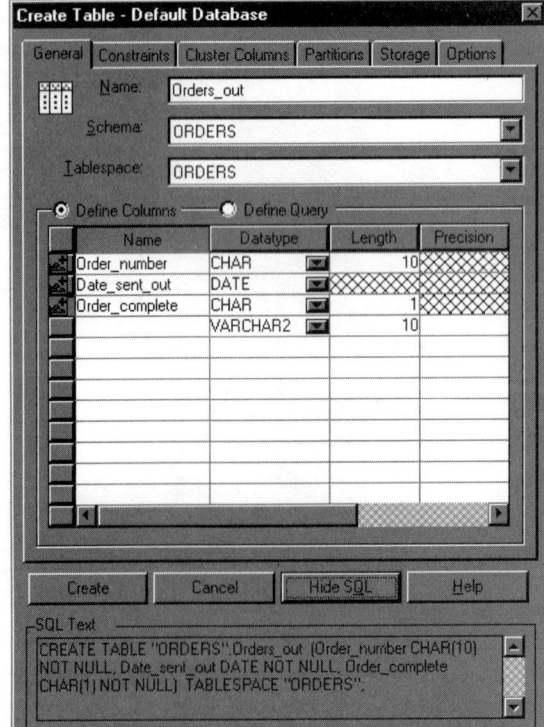

In Figure 4.13 we can see that it is very easy to complete the dialog boxes. Simply give the table a name and select a schema and tablespace from the drop down list. Then fill in the column names, select the datatype and scroll across to complete the other columns.

Pressing the *Show SQL* button will display the SQL statement that would create this table. It is not necessary to use the SQL, but saving it to a script file could be useful if it was necessary to recreate the database at a later stage.

Essential !

4.2.4   Table Storage

In Section 3.9 we saw that when we are defining a tablespace we must specify the size of the extents used for storing data. This approach would be reasonable if only one object type, say a table or index was stored in the tablespace. Unfortunately, this is very rarely the case and therefore we must use the storage options for the table and index, to explicitly state how to store this object.

There are two ways to define the storage requirements for a table in Oracle8:

8

Oracle

- fill in the boxes shown in Figure 4.14, click on *Explicit*;
- let the database calculate the storage requirements using the information supplied in Figure 4.10, click on *Auto Calculation*.

Figure 4.14 Table Storage Using the Explicit Method

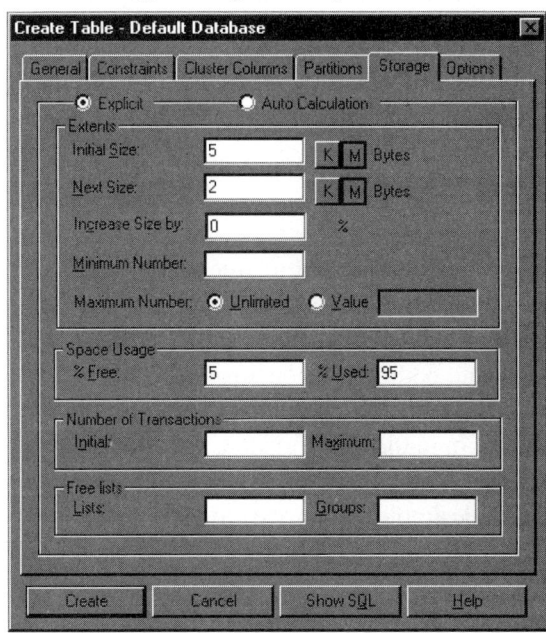

Which method you choose is a personal choice. Readers familiar with the Oracle database will probably choose the *Explicit* method. However, letting the system decide using the *Auto Calculation* takes the worry out of calculating the right parameter values. So what are the parameters that have to be defined?

This book is by no means a comprehensive reference to all the parameters, but it does highlight the important ones. On the *Explicit* screen shown in Figure 4.14 there are a number of parameters, but the following ones are the main ones to be concerned about.

All of the *Extent* boxes are important. The *initial* and *next size* are calculated as described in Section 3.9. Remember that if the table is static and unlikely to grow, you should try to size the first extent to hold the entire table. For volatile tables you can have as many extents as you like, but be aware that if there are many other tables using your tablespace, extra I/O may be required to retrieve all the rows in the table in the event of a full table scan, as illustrated in Figure 4.15 The number of extents available for this table is determined by the min and maximum values. As a guide, try to store the table in as few extents as possible and preferably set the *next size* equal to the *initial size*.

The *Increase Size By box* is the parameter PCTINCREASE if you were using the SQL CREATE TABLE command. If this value is set to zero, then every time a new extent is created its size remains constant, as specified by the *next size* value. Using a constant growth size ensures that the database grows at a predictable rate.

The *Space Usage* values, if not defined correctly, could cause your database to expand earlier than expected and use more space than you predicted. There are two values to specify, *%Free* and *%Used*, which equate to the SQL CREATE TABLE parameters PCTFREE and PCTUSED. To clarify these parameters, let us refer to Figure 4.15.

%Free determines the amount of free space that is left in every block which allows a row to grow. If your rows are static, or once they are stored, the contents never changed, then free can be set to a very low value, such as 3%. Today, it is quite common when a row is first stored to only supply some of the information. Later the row is updated with more information. If there is insufficient room in the block to store the additional data, then the new data is stored in another block and the two blocks are said to be *chained* together. This is very undesirable from a performance perspective and should be avoided. Therefore to avoid chained blocks, in this example *%Free* would be set to a high value of say 30% or 40%. Then all that space is available for storing the

extra data. It is especially important to use a high free value if the data that is likely to be added later is textual, because text data often occupies many kilobytes. The default value for *%Free* is 10% which may not be appropriate for some of your tables.   *will not!*

Figure 4.15 %Free and %Used Parameters

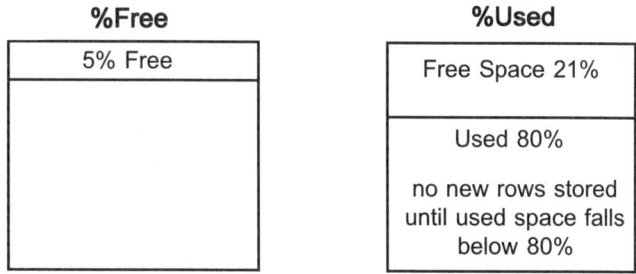

%Used or the CREATE TABLE parameter PCTUSED determines the point at which a block is available for storing new rows. The important thing to remember about this parameter is that it only takes effect when the block is full, as determined by the *%Free* value.

Referring to Figure 4.15, we have set the *%Free* value at 5% so that 95% of the block can be used for storing data. When the block is 95% full, if we set *%Used* to 80%, then this block only becomes a candidate for storing new rows, when the amount of used space is *less than* 80%. The default value for *%Used* is 40, which may be far too low for many tables. Here is a useful formulae for this parameter:

%Free + %Used <= 100

Other parameters that can be defined are related to transactions and the free list. These are parameters that can be left to their defaults and only require modification if your application warrants it.

4.2.5   Index Only Table

8

Oracle

Oracle8 introduced the concept of an *index only table*. An index only table is a table where the contents of the table are kept in a b-tree structure. Therefore the only blocks used to store the data are index blocks rather than table and index blocks.

Indexed only tables are ideal to use in applications where you are continually retrieving all the columns in a table or any spatial or online applications requiring fast retrieval times. For instance, in the example below, an index only table has been created on a table that translates location codes to a textual location.

At the time of writing, the only way an IOT (Indexed Only Table) can be created is by using the SQL CREATE TABLE command and specifying the keywords ORGANIZATION INDEX as shown below.

```
CREATE TABLE location_codes_iot
   (loc_code  VARCHAR2(4) ,
    location  VARCHAR2(15) ,
   CONSTRAINT loc_iot PRIMARY KEY (loc_code) )
       ORGANIZATION INDEX
           TABLESPACE indx ;
```

There are a few restrictions regarding the use of indexed only tables:

- a primary key must be defined;
- unique constraints may not be used;
- the table cannot be clustered, replicated or partitioned;
- no columns using the long, raw or long raw datatype.

Nevertheless, IOTs can prove very useful and these restrictions should not prevent many people from using them.

4.2.6   Create a Table Using a Query

So far we have created tables in the database by defining the columns, but a table can also be created by using a query expression. Referring back to Figure 4.13, one of the options is *Define Query*, which is the one to use for creating a table based on a query.

This technique is a useful one and is often used in Data Warehouse and Data Mart applications for holding summary information. Although the example shown here is a summary, you will see that there are many other occasions when this technique would be useful.

Suppose we want to know how much each of our stores sold for a special promotion that was running on a given day. Rather than search through all the data, we could use a table which already has the results precalculated. Using the CREATE TABLE AS clause, we can construct the query to join the tables and retrieve the data. Looking at the example below, we can see that our query returns several values; day, store and promotion. We obtain the totals for sales, unit_sales and cost by grouping the values by day, store and promotion.

```
CREATE TABLE sum_day_store_promo
  PCTFREE 0   TABLESPACE summary
  AS SELECT
      t.day, f.store_key, f.promotion_key,
      SUM(sales) as sum_sales,
      SUM(unit_sales) as sum_unit_sales,
      SUM(cost) as sum_cost
      FROM time t, fact f
        WHERE
            f.time_key = t.time_key
      GROUP BY t.day, f.store_key, f.promotion_key;
```

When we execute the SQL shown above, a table is created called sum_day_store_promo which contains six columns as they are named in the query, and it is populated with the results of the query. We have an instant table ready for use, whereas if we had defined it using the previous method, we would have to create the table and calculate the results and then insert those into the table.

One important point to remember with tables that are based on a query is that when the contents of the tables on which the query is defined change, no updates or changes are made to the table based on the query.

The queries used for query based tables can be simple or complex. The example above illustrates the use of functions like SUM and the GROUP BY clause. However, whether you use SQL Worksheet or the GUI to define the table, you always have to write the SQL for the query as illustrated in this example.

4.3 CONSTRAINTS

One of the major benefits of using a relational database is the ability to define integrity constraints on the data. These are very useful, as they cannot be overridden by anyone, not even the database engine itself. When integrity rules are defined, you can rest assured that your data must correspond to the rules.

However, it should be noted that in Oracle8 there is one possible way that an integrity constraint can be violated which is described in Section 4.3.8.

The Oracle database provides five different types of constraints:

- Not Null
- Unique
- Primary Key
- Foreign Key
- Check

Every constraint in the database has a name and can be defined either via an SQL statement or using the GUI window shown in Figure 4.16. Choose the constraint name wisely because this will be displayed if there is an error. A sensible constraint name helps to rapidly identify which constraint has been violated. Although the dialog box shown in Figure 4.16 is not difficult to use, this is the one time where experienced SQL users may prefer to write an SQL statement instead. Therefore, the SQL statements will also be included here.

At any time a constraint can be disabled. In Figure 4.16 all the constraints are by default enabled, which is why they all have a cross in the disable column. A checkmark in the disable column denotes a disabled constraint.

Figure 4.16 Constraint Dialog

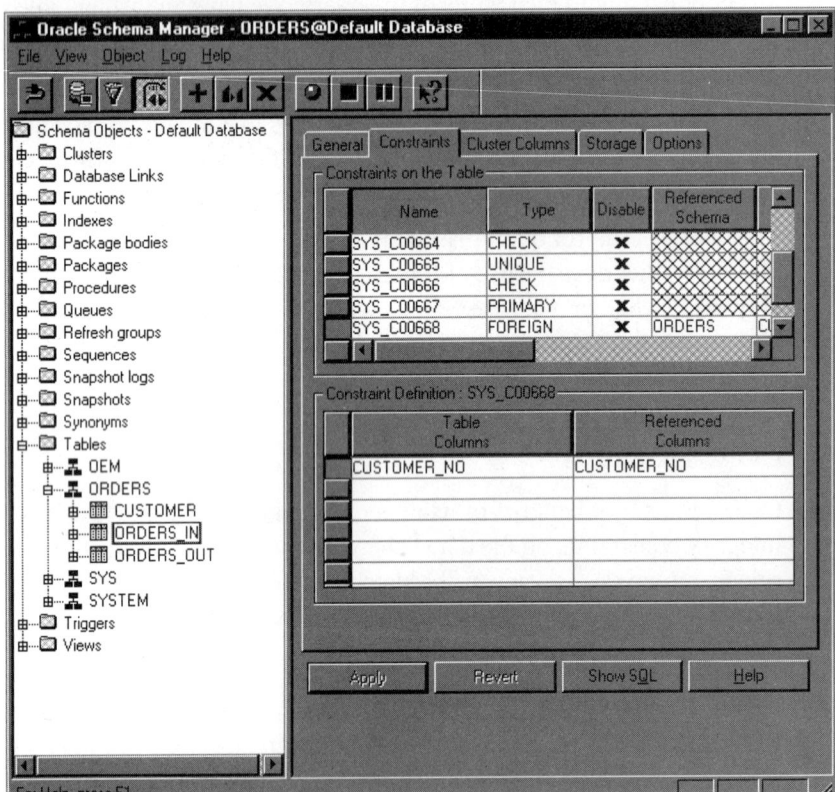

4.3.1   Not Null

The not null constraint checks that the value of a column is not null. In SQL, the constraint is defined using the NOT NULL clause.

```
CREATE TABLE orders_out
  (order_number  CHAR(10),
   order_type    VARCHAR(2)
   CONSTRAINT order_type_not_null NOT NULL);
```

From Schema Manager, a not null constraint is created from a table using the *General* tab, shown in Figure 4.17. X means that the column cannot be null.

Figure 4.17 Not Null Constraint

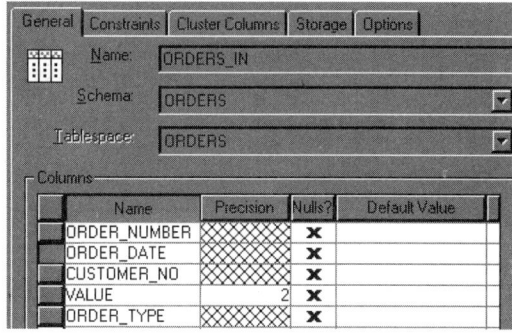

4.3.2 Unique

A *unique* constraint specifies that the value in this column must be unique within all the values in the table, that is, the order number must be unique across all orders. A primary key constraint defines a unique, non-null value, so it is much more commonly used than a unique constraint, which could contain null values.

4.3.3 Primary Key

The primary key is a very commonly used constraint, and when it is defined Oracle automatically creates an index on the columns referenced in the primary key to ensure fast evaluation of the constraint. The columns in a primary key must be both not null and unique. It is easily defined using the PRIMARY KEY clause.

```
CREATE TABLE orders_out
  (order_number  CHAR(10)
     CONSTRAINT orders_out_pkey PRIMARY KEY,
   order_type    VARCHAR(2));
```

Using the GUI in Figure 4.18, first give the constraint a name, such as Orders_out_pkey. If the constraint is violated, its name is displayed in Oracle error messages, so choose a name that indicates immediately which constraint has been violated for a table. If you don't give the constraint a name, then a name like SYS_C00665 as shown in Figure 4.16 will be allocated.

Next choose the type of constraint from the drop down list, which in this case is Primary. Then in the window below, choose the columns that this constraint is defined on. Press *OK* and the constraint has been defined.

Hint: If you make a mistake with the constraint definition, click the **icon with the right mouse button and select** *drop* **from the list to delete it.**

Figure 4.18 Primary Key Dialog

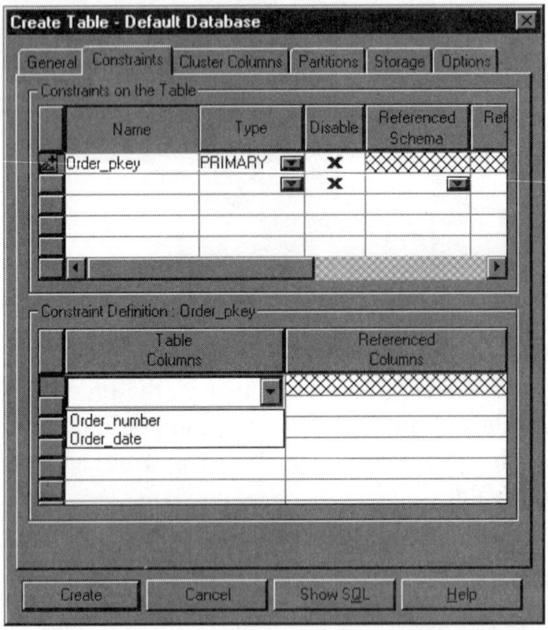

4.3.4   Foreign Key

Foreign keys are often defined in a relational database because they ensure that a value in one table corresponds to a value in another table, as illustrated in Figure 4.19. A common requirement is to ensure that the order_number used in the order_lines table matches an order_number for an order in the orders table.

This integrity check is implemented by defining a *primary key* on the table that is referenced, in this example, the *orders* table and a *foreign key* on the table where the match originates from (i.e. the *order_lines* table).

The SQL for this constraint definition does not use the clause foreign key; instead the keyword REFERENCES is used.

Figure 4.19 Foreign Key

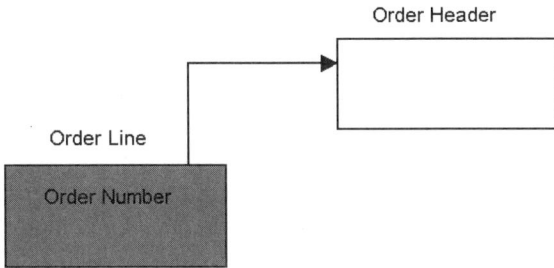

The SQL to create a foreign key constraint is shown below:

```
CREATE TABLE order_line
  (order_number  CHAR(10)
   CONSTRAINT order_line_fkey
    REFERENCES orders (order_number),
  order_value  NUMBER(8,2) );
```

The procedure for defining a foreign key is very similar to that for a primary key and this is where the GUI can help define the constraint.

Referring to Figure 4.20, first give the constraint a name, then pick the type of constraint, which in this case is FOREIGN. Now pick the schema in which the reference table resides, in this example ORDERS, and then select the table from the list, which is also called ORDERS. Now move down to the bottom box and select the column from this table that is to be checked and then the column from the referenced table. This highlights the major benefit of using this dialog box; you don't have to remember how to spell the column name, just select it from the drop down list.

Figure 4.20 Foreign Key Definition

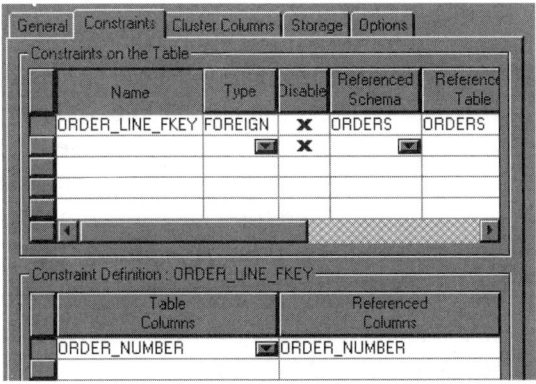

4.3.5   Check

Check clauses are used extensively because they are an excellent method for ensuring that a column value can only take one of a given range of values. Often developers put this type of check in the application, but it really should be in the database, because today users often have more than one tool that they can use to access and change data. Don't forget that even a power user could change data using SQL Worksheet. With the constraints in the database, you are guaranteed that invalid data cannot be entered. If the checks are only in the application then there is potential for breaching the required values.

The SQL for a typical CHECK constraint is shown below, where the column order_type can only take the values M, T or W.

```
CREATE TABLE orders
   (order_number   CHAR(10),
    order_type    VARCHAR2(1)
     CONSTRAINT order_type_check
        CHECK ( order_type IN ( 'M','T','W')) );
```

If you use the Storage Manager to define the constraint, as shown in Figure 4.21, then you will have to scroll across to find the check box. This is the one constraint where you have to explicitly write the evaluation clause, such as

order_type IN ('M','T','W')

Figure 4.21 Check Constraint Dialog

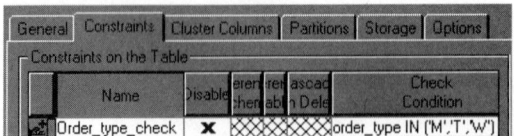

4.3.6   Deleting Constraints

Data that is part of a constraint definition cannot be deleted if it would violate the integrity constraint. For example, take our foreign key, that establishes a relationship between the orders and order_line. If the order was deleted without removing the order_lines, then we would have lines of an order without the order information. To prevent this situation, first the database will disallow any deletes on the parent. Therefore, the children in the relationship must be deleted first and then the parent can be removed.

If at any time a constraint is not required, it can be quickly disabled by clicking on the disable column as shown in Figure 4.21. A checkmark indicates that the constraint has been disabled. To remove the constraint, using the right mouse button, click on the gray box to the left of the constraint name, as shown in Figure 4.20. Then select *drop* or *drop cascade*. Drop cascade is used when you want to delete the parent and all of its children.

4.3.7   Constraint Evaluation

Prior to Oracle8 it was not possible to specify when a constraint was checked. Now as part of the constraint clause you can specify whether the constraint checking is immediate or deferred.

8
Oracle

An *immediate* constraint is evaluated at the end of the current SQL statement, whereas a *deferred* constraint is not evaluated until the transaction is committed. For performance reasons it is best to evaluate constraints immediately, otherwise data has to be reread to execute the constraint.

This feature in Oracle8 can currently only be defined via the SQL clause NOT DEFERRABLE and not via the Schema Manager.

```
CREATE TABLE orders
   (order_number  CHAR(10),
    order_type    VARCHAR2(1)
    CONSTRAINT order_type_check
       CHECK ( order_type IN ( 'M','T','W'))
       NOT DEFERRABLE );
```

4.3.8   Fast Constraint Creation

8
Oracle

There are times when you may want to enable a constraint, but you don't want to spend all the time checking the data because you know that none of the rows will violate the constraint. This is a common problem when a database is being reorganized. The solution to this problem is available in Oracle8, because now you can enable a constraint and request that no validation takes place upon the existing data, as shown in the example below using the SQL ENABLE NOVALIDATE clause.

```
ALTER TABLE fact
   ENABLE NOVALIDATE constraint fk_time;
```

Please be extremely careful when using this facility because it does rely on you knowing that the data currently residing in the database will not violate this constraint. The good news is that for very large databases, minutes and even hours could be saved during database reorganization because the constraints no longer have to be checked.

4.3.9   Enforced Constraint

8

Oracle

New in Oracle8 is the ability to *enforce* a constraint. An enforced constraint is just like an enabled constraint, except the database cannot guarantee that existing data in the database does not violate the constraint. A constraint is enforced using the

ALTER TABLE <table name> ENFORCE CONSTRAINT <name>;

4.4   INDEXES

An index is to a database what a gearbox is to a car. You could build and drive a car without a gearbox, but it would be inefficient and difficult to drive, to say the least. An index is a structure which eliminates the need to search every row in the table. Instead the index is searched, which greatly speeds up the response to database queries.

Defining indexes in an Oracle database is straight forward; about the only decision to make is which type of index has to be created:

- Sorted, or
- Bitmapped (new in Oracle 7.3).

Indexes can be defined either through the *Schema Manager* or directly using the SQL CREATE INDEX statement.

4.4.1   Sorted Index

The sorted index is the most commonly used index structure, especially since until recently it was the only type of index available. Creating one couldn't be easier, if we fill in the boxes shown in Figure 4.22. First give the index a name. Often DBAs use a naming convention that includes a suffix such as _IDX so that everyone knows that this is an index, or _N1, _N2 for the first and second nonunique indexes on a table and _U1 for unique indexes. Next, say in which tablespace the index is to reside; it can be a different tablespace than where the table is stored. Select the columns on which the table is to be indexed and press OK.

Another consideration is the size of the database block. The larger the block, the shallower the b-tree, thus improving read performance in the vast majority of cases.

If the index is created using the Schema Manager, before you select create index, position yourself in the navigator window on the table on which you want to build the index. When the box shown in Figure 4.22 is displayed, the table window will already be completed with this information.

An index can be defined as being unique by checking the unique box at the bottom of the window in Figure 4.22.

Figure 4.22 Create a Sorted Index

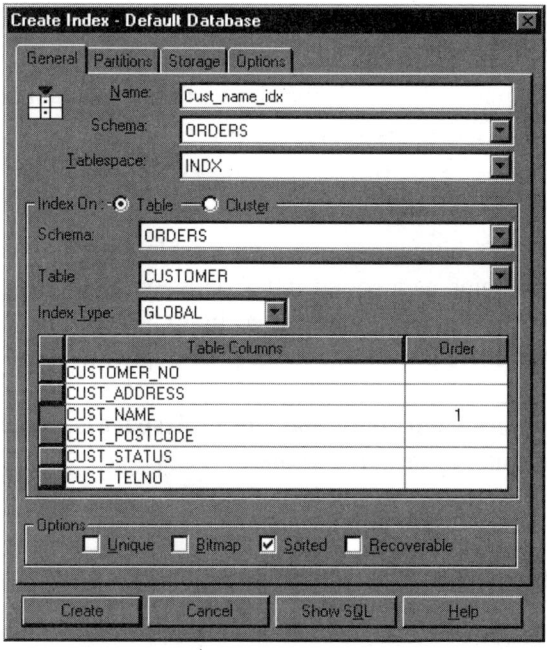

When we define the index we should also define how the index is to be stored in terms of the initial and next extents and %used, by clicking on the *storage* tab. The algorithm used for these values is the same as described previously for a table.

8

Oracle

When an index is defined using the Schema Manager dialog in Figure 4.22 it is built as an ascending index by default. Sometimes an index in descending order is required and it can be created by using the REVERSE clause on the CREATE INDEX statement as shown below.

```
CREATE INDEX cust_status_idx ON CUSTOMER
   (cust_status) REVERSE;
```

Existing indexes can be rebuilt by issuing an

```
ALTER INDEX cust_status_idx
   REBUILD REVERSE;
```

4.4.2   Bitmapped Indexes

A new type of index introduced in Oracle 7.3 is the bitmapped index. It is defined exactly the same as in Figure 4.22, except the *bitmap* box is checked instead of the *sorted* box in the options section at the bottom of the window.

Bitmapped indexes should be used when an index has a lot of rows but only a few unique values. Take our Customer table, which has a column called Customer status which can take one of four values. This would be an ideal candidate for this type of index. Bitmapped indexes store duplicate data much more efficiently than a conventional sorted index.

Creating a bitmapped index is the same as for a sorted index, but you include the keyword BITMAP as shown below.

```
CREATE BITMAP INDEX cust_status_idx ON CUSTOMER
            (cust_status) ;
```

You can create a bitmapped index on a table with unique values and it will work just the same as a sorted index. However, you could find that it takes much longer to create the bitmapped index. Therefore, only use bitmapped indexes when there are a large number of duplicate values.

Hint: Make sure plenty of temporary tablespace is available when creating bitmapped indexes on large tables.

4.5   PARTITIONING

8
Oracle

As databases grow in size, managing very large tables and indexes becomes a real problem for the DBA. A very welcome new feature in Oracle8 is the ability to partition a table or index across a number of datafiles, as shown in Figure 4.23. Partitioning is a very useful design technique, ideally suited to VLDB (Very Large Database) environment, but anyone can use it.

There are a number of reasons why a table would be partitioned. One is that maintenance can now be performed on a single partition rather than the entire table or index. Another would be that queries on ranges of data would now be restricted to searching specific partitions rather than all of the data. As you start to use partitions, other benefits specific to your application will no doubt appear.

Partitioning can be applied to either the table or the index or both. However, it usually makes sense to partition both the table and the index using the same range. A table or index is partitioned by specifying a partitioning criteria which is based on a range of values, determined by a *less than* clause. Each partition can have its own set of storage parameters, that is extents and %free. There is a limit on the number of partitions per table or index, but at 64000, I would be surprised if that didn't cater for most people's needs.

Figure 4.23 Partition

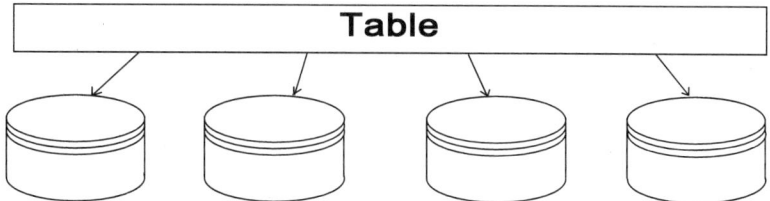

Anyone who has never used partitioning in a database may be looking at this section and thinking to themselves that this is going to be difficult. However, nothing could be further from the truth and here are some simple steps to follow to help you create a partitioned table.

1. Select the table to be partitioned.
2. Identify the column(s) which will be used to specify in which partition data resides. This is known as the *partitioning key.*
3. Decide how many partitions are required.
4. Create the tablespaces for each partition.
5. Define the partitioned table or index using SQL or the GUI shown in Figure 4.24.

Creating a partitioned table is not difficult, but no matter whether you use SQL or the GUI, it is a rather repetitive process, but really worth the effort. To understand the steps, imagine that we have an Orders table and we have decided to partition on the *month_ordered* column. Since this is part of creating a table, we select *Create Table* from within the Schema Manager and then click on the *Partitions* tab to obtain Figure 4.24.

It has been decided that the table will be split across 12 partitions, one for each month. The relationship is that a partition is mapped to a tablespace, therefore, its good design practice to name your tablespaces so that they are easy to relate to the appropriate partitions. For example, in Figure 4.24 the tablespaces have been named August, September, etc. and the partitions have been called Month8 and Month9.

One aspect of this process that is likely to catch everyone out the first time they try to do this, is that, before the partition can be created, the tablespaces must have previously been defined using the *Storage Manager* or SQL.

Figure 4.24 Creating a Partition

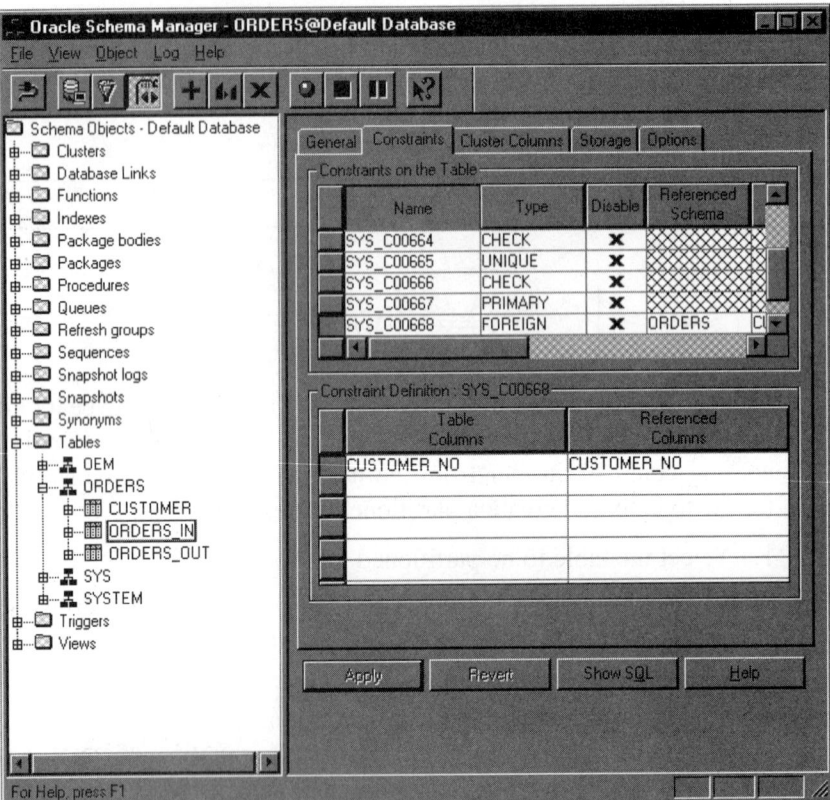

Now it is simply a matter of first selecting the columns on which to partition. In this example we are using only one, month_ordered. Then we click on the *Add* button, to reveal Figure 4.25. Most of the dialog here has been completed for us; all we need to supply is a name for the partition and the upper bound value for the partition range.

Since the range check is less than, be very careful defining each upper bound. Referring to our example where we are partitioning by month, assume that the month of August is allocated month number 8. Then the upper bound for this partition would be 9 because 8 is less than 9. If we used a value of 8, then because 8 is not less than 8, the data would be put in the next partition.

If required, each partition can have its own storage requirements, such as extents, and these are defined by pressing the *Storage* button. This process is now repeated for every partition and once they have all been defined, pressing *Create* in Figure 4.24 will create the partitioned table in the database.

Figure 4.25 Creating a Partition

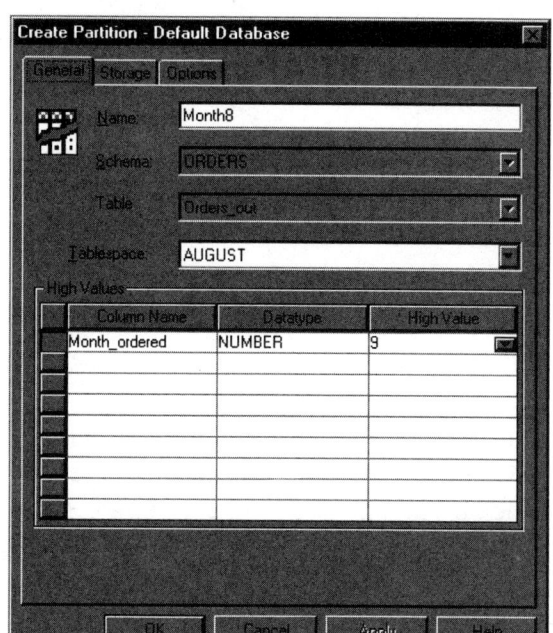

Hint: Don't be afraid to use different sized partitions (e.g, the December partition could be 1gb, but the one for August, a quiet time, is only 150mb).

Partitions can be defined using SQL and some readers may well prefer to cut and paste text a number of times rather than use the GUI to define it. An example of an SQL statement is shown below for a table called fact where we are using the time_key to partition. Note the power of the partitioning in Oracle8; we can use the TO_DATE function to translate our date into a format suitable for partitioning.

```
CREATE TABLE     fact
  (time_key       date,
   store_key      integer,
   unit_sales        integer,
   dollar_cost       number (6,2))
PARTITION BY RANGE (time_key )
  (PARTITION month9
    VALUES LESS THAN
      (TO_DATE('01-09-1997', 'DD-MM-YYYY'))
    PCTFREE 0 PCTUSED 99
    STORAGE (INITIAL 10M NEXT 10M PCTINCREASE 0)
    TABLESPACE september ,
```

```
PARTITION month10
 VALUES LESS THAN
    (TO_DATE('01-10-1997', 'DD-MM-YYYY'))
 STORAGE (INITIAL 1M NEXT 1M PCTINCREASE 0)
 TABLESPACE october );
```

The partitioned table is now defined. Whenever data is stored in the database, it will check the ranges to see in which partition to store the data.

4.5.1   Partitioned Indexes

8
Oracle

One of the big benefits of using partitions is that it can help the optimizer reduce the amount of data it has to scan. Suppose the query asks for all the orders within a given range of order numbers. If the table is partitioned on order number, and the requested range resides within one partition, then the optimizer knows only to scan that partition to find the requested data, thus saving a significant amount of system resources and improving query response time. This is just one example of how creating a partitioned index could improve access to information within your database. Four types of index can be created in an Oracle8 database:

- nonpartitioned;
- global prefixed;
- local prefixed;
- local nonprefixed.

A *nonpartitioned* index is the traditional type of index used before Oracle8. A *prefixed* index is one where the left-most columns of the index are the same as the columns used to partition the index (e.g., the table is partitioned on month_number and the first column of the index is also month number). A prefixed index is the one that you are most likely to use when partitioning tables, because then each index partition will only refer to data in that partition, as shown in Figure 4.26.

Figure 4.26   Prefixed Indexes

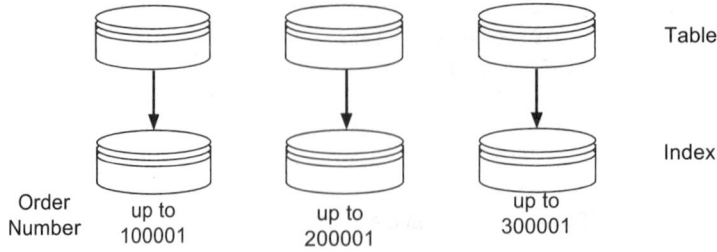

A *nonprefixed* index is where the columns used to partition the index do not match the columns used to partition the table (e.g., the index is partitioned on month_number and the table is partitioned on order_number). Implementing this type of partitioning, one index partition could point to any number of data partitions, as illustrated in Figure 4.27.

Figure 4.27 Nonprefixed Indexes

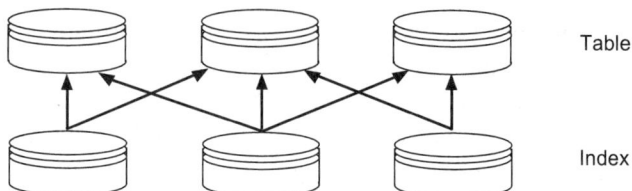

The final choice is to decide whether the index is to be of type:

- global;
- local.

In a *local* index, all rows in a table partition will have a corresponding index entry in the index partition. A *global* index can be unique or non-unique and is normally not partitioned the same as the table it refers to. Local indexes are the best ones to use because maintenance activities can be restricted to a single partition.

The partitioned index can be created using either SQL or via the Schema Manager GUI by selecting *Create Index* and then clicking on the *Partitions* tab, as shown in Figure 4.24 and then supplying the partition information as per the description for a table.

When you define a local partitioned index, as shown in the following SQL example, it is not necessary to specify the partition values, only the key.

```
CREATE bitmap INDEX grocery.fact_time_index
 ON fact
 (time_key )
  LOCAL
(PARTITION Imonth9    TABLESPACE index_september ,
 PARTITION Imonth10 TABLESPACE index_october);
```

These pages represent a brief introduction to partitioning and anyone building partitions into their database would be well advised to check the documentation for any restrictions and extra information that is not described in this text.

4.6   CLUSTERS

So far everything that we have stored in the database has been placed in its own extent. For instance, data from the orders table is held in one extent and the data for our customers is held in another extent. This approach usually works very well, but in some applications it could cause queries to take longer to respond, because I/O has to be performed to retrieve each segment separately. To avoid this problem, *clusters* can be created.

A cluster is an object in the database where like information is stored together based on a clustering key. For example, imagine an ordering system where there is an orders and an orders_line table. Now we know that every time an order is retrieved, we need to know the lines on the order. Therefore we can create a cluster to store all this information in one extent in the database as illustrated in Figure 4.28.

Figure 4.28 Clusters

Block

Order	Order Line	Order Line	Order Line	Order Line	Order Line

Clusters should be considered for tables that are queried and not frequently updated and tables that are often joined with other related tables.

Figure 4.29 Create a Cluster

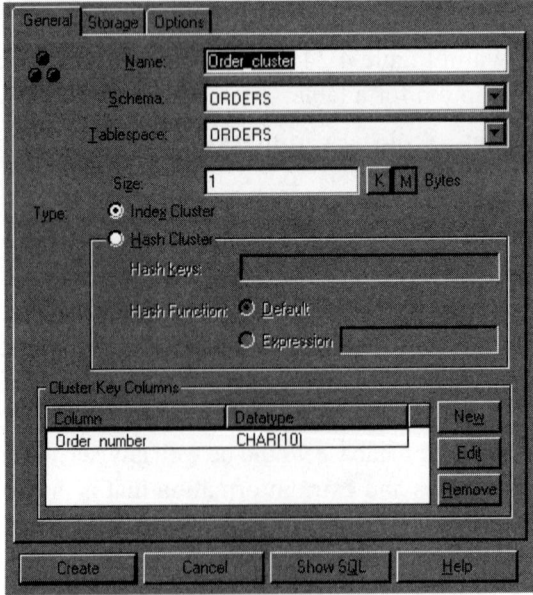

Several steps have to be followed, whether you use the Schema Manager or SQL, in order to create a cluster. If you are using the Schema Manager, then select *Create Cluster* which will display the dialog box shown in Figure 4.29.

First give the cluster a name and specify in which tablespace it is to be stored. Don't forget that like all the structures we have seen in this chapter, you can also specify its own storage options. The *size* value is very important because it states how much space is required to store all the rows for a particular cluster key value. Next, click on *Index cluster*, which is what this type of cluster is called.

The cluster key is defined by clicking on *New*, which displays Figure 4.30. Make sure you type in the correct name and its type and then press *Add*.

Figure 4.30 Define the Cluster Key

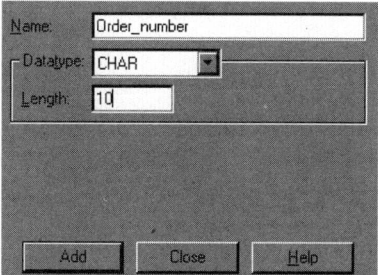

When you are finished defining keys click on the *Close* button. When finished defining the cluster click on the Create button shown in Figure 4.29. Clusters are considered a special type of object in the database and their existence can be checked in the Schema Manager by clicking on the Clusters name in the navigator window as shown in Figure 4.31.

Figure 4.31 Schema Manager and Clusters

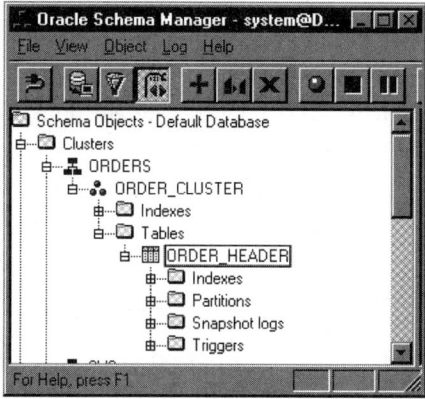

The final step is to create the tables that will reside in the cluster, so we return to the procedure we used for creating a table. This time we define the table as before, but if we were using the Schema Manager, then we would click on the *Clusters* tab to complete the dialog shown in Figure 4.32 by identifying which column in the table we were defining as the clustering column.

The definition of the table is complete and the cluster is now created. We will be able to see our table definition in two places in Schema Manager in the cluster hierarchy and under tables.

Figure 4.32 Define the Table in a Cluster

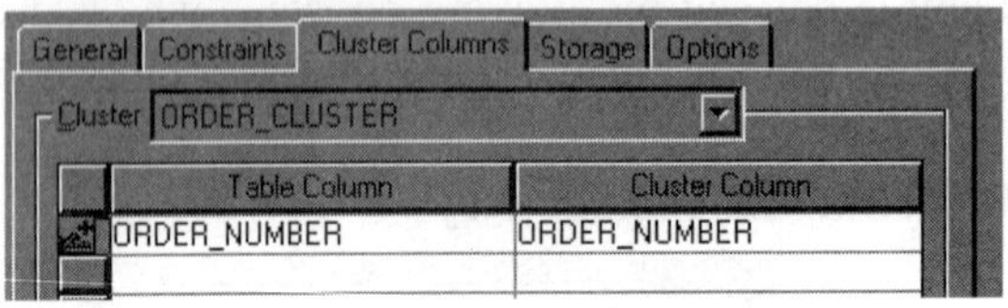

4.6.1   Hash Cluster

If you looked closely at Figure 4.29, then you may have noticed that one of the questions was whether to create an indexed or a hashed cluster. A hashed cluster is identical to the indexed cluster that we have just seen, except that a hash function is applied to the cluster key.

The reason for doing this is that by passing the value of the cluster key into a hashing algorithm, a block number is returned where the data is to be stored. This allows us to distribute data into different blocks. If there is a requirement to distribute the data across a range of blocks then the hash cluster should be selected, otherwise create an indexed cluster.

4.7   TRIGGERS

In today's databases, triggers are proving very popular for a variety of reasons. By implementing a trigger, you can guarantee that a given set of actions will occur when you insert, update or delete data. Triggers can be used to perform tasks like:

- cascading updates and deletes;
- summation updates;
- hidden deletes;
- preventing changes to data during certain hours;
- enforcing complex business rules on data.

Their use is widespread across a variety of applications. Since triggers can contain either SQL or the very powerful PL/SQL language, they can perform quite complex tasks. A trigger can be activated for a SQL insert, delete or update statement and you can declare whether the trigger must be performed before or after the statement.

So why use a trigger? First of all, by defining this code as part of the database, you are guaranteed that whenever certain actions are performed against a table, the trigger will always be fired. Therefore, the code is maintained in one place only, rather than in all the applications from which this action could be initiated.

But the real benefit comes when you have a specific task to perform. For example, suppose in your database that when an order is stored, the details are placed in six tables. That means that when an order is deleted, those six tables must be altered. Rather than tell every application to delete data from the six tables, a trigger is defined so that when the order is deleted, all data associated with that order is removed from the database. This type of trigger is called a *cascading delete*.

Other uses could be the maintenance of statistics or summary data. For example, every time a row is stored in a certain table, a trigger writes to another table recording some statistical data or updating a running total using a value from the row just stored. This is an example of a *summation update*.

Because you can write PL/SQL in a trigger, it could perform quite complex tasks like checking that the time at which the data is being changed is allowed or manipulating the data before it is placed inside the database. Hopefully this has given you some idea of how to use a trigger, but please don't get trigger happy and define too many because they could impact system performance.

A trigger can be created either using SQL or by selecting the trigger object in the Schema Manager. Usually the GUI is the preferred approach for defining a database object, but since the SQL or PL/SQL statements have to be manually entered as part of the trigger definition, there is no significant benefit in using the GUI dialog.

Using Schema Manager, select *Create Trigger* and the dialog box shown in Figure 4.33 appears. First give the trigger a name, and just like constraints, choose a meaningful name because if the trigger has an error, this is the name that will be displayed in the error message.

Next select on which table the trigger will be initiated. The actual SQL statements that must be executed by the trigger are entered manually into the very large box shown in Figure 4.33. No validation is applied to this box, therefore it is very important that it works. To avoid triggers failing due to bad SQL statements, here is a little tip. Write the SQL using SQL Worksheet and test it there first. When it works, copy the SQL into this box.

Figure 4.33 Create a Trigger

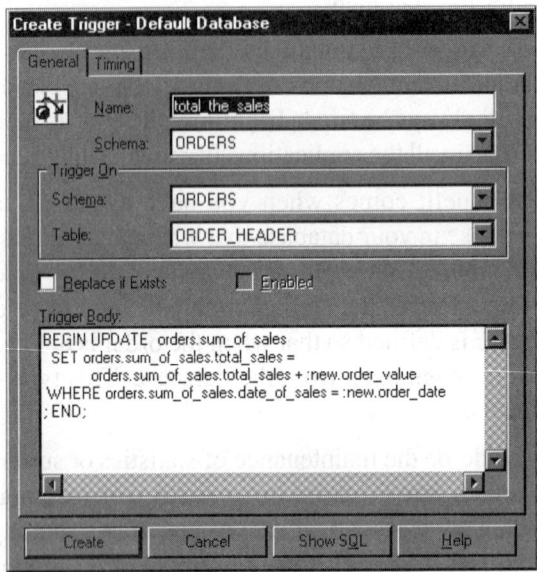

Figure 4.34 Trigger Timing

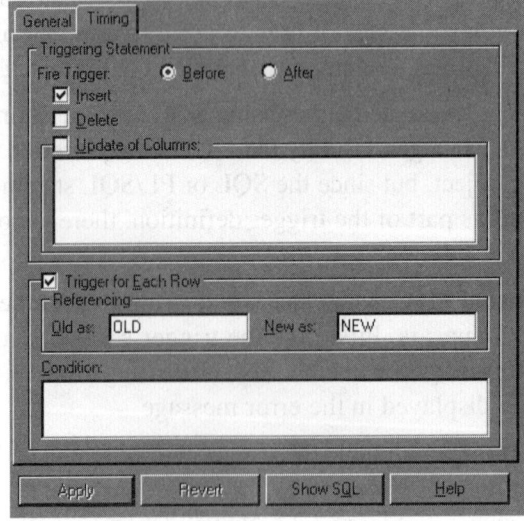

Before the trigger is created, the *Timing* tab must be pressed, which displays the dialog box shown in Figure 4.34. This box is extremely important, because it is here where you specify when the trigger is to be fired, that is, before or after the statement.

If the trigger is going to use data from the triggering table, then the trigger for each row box must be clicked and a prefix entered, which will identify the values from the triggering table. Referring back to Figure 4.33, this trigger is fired every time a row is inserted into the order_header table. It then updates a table called *sum_of_sales* with the value of the order for the date the ordered was placed. The value of the order is held in a column in order_header called *order_value.* If we then use the prefix of new as defined in Figure 4.33, the variable becomes *:new.order_value.* The colon is extremely important, without it, the trigger will fail. We can then update the correct row in *sum_of_sales* by selecting using *:new.order_date.* Obviously, these instructions cannot be written in SQL Worksheet and tested, but you could get the framework correct by supplying literals for the date and number and testing that first.

Once the trigger is created, it should be tested to see that it behaves as required. Once again, this can be done using SQL Worksheet as we can see below. Here we check the values in table *sum_of_sales*, before and after the new row has been inserted into *order_header.*

```
SQLWKS> SELECT * FROM orders.sum_of_sales;

DATE_OF_S  TOTAL_SALE
23-AUG-97    500.03
1 row selected.

SQLWKS> INSERT INTO order_header VALUES
        ('20A','23-AUG-1997',249.97);
1 row processed.

SQLWKS> SELECT * FROM orders.sum_of_sales;
DATE_OF_S  TOTAL_SALE
23-AUG-97    750
1 row selected.
```

Triggers are probably one of the hardest objects within the database to create because the triggering code has to be manually entered. Now if you are good at writing SQL then triggers won't be a problem. Otherwise, just allow a little extra time to create them. Even though they may take time to write and get working, the benefits that your database will see by using them far outweigh the creation time.

4.8   **VIEWS**

Another popular database object is the View, which is used extensively in databases. Unlike all the other objects that we have discussed, such as table and indexes and partitions that actually exist inside the database, views are logical objects. Therefore if you understand the internals of the database engine, then you could actually show where in the database an index is stored but not the view because it has no physical representation. A view is usually defined using a query that joins several tables.

Views are created in a database because:

- they offer a mechanism for restricting access to specific columns in a table;
- complex queries can be predefined using a view;
- data can be shown in a different format via a view;
- endusers who are not very sophisticated can view complex data through a simplified view.

A view at first glance looks very similar to a table and but for a few restrictions, you could insert, delete and update from a view as if it were a table.

Look at the example below. Suppose our endusers wanted to know how much business we have done with each supplier. They could type in the SQL SELECT statement shown below.

```
SELECT SUM( quantity * price)
  AS ordervalue , supplier.suppkey
    FROM supplier , lineitem
    WHERE lineitem.suppkey = supplier.suppkey
    GROUP BY suppkey ;
```

Alternatively, we could define a view called value_by_supplier and then the user would enter

```
SELECT * FROM value_by_supplier.
```

Don't you agree that it is much easier for the enduser to access the data via a view?

To create the view, the DBA would enter

```
CREATE VIEW value_by_supplier AS
  SELECT SUM( quantity * price)
  AS ordervalue , supplier.suppkey
      FROM supplier , lineitem
        WHERE lineitem.suppkey = supplier.suppkey;
          GROUP BY suppkey ;
```

This is a very simple example and the author has seen view definitions that span several pages of SQL and may join over a dozen tables. Since the bulk of the view definition is the SQL statement, creating the view via Schema Manager will require completing the dialog box shown in Figure 4.35. Unfortunately, the GUI won't help you write the SQL, so once again, you will have to enter it manually.

Figure 4.35 Views

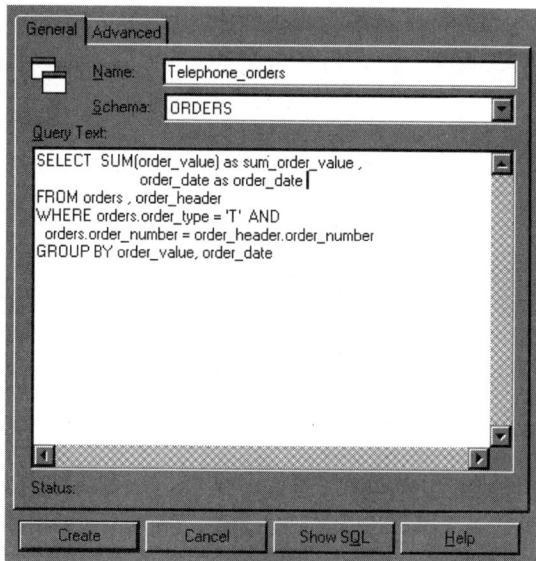

Views are primarily used for people to retrieve data. If a view contains a join, set operators, group functions, group by, connect by, start with or a distinct operator, then it cannot be used for inserts, updates or deletes.

4.9   SEQUENCES

How many times have you been developing an application where one of the columns has to increase in a sequence, such as an order or an invoice number? One would think that allocating the next number in a sequence would be an easy task. However, if you have ever had the misfortune to be given this task, you will know how difficult it is. Thankfully, this is a very easy problem to solve in an Oracle database because it has a special object called a sequence.

You can create as many sequences as you like and each one generates a unique integer number. A sequence is defined either in SQL or via the Schema Manager as illustrated in Figure 4.36. When a sequence is defined, you can specify its starting value, how it is to be incremented, what its maximum and minimum values are and whether it can cycle around when the maximum value is reached.

Figure 4.36   Create a Sequence

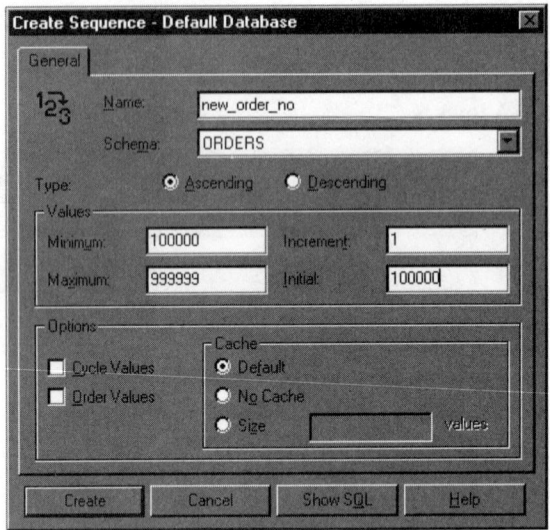

The sequence number is obtained in one of two ways. The next number is obtained by using the psedocolumn *nextval* and the current value by using *currval*. The number is obtained by calling the sequence and then the pseudocolumn. This means that a sequence can be used in a number of ways.

For example, it can be retrieved by requesting *nextval* by using the dummy table dual as shown below.

```
SELECT orders.new_order_no.nextval FROM DUAL;

NEXTVAL
----------
  100000
1 row selected.
```

Alternatively, it can be referenced directly in an SQL statement such as an INSERT or UPDATE.

```
INSERT INTO orders.orders VALUES
( orders.new_order_no.nextval , 'T');
```

The big benefit of using sequence numbers is in an environment where there are lots of users, all needing the next number for their transaction. It can be obtained without any locking conflicts, which is the problem that besets anyone who tries to implement this manually.

4.10   **SUMMARY**

This long chapter has introduced most of the objects that you can create in an Oracle database. Even using all these pages, we have only skimmed the surface on some of the functionality available with these features. Nevertheless, hopefully you will now appreciate what the Oracle8 engine has to offer.

5   SQL

This chapter will concentrate on how to use the SQL language against the Oracle database. SQL is to a database what wheels are to a car. Although in the beginning, database vendors had their own languages, today everyone communicates with the database using SQL plus their own special extensions.

A standard has been defined for the SQL language, therefore SQL written against one database engine should work against another database engine. In theory this is true, but every database vendor has extended SQL to support functionality in their own product. The Oracle8 server is no different, so don't be surprised if some of the SQL shown here works only against an Oracle8 database.

5.1   USING SQL

There are two tools available for writing SQL statements in Oracle:

- SQL*Plus;
- SQL Worksheet.

SQL*Plus can be found in the *Oracle for Windows NT* program group. Before it starts, the user is prompted to enter a username and password and then a new window is created, as shown in Figure 5.1, into which the SQL statements can be written.

Anyone who has used Oracle on a platform other than NT will probably feel right at home using SQL*Plus. It is a very good tool, and behaves and looks like a typical command line tool. The author prefers to use SQL Worksheet, but any of the examples here can be used in either of these tools.

In SQL*Plus no help is available, so make sure the documentation is handy so that syntax can be verified. There is also no ability to recall commands that have previously been entered, so if you use SQL*Plus, make sure that you keep script files to keep typing to a minimum.

Figure 5.1 SQL*Plus Tool

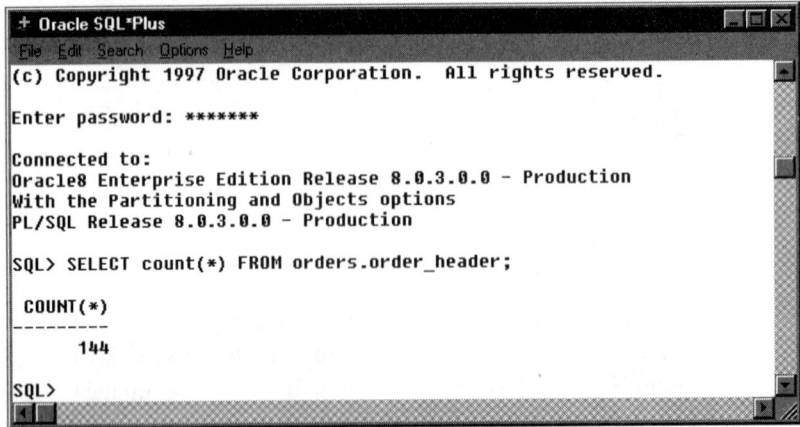

SQL Worksheet is one of the GUI tools provided as part of Oracle Enterprise Manager. It can be started independently from the Oracle Enterprise Manager program group or from the console. When it is started, and a valid username and password have been entered, the window shown in Figure 5.2 is displayed.

The top window displays the results of the query and the bottom window is where the SQL is entered. The results window is scrollable so it is easy to look back at previous results.

When SQL is entered into the bottom window, it is not executed until the execute icon ▓ is pressed. One of the nice features in SQL Worksheet is the ease with which SQL scripts can be saved and retrieved. To save the current SQL simply click on the Save ▓ icon, which will ask for the name and location of where the SQL is to be stored. Since the bottom window is a free text area, hopefully this will encourage you to add comments to your SQL statements so that people returning to the commands later will know why they exist.

The commands entered can often be retrieved from the output window. However, too much output could lose a few commands, so click on the ▓ icon to display a list of previous commands. Select the one you require from the list and press the *Get* button.

Hint: Using *Save Output As* will save the entire contents of the output window, not just the lines currently visible.

The size of each window can be adjusted by dragging the mouse over the center dividing line so that a double line with arrows at the top and the bottom appear. Click on the mouse and drag the box to resize it.

Figure 5.2 SQL Worksheet

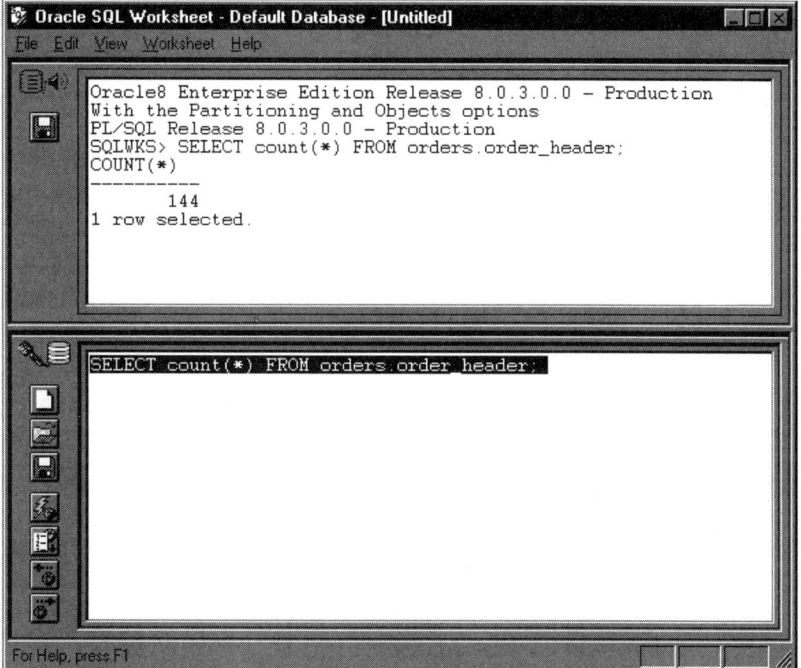

Writing SQL statements via SQL Worksheet is so easy that you will quickly build up a library of SQL scripts. Changing any statement merely involves moving the mouse to the appropriate place in the window, clicking, and then entering the new characters.

Now we will see how to access and manipulate data using SQL. All the following examples will consist only of the SQL statements, which could easily be entered in either of the two tools described here.

5.2   ACCESSING DATA

Now it is time to see what is involved in retrieving data from our database.

5.2.1   Comments

How many times have you heard somebody say, if only they had written a comment with this code, we might understand what it is doing. As you start to write SQL scripts, comments will need to be included. This can be achieved by using any of the following methods:

```
REM This is a comment
-- This is a comment
/* This is a comment */
```

5.2.2   Starting a Transaction

All work against a database is performed within the realms of a transaction. A transaction has a start point, includes a number of SQL statements and upon completion of the transaction, requires you to say whether to COMMIT, that is keep all the changes, or ROLLBACK, undo all the changes, back to the start of the transaction.

Transactions are invaluable in the database world because they give the user the ability to revert changes. For example, imagine a telephone ordering system, where, right in the middle of the order, the customer changes his mind and decides not to place the order. The operator presses the cancel order key, which instructs the database to rollback the changes it has made and return the database to the state it was at prior to the start of this order. Without a transaction, this would be a complex operation.

Whenever you do any work inside the database that changes its contents, the previous contents of the record are written into a rollback segment. These are then used if you decide to rollback a transaction. Since all your changes go into the rollback segments, it is very important that you have sufficiently sized rollback segments to hold of all of your changes.

There are two types of transactions:

- read only;
- read write.

By default, a transaction in SQL is started as read write, which means that anyone in this type of transaction can both read and write data. Anyone using a read only transaction is only allowed to read data.

A transaction is either started implicitly by the use of an SQL statement, or it can be explicitly started with a

```
-- Example of a Read Only Transaction
SET TRANSACTION READ ONLY;

-- Example of a Read Write Transaction
SET TRANSACTION READ WRITE;
```

The transaction is finished by using the COMMIT or the ROLLBACK statement. A typical application will use many transactions and there is no limit to how many are created. However, when writing transactions always try to keep them as short as possible. This will reduce the likelihood of a lock conflict with another user.

Savepoints

Sometimes you don't want to undo all the changes that have been made in a transaction and would prefer to rollback to a point within the transaction instead. This is possible with the Oracle8 database using a facility known as savepoints. Referring to Figure 5.3, the transaction is started and then a number of SQL statements are issued. At key points, save points are marked using a SAVEPOINT statement. Then, when we decide to rollback, we only rollback to a savepoint instead of all the way back to the start of the transaction.

The undo of only some of the changes is achieved by using the ROLLBACK TO SAVEPOINT statement.

Shown below is an example where a read write transaction is started.

Figure 5.3 Savepoints

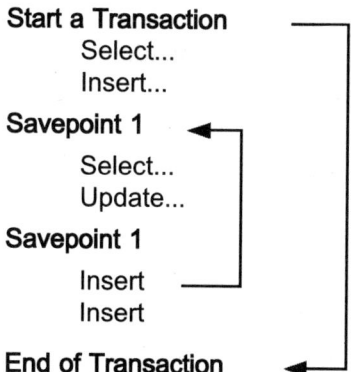

```
/* Savepoint Example */
SET TRANSACTION READ WRITE;
SELECT COUNT(*) FROM orders.order_header;

SAVEPOINT insert_header;

INSERT INTO orders.order_header
  VALUES ('LILIAN','1-SEP-1997',1);

SAVEPOINT insert_customer;
INSERT INTO orders.customer
  VALUES ('lhobbs','Lilian Hobbs','My Address',
          'SO23 1TQ','123',1);
```

```
ROLLBACK TO SAVEPOINT insert_customer;
COMMIT;
```

The first savepoint called insert_header is defined after the first select statement. Another savepoint is defined just prior to the insert of the customer record. Therefore, in this example we could insert the order header row and then back out the customer that was just inserted.

5.2.3   Retrieving Data

Probably the most used SQL statement is the SELECT command for retrieving information from the database. It can be one of the simplest or most complex statements that you may ever write. Shown here are some of the ways it can be used to retrieve information. For the reader who needs to write far more complex SQL instructions, it is recommended that the Oracle documentation is consulted.

Simple Retrieval

The basic format of the SELECT statement is SELECT some data from one or more tables that match a given condition.

```
SELECT * FROM orders.customer WHERE
  customer_no = 'lhobbs';
```

Where the FROM clause identifies the table and the WHERE clause the selection criteria.

Group By

The GROUP BY clause is a convenient way to group together data that has an aggregate function like SUM applied to it. In the example shown below, a list of the total value of orders taken for each date is generated.

```
SELECT order_date, SUM(order_value)
  FROM orders.order_header
   GROUP BY order_date;

ORDER_DATE  SUM(ORDER_VALUE)
----------  ----------------
23-AUG-97        9264.48
01-SEP-97              7
2 rows selected.
```

The GROUP BY clause is very popular and can be used with other functions like COUNT, MIN and MAX.

Having

Sometimes the GROUP BY clause does not restrict the data sufficiently, which is when the HAVING clause is required. Using the previous example, suppose we are only interested in the value of orders taken after August 31. Then the query is written as:

```
SELECT order_date, SUM(order_value)
  FROM orders.order_header
   GROUP BY order_date
    HAVING order_date > '31-AUG-1997';

ORDER_DATE  SUM(ORDER_VALUE)
----------  ----------------
01-SEP-97            7
1 row selected.
```

Sorting

Since data inside the database is stored in a random order, there is often a requirement to present the data in some sorted form. This is achieved by using the ORDER BY clause. Data can be sorted into either ascending (ASC) or descending (DESC) order.

```
SELECT cust_name FROM orders.customer
  ORDER BY cust_name DESC;

CUST_NAME
---------
Paul Hobbs
Paul Gaffer
Louise Wiles
Lilian Hobbs
4 rows selected.
```

If no sorting sequence is specified, the default order is ascending.

Retrieving only n rows

There are times when, rather than viewing the entire contents of a table, only a sample of the rows that satisfy the selection criteria are required. This can be achieved by using the ROWNUM clause. As a row is returned by a query, it is allocated a unique number starting from one. By including ROWNUM in the WHERE clause, it is possible to specify how many rows to display.

Referring to the previous example, to see only the first two rows returned the SQL would be:

```
SELECT cust_name FROM orders.customer
 WHERE ROWNUM <3
  ORDER BY cust_name DESC;

CUST_NAME
-----------
Paul Hobbs
Lilian Hobbs
2 rows selected.
```

Rename a column

There are times when it is very useful to rename a column or give a column a name such as when an aggregate operation like SUM is performed. Columns are renamed using the AS clause. In the example below, we can see how the result of the SUM has been placed in a column called value.

```
SELECT order_date AS date_in ,
    SUM(order_value) AS value
 FROM orders.order_header
  GROUP BY order_date ;

DATE_IN     VALUE
---------   --------
23-AUG-97   9264.48
01-SEP-97      7
2 rows selected.
```

Relational Operators

There are quite a number of operators available for use in SQL queries. These are shown below.

=	Equal To	<>	Not Equal To
>	Greater Than	<	Less Than
>=	Greater Than or Equal	<=	Less Than or Equal
IN		ANY, SOME	
ALL		BETWEEN	
EXISTS		LIKE	
IS NULL		NOT	
AND		OR	

Partial Matching

Queries usually rely on matching an entire column value, but what if you are only interested in, say, orders that contain the letter A in the order_number?

Queries of this type are possible using the LIKE clause.

```
SELECT count(*) FROM orders.order_header
  WHERE order_number LIKE '%A%';
```

A % value means that any number of characters are valid and an underscore uses only 1 character. In the previous example, an order number with any number of characters before or after the letter A would be returned, whereas in the example below, only order_numbers whose second character begins with 4 are reported.

```
SELECT count(*) FROM orders.order_header
  WHERE order_number LIKE '_4%';
```

Distinct

The DISTINCT clause is very useful to eliminate duplicate values in a table from a query. Take the example shown below; rather than listing every order date, of which there could be many for the same day, the DISTINCT clause removes all of those duplicates and returns just two dates.

```
SELECT distinct(order_date) FROM orders.order_header;

ORDER_DATE
----------
23-AUG-97
01-SEP-97
2 rows selected.
```

Not Null

Null values are often used in relational databases. If a column in a table is not given a value initially, then it is said to be null. Applications often rely on performing null checks and a query can ask whether a column IS NULL or is NOT NULL.

```
SELECT distinct(order_date)
   FROM orders.order_header
    WHERE order_value IS NOT NULL;
```

To insert a null value into a row the NULL clause is used.

```
INSERT INTO orders.customer VALUES
 ('www1','Internet Made Simple',NULL,
    NULL,'01234 56789','1');
```

Existence

Sometimes one needs to know if a row does or does not exist. Take the example shown below, where we are going to display the order_number of any row in the order_header table that does not have a corresponding row in the order_line table.

```
SELECT orders.order_header.order_number
  FROM orders.order_header
   WHERE NOT EXISTS
       (SELECT orders.order_line.order_number FROM
         orders.order_line
          WHERE
            orders.order_line.order_number =
            orders.order_header.order_number);
```

Existence tests can be either NOT EXISTS, as above, or EXISTS.

Functions

When it comes to functions, the Oracle8 user is spoiled with choices, because there is a vast number to choose from. The functions can be broken down into a number of categories:

- Number
- Character
- Date
- Conversion
- Group
- Other

Nothing special has to be written to include the function in a SQL statement. It is specified with the column to which it refers.

```
SELECT MAX(order_value) FROM
  orders.order_header;
```

For a complete list of functions, please refer to the Oracle documentation.

Take care when using functions because they may disable an index and therefore affect performance.

The *number* functions all expect to be given a numeric value, and they return a numeric value. The functions available range from scientific ones like COS (cosine of an angle) and SQRT (square root) to ROUND (round a number to a specified number of decimal places) and ABS (return the absolute value of a number).

The *character* functions are always popular, because they not only perform string manipulation, like changing everything to lowercase, but they also convert characters into numbers. Here are some examples of how to use some of the character functions.

```
-- Join two characters together
SELECT CONCAT(cust_name, cust_postcode) FROM
  orders.customer;

CONCAT(CUST_NAME,CUST_POSTCODE)
-------------------------------
Lilian HobbsSO23 1TQ
Paul HobbsRG23 1TQ
Louise WilesSW23 1TQ

-- Number of characters in a string
SELECT LENGTH(cust_name) FROM
  orders.customer;

LENGTH(CUST_NAME)
-----------------
      12
      10
```

The *conversion* functions enable a column to be converted from one datatype to another, such as from a DATE datatype to a VARCHAR2 using the function TO_CHAR, or from a number to a character string using the function TO_NUMBER.

```
SELECT TO_NUMBER(cust_status) FROM
  orders.customer;
```

The *other* functions include the ability to return the least value in a list, function LEAST, and the value to return whether or not a column is null using the NVL function.

```
SELECT customer_no,
  NVL(cust_address, 'no address supplied')
    FROM orders.customer;

lhobbs My Address
phobbs My Address
lwiles My Address
mlarge My Address
www1   no address supplied
5 rows selected.
```

The ever popular *group* functions are always being used in SQL statements. They comprise of functions like AVG, COUNT, MIN, MAX and SUM.

```
SELECT order_date, SUM(order_value)
FROM orders.order_header
 GROUP BY order_date;

ORDER_DAT SUM(ORDER_VALUE)
--------- ----------------
23-AUG-97          9264.48
01-SEP-97                7
2 rows selected.
```

Working with Dates

With the year 2000 approaching, dates which were once considered a routine item inside the database are now attracting lots of attention. Databases are often asked to manipulate dates and Oracle8 provides a comprehensive range of functions and facilities to make working with dates easy.

All of the date functions, expect the column to be of the DATE datatype, and they all except function MONTHS_BETWEEN, return their results as a date. With careful use of other functions and the initialization parameter NLS_DATE_FORMAT, working with dates couldn't be simpler.

Oracle8 provides a number of date functions, which includes ADD_MONTHS, LAST_DAY, MONTHS_BETWEEN, NEXT_DAY and SYSDATE. SYSDATE returns the current date and time.

```
SELECT sysdate, LAST_DAY(sysdate) FROM dual;
SYSDATE     LAST_DAY_0
---------   ---------
30-AUG-97   31-AUG-97
1 row selected.
```

One of the really nice features in Oracle8 is that dates can be displayed in an extensive range of formats. When the database is first created, the initialization parameter NLS_DATE_FORMAT advises how dates will be displayed. By using the ALTER SESSION command it is possible to change that format. In the example below, instead of dates being displayed as DD-Month-YY, we use the ALTER SESSION command to display dates using only the day. Then when we use the function LAST_DAY to find out when the last day is in the current month, it returns the value as the day, which in this case is Sunday.

```
ALTER SESSION SET NLS_DATE_FORMAT = 'Day';
SELECT sysdate Today,
 LAST_DAY(sysdate) "Last Day" FROM dual;

TODAY     Last Day
--------  --------
Saturday  Sunday
```

In the SQL Language Reference Manual all the different date format options are described, providing you with a wealth of options for displaying not only the date, but also the time.

```
ALTER SESSION
SET NLS_DATE_FORMAT = 'YYYY-MON-DD HH24 MI SS';

SELECT sysdate "Current Date/Time" FROM dual;
Current Date/Time
-------------------
1997-AUG-30 09 51 38
```

Since the format of dates can be changed during a session, this means that users can view dates according to their own specific requirements. Some of the date formatting options are:

YYYY	4 digit year
MM	2 digit month
MON	Abbreviated month name
MONTH	Full month name
DD	2 digit day
DDD	Day in the year
DAY	Day name
HH	Hour of the day
SS	Seconds of the day

Hint: Use these formats to convert dates into numeric values to simplify calculations like how many days the account is overdue.

Formatting Options

In some of the examples shown in this chapter, you may have noticed that the output had been reformatted and here are some examples of what can be achieved.

```
-- Change the Heading of a Column
SELECT order_value 'Value of Order'
  FROM orders.order_header;

Value of Order
--------------
     10.25
```

This is the one time when SQL*Plus offers more formatting options than SQL Worksheet. Therefore, if you want to use SQL to generate some reports, this would be when it would be a good time to use SQL*Plus. For instance, the COLUMN command enables you to define, once only, what the heading should be for this column, instead of having to specify it every time.

```
SQL> COLUMN order_value HEADING 'Value of Order';
SQL> SELECT order_value FROM orders.order_header;

Value of Order
--------------
        10.25
```

From the SQL*Plus window, if you click on *Options* and then *Environment*, all the formatting and other options are shown, so they can be changed using the dialog shown in Figure 5.4. For example, here we are setting the underline character to be the equals sign.

Figure 5.4 Formatting Options in SQL*Plus

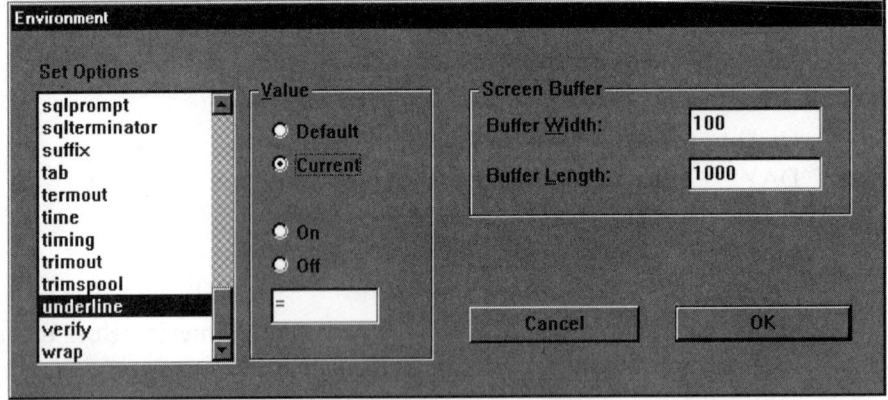

Alternatively, these options can be set using their own commands as illustrated below:

```
-- Set the Underline character to =
SET UNDERLINE =
```

Other useful formatting options include the ability to set a BREAK, define spacing options and even COMPUTE statistics at a break point. In the SQL*Plus documentation there is an extensive range of examples, displaying what it is possible to achieve.

Table Alias

Another useful technique to learn is when to use a table alias. Table names can be quite long, but an alias allows you to abbreviate it to something as short as a single character.

A technique the author often uses is to select a character that corresponds to the table name. Therefore C is used for Customer and O for Orders. An alias doesn't have to be that short; it's your decision as to what to use. An alias is usually used when tables are being joined together, or the same column is in two tables and you need to identify which column is to be displayed.

In the example below, the table order_header is given the alias OH and the table orders the alias O. The column order_number appears in both tables, therefore to use the one in the order_header table the alias "oh" is prefixed before the column name.

```
SELECT oh.order_number, order_value, order_type
  FROM orders.order_header oh, orders.orders o
    WHERE oh.order_number = o.order_number;
```

5.2.4   Joining Tables

One of the reasons that relational databases have become so popular is the flexible way that data can be retrieved. Gone are the days when the only way that data could be accessed was by the paths defined by the DBA. Today you can retrieve and manipulate the data however you like.

Multitable Joins

Joining tables in a relational database is done all the time and it isn't restricted to tables. A join can be performed between tables, views and snapshots. A simple join involves joining two or more tables on one or more common columns.

```
SELECT oh.order_number, order_value, order_type
  FROM orders.order_header oh, orders.orders o
    WHERE oh.order_number = o.order_number;
```

Outer Join

Another useful type of join is the outer join. This is used when two tables are joined together and one of the tables cannot match all of its rows with the other table. In the previous example, we only retrieved those rows that had the same order number in the orders and order_header table. But suppose we wanted to know the rows in the order_header table that do not have a matching row in the orders table. This can be achieved by using the *outer join* operator, which is denoted by including (+) in the SQL.

```
SELECT oh.order_number, order_value, order_type
  FROM orders.order_header oh, orders.orders o
    WHERE oh.order_number = o.order_number (+);
```

Union

The union operator allows tables to be joined together without the need for a selection criteria. Two types of union are allowed. UNION, which joins the tables and removes duplicate values, and UNION ALL which does not eliminate the duplicate rows.

In the example below, the two tables are joined together and the duplicate rows in the order_lines table are removed.

```
SELECT order_number "order #" FROM
  orders.order_line
 UNION
SELECT order_number FROM orders.order_header;

order #
-------
20A
21A
22A
23A
24A
25A
6 rows selected.
```

If the clause UNION ALL were used, then all the rows in both tables would be displayed.

Subqueries

The ability to query the database and include a subquery allows for very powerful SQL statements to be created. This is because the results of the subquery can be used to determine which rows are displayed from the main query.

In the example below, first a search is made for location codes beginning with R, then the location codes are used to determine which order headers should be reported.

```
SELECT * FROM orders.order_header
 WHERE order_location =
    (SELECT loc_code FROM orders.location_codes_iot
     WHERE loc_code LIKE 'R%')

ORDER_NUMBER  ORDER_DATE  ORDER_VALUE  LOC
------------  ----------  -----------  ---
100000        30-AUG-97   10.34        RDG
100001        30-AUG-97   10.34        RDG
2 rows selected.
```

Dual Table

A special table called DUAL is provided by Oracle. It only contains one column and it can be used to obtain the current date, rather than by querying one of the other tables.

```
SELECT sysdate FROM dual;

SYSDATE
-------
10-AUG-97
1 row selected.
```

5.2.5   Keywords and Reserved Words

When writing SQL you must be very careful not to use any keywords or reserved words. Examples of a *reserved word* are ORDER, NUMBER and DELETE. No object can be created in the database that uses a reserved word, or the following error will be generated:

```
CREATE TABLE order
  ( ord_no VARCHAR2(5),
    ord_dt DATE);

 ORA-00903: invalid table name
```

There is a long list of reserved words in the SQL Reference Manual.

A keyword is similar to a reserved word in that it has special meaning, such as CHECKPOINT or CURSOR. Objects can be created that use keywords, but this is not recommended.

It is a good idea when naming objects to stay well away from keywords and reserved words, because otherwise your SQL could be quite confusing to read. However, sometimes it is difficult; in a telephone ordering system it is very natural to create a table called order, but this is not allowed since order is a reserved word.

If an object must be created using a reserved word, this can be done by enclosing the word within quotes as shown below.

```
CREATE TABLE "order"
  ( ord_no VARCHAR2(5),
    ord_dt DATE);
Statement processed.
```

However, all subsequent references to the object must then be enclosed within quotes.

```
DROP TABLE "order";
```

5.3   DATA MANIPULATION

So far we have seen how to retrieve data from the database, but before we can do this, some data must be stored. In Chapter 6 we will see how to use tools like SQL*Loader for storing data, but the majority of inserts will come from using the SQL commands STORE, INSERT and UPDATE.

Whenever data is changed in the database, it must be done within a read write transaction. Fortunately, Oracle8 always starts a read write transaction, but to keep your changes don't forget to issue the COMMIT statement at the end of the transaction.

5.3.1   Storing

Rows are stored in the database using the INSERT statement. If you are going to store a value in every column, then the list of columns can be omitted.

```
INSERT INTO orders.location_codes_iot
  VALUES ('TVP','Reading HQ');
```

However, if you plan to only insert data for some of the rows in the column, then each column must be specified. In the example below, the table actually has four columns, but we are only inserting data into two of them. The omitted values will be given a null value.

```
INSERT INTO orders.order_header
  (order_number, order_date)
    VALUES ('100005',sysdate);
```

Another useful tip is that the values to be inserted can come from either another table or the same table. This technique can be very useful if anyone is trying to create some test data and needs to populate a table.

```
INSERT INTO orders.order_header
  SELECT * FROM orders.order_header;
154 rows processed.
```

In the example above we have been able to insert 154 rows, and if we repeated the instruction, then next time 308 rows would be inserted.

5.3.2   Updating

Once data is in the database, it usually has to be changed, and this is achieved using the UPDATE statement. An update can be applied to one or more rows or an entire table.

```
UPDATE orders.order_header
  SET order_location = 'POT'
   WHERE order_location IS NULL;
```

5.3.3   Deleting

Data is removed from the database using the DELETE command. All the rows in a table can be deleted or specific rows can be selected.

```
DELETE FROM orders.order_header
WHERE order_location = 'POT';
```

Hint: If all the rows have to be deleted, use the TRUNCATE TABLE statement which deletes the rows much quicker than the DELETE command. A TRUNCATE TABLE command works almost instantly.

5.4   PL/SQL

PL/SQL is an extension to the SQL language that allows you to almost write a program using SQL and other statements. PL/SQL is a block structured language that consists of a

```
DECLARE      (declarations)
BEGIN
             (statements)
EXCEPTION    (handling)
END
```

One way to think of PL/SQL is to imagine a good old fashioned programming language like COBOL or BASIC. Where you can define variables and the flow of the program depends on certain conditions and what to do in the unlikely event of an error. Now imagine taking that program and storing it inside the database. Then to execute the program you call it from any application. PL/SQL is an incredibly powerful language, which Oracle applications use extensively.

The benefits of using PL/SQL are:

- supports SQL;
- improved performance;
- higher productivity;
- support for object-oriented programming;
- integration with Oracle applications.

Probably the best way to learn about PL/SQL is to work through an example. What has been written here merely skims the surface of what is possible in PL/SQL. The goal of this section is to give you an appreciation of what it can do. To find out more, please refer to the PL/SQL manuals.

Displaying Results

When a query is executed outside of PL/SQL, the contents of the rows are automatically displayed, but this is not the case in PL/SQL. In order to see the contents of a row, a package called DBMS_OUTPUT must be used, which displays the results upon completion of the SQL statement.

Before it can be used, output must first be enabled by calling

```
SET SERVEROUTPUT ON;
```

Then for each line to be displayed, the package DBMS_OUTPUT is called, passing in the values as one long text line. Therefore if multiple values have to be displayed you will need to use the || operation. In the example shown below, the text 'row from cursor' is output, along with the contents of the variable this_order.

```
DBMS_OUTPUT.PUT_LINE
     ('row from cursor: ' || this_order);
```

A complete example showing the use of this feature is shown in the cursor section.

Variables

Within a PL/SQL block, variables and constants may be defined using the DECLARE statement before the BEGIN block. In our example we have declared two variables and one constant.

```
DECLARE
  counter NUMBER := 1; -- counter
  orderval NUMBER (4,2); -- local value of order
  maxloop CONSTANT NUMBER :=10; -- control the loop
BEGIN
  FOR i IN 1..maxloop LOOP
    counter:= counter +1;

  END LOOP;
END;
```

The first variable is called counter and has been assigned an initial value of 1. The next variable is called orderval and it has no initial value, but is available for use in the BEGIN/END block. A constant called maxloop has been defined with a value of 10. Any number of variables can be specified in the declaration area for use within the main block of the procedure.

As with any program, if you plan to have a number of variables, then please add some comments so that people know what the variables are supposed to contain. If nothing else, the original author will appreciate some comments when he or she visits the procedure months or even years later.

Cursors

Whenever data is retrieved from the database, Oracle always uses a cursor. Even a query returning one row will have a cursor created, but because this is done behind the scenes without you knowing, it is known as an *implicit* cursor.

The users can define their own cursors and these are called *explicit* cursors. They are used when you have to work with a number of rows that have to be processed individually. In order to use a cursor, several steps must be followed.

1. Declare the cursor.
2. Open the cursor, which actually identifies the data.
3. Retrieve each row from the cursor.
4. Close the cursor when done.

The declaration of the cursor simply states the query and gives the cursor a name which is used to manipulate it. The cursor is not created until it is opened, so it is at that point that the contents of the cursor are formed. Once opened, each row is retrieved from the cursor using the fetch statement. Some form of loop is normally required to process each row in the cursor. When you have finished working with the cursor, don't forget to close it.

```
SET SERVEROUTPUT ON;
DECLARE
  this_order
       orders.order_header.order_number%TYPE;
  this_value orders.order_header.order_value%TYPE;

  CURSOR today_orders IS
    SELECT order_number, order_value FROM
      orders.order_header
    WHERE
       TO_CHAR( order_date , 'DD-MON-YYYY') =
              '31-AUG-1997' ;
```

```
BEGIN
 OPEN today_orders;
 LOOP
   FETCH today_orders INTO this_order, this_value;
    DBMS_OUTPUT.PUT_LINE
   ('row from cursor: ' || this_order
    ||this_value);
   EXIT WHEN today_orders%NOTFOUND;
 END LOOP;
 CLOSE today_orders;
 END;
```

In this example, the first two variables are declared to hold the data retrieved, then the cursor is defined. The cursor is opened within the BEGIN block and then within the loop, each row is fetched and the contents are placed in the variables defined previously. The "exit when" clause is used to terminate the loop when all the rows have been fetched, and then the cursor is closed.

This is an example of a simple cursor; obviously in the real world, there would be extensive operations performed within the cursor.

Conditional Blocks

If only everything was executed in order, and nothing was repeated, then we wouldn't need conditional block processing. When writing PL/SQL, it is inevitable that one of these constructs will be required. For instance, in the previous section on cursors, a loop block was required to process each individual row in the cursor. Once those rows are extracted, then blocks like IF THEN ELSE are needed to determine the actions that need to be taken. PL/SQL provides us with a number of different types of conditional blocks to choose from:

- IF THEN ELSE
- LOOP
- FOR LOOP
- WHILE LOOP
- GOTO
- NULL

IF THEN ELSE

The IF THEN ELSE block enables us to select processing, dependent on a value. It can be used in various forms, such as IF THEN, IF THEN ELSE and IF THEN ELSIF. In the example below, a single row is retrieved and then it is analyzed to see if it is a telephone order.

```
SET SERVEROUTPUT ON;
DECLARE
  type_of_order orders.orders.order_type%TYPE;
  ord_no orders.orders.order_number%TYPE;
BEGIN
  SELECT order_number, order_type
    INTO ord_no, type_of_order FROM orders.orders
    WHERE ROWNUM<2;

IF type_of_order = 'T' THEN
  DBMS_OUTPUT.PUT_LINE
    ('Telephone Order : ' || ord_no);
ELSE
  DBMS_OUTPUT.PUT_LINE
    ('Direct Order : ' || ord_no);
END IF;
END;
```

Loops

There are several different types of loops that can be used. We have already seen the LOOP-END LOOP in the cursor example, where it loops forever until the EXIT WHEN %NOTFOUND action. Care should be taken when using this type of loop because it could loop forever if the exit clause is omitted.

Far more popular is the WHILE-END LOOP which loops until a condition is met.

```
WHILE order_type = 'T' LOOP

  statements;

END LOOP;
```

Another type of loop is the FOR LOOP, which enables you to control the number of iterations using a counter.

```
FOR i IN 1..maxloop LOOP

    counter:= counter +1;

  END LOOP;
```

A GOTO statement is also provided which enables you to specify a label and then jump to that label in the BEGIN END block. Depending on your views, some people believe that a GOTO is a dreadful statement and should never be used. Others will disagree and declare that at times it can be extremely useful. The author will let you decide whether a GOTO will appear in your PL/SQL.

Packages and Procedures

So far we have seen how to write a PL/SQL block, but we haven't saved it in the database so that it can be regularly used. This is where we have to create a package and a procedure. By using packages and procedures, common functions can be stored in the database and shared with everyone. By storing them in the database they are held and managed in one place. Another big benefit of using them is that the procedures are compiled and stored in the SGA which makes them very efficient to use.

A package is a schema object that groups together the components of PL/SQL. A package is normally made up of two parts, a *specification* and a *body*, although sometimes the body is not required.

A procedure is a group of SQL statements. It is best to keep procedures short and dedicated to performing a specific task. For example, the one below returns today's date.

```
CREATE PROCEDURE today_date (thedate DATE)
  AS
   today DATE;
   BEGIN
    SELECT sysdate INTO today FROM dual;
END today_date;
```

There is no restriction on the number of procedures that can be defined, and normally they will be a bit more complicated than described here.

All the procedures are brought together inside a package. In the example below, only one procedure has been included in the package.

```
CREATE PACKAGE general_routines
  AS
   PROCEDURE today_date (thedate DATE);
END general_routines;
```

The example shown here was created directly in SQL Worksheet, but it could be done using Schema Manager. However, the GUI doesn't facilitate easy package creation because you still have to write the PL/SQL block, as you can see in Figure 5.5.

One of the really useful aspects to working with procedures and packages via the Schema Manager is that a package can, by pressing the *Recompile* button, be checked for any errors. If errors do occur during the compilation, then click on the Show Errors button, which will only be available if there are errors. See Figure 5.6 which displays the problems with the package.

Figure 5.5 Create a Package

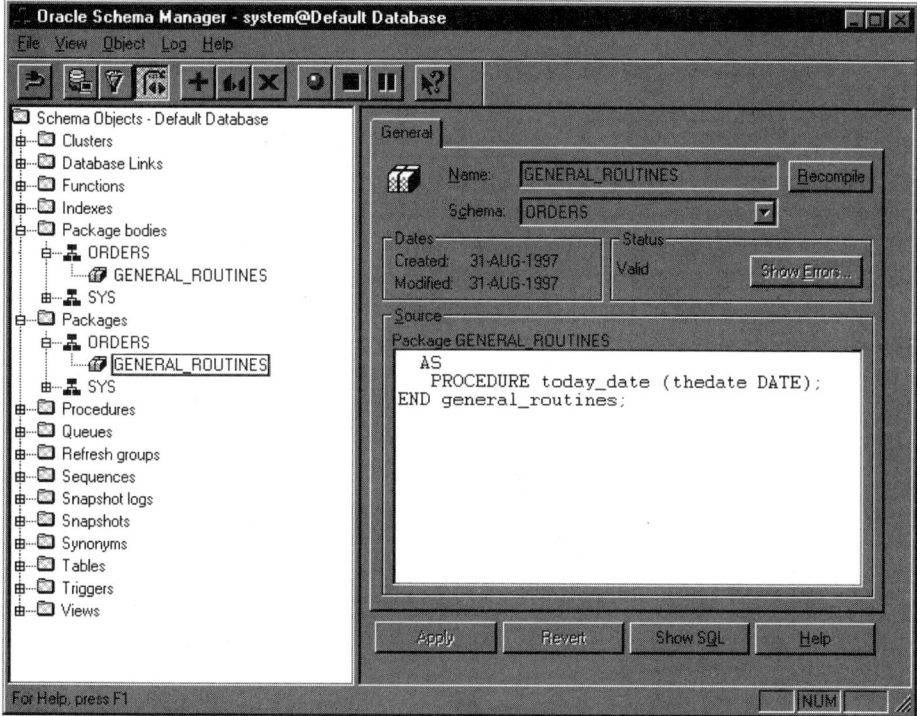

The examples shown here are very simplistic. In reality, a procedure will include variables, SQL statements, conditional blocks and exception handling. It should be noted that the exception handling in PL/SQL is very sophisticated and a number of exceptions can be trapped and actions performed.

Figure 5.6 Errors in a Package

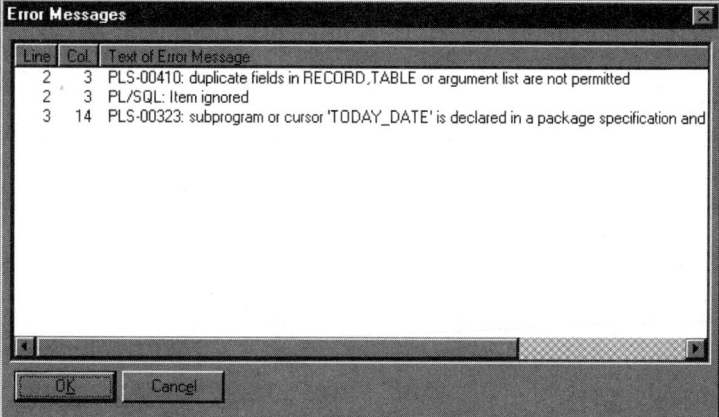

5.5   **OPTIMIZER**

Ask any DBA which part of the database they dislike and chances are they will reply, the optimizer. This is really a bit unfair, because the optimizer is an amazing component of a relational database and it does differentiate between the database engines in the market place.

Before relational, databases didn't need optimizers, because the only way the data could be retrieved was by access paths, previously defined by the DBA. All that changed with the introduction of relational databases, because now a mechanism was needed to join and retrieve data from tables, where no access path had been clearly defined. This is when the optimizer was born.

The role of the optimizer is to review an SQL statement and then decide which is the best way to retrieve the data. To be fair, the optimizer usually gets it right and does a really good job. Unfortunately, when it chooses a bad retrieval strategy it can means that a query takes minutes to return its row instead of seconds. If this occurs too often, the users become annoyed and this is why the optimizer is so disliked.

Two optimizers are available within Oracle8; *rule* and *cost* based. The cost based optimizer is the one to use and the rule based one exists to support older applications.

The cost based optimizer cannot make good decisions unless it has some statistics about your data. Therefore, it is very important to run the ANALYZE statement regularly if your data is volatile, to ensure that the optimizer is using good data. Chapter 6 describes how to use the ANALYZE command without having to read all of the data, which could be very time consuming in a very large database.

To use the cost based optimizer, check that the initialization parameter OPTIMIZER_MODE is set to COST. Alternatively, a value of CHOOSE will allow the optimizer to use either rule or cost basis depending on the query.

Another important point to bear in mind is that if any statistics exist for any table in the join, the cost based optimizer will be used, even though all the table statistics may not be available.

5.5.1   **Query Plans**

When a query takes a long time to complete, the first question asked is what is the optimizer doing? This information is available from the query execution plan. Before query execution plans can be retrieved, a special table called the

PLAN_TABLE must be created in the database by running the SQL script *utlxplan.sql* which can be found in *oracle_home\rdms80\admin*.

A query plan is obtained by using the EXPLAIN PLAN command with the SQL statement. Don't worry, the SQL statement included in the EXPLAIN PLAN is not executed. All this statement does is decide how the query would be executed, and it then writes this information into the PLAN_TABLE. This is why it is important to set the column statement_id to a sensible value so that the execution plan can be easily found.

```
EXPLAIN PLAN
  SET statement_id = 'orders'
  FOR
    SELECT * FROM orders.order_header
    WHERE order_location = 'SOT';
```

Hint: Keep the number of execution plans held in the PLAN_TABLE to a minimum.

Now that the strategy is in the PLAN_TABLE, it must be queried so that we can see the execution plan. This requires a statement as shown below, to display it in a readable format.

```
SELECT id, parent_id,
  lpad(' ', 2*(level-1))||operation||' '||options||'
    '||object_name||' '||
  decode(id, 0, 'Cost = '||position) 'Query Plan'
FROM plan_table
 START WITH id = 0 and
   statement_id = 'orders'
 CONNECT BY prior id = parent_id and
   statement_id = 'orders';
```

If we perform an explain plan for the two tables that were joined in the multitable join Section 5.2.4, then the results are shown below.

```
ID    PARENT_ID Query Plan
------- --------- ----------------------------------
   0          SELECT STATEMENT   Cost = 4
   1        0 HASH JOIN
   2        1 TABLE ACCESS FULL ORDERS
   3        1 TABLE ACCESS FULL ORDER_HEADER
4 rows selected.
```

This query is executed by doing a *table access full* on each of the tables, which means they are sequentially scanned. The resulting keys are then joined using a *hash join*. There are some 30 different operations that the optimizer can do, and these include index range scan, merge join, outer join, sort aggregate, union and view.

Hint: Read the results of the query plan from the bottom up.

When analyzing plans, look for access paths that are likely to take a long time, like *table access full* instead of *index unique scan,* which is searching via an index.

When you have finished with the information in the plan_table, it can be quickly removed using the TRUNCATE TABLE command.

In 8.0.3. there are no GUI tools available to display the query plans or assist with creating them.

5.5.2   Hints

When the optimizer does choose a bad strategy, then the only way to prevent it doing that again is to use what is known as a hint. Hints are written in the SQL statement to influence the optimizer to execute the query differently.

Hints can be used to change strategies chosen by the cost based optimizer. Unfortunately, they have to be written as part of the SQL and are therefore embedded in the statement. A hint is written like a comment and is enclosed between /*+ */. The + sign is very important, because it is this, which tells the optimizer that it is looking at a hint and not a comment.

There are some two dozen hint keywords that can be used to influence the optimizer, some of them are listed here:

ALL_ROWS	optimize for all rows quickly
AND_EQUAL	perform and equal operation on indexes
CACHE	keep blocks from table scan in memory
CHOOSE	optimizer to select rule or cost based
CLUSTER	use a table access cluster method
FIRST_ROWS	optimize to return the first rows quickly
FULL	use table access full method
HASH	use table access hash method
HASH_AJ	use a hash antijoin
INDEX	use these indexes
INDEX_ASC	use this index

INDEX_DESC	scan index in descending order
INDEX_FFS	use a fast full index scan
MERGE_AJ	merge anti-join
NOCACHE	don't keep blocks in SGA
NOPARARREL	don't execute in parallel
ORDERED	influence the order in which tables are joined
PARALLEL	execute in parallel
ROWID	use table access by rowid
RULE	use the rule based optimizer
STAR	use a star query
USE_HASH	do a hash join
USE_MERGE	use a merge join
USE_NL	use a nested loop

A hint is written in the SQL as illustrated below. In this example the optimizer is told to join the tables as per how they are referenced in the query. Therefore it reverses the order compared to its normal strategy.

```
SELECT
/*+ ORDERED */
oh.order_number, order_value, order_type
  FROM orders.order_header oh, orders.orders o
  WHERE oh.order_number = o.order_number;

ID     PARENT_ID Query Plan
-------- --------- ------------------------------
    0            SELECT STATEMENT  Cost = 4
    1        0 HASH JOIN
    2        1 TABLE ACCESS FULL ORDER_HEADER
    3        1 TABLE ACCESS FULL ORDERS
4 rows selected.
```

Hints can be very useful, but they should be used with care, especially as they are embedded in the SQL. It is a good idea to try to keep a log of all the hints that have been used and where. Every release of the Oracle server will see some changes made to the optimizer. If it is known where the hints are, they can be checked to see if they are still required.

5.6   **SUMMARY**

This chapter has attempted to provide an appreciation of how SQL can be used against an Oracle database. Today SQL is so powerful through facilities like PL/SQL that virtually an entire program can be written as part of the database. We have only scratched the surface here of what is possible, so don't be surprised if you discover other things that you can do in SQL.

6   Database Management

Most people are concerned with building and tuning a database. However, one can design and tune the biggest and fastest database in the world, but if it is too difficult to manage, it won't support your business. Instead, it will be a millstone around the DBAs neck. In this chapter, we will look at the various techniques that are available for managing the database.

6.1   ORACLE ENTERPRISE MANAGER

When it comes to managing the database, various methods are available. However, this is NT, and on NT one expects to use a graphical interface. Therefore, whenever possible, GUI tools will be used to perform the task, but there could be an alternative command using tools like Server Manager and SQL*Plus.

Throughout this book we have seen the graphical tools that are part of Oracle Enterprise Manager. So far, tools like SQL Worksheet and Schema Manager have been started directly and not invoked from the Enterprise Manager console. When we are managing the database some of the tasks can only be started from the Enterprise Manager console and as we progress through this chapter you should begin to appreciate the tasks that ideally should be started from the console.

Oracle Enterprise Manager is started by selecting *Enterprise Manager* from the *Oracle Enterprise Manager* folder. Before it can be used some setup is required because Enterprise Manager is more than just a launching vehicle for graphical tools. It holds details about the backups that have been taken, the database and scripts for performing various tasks. All this information is held in its own repository, which of course, is an Oracle database. Therefore, it is suggested that the database you connect to when using Enterprise Manager is one that is used specifically for this tool, thus keeping your data in a separate database. One very good reason for using this approach is that you will not be able to use the Backup facility in Enterprise Manager unless you have two databases, that is one for Oracle Enterprise Manager and the database with your data that is to be backed up.

6.1.1   Enterprise Manager User

Before the console can be used, some setup must be completed which involves creating an NT user that is given the User Right to *logon as a batch job*, as illustrated in Figure 6.1. This user is then configured in the *Preferences* section for this node, using the username and password for the NT user that has just been created.

Figure 6.1 NT User

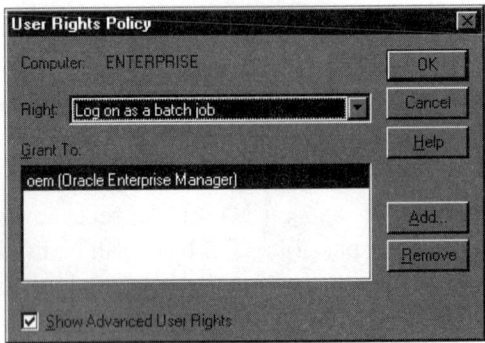

It is also a good idea to create a special user for all administration work for the database giving it the same username as the NT user just created. The steps for doing this are described in section 7.1.1.

6.1.2   Creating the Enterprise Manager Repository

The setup required to use Enterprise Manager is minimal. Once you have the database, simply start the tool and you will be prompted as to whether or not the catalog should be created, as shown in Figure 6.2. This is a one off operation and this message will only appear again if you accidentally logon using a different username.

Without the catalog it will not be possible to use the Enterprise Manager to its full potential. This step should take less than a minute to complete so it is worth waiting.

Figure 6.2 Creating the Repository

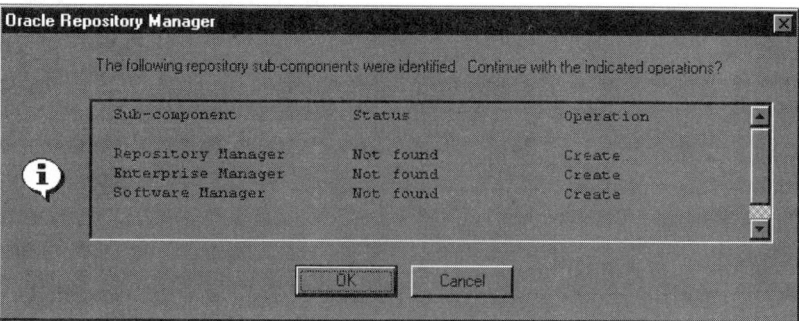

6.1.3   The Discovery Process

In order for the discovery process to succeed, the *OracleAgent* service must be running. When the Enterprise Manager starts, the first step is to run the *Discovery* process which searches for databases on the specified nodes.

Figure 6.3 Discovery Process

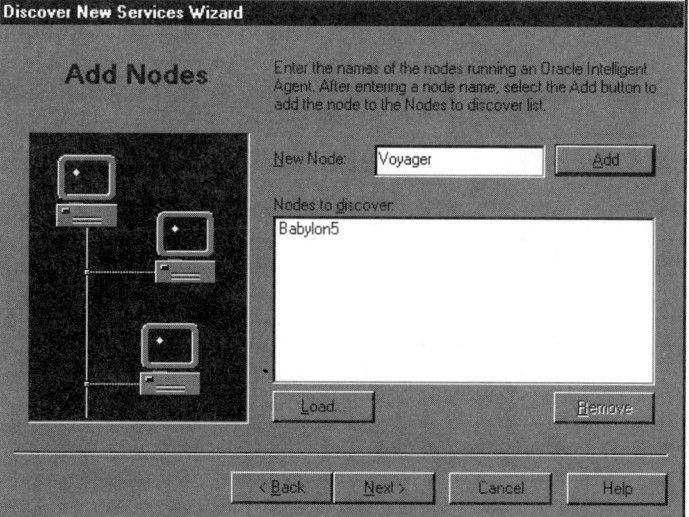

Although all the examples in this book refer to a single node, one of the great strengths of the Enterprise Manager is the ability to manage databases anywhere on the local or wide area network. All that is required is that on each system where you want to perform system management, its node has gone through the *discovery process*. This involves nothing more than selecting *Navigator* from the strip menu on the Enterprise Manager console and then selecting *Service Discovery*. From here you would pick *Discover New Services* and specify the nodes that you wish to manage or view, as per Figure 6.3.

The discovery process only needs to be run if the databases change on the machines that are being monitored, or new machines are added to the hardware configuration.

6.1.4   Jobs

Jobs are an integral part of the Enterprise Manager console because that is where tasks can be scripted and run at specified times. When administering a database, if a script to complete a task can be written, saved and then scheduled to run at specific times, this removes a lot of worry for the DBA. One very important reason for using this feature is that it means the DBA can go home to sleep knowing that, for example, the backup of the database has been scheduled to run at 0200.

A good method to test that the job part of Enterprise Manager has been setup correctly is to create a simple job and run it through the console. It is very important to check that the agent is functioning correctly because otherwise it will not be possible to perform tasks like backing up the database.

Figure 6.4 Create a Job Step 1

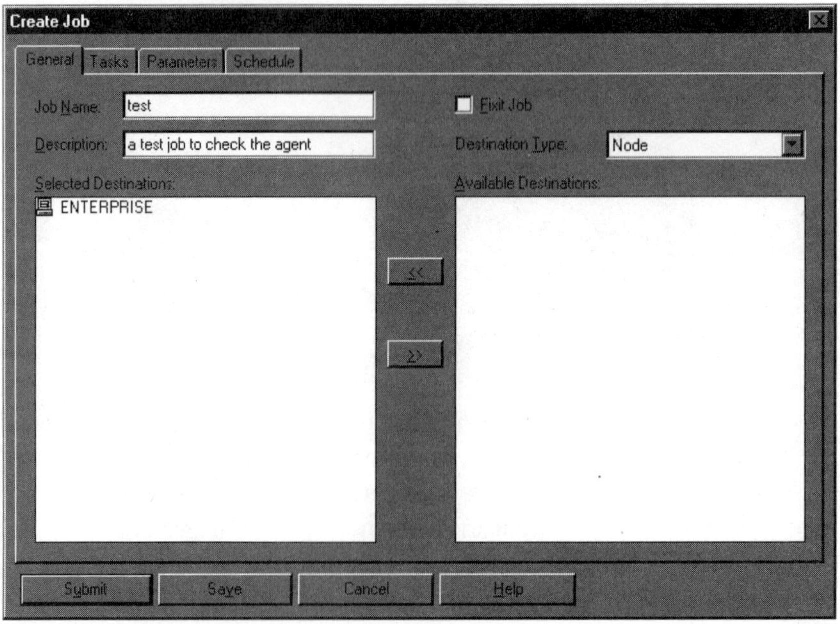

Therefore, make sure that jobs are running without any problem. A simple technique for testing the job facility is to execute a directory command on one of the folders on the system.

To create a job, select *Job* from the strip menu and then select *Create Job* from the menu. Every job must be given a name, and since this is not a database job, you must select the destination node on which the job must be run, as shown in Figure 6.4.

Next select the *Tasks* tab and choose the type of operation to be performed. In Figure 6.5 we have selected to *run an operating system command*, but as you can see we have a wide choice of options available.

Figure 6.5 Create a Job Step 2

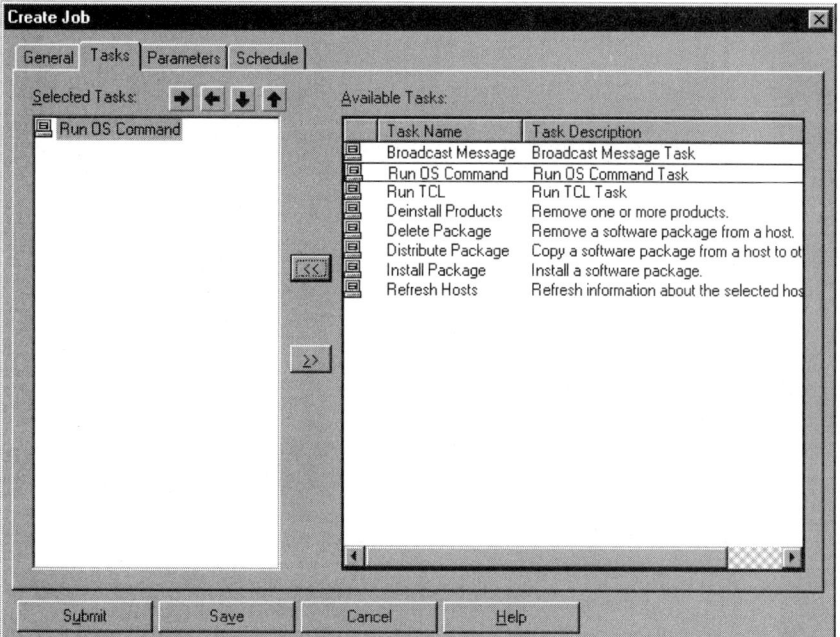

The *Parameters* tab, as shown in Figure 6.6, is where you actually enter the command to be run. In our example this is a simple MSDOS dir command. However, in a production environment it is most likely to be a script file that must be run. A number of script files are already available on the system and will be used when tools like the tablespace analyzer are used.

Finally, press the *Submit* button to say when the job is to be run. If the job is submitted immediately, then its progress will be shown on the console in the job window, otherwise it can be scheduled to run at a specific time.

Figure 6.6   Create a Job – Parameters

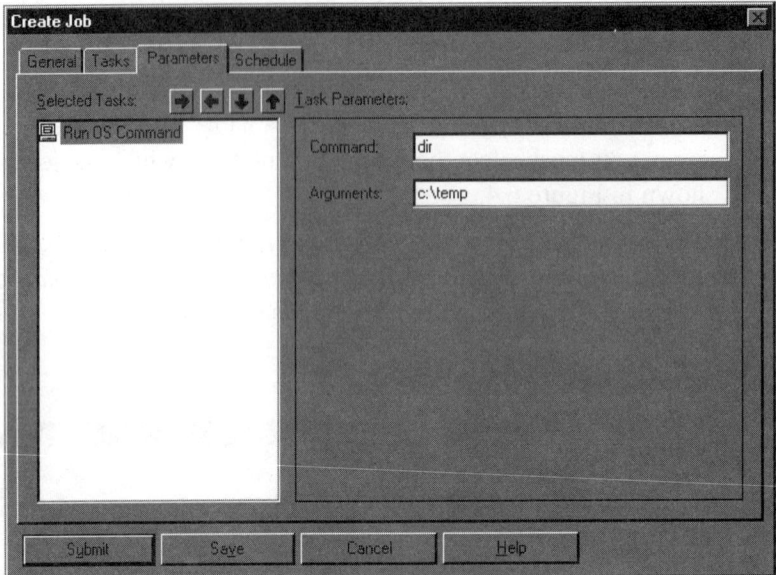

Figure 6.7 shows the job window, where three options are available for monitoring jobs. A user can:

- see jobs currently running from the *Active Jobs* tab;
- review which jobs have been run from *Job History*;
- maintain a list of jobs in the *Job Library*.

Figure 6.7   Job History

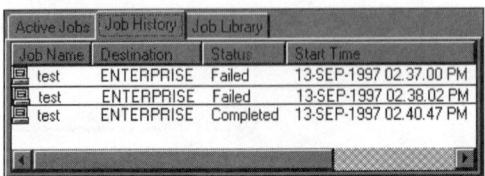

In Figure 6.7 we have clicked on the *Job History* tab to see when the jobs were run and whether they were successful. For any job, double clicking on the entry will display the execution log. This is especially important to use when a job has failed because this is where the reason for failure will be given.

Anyone who has ever managed a large system will tell you how important script files which execute specific tasks are to the system. From within the console, scripts can be run and saved. In Figure 6.8 we see a sample from the Job Library. It is worth building up a library of useful tasks. But please give them sensible names so that they are easy to find and use.

Figure 6.8 Job Library

6.1.5   Events

Another useful feature available in Enterprise Manager is the ability to define *events*. Only a few basic events are supplied with Enterprise Manager, such as database is up or down. However, if the performance pack is purchased then many other events are available, including performance and space usage statistics. When an event occurs an operator can be contacted using various methods, like e-mail or paging, and a script can be run. Otherwise, the console can be checked for the status of the event.

Figure 6.9 Define an Event

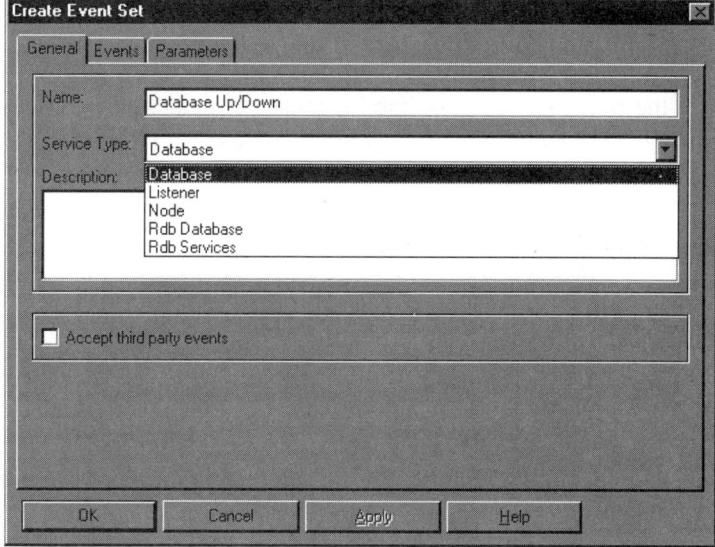

To create an event, click on *Event* in the strip menu and then select *Create Event Set*. Figure 6.9 appears where the event is given a name and the type of event is selected from the drop down list.

The event to be monitored must be chosen from the list shown in Figure 6.10. The list here is quite comprehensive because the Performance Pack is installed, otherwise there would only be a few events available. One should also be aware that this list will vary depending on the type of event requested.

Figure 6.10 Select the Event

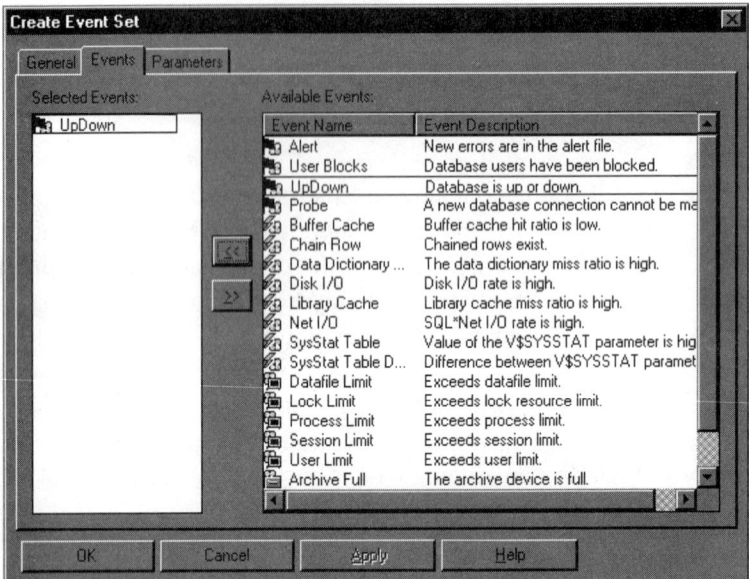

Once the event has been defined it must be registered by clicking on *Event* from the strip menu and then *Register Event Set*. Figure 6.11 is displayed where you must specify to which groups this event applies.

Figure 6.11 Register the Event

Once registered, the event is continually monitored as per the frequency specified. Therefore at any time one can see the status of the events by referring to
the event window, a sample of which is shown in Figure 6.12.

Figure 6.12 Status of an Event

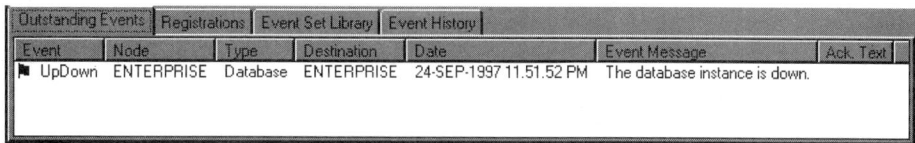

6.1.6 Console

The console of Enterprise Manager is where everything happens. From here
you can see the databases that are to be managed in the navigator window. A
map can be created to enable you to graphically see your configuration. Then
using drag and drop, a database can be selected from the navigator window
and then dropped onto the map to register the database at that location. Jobs
can be created and scheduled using the job window and the event facility will
advise you when specific events occur. The console really becomes the control room where you can monitor all of your databases.

In Figure 6.13 we can see an example of the console. The discovery process
has identified a database on the machine called Enterprise, but in a production
environment one would expect to see databases discovered on many machines.
The map shows us that these databases are located in the southern part of the
United Kingdom. The database called Enterprise has been dragged and dropped
onto the group called Lilian's office. An event has been created which monitors the state of that database, therefore if we click on the icon for Lilian's
group we can see that the database is currently not started, as illustrated in
Figure 6.14, but when it is open then the database has a green flag as shown in
Figure 6.15.

Four windows are shown in Figure 6.13. The first one on the left is known as
the *Navigator* window, to its right is the *Map* window, underneath the navigator window is the *Job* window and underneath the map window is the *Events*
window.

One can now begin to see the benefits of this tool for administering the database. Maps can be created for areas of your network and then you can monitor
aspects of your system. You also have the ability to schedule jobs to run at
specific times and be advised when important events occur, like the database
going down. Enterprise Manager makes managing both local and remote
databases easier.

Figure 6.13   Enterprise Manager Console

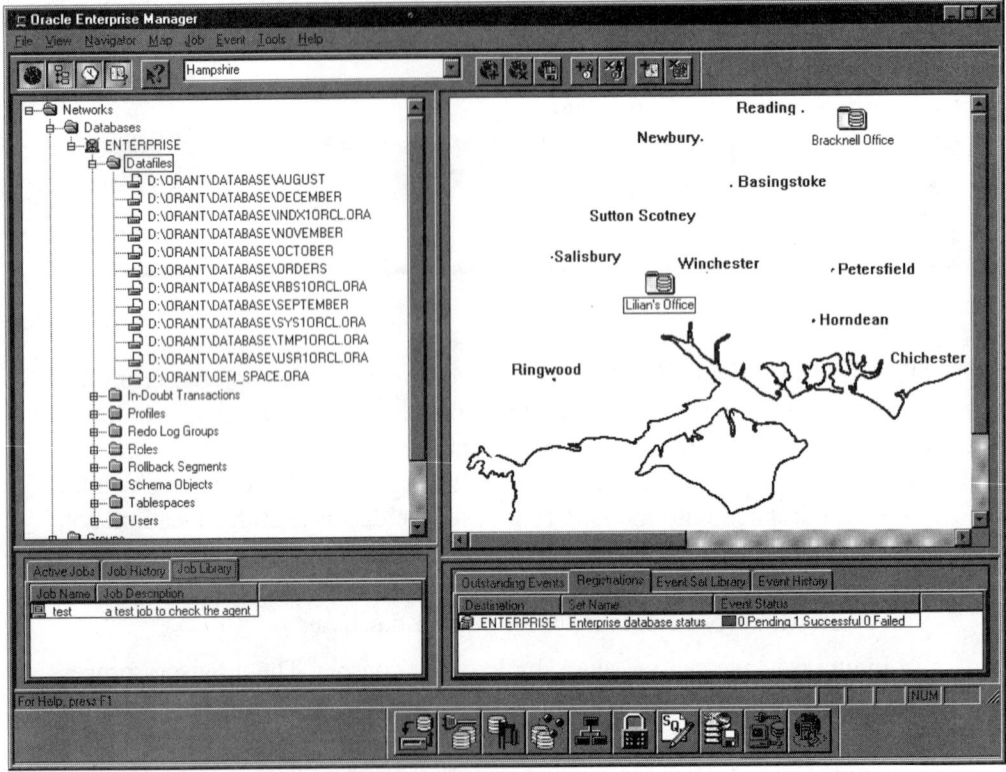

Figure 6.14 Database Is Closed

Figure 6.15 Database Is Open

6.2   DATABASE SERVICES

Whenever you logon to one of the databases you are prompted for a user-name, password and which *service* you would like to use. It is important to create a service for each Oracle instance you want to logon to, including any instances on a remote computer. A service is created by selecting the *Oracle Net8 Easy Config* program from the *Oracle for Windows NT* folder. Then an easy to follow wizard is provided to create the service. The first screen is shown in Figure 6.16.

Figure 6.16   Create a Database Service

8

Oracle

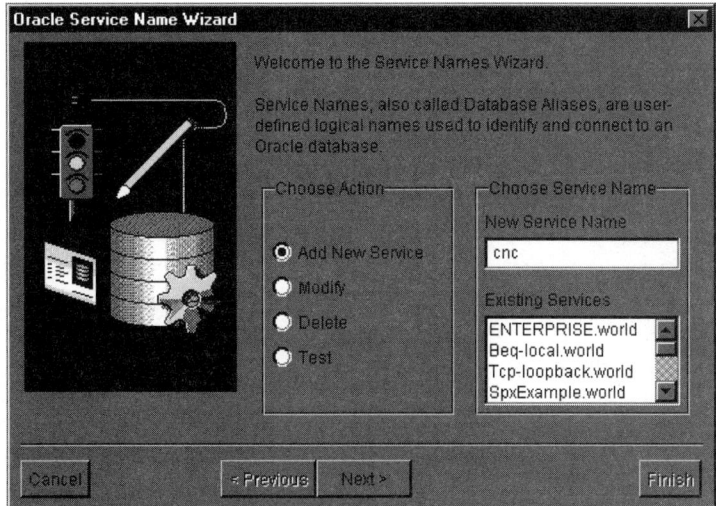

Simply give the service a name which easily identifies it, such as the instance name. Choose which networking protocol to use, such as TCP/IP, or if the database is on the local machine, use Bequeath. Then advise on which machine the database is located and the instance to be used. The final step is to test the service using a valid username and password to logon to the database. Any number of services can be defined and they are all managed using the same tool.

Once services have been created they provide a mechanism to administer and use any database as if it were local. For example, a user can start *SQL Worksheet* and at the logon prompt specify a database service for a remote database. When SQL Worksheet starts, you will be connected to the remote database and can write SQL commands as if you were accessing a local database.

6.3 INSTANCE OPERATIONS

The instance is an essential part of the Oracle database and, depending on its status, determines what the user can do. An instance, as we saw in Section 2.5.1, can be in one of four states:

- started;
- mounted;
- open;
- shutdown.

When administering the database, it will have to be started in certain modes to perform certain tasks. Most tasks can be completed in the *open* mode, but to perform certain backup and recovery operations it must be in the *mount* state.

Hint: To change the status of the instance, click on the right button when the mouse is over the database name in the Enterprise Manager console.

To check the state of the database, one would normally start the *Instance Manager*. However, if a database up/down event has been defined for the database, then we can observe in the navigator window of the Enterprise Manager console, as shown in Figure 6.17, the state of the database.

Figure 6.17 Instance Status

6.4 ROUTINE MAINTENANCE

When it comes to managing the database, the first task that everyone thinks of is making backups. However, there is more to managing the database than that. Other tasks that need to be performed include:

- collecting statistics for the optimizer;
- checking space usage;
- removing chained rows;
- archiving the redo logs.

By using the Enterprise Manager, these tasks can be scripted and run on a regular basis.

6.4.1   Collecting Optimizer Statistics

One of the key differentiators between relational databases is the optimizer because it is the optimizer which decides how a query should be executed. In order to choose a good execution strategy, the optimizer uses sophisticated mathematics, which includes using data from an SQL ANALYZE statement. The collection of these statistics is possible using one of two methods, either by specifying the command in SQL Worksheet or SQL*Plus or by using the graphical tool Tablespace Manager, which is part of the optional Performance Pack.

If manually executing the SQL ANALYZE statement is the preferred method, then this task would be an ideal candidate for creating a job in the console and scheduling it to run on a regular basis.

If the Performance Pack has been purchased, then the *Tablespace Manager* can be used, because it provides an easy to use interface which submits a job that is run by the console.

The statistics can be collected on tables, views, clusters and indexes, and the first important decision is whether the statistics are estimated, or computed by actually reading all of the data. For large tables it is suggested that the statistics are estimated by specifying a sample of data to analyze, otherwise the time required to complete the task could be excessive. The information collected is stored in some of the data dictionary views, which can then be queried, or alternatively, they can be viewed graphically using the Tablespace Manager.

Tablespace Manager

To use the *Tablespace Manager* to collect the statistics, first start the application from the Enterprise Manager console. Next select the object to be analyzed and then select *Tablespace Analyzer* from *Tools* in the strip menu. This will result in the first window of the Tablespace Analyzer being displayed as shown

Figure 6.18 Tablespace Analyzer

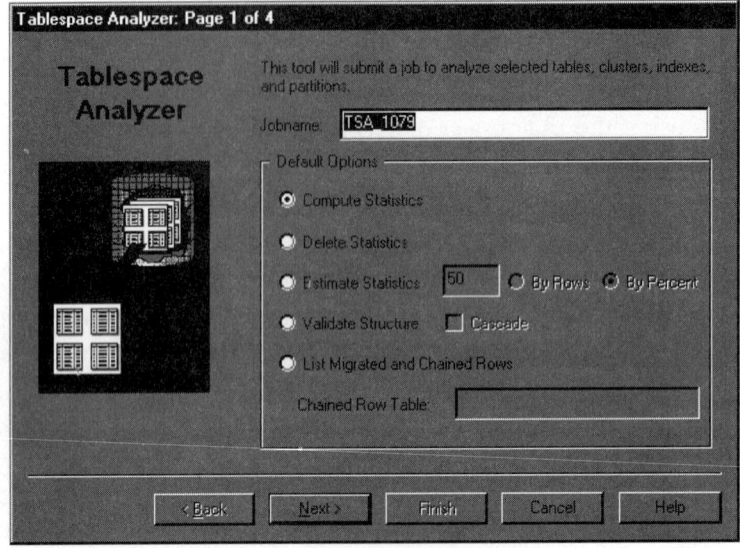

in Figure 6.18. From here you can specify whether or not to compute the statistics and if only a sample is to be read, then how large that sample should be. Clicking on the *Next* button will prompt you for the database to be analyzed and then when the job is to be run. If *immediate* is selected, then the job will automatically run through the console.

Collect and Reporting using SQL

Alternatively, the database can be analyzed manually using the SQL ANALYZE statement. It is this command that the Tablespace Manager is using, but because the interaction with the user is via the GUI the statement is hidden inside the job that it submits to the console. When you review the log for the job then you can see the ANALYZE statement that was used.

The statement has few options, as can be seen below, and it must be called for every object requiring analysis.

```
SQL> ANALYZE TABLE orders COMPUTE STATISTICS;
```

Once the data has been collected, the information can be viewed in the data dictionary table DBA_TABLES, as shown below, or by clicking on the *Space Usage* tab in Tablespace Manager to display Figure 6.19.

```
SELECT table_name, num_rows, blocks,
   empty_blocks, avg_row_len FROM
   DBA_TABLES WHERE tablespace_name = 'ORDERS';
```

There are manu other useful columns in this table, so take a moment to see what other information may be useful to you and then include that in a job that is run regularly. Ideally this job should be put in the job library, otherwise maintain a SQL script in a safe place.

Figure 6.19 Database Statistics

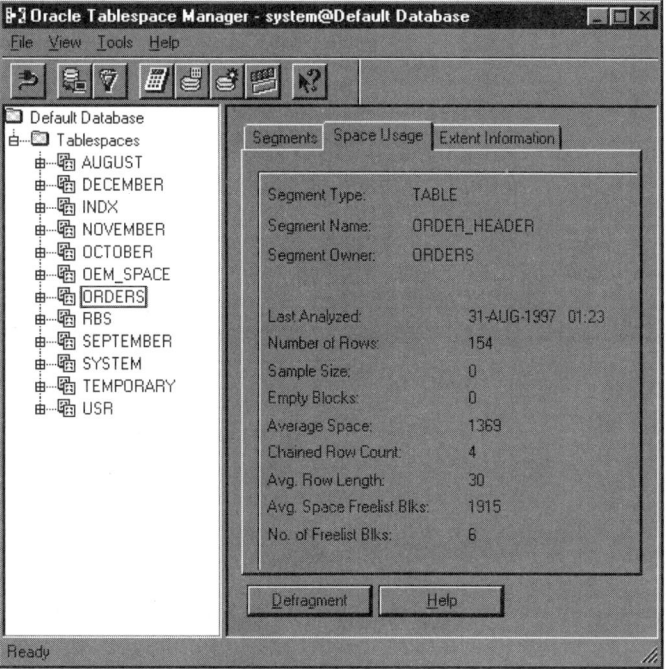

Hint: If a table or index does not display any statistical information, it has not been analyzed.

6.4.2   Checking Space Usage

It is very important to check that the database does not run out of disk space and this is where the Tablespace Manager and Storage Manager are useful.

When the *Tablespace Manager* is started, it displays an overview of space usage by tablespace, as shown in Figure 6.20. Then by selecting a specific tablespace, it is possible to view how much space each of the objects being stored in that area is using. Figure 6.20 tells us that the ORDERS tablespace is only using 33% of the available space. If we click on the tablespace ORDERS, Figure 6.21 appears, which tells us which objects are in that area and in which blocks they are stored.

Figure 6.20 Database Space Usage

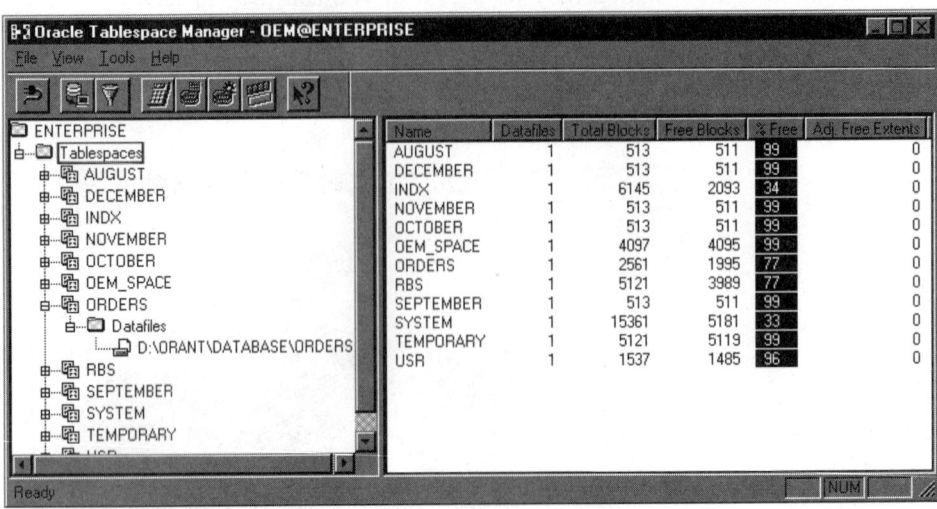

As you select each object in the list in the right window, the display adjusts to report the blocks being used by that object. For example, we can see in Figure 6.21 where ORDER_HEADER has been selected, that all these blocks are together. The segment information area is worth reading, because it advises how many blocks have been allocated to this object and how many extents it is using.

If you click on the tab *Space Usage*, you can see how many rows are in this object, what its average size is and other useful information, as shown in Figure 6.19. All of this data can be extremely useful to the DBA when trying to size a database.

Another useful display is generated when multiple objects are selected from the list shown in Figure 6.21. When this occurs, the tab *Selection Tally* will appear and clicking on it will display Figure 6.22.

If you don't have the Performance Pack on your system, an overview of the space used by tablespaces and datafiles can be obtained by starting the Storage Manager as shown in Figure 6.23. The Storage Manager lets us see at a glance how much space is being used in an area. However, it doesn't allow us to drill down to see which component is using the most space.

Alternatively space information can be found by querying the data dictionary table DBA_FREE_SPACE to report the amount of free space in each tablespace. A sample query is shown next.

Figure 6.21 Individual Space Usage Within a Tablespace

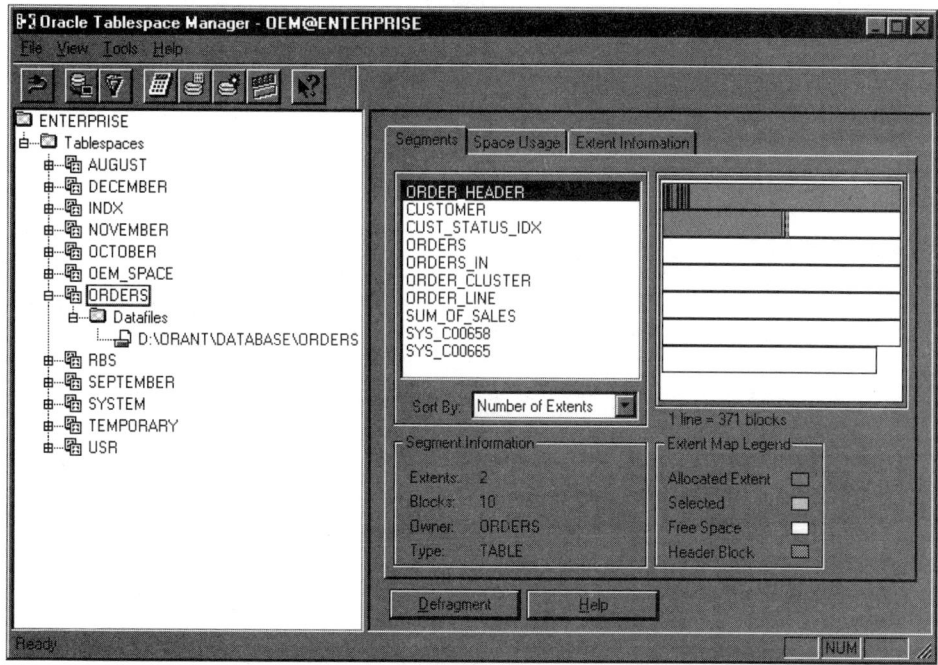

Figure 6.22 Selected Tally Area Display

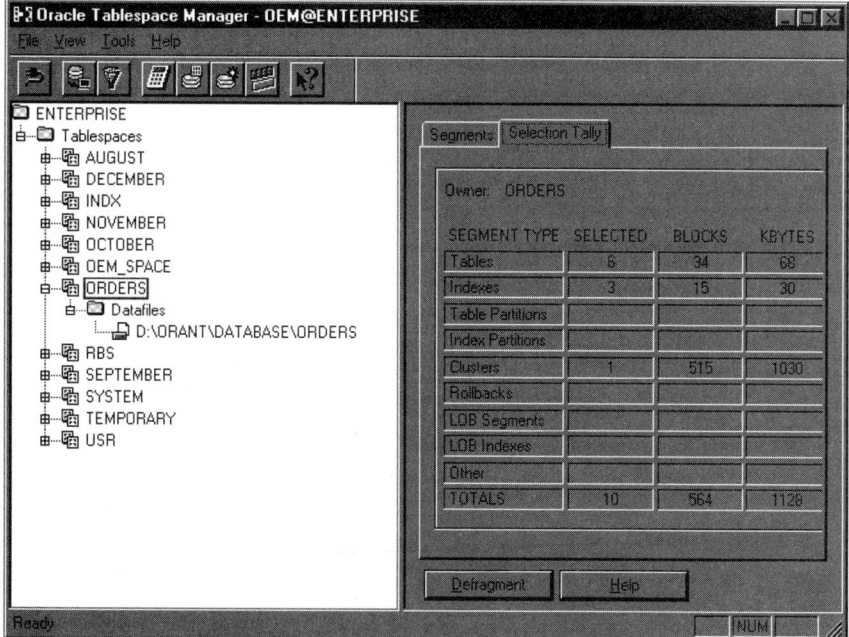

Figure 6.23 Space Usage Using the Storage Manager

```
SELECT tablespace_name, bytes, blocks
   FROM DBA_FREE_SPACE;

TABLESPACE_NAME                              BYTES       BLOCKS
-----------------------------             ----------   --------
SYSTEM                                    10610688       5181
TEMPORARY                                 10483712       5119
INDX                                       4286464       2093
```

Figure 6.23 is merely providing a visual representation of the information that is reported in this SQL statement. Hopefully you will agree that the visual tool has far more impact than a large number.

6.4.3   Chaining and Migration

In Figure 6.18 one of the options was to identify if there are any *chained rows* in the database. A row is chained when it expands and can no longer fit into the current block. When this occurs it can impact performance because instead of one read to find the row, another is required to retrieve it from its current location. Chained or migrated rows should not occur unless rows have expanded in size when they have been updated.

To find out how many chained rows exist in the database, the script *utlchain.sql*, which can be found in *%oracle_home\rdbmsxx\admin* and which creates a table in the database called CHAINED_ROWS, must be executed.

Chained rows can be identified by selecting this option from the *Tablespace Analyzer* or by using the SQL ANALYZE statement as illustrated below.

```
SQL> ANALYZE TABLE order_header LIST CHAINED ROWS;
```

The rowids of every chained row is put into this table. Using this information, the specific rows can be removed from the database and reinserted so that they are no longer chained. This method avoids reorganizing the entire table and therefore significantly reduces database maintenance time.

6.5   REORGANIZING THE DATABASE

Sometimes the rows in a table are not stored optimally; for example, many of them could be chained or the rows are stored in many extents and there are free space gaps between them. These are just two of the many reasons why the DBA might decide to reoganize a table in the database.

Rather than the DBA writing a script to perform this task, the Tablespace Manager will do it for you. First select the object you want to reorganize from the navigator window. Then select the *Tablespace Organizer* from *Tools* on the strip menu, and the dialog box show in Figure 6.24 appears. Select the task to be performed and then select which tables are to be reorganized by selecting them as shown in Figure 6.25. Finally, check that the correct tables are being reorganized as shown by the Summary box in Figure 6.26.

When the *Finish* button is pressed, a job is submitted to the Enterprise Manager console. Then just sit back and wait for the job to finish.

Figure 6.24 Reorganizing the Database

8
Oracle

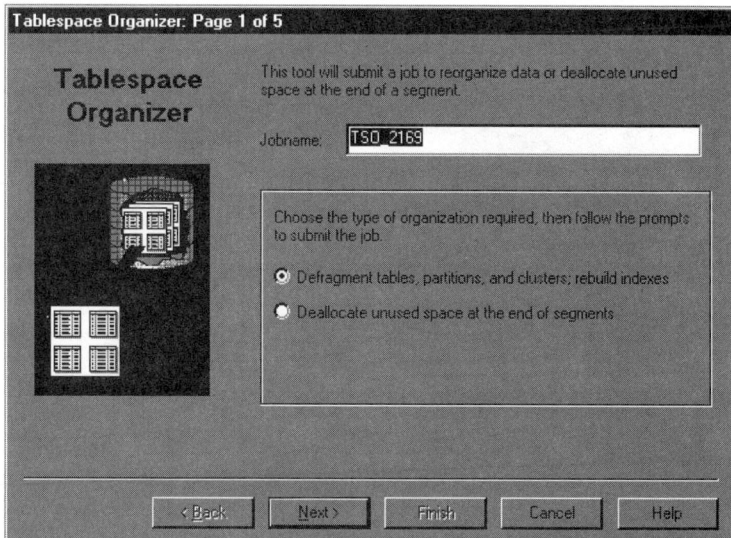

Hint: Before any maintenance work is done on the database always ensure that a backup is available that can be used to restore the database should the reorganization fail. Never assume that a script file will work; gremlins are always lurking around the corner waiting to catch you off guard!

Figure 6.25 Select Objects to Reorganize

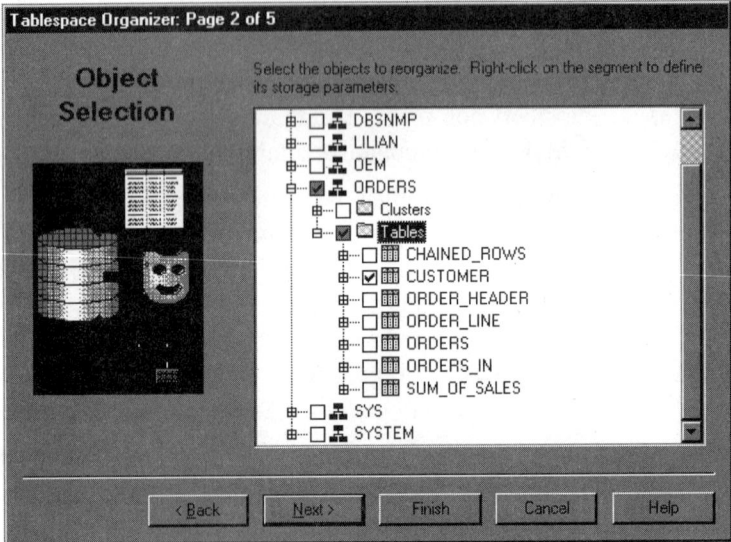

Figure 6.26 Summary Job Information

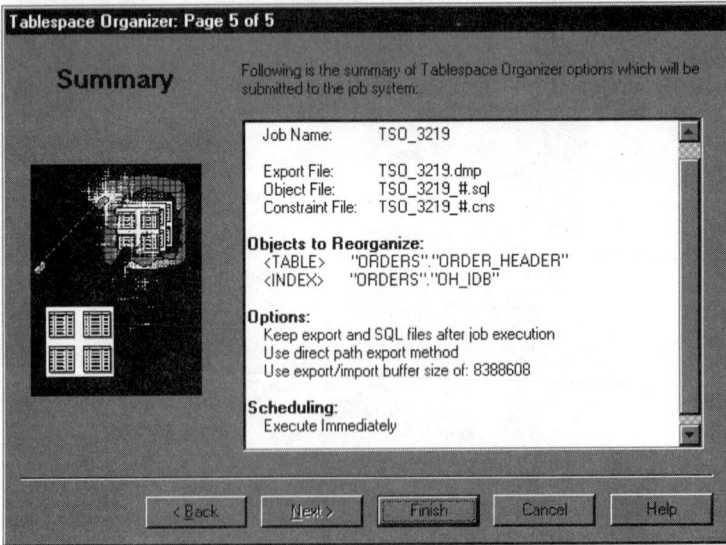

You may have also noticed a *Defragment* button on Figure 6.21. This can be pressed to defrag the specific object by submitting a job to the console.

Reorganizing parts of a database are inevitable for some databases. The situation arises for a variety of reasons, such as performance problems or changes to the way the company does business. When the need does arise to reoganize the database, don't be alarmed. Instead, carefully plan out what needs to be done, estimate how long it will take and the resources required to complete the job, then create a small environment where you can build and test the scripts needed to perform the task.

Don't ever approach a database reorganisation without a backup of the database and scripts that have never been tested. This is a recipe for disaster and overrunning the time available. Most database reorganizations have to be executed in a small maintenance window and if the production system is unavailable because your scripts are failing to run, this is not the way to get noticed by senior management within your company!

We have seen here a method for reorganizing the database using the assistants that Oracle provides. Many DBAs like control over the operation and prefer to write the scripts themselves. There is nothing wrong with this approach and for a large, complex database it may be the safest option.

6.6   ALTERING THE DATABASE

One of the reasons relational databases have become so popular is the ease with which they can be changed. In the early days, database systems were very rigid objects which could not be changed easily. For example, just adding a new column to a record would be a major exercise that could even result in recompiling all the applications. Today we add columns to a database without thinking of what the database is doing for us behind the scenes. Since databases are continually evolving in order to support businesses that are forever changing, one of the great strengths of the Oracle database is the ease with which it can be modified.

Whenever any significant changes are made to the database don't forget to take a backup and, if appropriate, update the initialization parameter file and create a new stored configuration.

6.6.1   Adding a Column

One of the most common alterations made to a database is adding columns to an existing table or adding a new table to the database. One of the reasons relational databases are so popular is the ease with which the database structures can be amended.

A new column can be added to a table using either SQL or the Schema Manager. From within Schema Manager, all one has to do is display the table and then add the column at the bottom of the list. In Figure 6.27 a new column CUST_REGION has been added. The SQL to add a column can be displayed by clicking on the *Show SQL* button.

New columns can be added to the database at any time. No reorganization of the data is required, therefore existing applications are not invalidated.

Figure 6.27   Add a Column to a Table

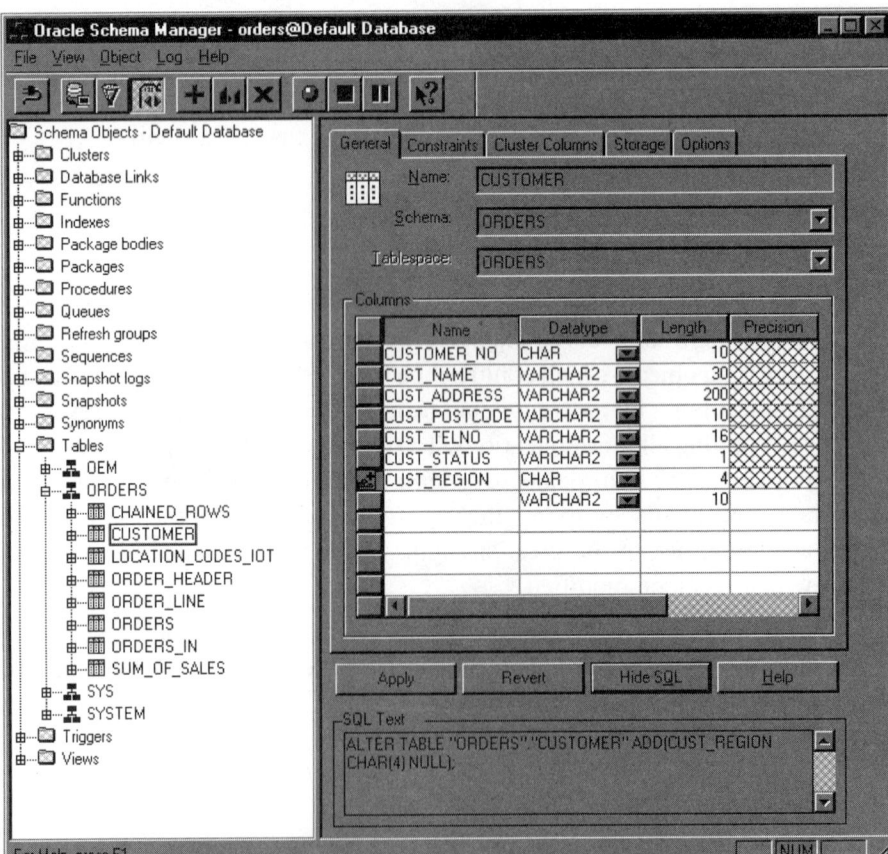

6.6.2   Adding Rollback Segments

Rollback Segments are a very important part of the database because they hold the contents of a transaction prior to it being committed to the database. Therefore, if a transaction has to be undone, the contents of the rollback segment are used to return the database to the state it was in prior to the start of the transaction.

Sometimes more rollback segments have to be added to the database, and this can be accomplished using the *Storage Manager*. Simply click on *Rollback* in the strip menu and then select *Create*. Figure 6.28 appears, allowing you to specify the name of the rollback segment and the tablespace where it is to reside.

The size of the rollback segment can be specified by clicking on the *Extents* tab. Clicking on the Create button adds this rollback segment to the database. To confirm that the rollback segment is now available, click on *Rollback Segments* in the Navigator window and the status of all the rollback segments will be shown, as illustrated in Figure 6.29.

Figure 6.28 Add a Rollback Segment

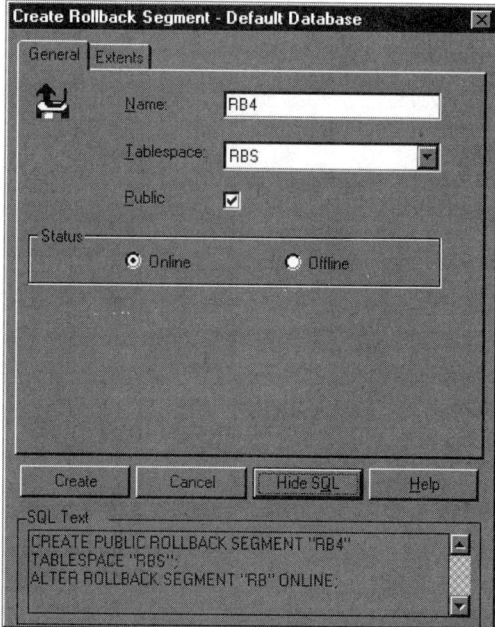

Figure 6.29 Rollback Segments

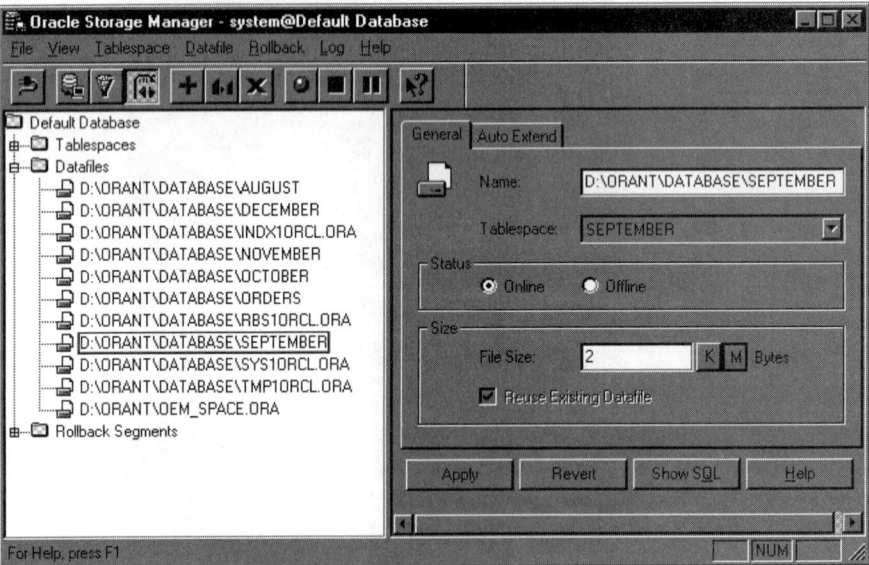

6.6.3   Altering Datafiles

Datafiles rarely need altering, but the one change that is likely to be required is to increase the size of the datafile. This task can be achieved using the Storage Manager. Suppose we want to increase the size of the datafile called September. Referring to Figure 6.30, we select the datafile from the Navigator window, which displays the characteristics of this datafile in the right window. The size of the datafile is now entered as 2 megabytes. Clicking on the apply button will increase the size of the datafile.

Figure 6.30 Change a Datafile

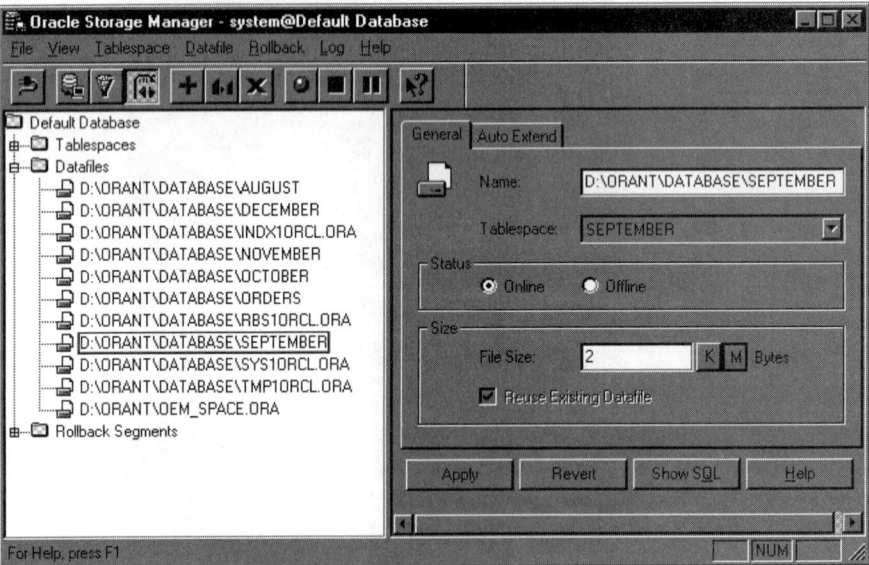

By default, a datafile is created without the ability to automatically extend if it runs out of space. Therefore the other change that may be required is to turn on the auto extend feature for an area. This is achieved by clicking on the *Auto Extend* tab and clicking on the box to enable it, then pressing the *Apply* button.

6.6.4   Changing the Redo Log

The redo log is a very important component of the database because it is where a copy of all the changes made to the database are stored. Therefore, when the redo logs are joined with a database backup, a restored database can be recovered to a specific point in time. Trying to predict the size of the redo log is not an easy task, especially when a business is working at peak loads.

If another redo log is required, one can easily be added using the *Backup Manager* tool. By selecting *Database* from the strip menu and then *Add Log Group*, Figure 6.31 must be completed to create the additional file. The name of the new file is specified in the *New Member* box and then the *Add* button is pressed. When the *Create* button is pressed, the new redo log will be created as a new group. To check the state of the redo logs, just click on *Redo Log Groups* in the navigator box, as illustrated in Figure 6.32.

Figure 6.31   Add a Redo Log File

Another very useful feature available to the DBA is the ability to create a mirror copy of the redo log on another disk which is automatically maintained by the Oracle8 database. These files are created by selecting *Database* from the strip menu and then *Add Log Member.* All that is required is the name of the file, including the directory and where it is to be stored, as shown in Figure 6.33.

Figure 6.32 Status of the Redo Logs

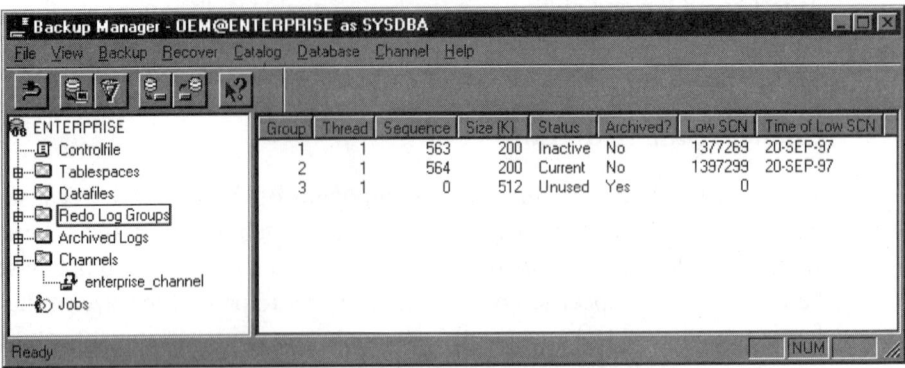

Figure 6.33 Add a Redo Log Member

Other tasks that can be performed upon the redo log files from the Backup Manager are:

- force a checkpoint;
- switch to a new logfile;
- delete a logfile;
- startup and shutdown the database.

Think of the Backup Manager as more than just a backup tool.

6.7 DELETING

There will come a time in the database when you decide that something is no longer required. It could be that a table or index is no longer needed or even the database itself.

To remove objects like tables and views from the database the *Schema Manager* should be used. Of course they can be deleted using the appropriate ·

DROP command in SQL, but this is NT and we should be using a graphical interface to complete tasks like this.

6.7.1   Deleting an Object

To delete an object like a table, view or index from the *Schema Manager*, click on *Object* in the strip menu at the top and then select *Remove*. You will now be prompted, as shown in Figure 6.34, as to whether the object should be removed. Simply confirm yes, and the object and all of its dependencies such as constraints and triggers will be removed from the database. This is a permanent operation, so once it is deleted there is no going back, unless you return to a backup of the database.

Figure 6.34 Remove an Object from the Database

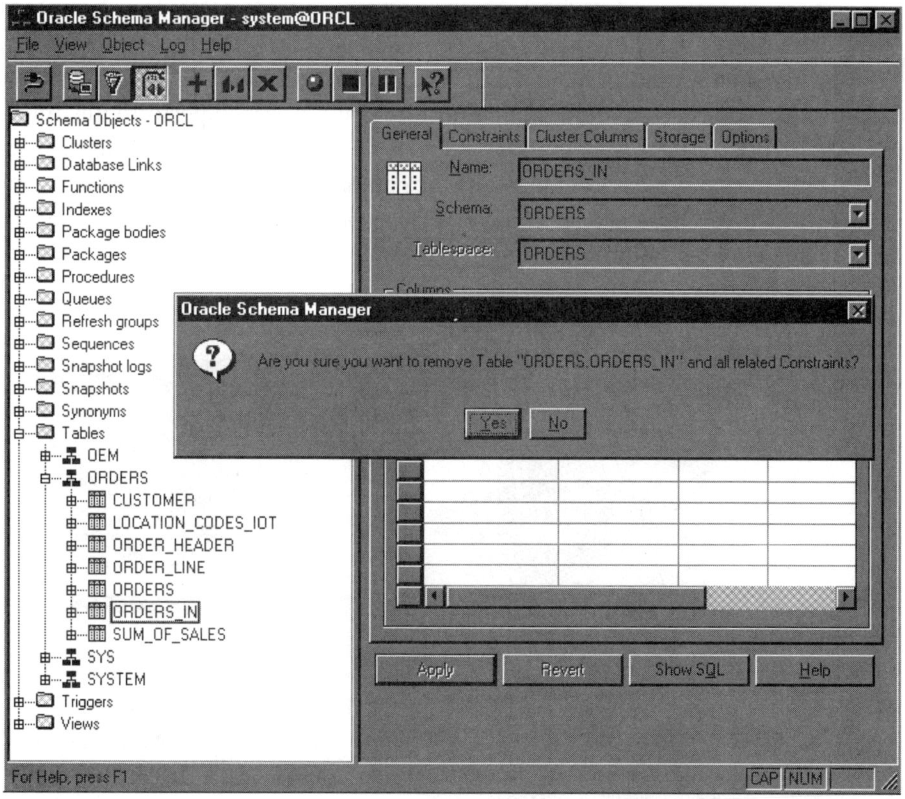

6.7.2   Truncating a Table

It is not uncommon to want to remove all the rows from a table but leave the table in the database. Some SQL programmers will suggest using the SQL DELETE statement to remove all the rows. This method works, but if the table is large it can take some time. A much quicker method is to use the SQL TRUNCATE statement which very quickly removes all the rows in a table.

One big disadvantage of using the TRUNCATE statement is that the operation is not recoverable. Once executed, that is it, and it cannot be undone. The significant gains in deletion time are why this statement is used.

```
SQL> TRUNCATE TABLE order_header;
```

6.7.3   Deleting the Database

To remove a complete database, the best method is to select *Database Assistant* from the Oracle for Windows NT folder. We first met this tool in Chapter 2 when we used it to create the database. Most people will probably remember it as a database creation tool and forget that it can also perform this important job. It is best to use this tool because it will remove everything associated with the database, rather than just the database files. Remember that a database consists of physical files and NT services and for completeness all these components must be removed.

8

Oracle

Figure 6.35 Deleting a Database

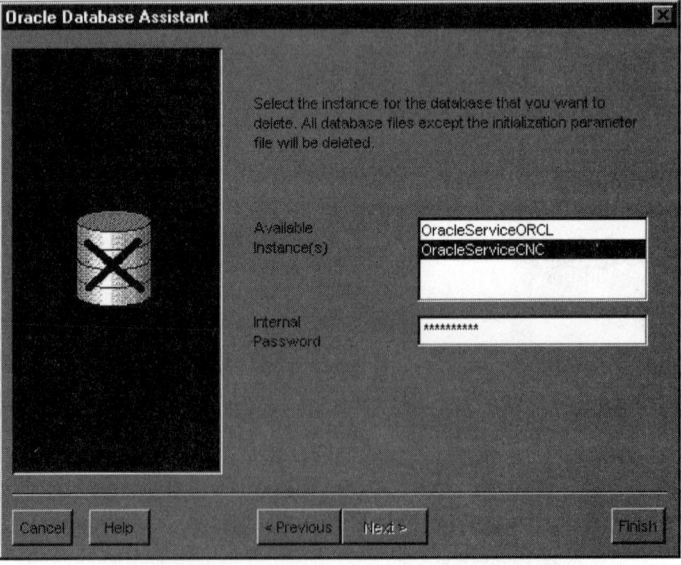

6.7.4   Deleting a Service

When the database is deleted, the NT services associated with that database should be removed if the database will never be used again. If the database is deleted using the Database Assistant, then the services will be automatically removed. If the database is deleted manually the services can be removed using the ORADIM80 utility at a DOS prompt, as shown in Figure 6.36.

8

Oracle

Figure 6.36 Remove an NT Service

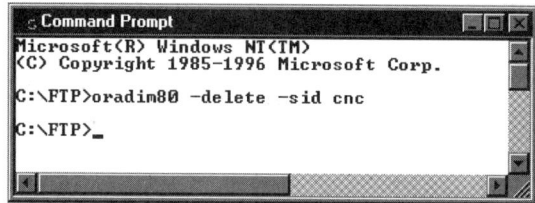

Hint: When the command is executed, the prompt immediately returns. Please wait a while before checking to see that the service has been deleted, because the task is run in background and takes a little while to complete.

6.8   SQL*LOADER

When a database is being created, everyone tends to concentrate on the physical design and the subsequent tuning of the database. Only when all that work is completed do people turn their attention to loading the database with data. This is when they discover that loading the data, especially if the database is many gigabytes, could take many, many hours.

Sometimes a custom written program is used to insert the data into the database. Although this may sound like an attractive solution, the time required to load the data using SQL INSERT statements can easily exceed the available time.

Therefore the fastest way to insert data into the database, from an external file, is to use the utility called SQL*Loader, which loads data very quickly in a wide variety of formats, such as delimited, fixed and variable. The utility is used in one of two modes:

- conventional path;
- direct path.

Whenever possible, the *direct path* method should be used as it bypasses the SQL layer and does not write entries into the redo logs. Since it is working at a very low level, the performance of SQL*Loader is extremely good.

Conventional path is only used in a few circumstances, such as when data is being loaded into a clustered table, loading into an indexed table that must remain accessible or the need to apply SQL functions to the data fields.

Before SQL*Loader can be used, a control file must be created which tells the utility in what format to expect the data. The control file must match your data precisely or data cannot be loaded. This is the most difficult part of using the tool and, unfortunately, even the GUI can't help you here because it too asks for the control file, expecting it to have been prepared previously.

The control file consists not only of the format of the file to be loaded, but also parameters on how the job is to be run. It could even include the data to be loaded, but it is best to keep the data and the control file separate.

In the example shown below is a control file for a fixed length file.

```
---
---   Load FACT table with fixed length records
---
options (direct = TRUE , parallel = FALSE)
-- unrecoverable
load data
infile 'fact.dat'
into table fact

reenable disabled_constraints

(  time_key
     position (1:12) date(12) "DD-Mon-YYYY",
   store_key
     position (13:16) integer external ,
   product_key
     position (17:21) integer external ,
   promotion_key
     position (22:26) integer external ,
   dollar_sales
     position (27:32) decimal external ,
   unit_sales
     position (33:36) integer external ,
   dollar_cost
     position (37:42) decimal external ,
   customer_count
     position (43:46) integer external )
```

It begins by telling us that the direct path method should be used, but parallel loading should be disabled. Next it advises to load data from a file called fact.dat into a table called fact. By default, SQL*Loader disables constraints on a database during loading. Therefore, by specifying the clause *reenable disabled_constraints*, they will be turned back on after the load. An alternative and faster method for reenabling constraints without incurring the overhead of evaluating them again, is to issue the SQL statement ALTER TABLE ENABLE NOVALIDATE after the load, which is described in section 4.3.8.

Comments can be placed in the control file using a --.

Next we must tell SQL*Loader how the file is formatted. Because this is a fixed length file, we must advise exactly where the data is stored in the file. The first column is a date, so we must tell Oracle how dates are to be represented. The other columns are numbers.

A very popular format for input files is delimited files, where the data is delimited by a character such as a comma. The following example illustrates how to define a control file for a delimited file.

```
---
---   Load STORES table with delimited records
---
options (direct = TRUE , parallel = FALSE)
--- unrecoverable
load data
infile 'store.dat'
into table store
reenable disabled_constraints
fields terminated by ','
optionally enclosed by "'"
(
     store_key                integer EXTERNAL,
     store_number             ,
     store_name               char,
     zipcode                  char,
     city                     char,
     county                   char,
     region                   char,
     finance_services_type    char,
     floor_plan_type          char,
     frozen_sq_ft             ,
     grocery_sq_ft            ,
     meat_sq_ft               ,
     manager                  char,
     open_date                date(20)   "DD-Mon-YYYY",
     last_remodel_date        date(20)   "DD-Mon-YYYY"

                              terminated by ' ')
```

Once again the control file begins with the parameters for the load. However, this time, because this is a delimited file, we must use the clause *terminated by* to advise what the delimiting character is. Since each piece of data is seperated by a comma, there is no need to specify the position of the data in the file. Instead all we have to specify is the datatype. In this example, the first column is a date; the subsequent fields have no type defined, therefore they are assumed to be numeric. Text fields are denoted by the use of the char datatype and at the end of the file there are some more dates.

The control files shown here provide only a hint of what is possible using this tool. There is a huge section in the Oracle documentation devoted to how to make the best use of this tool. Once the control file has been defined the data can be loaded, either using the GUI or via the command line. To use the command line, enter:

```
sqlldr80 grocery/grocery, control=d:\promotion.ctl
     log=d:\promotion.log data=d:\promo.dat
```

While the data is being loaded, a log file is maintained so that you can see how the load progressed. If there are any records that generate an error during the load process, they are stored in a file pointed to by the parameter BAD. If records have to be rejected by the load process, they are placed in the file pointed to by the parameter DISCARD.

Depending on the hardware configuration, another feature that can improve the load time is the ability to load the data in parallel using the parameter PARALLEL.

Once the data has been loaded, check the log file to verify that no errors occurred during the load.

Rather than use the command line version of SQL*Loader to load the data in the database, it can be invoked from the *Backup Manager* by selecting *Data* from the strip menu and then *Load*.

The first question asked by the wizard in Figure 6.37 is the name of a valid control file. Unfortunately, the wizard doesn't help you define the control file; that task must have been completed prior to starting the tool. If a valid control file does not exist, you won't be able to proceed beyond this point.

Hint: Make use of the *Browse* feature if you cannot remember the name and location of the file.

Figure 6.37 SQL*Loader Select the Control File

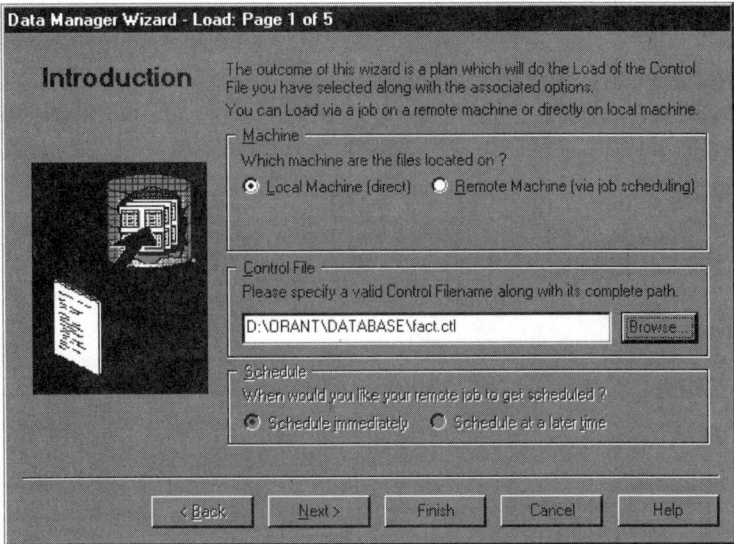

Figure 6.38 Name the Log Files

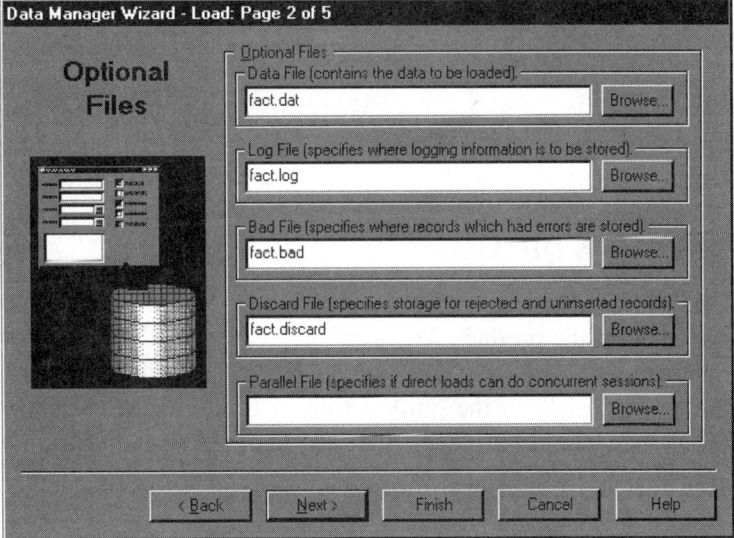

Moving on to the next screen, Figure 6.38, you are prompted for the name of the data file to be loaded and the names for the log, bad and discard files. Specifying these files takes very little time and if any errors occur they can be used to input the data next time around, rather than having to reload the entire file again.

Figure 6.39 is an extremely important screen, because it is here that the direct path option is selected. This is also the place where other parameters allow you to skip through the data if this is a restart operation.

Before submitting the job, a summary window displays all the options that have been selected. Once confirmed, the job is automatically started.

Figure 6.39 Specify Direct Path

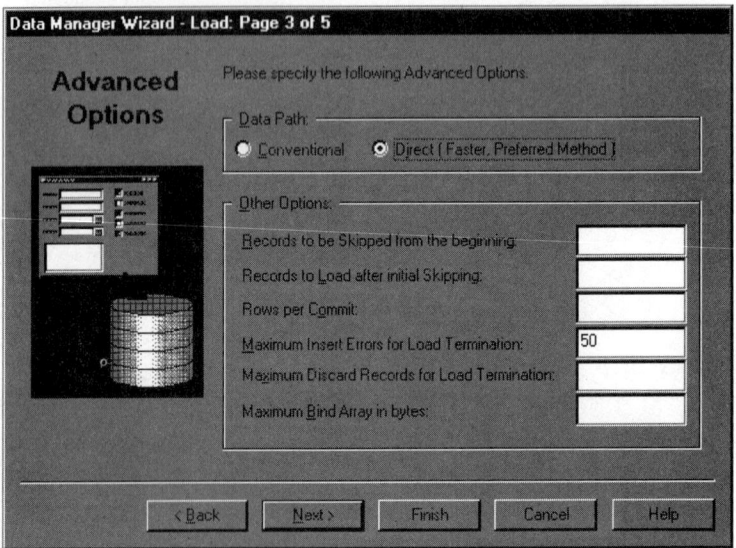

6.9   THE DATA DICTIONARY

One of the advantages of using the NT platform is the user is shielded from the detail of the product. Anyone who has used earlier versions of the Oracle database will be used to querying the internal data dictionary while managing the databases. With the introduction of Enterprise Manager, queries which previously would have been done via SQL are now displayed graphically.

However, some people still prefer to use SQL rather than GUI tools. Within the Oracle documentation all of the data dictionary tables and views are documented and there is nothing wrong with querying them. Sometimes, the information is not available in the GUI, therefore an SQL query is the only way to obtain the information.

Some of the tables that provide storage information are:

- DBA_TABLESPACES
- DBA_FREE_SPACE
- DBA_ROLLBACK_SEGS
- DBA_SEGMENTS
- DBA_EXTENTS

Following are some examples of the type of queries that are possible against the data dictionary.

Free Space by Tablespace

To find out how much free space is in a tablespace, table DBA_FREE_SPACE is queried.

```
SQL> SELECT tablespace_name, SUM(bytes) FROM
   DBA_FREE_SPACE
     GROUP BY tablespace_name
     ORDER BY tablespace_name;


TABLESPACE_NAME           SUM(BYTES)
---------------           ----------
AUGUST                       1046528
DECEMBER                     1046528
INDX                         4286464
NOVEMBER                     1046528
```

Number of Extents in a Tablespace

The number of extents in a tablespace, query table DBA_EXTENTS.

```
SQL> SELECT tablespace_name, COUNT(*)
   FROM dba_extents  GROUP BY  tablespace_name;


TABLESPACE_NAME           COUNT(*)
---------------           ----------
INDX                           162
ORDERS                          11
RBS                              6
SYSTEM                         427
```

Status of the Database Usernames

What is the status of all the database usernames?

```
SQL> SELECT username, account_status FROM
   DBA_USERS;

USERNAME                        ACCOUNT_STATUS
------------------              --------------------
SYS                             OPEN
SYSTEM                          OPEN
DBSNMP                          OPEN
OEM                             OPEN
ADMIN                           OPEN
ORDERS                          OPEN
LILIAN                          EXPIRED & LOCKED
7 rows selected.
```

List of Roles in the Database

To list all the roles that have been defined, enter this query.

```
SQL>  SELECT role  FROM DBA_ROLES;

ROLE
---------
CONNECT
RESOURCE
DBA
SNMPAGENT
```

Table Information

There is a wealth of information held in the data dictionary about the tables and indexes that have been defined. Table information is in DBA_TABLES and index information is in DBA_INDEXES.

The query below displays the pctfree value for the table.

```
SQL> SELECT table_name, pct_free  FROM DBA_TABLES;

TABLE_NAME                      PCT_FREE
-------------                   ----------------
ORDERS_IN                              20
ORDERS                                 10
ORDER_LINE                             10
```

The examples shown here have not even skimmed the surface of what can be done with the internal data dictionary. There is a wealth of information which, if you know where to look, can prove invaluable. However, since the vast majority of the information that you need to manage the database is displayed in the GUIs, one could say that this approach is for the diehard SQL person. If you want to be modern and make life easy, then use the GUI approach.

6.10   SUMMARY

Anyone who has ever had to manage a database will tell you that it is not a trivial task. In this chapter we have seen how, through the use of tools like the Enterprise Manager and the wizards, database management needn't fill you with trepidation. Simply answer the questions and then let the system schedule the job for you. Of course, for those who prefer total control over the management tasks, that is available as well.

The one important point to remember about managing a database is to perform the tasks regularly and you shouldn't be caught off guard by some surprises.

7   Security

Often the information held inside databases is not for everyone to see. In this chapter we will learn about the various security mechanisms that are available, such as Oracle usernames, and how to restrict access to certain tables and the actions that a user can perform.

7.1   DATABASE USERS

Before anyone can access anything inside the database, they have to logon. In Oracle 8.0.3 this would be using an Oracle username and password as shown in Figure 7.1. This username and password is completely different from the username and password that you used to logon to NT. There is no direct relationship between these two usernames and they are maintained using different tools. Database users can be created using SQL, but the examples shown here will use the *Security Manager* GUI.

Figure 7.1 Oracle Database Logon

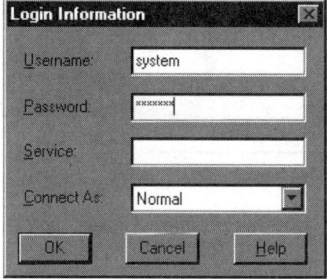

Having to maintain two sets of usernames and passwords can be viewed as a lot of extra maintenance. Oracle8 provides a very useful facility where access to the database can be granted dependant on your NT username. If the initialization parameter OS_AUTHENT_PREFIX="" and a username is created in the Oracle database with a password type of external that is identical to your NT username. Then you can immediately logon to the database. According to the NT documentation this feature should be available, but in Oracle 8.0.3 it is not yet available.

An important decision for the DBA is how usernames will be allocated and maintained. Your organization may already have defined a strategy for database access. If not, then some of the options are:

- give each user his or her own username;
- allocate usernames by group and task (e.g., account clerk and account supervisor);
- create an Oracle username that corresponds to the user's NT username.

One very nice aspect of the Oracle username and password is that they are not case-sensitive, unlike an NT username and password which must be entered precisely using the correct case. Therefore, provided you remember them, you can login.

When the Security Manager is started, Figure 7.2 is displayed. Take a moment to check the box on the right hand side, which displays the username that you used to logon to the database.

Figure 7.2 Security Manager

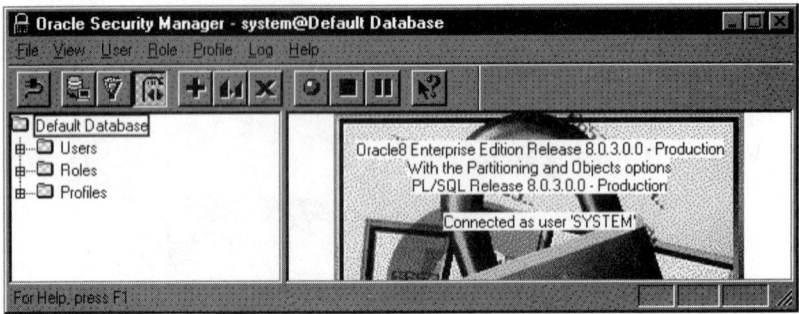

Hint: If all the tabs described here are not available, click on *View* in the strip menu and then *Advanced Mode* or click on the  icon.

In the left window, the navigator is poised, waiting to show us the users, roles and profiles that have been defined. Existing users can be modified by clicking on *Users* and then clicking on the username requiring modification. To create a new user, click on *User* in the strip menu and then select *Create*.

Several usernames are created automatically by Oracle when it is installed. The most powerful username is *internal*, which is used for managing the Oracle instance. Another powerful user is *system*, with a password of manager, which can be used to create objects in the database and the user *sys*. The first time you connect to the database, these passwords should be changed from their system defaults so that database security is not compromised.

7.1.1   Create an Oracle User

Creating a new user requires completing the four tabs shown in Figure 7.3, which are General, Roles/Privileges, Object Privileges and Quotas. Referring to Figure 7.3, first the user must be given a name and a profile, which is described in Section 7.3.

Figure 7.3 Security Manager

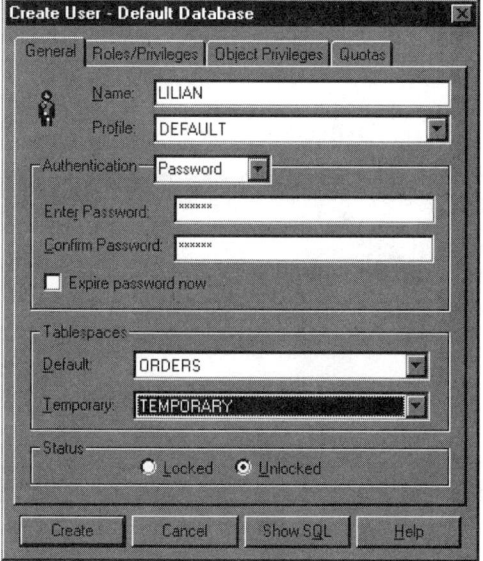

If password is selected, then the password is typed in the boxes shown in Figure 7.3. This means that all passwords are managed by the Oracle8 server. An external password is validated by the operating system, but this option is not available in 8.0.3.

In previous chapters we have seen that, whenever an object is defined in the database, we can specify into which tablespace that object is stored. The same is true for a user; we must say what their default tablespace is for storing data and which tablespace they should use for temporary segments they may create while accessing the database.

Finally, new for Oracle8 is the ability to lock an account. Once locked, the account cannot be used and attempts to do so will be greeted by the message shown in Figure 7.4.

Figure 7.4 Locked Account

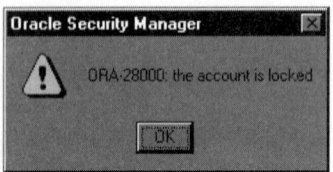

If you click on the *Users* name in the navigator window you can easily see the current status of all user accounts, including whether they are locked, as shown in Figure 7.5. See how user LILIAN prominently stands out as being locked with the red icon next to it. All the other users have an open lock icon, to denote their accounts are available for use.

Figure 7.5 User Overview

Oracle Security Manager - internal@Default Database

File   View   User   Role   Profile   Log   Help

Username	Account Status	Expire Date	Authentication	Default Tablespace	Temp Tablespace
ADMINISTRATOR	OPEN	None	External	ORDERS	TEMPORARY
DBSNMP	OPEN	None	Password	SYSTEM	SYSTEM
LILIAN	EXPIRED_LOCKED	00 000 0000	Password	ORDERS	TEMPORARY
OEM	OPEN	None	Password	OEM_SPACE	TEMPORARY
ORDERS	OPEN	None	Password	ORDERS	TEMPORARY
SYS	OPEN	None	Password	SYSTEM	TEMPORARY
SYSTEM	OPEN	None	Password	USR	SYSTEM

For Help, press F1

7.2   ROLES

A very popular feature in the Oracle database is the ability to define roles. Normally the rights to access an object and how it can be manipulated have to be allocated individually which becomes very tedious, especially when you have as many privileges as the Oracle8 server allows. The solution to this problem is to create a role which is allocated certain privileges. If the role is assigned to any users, then when those users logon, they are automatically granted all the privileges for that role.

Figure 7.6 Roles

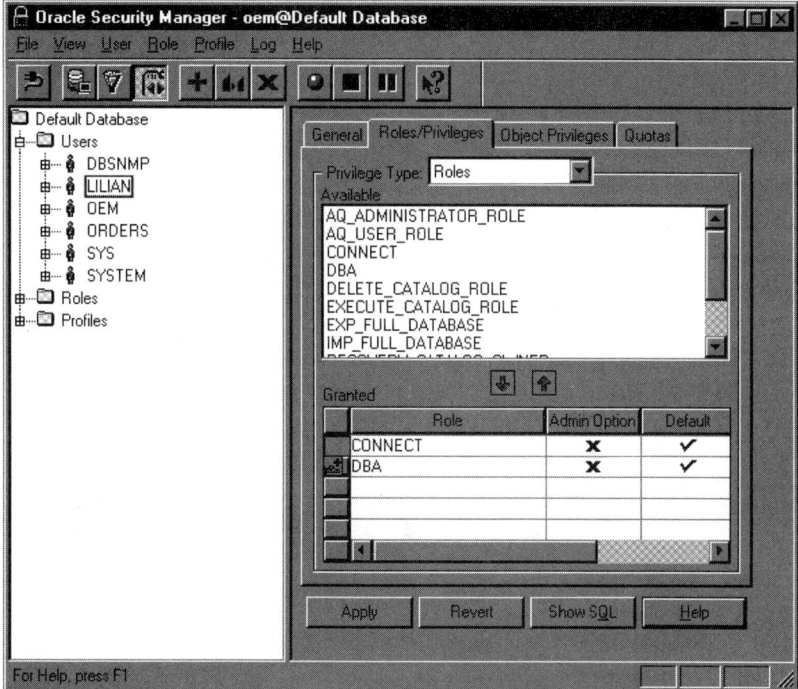

A number of roles are created when Oracle8 is installed, which may prove adequate for your needs. For example, when the DBA role is granted to a user that user can perform DBA type operations like CREATE TABLE, whereas a user with the EXP_FULL_DATABASE can only backup and select any table or execute a procedure.

Roles are allocated to a user, as shown in Figure 7.6, by pressing the Roles/Privileges tab when a user is selected from the navigator window.

First check that the drop down list is on Roles. Now select each role and then press the down arrow to grant this role to the user or use the up arrow to remove it. The role now appears in the box at the bottom. By default there is an X in the *Admin Option* column because granting the admin option with a role makes a very powerful user. When the Admin Option is available, the user not only has all the rights and privileges of the role, but can also grant or revoke the system privilege or role to any other user and can alter or drop the role. This makes an extremely powerful user, so be very careful about granting this privilege.

Figure 7.7 Security on a Role

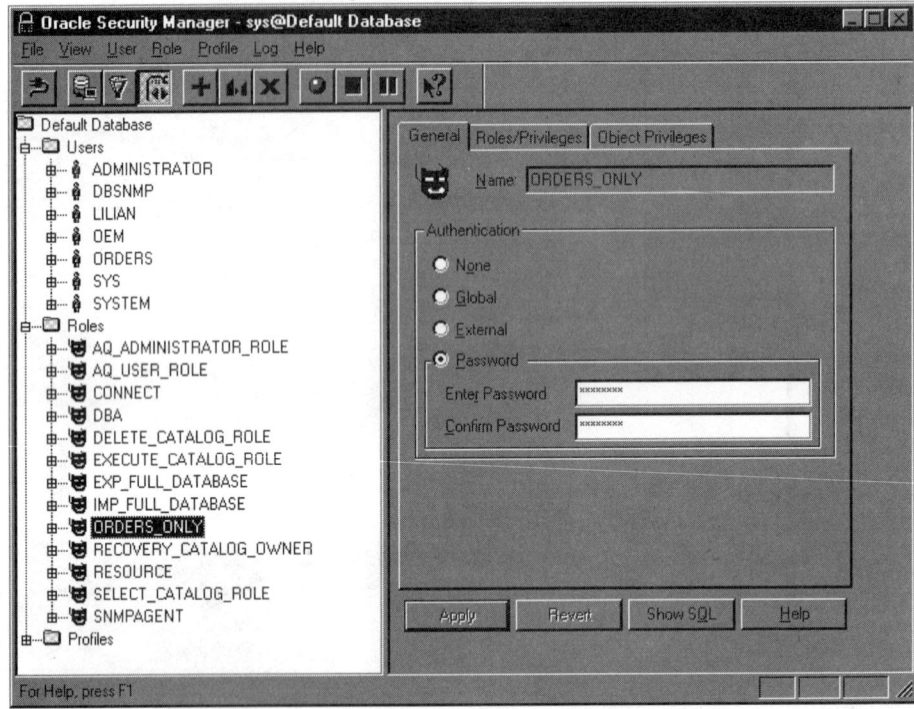

In Figure 7.7 is the first dialog box to create a new role. The role is given a name, and one very useful feature is the ability to specify a password which must be entered to use the role. The password is created using the IDENTIFIED BY clause as part of the SQL SET ROLE statement as shown below.

```
SET ROLE orders_only IDENTIFIED BY orders;
```

If the default box does not contain a checkmark, then the SET ROLE must be used in SQL to use the role.

7.3   PROFILES

With the proliferation of PCs in the workplace, there has never been a better reason to restrict the system resources that a user has access to. Oracle8 allows a number of profiles to be defined, which contain the information shown in Figure 7.8. The profiles are created separately by selecting *Profile* from the strip menu and then selecting *Create*. Once defined, the profile is then allocated to a user.

As we can see in Figure 7.8, some very useful parameters can be set, such as how much CPU time a user is allowed to consume or how long a user can be connected. Idle time could be useful to prevent users leaving their screens idle.

Figure 7.8 Profiles

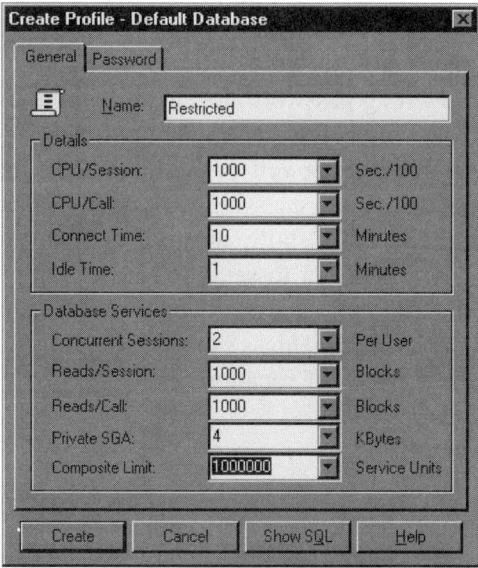

It is very easy with PC tools today, to generate runaway queries against the database. Setting parameters like the number of database blocks that can be read in a call can help prevent this type of problem.

If you are concerned about users consuming too many resources, consider creating a range of profiles from low to high powered users. However, be prepared for calls to the help desk if users suddenly find their jobs are failing.

When Oracle8 is first installed there is only one profile available, called Default which has unlimited resource utilization. If there is no need to restrict usage, then no action is required in this area, because every user will be given the default profile automatically, which allows them unlimited resource access.

7.3.1   Password Control

It is now possible in Oracle8 to have much greater control over a user's password, which is controlled as part of the profile definition, by clicking on the *password* tab. Now you can state whether a password expires; in Figure 7.9 we have set password expiration to 30 days. If new passwords are demanded by the system, a history can be kept of passwords previously used. This is very good for system security because it prevents the user from keeping the same password. However, it often annoys the end-user because they have to keep thinking of a new password!

If the *Enforce Password Complexity* box is enabled, then every password is checked to see if it can be easily guessed.

The final new feature is the ability to lock the account if the user keeps specifying the wrong password. In Figure 7.9, the user is allowed 6 attempts to enter the password before the account is locked. If you are concerned about security, keep this number very low, like three. If the value is kept very low, the chances of somebody guessing your password in three attempts is highly unlikely (unlike in a TV show, where they always work the passwords out right away). A reason not to set it too low, is that the help desk will keep receiving calls asking for users' accounts to be unlocked because they have forgotten their password. This is especially a problem when people have come back from a few weeks of vacation.

Figure 7.9 Passwords

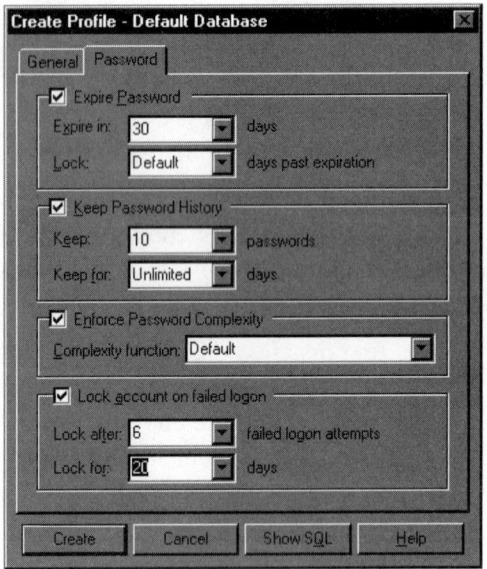

7.4   SYSTEM PRIVILEGES

Throughout this book we will come across some very powerful tasks that can be executed against the database which enable the user to add and remove data. Obviously, we don't want to give every user of the database the right to execute those commands. Therefore, for every user we can specify, via the system privileges, the tasks that user may perform. Oracle8 has a large number of privileges that can be granted, some of these listed in Figure 7.10. It is worth taking some time to review the list of privileges to see what is available. For example, in Figure 7.10 we can see a sample of the objects we are allowed to create, such as create table.

Figure 7.10 System Privileges

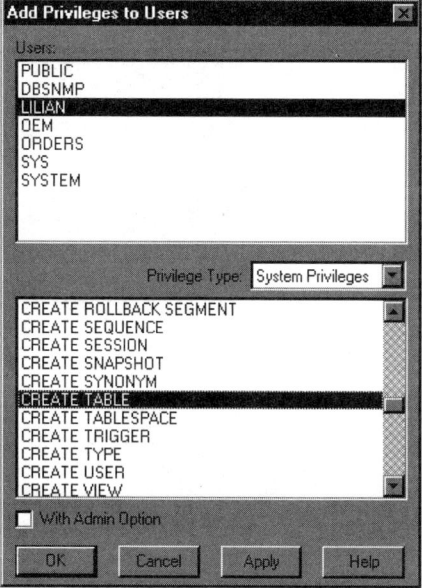

To add a privilege to a user, referring to Figure 7.11, click on the *Roles/Privileges* tab for a user. From the drop down list, change it from Role to System Privileges.

Now review the list of privileges, and to give a user the right to execute that task, simply select the privilege and then press the down arrow button to grant it to the user. Continue this process for every system privilege. Since there are a lot of privileges this can be a very time consuming task, so see if there is a role that can be granted instead that has those privileges.

If this method sounds a little tedious, there is an alternative method for granting privileges to a user. This time click on *User* from the strip menu and then select *Add Privileges to User* which displays Figure 7.12. Using this dialog box, all the privileges to be granted can now be selected using the shift or control keys as per standard Windows selection techniques, which is much faster than doing it individually. When all the privileges have been selected, click on the *Apply* button and they will all be granted to the user.

Figure 7.11　Grant Privileges to a User

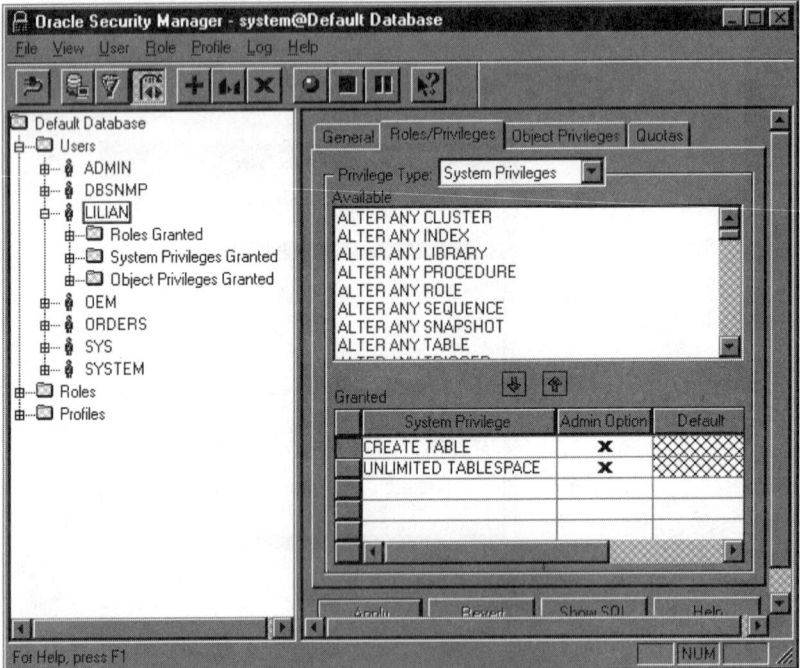

To check that the privileges have been granted correctly, return to the navigator and expand the username to see the privileges that have been assigned.

Figure 7.12 Add Privileges to a User

```
┌─ Oracle Security Manager - system@Default Database ──────────── _ □ X ┐
│ File  View  User  Role  Profile  Log  Help                            │
│ ┌──┬──┬──┬──┬──┬──┬──┬──┬──┬──┬──┐                                     │
│ │ ⤴│ 🗗│ 🔽│ 🖼│ +│ ⊷│ X│ ●│ ■│ ‖│ ▶│                               │
│ └──┴──┴──┴──┴──┴──┴──┴──┴──┴──┴──┘                                     │
│ 🗀 Default Database        ┌─General─┬ Roles/Privileges ┬ Object Privileges ┬ Quotas ┐ │
│ ├─🗀 Users                 │                                              │ │
│ │  ├─👤 ADMIN             │ ┌ Privilege Type: │System Privileges  ▼│     │ │
│ │  ├─👤 DBSNMP            │  Available                                    │ │
│ │  ├─👤 LILIAN            │  ┌──────────────────────────────────────┬─┐ │ │
│ │  │  ├─🗀 Roles Granted  │  │ALTER ANY CLUSTER                      │▲│ │ │
│ │  │  ├─🗀 System Privileges Granted │ALTER ANY INDEX            │ │ │ │
│ │  │  └─🗀 Object Privileges Granted │ALTER ANY LIBRARY         │ │ │ │
│ │  ├─👤 OEM               │  │ALTER ANY PROCEDURE                    │ │ │ │
│ │  ├─👤 ORDERS            │  │ALTER ANY ROLE                         │ │ │ │
│ │  ├─👤 SYS               │  │ALTER ANY SEQUENCE                     │ │ │ │
│ │  └─👤 SYSTEM            │  │ALTER ANY SNAPSHOT                     │ │ │ │
│ ├─🗀 Roles                │  │ALTER ANY TABLE                        │▼│ │ │
│ └─🗀 Profiles             │  └──────────────────────────────────────┴─┘ │ │
│                           │            ┌───┐ ┌───┐                       │ │
│                           │            │ ⬇ │ │ ⬆ │                       │ │
│                           │  Granted   └───┘ └───┘                       │ │
│                           │  ┌──────────────────┬─────────────┬────────┐ │ │
│                           │  │ System Privilege  │ Admin Option│ Default│ │ │
│                           │  ├──────────────────┼─────────────┼────────┤ │ │
│                           │  │CREATE TABLE       │      ✗      │▨▨▨▨▨▨▨│ │ │
│                           │  │UNLIMITED TABLESPACE│     ✗      │▨▨▨▨▨▨▨│ │ │
│                           │  │                   │             │        │ │ │
│                           │  │                   │             │        │ │ │
│                           │  └──────────────────┴─────────────┴────────┘ │ │
│                           │  ◄                                         ►  │ │
│                           │ ┌Apply┐ ┌Revert┐ ┌Show SQL┐ ┌Help┐          │ │
│ ◄                      ►  │ ◄                                         ►  │ │
│ For Help, press F1                                            │NUM│      │ │
└───────────────────────────────────────────────────────────────────────┘
```

7.5   OBJECT PRIVILEGES

The last set of privileges we can define is the actions that we can apply to objects like tables in the database. So far we have secured the database against unauthorized use through a username and password. We have prevented users from performing actions like creating or dropping data, but we haven't done anything yet to stop people from actually looking at data that they do not have the right to see.

By assigning object privileges, we can control precisely what people can do and see inside the database. There is a wide range of objects that we can secure, as shown in Figure 7.13.

Figure 7.13 Object Privileges

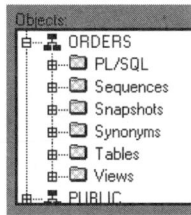

DBAs will want to define which tables a user can access. But as we can see in Figure 7.13, we can also specify which PL/SQL packages can be executed and how snapshots and views can be accessed, as well as the views they can use.

There couldn't be an easier way to assign these privileges. First click on the *Object Privileges* tab, which will display the dialog box shown in Figure 7.14. Move to the object pane on the left and click on the schema and then the object to which you want to assign privileges, which in this example is Tables. Now scroll down the list to find the table of interest and when you select it, the available privileges will appear in the right window.

Click on the privilege and use the down arrow to grant it. The assigned privilege will now show in the bottom window so you can double check that it has been assigned correctly. If at any time you change your mind about assigning a privilege, press the up arrow key to remove it.

In this example we have been given the right to alter, insert, select and update data from the Customer table, but we cannot delete it.

Of course, there are SQL commands to assign these privileges, but surely you will agree that this is much easier than trying to remember the actual SQL.

Figure 7.14 Object Privileges

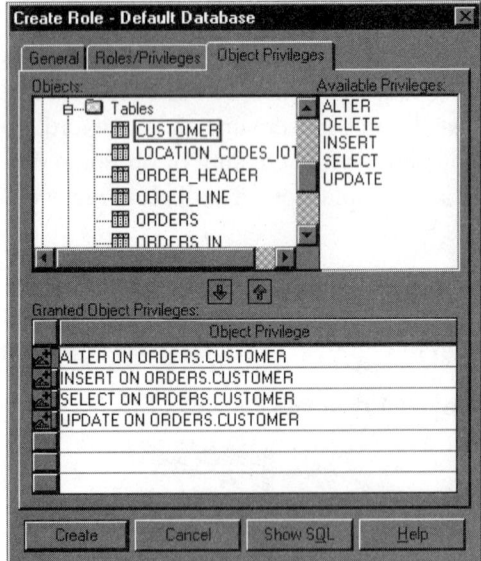

There is another way the privileges can be assigned and that is to select *User* from the strip menu, then select *Add Privileges to User* and scroll down the list in the middle to reveal Object Privileges. Then select, as was described in the previous section. Once again, using this method multiple access rights can be assigned and granted by using a few clicks on the keyboard and mouse.

Figure 7.15 Assign Object Privileges

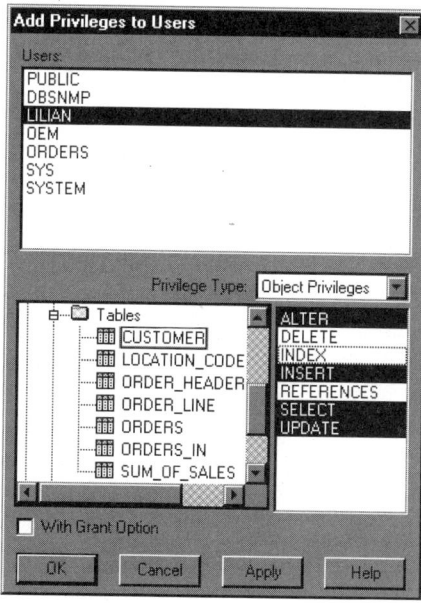

7.6 SUMMARY

Oracle8 provides a very comprehensive range of security mechanisms to ensure that unauthorized access and retrieval of information is kept to an absolute minimum. The Security Manager GUI really does make the whole process of securing the database much easier and quicker to execute. Nevertheless, don't underestimate the time and effort that is required to maintain a secure site. But if you make use of features like Oracle roles, then securing the database should be a pleasure and not a chore.

8 Backup and Recovery

This chapter is dedicated to one of the most important tasks for anyone responsible for managing a database: Backup and Recovery. The number of different options and methods for backing up is quite extensive in Oracle8, therefore what is written here is by no means a definitive list of features. The aim of this chapter is to provide only an appreciation of what is possible because entire books have been devoted to this subject.

8.1   BACKING UP THE DATABASE

Ask DBAs what is the first management task they think of in respect of a database and the chances are that they will say backup. Backing up the database is one of the most important tasks that a DBA or Operations department has to perform. When we backup the database, a copy of the database is taken and stored somewhere else, so that if there are any problems with the master database, the backup copy can be used instead.

It is very important to develop and implement a backup strategy that is most appropriate for the way that you do business. Once the plan has been agreed upon, ask yourself this question; "how much information will we lose if we have to restore the database?" If the answer is "some", then the strategy is unsuitable and it must be revised. The objective of any backup strategy is to ensure that absolutely no data is lost from the database. Most businesses cannot afford to lose any data for some of the following reasons:

- financial loss, business could go into bankruptcy;
- legal requirement to hold data;
- customers will not return for repeat business.

An organization's attitude towards backup can be very interesting to observe. If we write an important letter, then as a matter of course we make a duplicate copy and file it somewhere safe. Yet to be honest, if we didn't make that duplicate copy it probably wouldn't matter. However, businesses regularly store vast quantities of important information in their databases and don't make a copy of it, not for hours, days, weeks or sometimes even months. If anything were to happen to that data their business could be in financial ruin, but that doesn't seem to worry them. Sometimes, it seems like the mentality of "it won't happen to me" persists in the world of backups.

You would think that backups were difficult to take and that is why people forget to do them, but that couldn't be farther from the truth. In an Oracle environment, a backup is nothing more than making a copy of all the files that comprise the database. The problems start to arise when:

- you try to find a convenient time to make the backup;
- you try to find space to store the backup;
- the database is in constant use.

Prior to Oracle8, a backup of the database was usually taken by using commands in the Operating System language to copy all the database files. Therefore it was necessary to create quite sophisticated script files to perform these tasks. It is understandable that an organization's backup methods may not have been completely satisfactory.

All that has changed with Oracle8 because there is now a utility known as the *Recovery Manager* which allows you to backup and recover the database. The recovery manager can be used via its command line interface, the application RMAN80 or by calling the GUI tool *Oracle Backup Manager*, part of Oracle Enterprise Manager, which must be started from the console.

The database can be managed by other means, but if the *Recovery Manager* is used, it provides an easy interface to select which parts of the database to backup. Other advantages include the ability to backup only those parts of the database that have changed, create a compressed backup and maintain a catalog of what has been backed up.

Before the database can be backed up, when the users logon to the database, they must connect as SYSDBA. They will be logging on from the Enterprise Manager console, using the special username setup for this purpose. The SYSDBA system privilege must be granted to these users. This can be achieved by following two simple steps. First, change the initialization parameter REMOTE_LOGIN_PASSWORDFILE to EXCLUSIVE. Then start the *Security Manager* and logon using the internal username. Select the Enterprise Manager username and grant the SYSDBA system privilege to those users, who will now be able to connect as SYSDBA. This process is described in more detail in section 7.4. Previously we had always connected as Normal and this suffices for most operations, except tasks like backup.

When the *Backup Manager* starts you will be prompted, as shown in Figure 8.1, to select the required backup method. Irrespective of which method is chosen, the Backup Manager tool is started. However, far more facilities are available if the Oracle8 Recovery Manager is chosen, therefore it is suggested that this method is always used to backup the database.

Figure 8.1 Select Backup Method

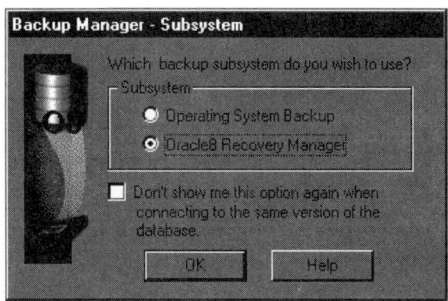

8

Oracle

Hint: Although it says Recovery Manager, don't worry, the Backup tool is started.

8.1.1   Backup Strategy

The aim of your backup strategy is to ensure that the backup can be completed in a timely fashion, without disruption to the business and without loss of data. When it comes to recovery, the available backups should be able to recover the system quickly and accurately. Various types of backup are possible and this is why determining the correct backup strategy is important.

The possible options are:

- complete backup;
- incremental backup;
- backup specific tablespaces or datafiles;
- image backup;
- archive the redo log;
- control file backup.

Deciding which one of these to use depends on your business requirements, available time and resources. Some people prefer to make a complete backup, because then they only have to restore the database. Although complete backups take time and potentially lots of disk space, they do give a feeling of reassurance because you know that in the backup file is everything that you need.

Incremental backups are extremely useful for large databases because an incremental only contains the changes since the last backup. Therefore, a complete backup could be taken once a week, say on Sunday night, and then daily incremental backups. If the database had to be restored, you would have to restore using both the complete and incremental backup. Although this is not difficult, it does add a little complexity to the operation and therefore may discourage some DBAs from using this option.

A similar problem arises if backups are taken which includes only specific tablespaces and datafiles. One has to be extremely careful that the correct version of the files is restored.

Finally, don't forget that if archivelog mode is enabled, the redo logs must be archived and these files are just as important as the backup files.

Whatever backup strategy you choose, which will probably be a combination of some of these options, do check that the backup procedure:

- is appropriate for your business;
- works;
- has a script or job to execute the task;
- will allow the database to be restored.

It is no good waiting until a disaster occurs to find out that there is a flaw in your backup strategy. Backups are an essential insurance policy for the database, which you hope that you never make a claim on.

8.1.2   Backup Manager

When the *Recovery Manager* is selected in Figure 8.1, the application that is actually started is the Backup Manager shown in Figure 8.2. From the navigator window one can see the tablespaces and datafiles in the database, the redo logs, where the archived redo logs are located and the channels and jobs that have been defined. The navigator window contains some very useful information and the DBA should remember that it can be consulted to verify the state of the database. For example, suppose one needs to know what redo logs are available; well, the information is available here.

Tasks are started from the strip menu at the top of the window, such as backup, restore and change the state of the database.

Figure 8.2 Backup Manager

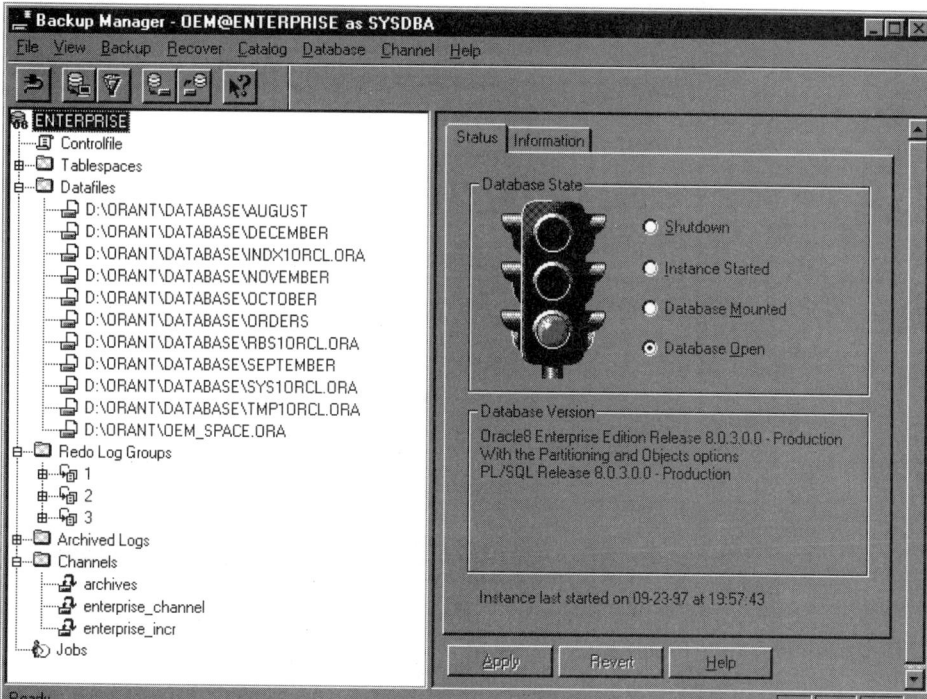

8.1.3   Define a Channel

Before a database can be backed up, a channel must be defined. This may
seem like a strange name, but it is nothing more than the place where the
backup file is to be placed. A channel can be defined for a specific database or
it can be generic for all databases to be backed up. It is created by selecting
Channel from the strip menu in the *Backup Manager* and then selecting *Create*.
The dialog box shown in Figure 8.3 appears which must be completed.

In this example we have created a channel specifically for the database on the
machine called enterprise. We have the choice of backing up to tape or disk,
but we have chosen disk. Then we specify the folder or directory in which the
backup is to be placed, which in this example is E:\DB_BACKUP, and how
the file will be named.

When naming backup files it is extremely important to choose a meaningful
name. The channel name refers to the actual name given to the file on disk or
tape. The tag name is the one that is most likely to be used to identify the
backup file to be restored. Although we will see in Section 8.3.1 an automatic
recovery, if we have to identify which backup files are needed for recovery,

Figure 8.3 Define a Channel

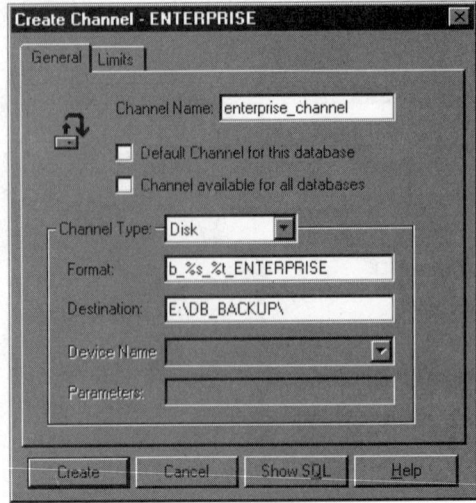

Hint: Press the Help button to see the available formatting options.

---

sensible names make the task easier and are an example of good database administration practice.

In Figure 8.3 the file has been named as a b for backup, followed by a backup set number (%s), which will start at 1, then a timestamp (%t), followed by the word ENTERPRISE to identify which database this backup belongs to. Rather than use the timestamp in the backup file name, which may not help identify when this backup was taken, you may prefer to include the date and time in your own format as part of the backup name. If this approach is taken the channel details must be updated every time a backup is made. Otherwise, one has to rely on the date and time given to the file, and if the file is moved around the system that could change, thus providing false information as to which time the backup was made.

8.1.4   Recovery Catalog

Oracle

The recovery catalog is maintained by the Backup Manager and it must reside in a database other than the one being backed up. The recovery catalog contains information such as:

- the physical structure of the database;
- information on what is in the backup and when it was taken;
- details of archived redo logs.

It is not mandatory to have the recovery catalog, but it does make life considerably easier and takes some of the risk out of restoring databases. Before the recovery catalog can be used, the script *catrman.sql*, which resides in *$oracle_home\rdbmsxx\admin*, must be run.

Hint: Run the script from SQL*Plus rather than SQL Worksheet because the script has a lot of work to do.

The first time the *Backup Manager* starts, in order to use the catalog, the catalog connect string must be specified, which tells it in which database the catalog is held. Simply click on *Catalog* in the strip menu, then select *Connect String* and enter the username, password and database service name. Once this has been setup this database will always use this catalog. To actually use the catalog, click on *Catalog* again in the strip menu and then select *Use Recovery Catalog*. A checkmark appears beside the catalog when it is in use.

Whenever a backup is made, details are written into some of the data dictionary views. These tables can be queried using SQL, thus enabling you to generate your own reports. Some of the useful tables to query are:

V$BACKUP_DATAFILE	contains details of each backup taken
V$ARCHIVED_LOG	contains information on the archived redo logs
V$BACKUP_SET	contains backup set information

Finally the database that is to be backed up, must be registered in the recovery catalog. This only has to be done once, unless any structural changes are made to the database, in which case it must be *resync*. To register, simply click on *Catalog* in the strip menu and then click on *Register* and Figure 8.4 will appear. Click on *yes* and a job is submitted for the registration process and by checking its log one can see whether it was successful or failed.

Figure 8.4 Register a Database in the Recovery Catalog

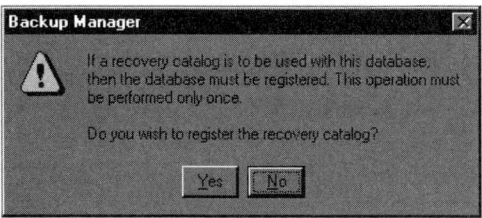

Hint: Don't forget to backup the database where the recovery catalog is stored. This is achieved by reversing the process as to which database holds the catalog.

8.1.5   Recovery Manager CLI

Almost all of the examples shown in this chapter will use the GUI version of Recovery Manager. Alternatively these steps can be executed via the CLI version of the Recovery Manager as shown in Figure 8.5. Additional functionality is available via the CLI, which includes the ability to generate reports and store scripts inside the catalog.

To use this utility, one has to specify which database is to be backed up, known as the *target*, and where the catalog is held, known as the *rcvcat*. For each database a valid username and password must be specified as shown below.

Figure 8.5 Using the CLI of Recovery Manager

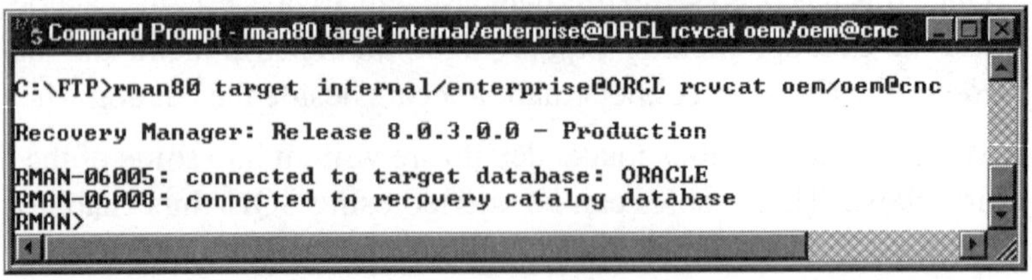

```
Command Prompt - rman80 target internal/enterprise@ORCL rcvcat oem/oem@cnc

C:\FTP>rman80 target internal/enterprise@ORCL rcvcat oem/oem@cnc

Recovery Manager: Release 8.0.3.0.0 - Production

RMAN-06005: connected to target database: ORACLE
RMAN-06008: connected to recovery catalog database
RMAN>
```

Reports

A number of different types of reports are available from the CLI version, using either the *report* or the *list* command. Report is the best command to use because it actually queries the database, whereas list merely reports what it finds. For example, a version of the *report* command will advise of any database that has not been backed up in the last *x* days. Therefore, using the report command you can:

- identify backup sets that are no longer required (Figure 8.6);
- check if any database is not recoverable (Figure 8.7);
- see whether anything needs to be backed up;
- report on the schema (Figure 8.8).

Figure 8.6 Obsolete Backup Report

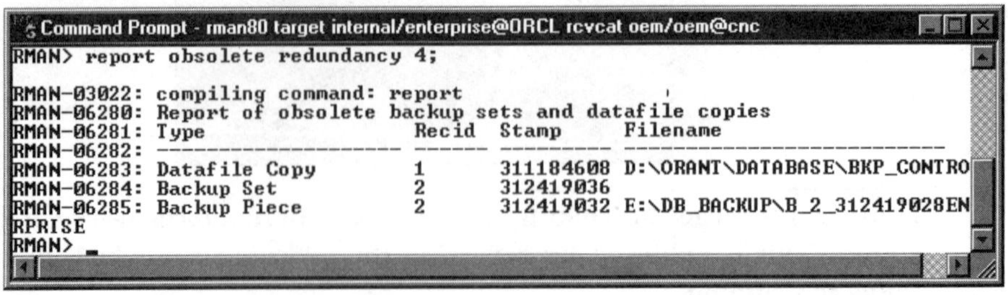

```
Command Prompt - rman80 target internal/enterprise@ORCL rcvcat oem/oem@cnc

RMAN> report obsolete redundancy 4;

RMAN-03022: compiling command: report
RMAN-06280: Report of obsolete backup sets and datafile copies
RMAN-06281: Type            Recid  Stamp      Filename
RMAN-06282: -------------   -----  ---------  --------------------------------
RMAN-06283: Datafile Copy    1     311184608  D:\ORANT\DATABASE\BKP_CONTRO
RMAN-06284: Backup Set       2     312419036
RMAN-06285: Backup Piece     2     312419032  E:\DB_BACKUP\B_2_312419028EN
RPRISE
RMAN> _
```

Figure 8.7 Unrecoverable Database Report

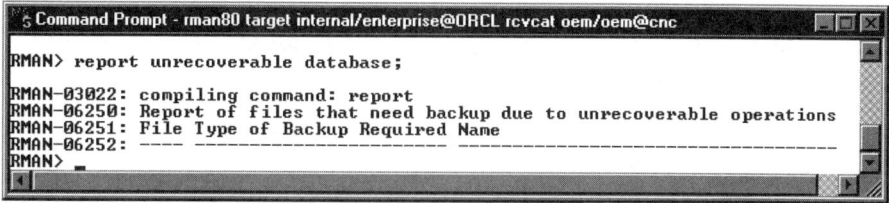

```
Command Prompt - rman80 target internal/enterprise@ORCL rcvcat oem/oem@cnc

RMAN> report unrecoverable database;

RMAN-03022: compiling command: report
RMAN-06250: Report of files that need backup due to unrecoverable operations
RMAN-06251: File Type of Backup Required Name
RMAN-06252: ---- ------------------------ ------------------------------------
RMAN>
```

Figure 8.8 Schema Report

```
Command Prompt - rman80 target internal/enterprise@ORCL rcvcat oem/oem@cnc
RMAN-06290: Report of database schema
RMAN-06291: File K-bytes     Tablespace        RB segs  Name
RMAN-06292: ----  --------   ---------------   -------  ------------------
RMAN-06293: 1       30720    SYSTEM            YES      D:\ORANT\DATABASE\SYS10
RCL.ORA
RMAN-06293: 2       10240    RBS               YES      D:\ORANT\DATABASE\RBS10
RCL.ORA
RMAN-06293: 4       10240    TEMPORARY         NO       D:\ORANT\DATABASE\TMP10
RCL.ORA
RMAN-06293: 5       12288    INDX              NO       D:\ORANT\DATABASE\INDX1
ORCL.ORA
RMAN-06293: 6        8192    OEM_SPACE         NO       D:\ORANT\OEM_SPACE.ORA
RMAN-06293: 7        5120    ORDERS            NO       D:\ORANT\DATABASE\ORDER
S
RMAN-06293: 8        1024    AUGUST            NO       D:\ORANT\DATABASE\AUGUS
T
RMAN-06293: 9        1024    SEPTEMBER         NO       D:\ORANT\DATABASE\SEPTE
MBER
RMAN-06293: 10       1024    OCTOBER           NO       D:\ORANT\DATABASE\OCTOB
ER
RMAN-06293: 11       1024    NOVEMBER          NO       D:\ORANT\DATABASE\NOVEM
BER
RMAN-06293: 12       1024    DECEMBER          NO       D:\ORANT\DATABASE\DECEM
BER
RMAN>
```

Scripts

Scripts to perform tasks like backup and restore can be held in the catalog. If the database is managed via the GUI version then creating scripts is not required because they are automatically stored in the catalog. Four sample scripts are provided in *$oracle_home\rdbmsxx\rman* and a sample of one of them is shown below.

```
run {
    allocate channel t1 type 'SBT_TAPE';
    allocate channel t2 type 'SBT_TAPE';
    setlimit channel t1 kbytes 2097150;
    setlimit channel t2 kbytes 2097150;
    backup
      incremental level 0
      filesperset 5
      format 'df_%t_%s_%p'
      (database);
    sql 'alter database open';
}
```

Some people prefer to write their own scripts so they have more control over the process. For those folks a comprehensive scripting language is available which includes the backup and restore commands.

8.2   BACKUP METHODS

Now that we have finished all the preparatory work, let us look at some of the possible methods that can be used to backup the database. Unless otherwise stated, these tasks are initiated using the Oracle8 Recovery Manager.

8.2.1   Complete Backup

8

Oracle

A complete backup can be taken using the *Backup Wizard*. It is started by selecting *Backup* from the strip menu and then *Backup Wizard.* Figure 8.9 will appear, where you select *Database* for a complete backup.

Figure 8.9 Complete Backup

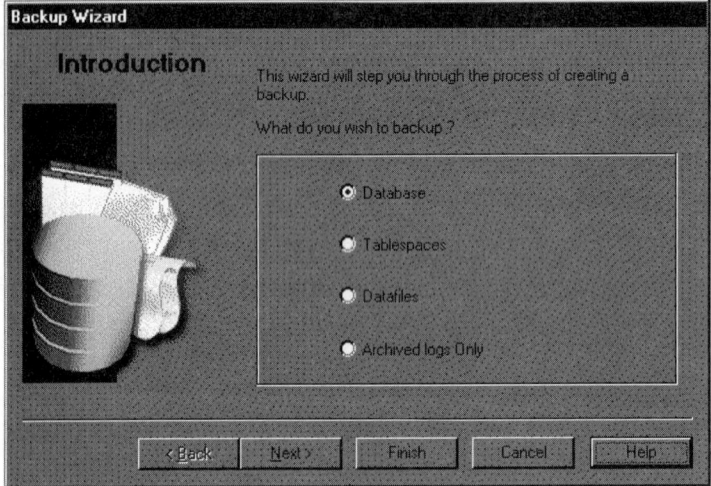

Next, in Figure 8.10 you will be asked whether the archived logs are to be included in the backup. Note that if you click the box at the bottom, the archived files will be deleted once they have been included in the backup.

Figure 8.10 Archived Log Files

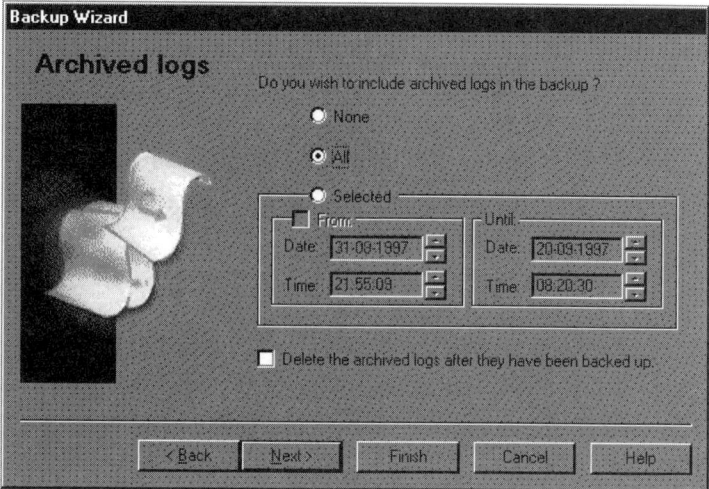

In section 8.1.3 we defined the channels; in Figure 8.11 we must select which channel to use.

Figure 8.11 Select the Channel

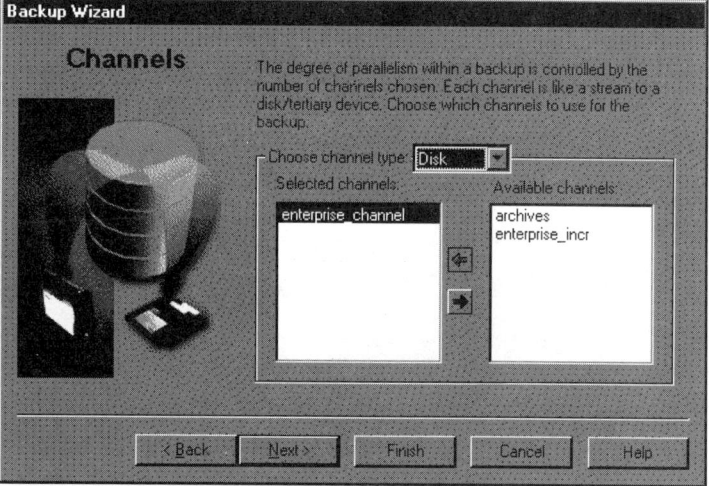

One of the most important questions asked during this process is what tag name to give this backup. Please give it some careful thought because if a manual recovery is ever performed, it is this description that will appear during the recovery process.

The level specified in Figure 8.12 must be zero because it is a full backup. It is only set to a nonzero value when an incremental backup is made.

Figure 8.12 Backup Tag Name

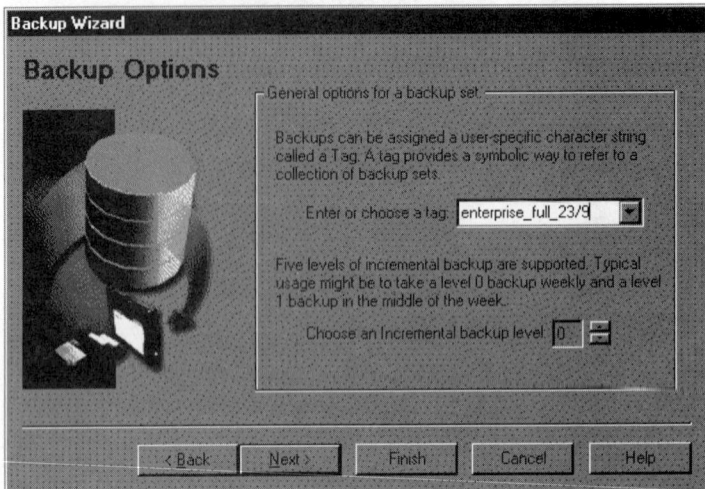

The next question that will be asked is how many files are to be included in the backup set. By restricting the number of files per backup set, the time taken to complete a backup can be improved by forcing it to use many channels instead of one.

By using the wizard, you can then schedule when the backup is to be made; by default it assumes that you want to start it now. However, you can schedule it to run on certain days of the week, or at specific times, by supplying the information requested in Figure 8.13.

Figure 8.13 Schedule the Backup

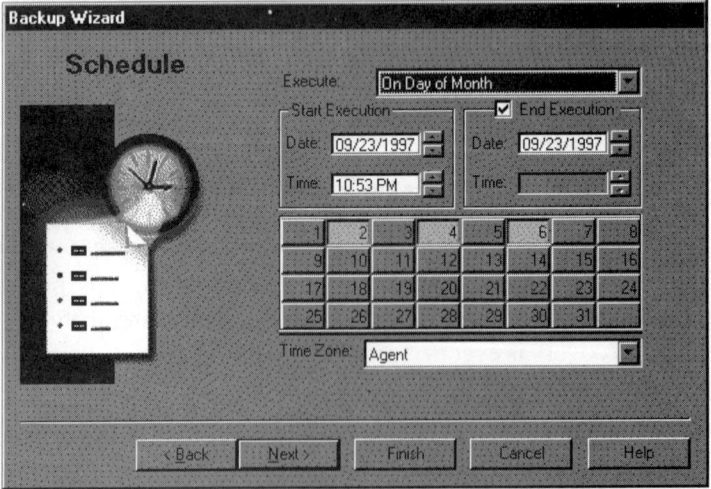

Referring to Figure 8.13, here we have decided to schedule the job to run on certain days in the month. A calendar for the current month is displayed and you simply select on which days it is to run and at what time. If you request the backup to be run by day, this window would show the days of the week instead of a calendar.

Figure 8.14 Saving the Job to the Library

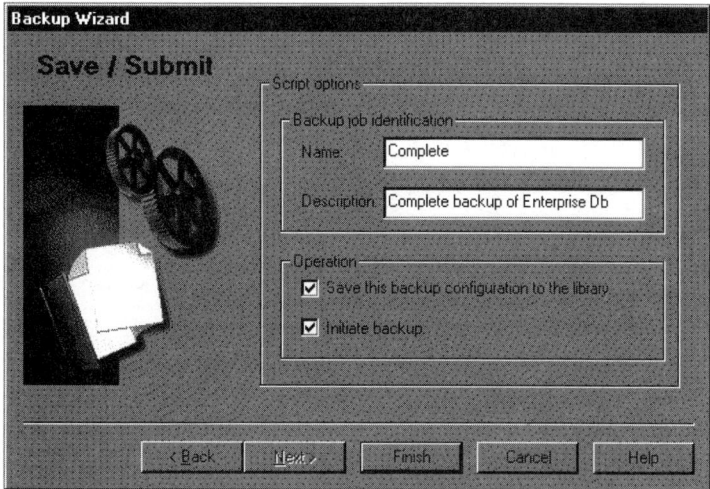

Finally, Figure 8.14 will appear requesting the name you would like to give this job and whether to save this job in the job library. Note that this is a different job library from the one that is part of the Enterprise Manager Console. Whenever the backup has to be run, this job can be called and executed from the navigator window jobs section, which is shown in Figure 8.2. When the job has completed, Figure 8.15 shows the backup file created by this job.

Figure 8.15 Database Backup File

The database that was backed up was actually using 89Mb of disk space; fortunately, the backup file is compressed and therefore uses a little under 21Mb of space. This is another excellent reason for using the Recovery Manager.

8.2.2   Incremental Backup

8

Oracle

Databases are typically very large and therefore one doesn't always want to backup the entire database, especially if only part of the database has changed. One solution to this problem is to use an incremental backup, which only backs up the changes that have been made to the database. Instead of one huge backup file, a much smaller one, containing all the changes since the last backup, is created. If your database is large with only a small percentage of the database changing, then incremental backups should be included in your backup strategy.

Figure 8.16 Incremental Backup

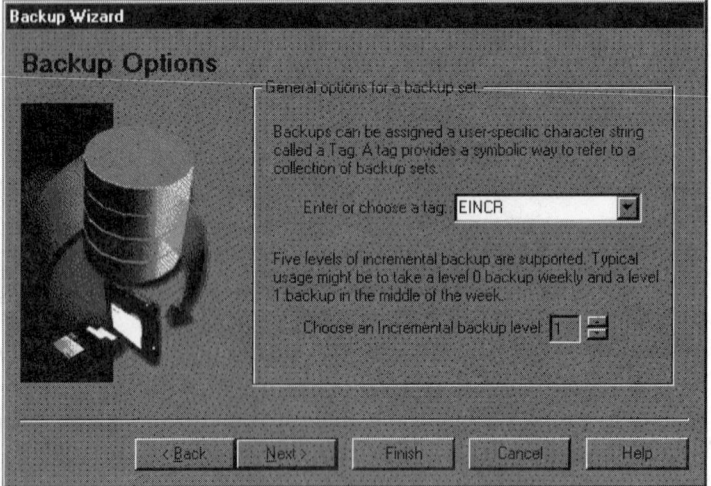

An incremental backup is defined using the same approach as a complete backup until the screen shown in Figure 8.16 is displayed. It is the backup level which determines whether this is an incremental backup. A value of zero denotes a full backup and a nonzero value represents an incremental backup. It is important to select the correct incremental backup level because it determines exactly what is put in the backup file. One scenario is to use level 1 for the midweek incremental backup and level 2 for a daily incremental backup.

Figure 8.17 Incremental Backup

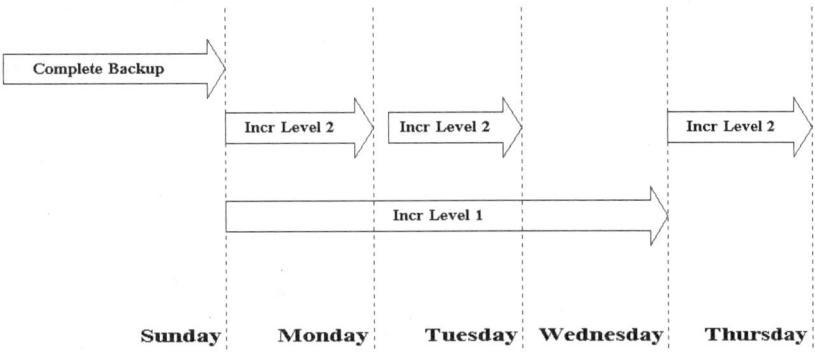

To clarify how the backup level is specified, let us refer to Figure 8.17. A complete backup is made on Sunday; this is our level 0. At close of business on Monday a level 2 incremental backup is made, which backs up all the changes since Sunday. On Tuesday another level 2 incremental backup is made, which will contain all the changes to the database since Monday. On Wednesday a level 1 incremental backup is made; since 1 is greater than zero, but less than 2, all the changes since Sunday will be placed in this backup file. On Thursday a level 2 backup is made, so the most recent backup with a value less than or equal to 2 is the level 1 backup from Wednesday, so this backup will contain all the changes since Wednesday.

Using this approach may at first seem complicated, but when automatic recovery is used, the recovery manager will decide for itself which complete and incremental backups are needed to recover the database.

8.2.3 Tablespace Backup

Another possibility, instead of making an incremental backup is to backup specific tablespaces. Suppose a number of changes have been made to the database but they have all been in specific tablespaces. To save time, only those tablespaces are backed up. A tablespace backup is created by using the *Backup Wizard* which is selected from *Backup* on the strip menu, and then selecting *tablespaces* from Figure 8.9. The dialog is almost identical except for Figure 8.18, where you specify the tablespaces to be backed up. In this example we have selected only one tablespace, but you can choose as many as you like. Continue answering the questions as described for a complete backup and the backup will be executed.

Figure 8.18 Backup only Tablespaces

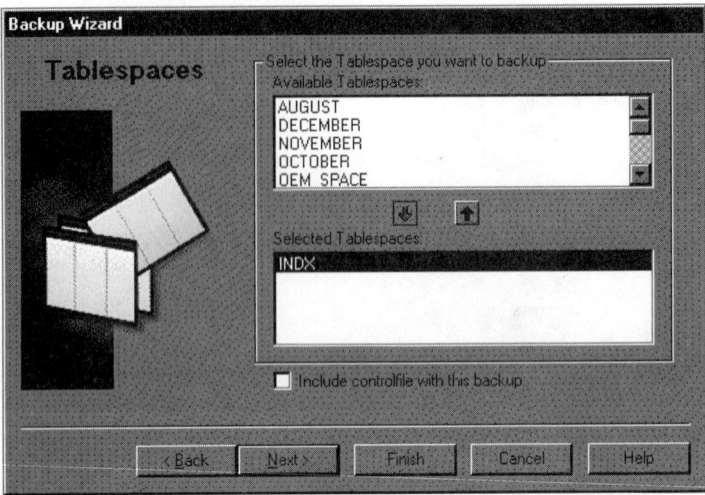

8.2.4   Datafiles Backup

An alternative to backing up specific tablespaces is to backup specific datafiles instead. The process is identical to that for a tablespace backup, as
described in 8.2.3, and the reasons would be the same for selecting this type
of backup.

Figure 8.19 Datafile Backup

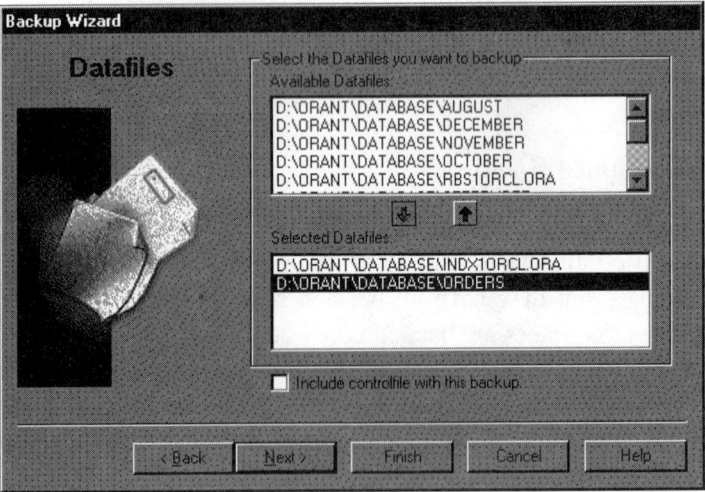

Figure 8.19 illustrates how to specify which datafiles are to be backed up.
Simply select the datafiles and press the down arrow key to include them in

the backup. Again, answer all the questions as per a complete backup and then the backup will be made.

8.2.5   Backup the Archived Redo Logs

In Section 3.4 we met the redo logs, which contain all the changes to the database. To perform a point in time recovery, we have to use the redo logs to return the database to a state after the last backups were taken. However, since we only have a limited area available for the redo log and there is most likely to be more data placed in the redo logs than we have available space, the redo logs are regularly archived by the archivelog process. This results in a number of files being created in the archive directory. Referring to Figure 8.20, we can see some of the files created by this archiving process. These are extremely valuable files and they should be backed up regularly as part of the backup strategy.

Figure 8.20 Archived Redo Log Folder

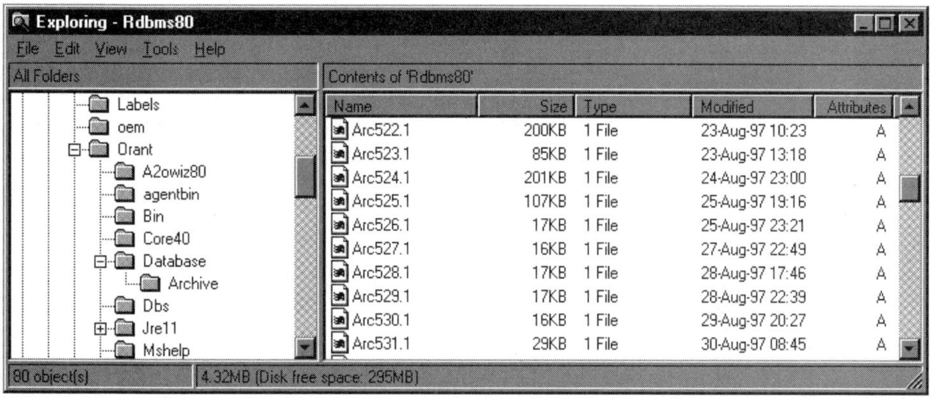

Whenever we execute a backup, we are usually asked (see Figure 8.10) if the archived redo logs should be included. If we back them up during this process, then we are guaranteed that the archived redo logs are an integral part of our backup strategy. Otherwise a separate job has to be run to backup the redo logs and this could easily be forgotten or overlooked.

8.2.6   Backup Control Files

The control files are a very important component of the database. They are automatically backed up during a complete backup, but sometimes you may want to make a backup of only the control files. Without them the database cannot be started and since they are so small it is easy to look after them.

The control files can only be backed up using the *Operating System Backup* rather than Recovery Manager. Therefore to start the utility choose *Backup Manager* in the Enterprise Manager console, then when Figure 8.1 appears, choose Operating System. A slightly different version of the *Backup Manager* is displayed and from *Backup* on the strip menu select *Backup Control File* and Figure 8.21 will appear. Specify the name and location of the backup file and the tool does the rest.

Figure 8.21 Backup the Control File

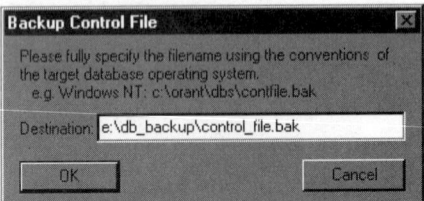

8.3   RECOVERING THE DATABASE

It is probably fair to say that when a backup and recovery strategy is being designed the majority of the time is spent reviewing the backup methods and creating the scripts required to complete those tasks. When all that work is done, then people focus on the recovery process. Perhaps it is because they think that they will never have to recover the database, but the recover aspect of management is just as critical as the backup process. Please spend just as much time reviewing and testing the recovery procedures as you do with the backup tasks.

Database recovery is achieved by using the Backup Manager, which we met in the previous chapter. Ideally the recovery catalog, described in Section 8.1.3 will have been setup to facilitate easier recovery operations.

One method of recovering the database is to use the *Restore Wizard*, which is selected from *Recover* on the strip menu of the *Backup Manager.* If the database instance is in the *open* state, then only tablespace or datafile recovery is allowed. To perform a complete recovery the database must be in the *mount* state. A quick method for changing the state of the database is to use the *Backup Manager.* Simply click on *Database* on the strip menu and then select *Shutdown*; you will be asked how to shutdown the database. The database can then be started in *mount* mode again by selecting *Database* and then *Startup.*

8.3.1   **Complete Recovery**

A complete recovery of the database is the method that is most frequently used. Using the *Backup Manager*, select the *Recover Wizard* and when Figure 8.22 appears choose *Database*.

Figure 8.22 Complete Recovery

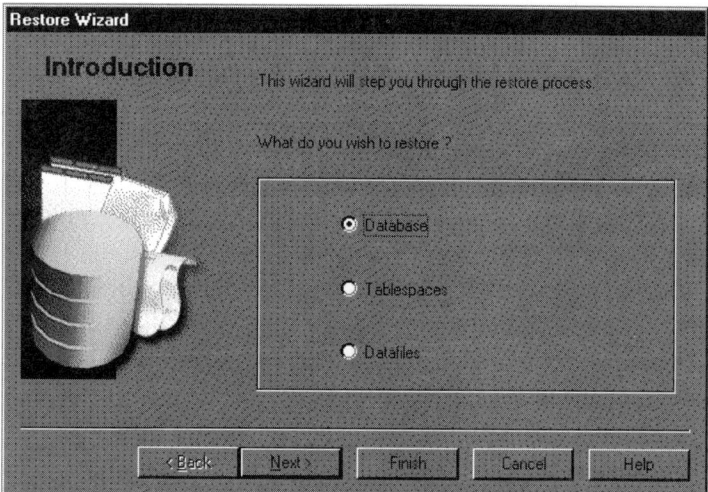

All of the datafiles are then listed as shown in Figure 8.23 and if necessary, they can be moved to another location by specifying the filename and location in the "new name" box. Otherwise they will be restored back to their original home. The next question is whether the restore should be up to the most recent point in time, which is the default because that is what you will usually require. Then choose the channel, which is normally the one that was used to backup the database. Once the *Finish* button is pressed, the restore begins. You can then refer to the Oracle Enterprise Manager console, to see the job running. Everything is now done for you; the catalog is consulted and the appropriate complete and incremental backups are selected and run. Just sit back and watch the database restore before your very eyes. It is not even necessary to delete the old database, the job that has been scheduled will do all that for you.

We can see whether the restore was successful by checking the Job History window shown in Figure 8.24.

Hint: Always confirm that the job did complete successfully by checking the log rather than relying on the status in the Job History window.

Figure 8.23 Specify Datafile Location

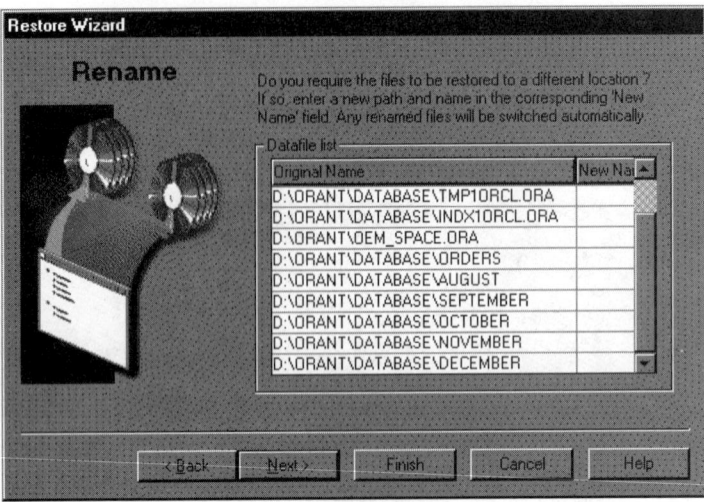

Double clicking on this entry will show us the actual script that was used and the backups that were restored, as illustrated in Figure 8.25.

Figure 8.24 Job History

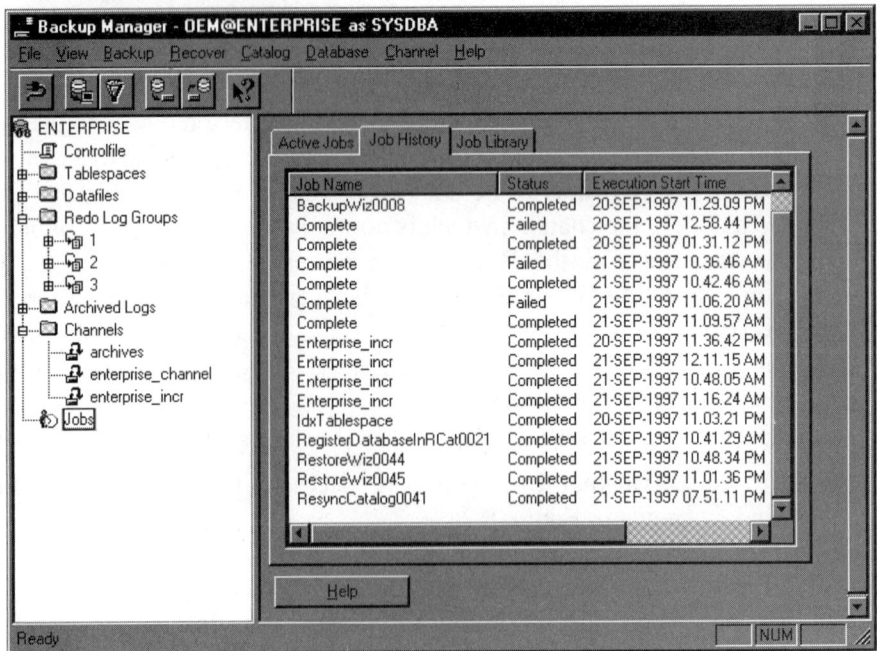

Figure 8.25 Recovery Job Log

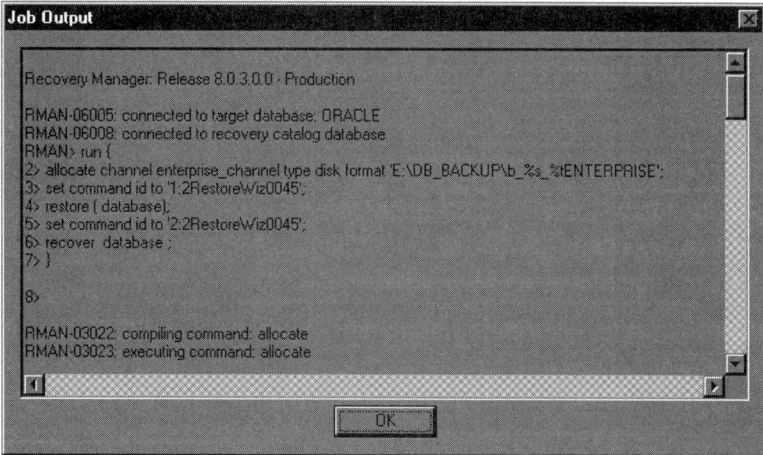

8.3.2   Tablespace and Datafile Recovery

The same technique can be used to perform a recovery of specific tablespaces or datafiles. If you are certain that the database will be correct if only part of it is restored, then by all means use this method. However, you must be absolutely certain, because to restore data without its indexes, for example, will leave you with a corrupt database. Alternatively, the database might not be corrupt, but the data could be invalid. For example, suppose an order is stored in two tablespaces called orders and delivery, and only one of the tablespaces is recovered instead of both of them. Incorrect data would then be stored inside the database.

Tablespace and Datafile recovery are extremely useful, especially with respect to large databases. Therefore, whenever you use this technique, before you start, use the "crossing the road" method, which is stop, check that this is correct, check again and then proceed.

8.3.3   Point-in-Time Recovery

There are times when you don't want the database to be restored back to its original state, but to a specific point in time. Suppose, for example, that somebody ran a batch job twice which put duplicate entries in the database.

Figure 8.26 Recover to a Specific Time

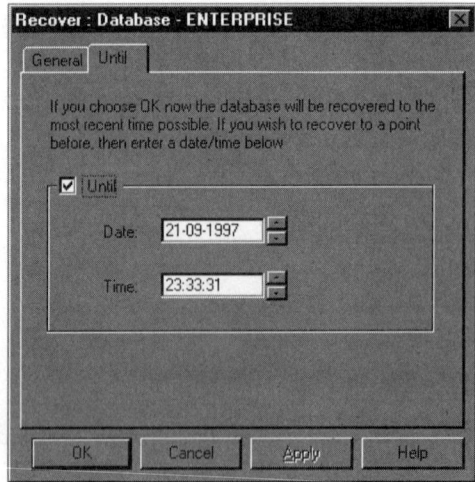

We know that the first batch job finished at 23:33:31 and the second batch job started at 23:35. In this instance, we would want to recover the database to 23:33:31. To perform a point-in-time recovery, start the *Recovery Wizard*, answer all the questions, and when Figure 8.26 appears, specify the time to recover to. This type of recovery is rarely needed, but you would be well advised to know how to do it in case the need ever arises.

8.3.4   Manual Recovery

Until now all the recovery methods have used the automated process which selects the files to restore and recover. Sometimes the database has to be recovered manually, and this can be done via the *Backup Manager* by selecting *Restore* from *Recover* on the strip menu. A single box is displayed, in Figure 8.27 and each of the tabs must be pressed to supply the required information.

In section 8.2.1 we entered a tag when the backup was created; this must be selected from the drop down list available on the *General* tab. Clicking on the *Rename* tab allows you to locate the restored files in a different directory. You must click on the *Channels* tab to specify which channel to use and only click on *Until* if a point-in-time recovery is required.

When the *OK* button is pressed, the database is restored and then a manual recover can be started by selecting *Recover* from the *Recover* option on the strip menu if the *recover object after restore* wasn't clicked at the bottom of the window in Figure 8.27.

Figure 8.27 Manual Recovery

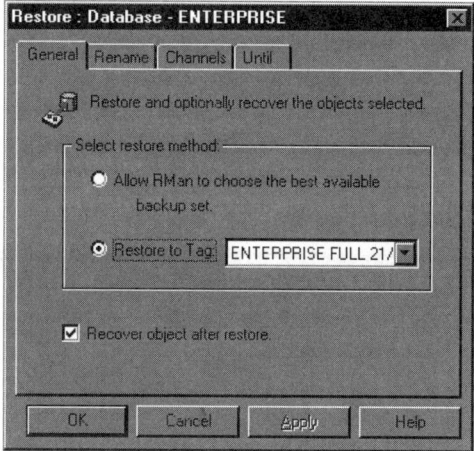

8.4 IMPORT AND EXPORT

So far all we have seen is the backup and restore capabilities of the Oracle database. However, there is another utility that can be used, called import and export. In Chapter 6, when we were reorganizing the database, the import and export utility were being used by the jobs to execute the command.

One of the attractions of using this utility is that, unlike the SQL*Loader utility which we saw in Section 6.8, this tool requires no control file and therefore no setup. Also, this tool will both unload and load data, whereas SQL*Loader will only load data.

So who would use the import and export tool? Well, we have already seen some of the database reorganization options using the utility. Developers may find it useful to maintain copies of their data. Instead of backing up an entire database or tablespace, they could copy only the objects in the database of specific interest to them.

8.4.1 Export

The *export* command is available by starting the *Oracle Data Manager* tool from the Enterprise Manager console. Just like the Backup Manager, this tool cannot be run standalone and must be invoked from the console. When the Data Manager is first started, Figure 8.28 appears. At first glance, the navigator window of Figure 8.28 may seem a bit confusing, because it lists users rather than tables. However, using the wizard, it is easy to specify which tables are to be exported.

A very important point to note about the Export tool is that it is devoted to copying data from the database into an external file, leaving the original data still inside the database. Therefore, there is no need to worry about data being deleted from the database when this option is used.

Figure 8.28 Export Navigator

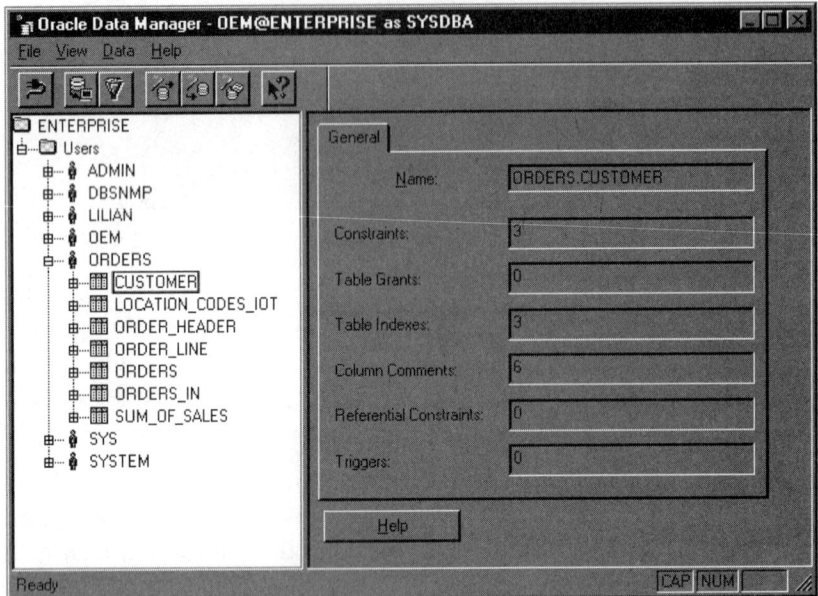

The *export* command can be found by clicking on *Data* in the strip menu and then selecting *Export*. Figure 8.29 will appear. This is the first window of many, which will allow us to export the database.

The first question asks where the export file is to be located. Put your export files in a safe place, especially if you plan on keeping them for any long period of time.

Now the moment has arrived to specify which objects are to be exported. As we can see from Figure 8.30, using the wizard makes this very easy. Simply select the objects using the right-hand window and click on the arrow key to send it to the selected area.

Figure 8.29 Location of Export File

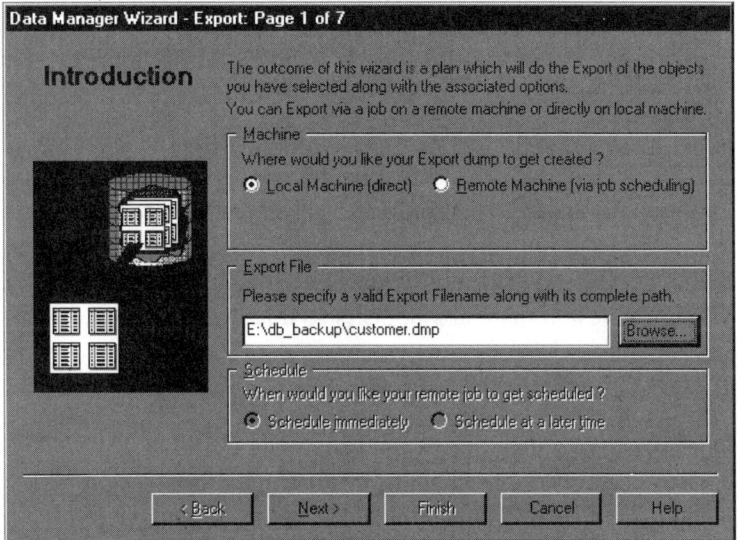

Figure 8.30 Select the Objects to Export

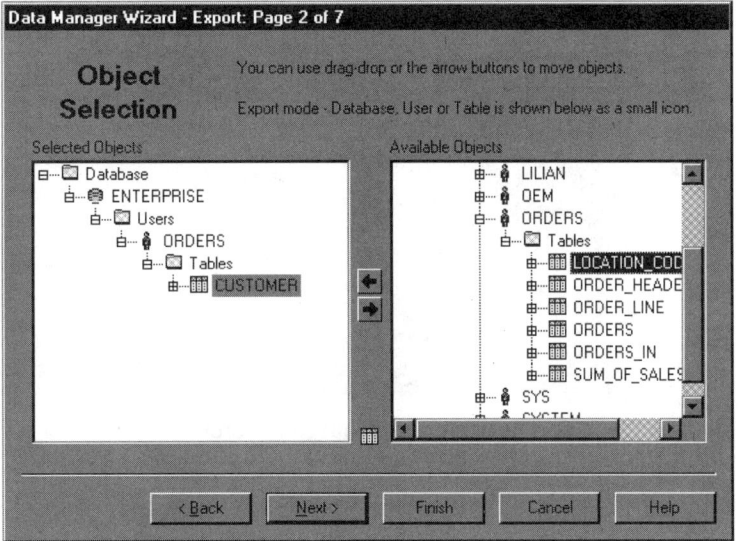

Hint: Select the user to export all the tables for that user instead of specifying them individually.

There are a number of advanced options which may be specified during the export, such as whether the privileges and indexes should be exported. But the most important box to check is the one at the bottom marked *Direct*. The first time we met the direct path facility was in Section 6.8 with regard to SQL*Loader. The export utility can also take advantage of Direct Path and this should always be selected so that your operations run as quickly as possible.

There are seven dialog boxes in the export wizard, so clicking on the *next* button will display another screen of advanced options and some tuning options. Finally, the summary screen will appear where you can check exactly what is being exported. Clicking on the *Finish* button starts the export and Figure 8.32 automatically appears so that you can monitor the progress of the export job.

Figure 8.31 Export Advanced Options

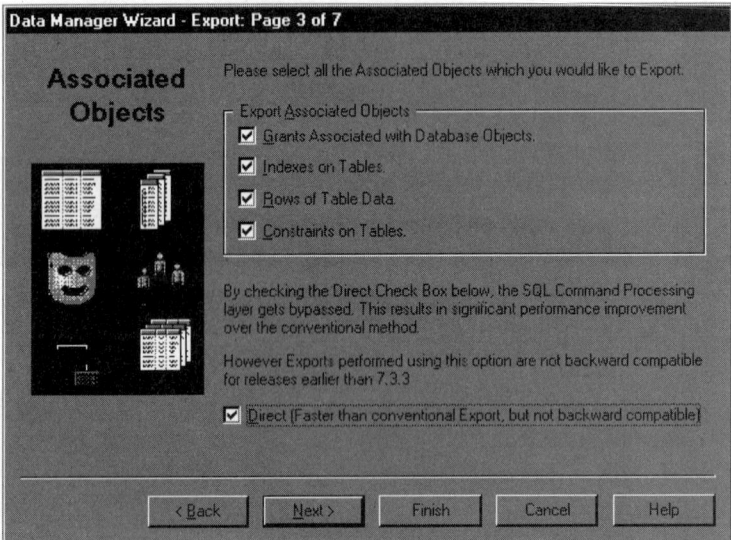

When the export job is run, it behaves differently from other jobs that we have seen. The export job is run immediately, there is no option to schedule the job, or to run it later or even save it as a job. Although the Data Manager must be started from the console, the export job does not run through the console, therefore it will not appear in the console Job window.

Figure 8.32 Export Job Progress

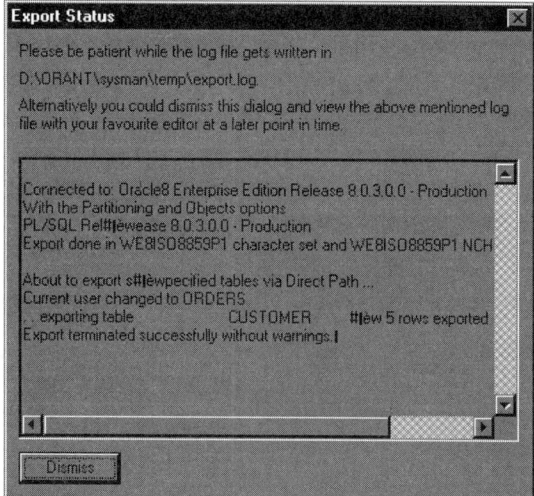

When the job has finished, the *Dismiss* button must be pressed to remove the window; however, this log file can still be viewed as it resides on your system. The exported data will reside in the file in the folder specified earlier.

Hint: Don't forget to delete the exported files when they are no longer required.

8.4.2   Import

The Import option reverses the process we have just seen and one could think of it like SQL*Loader. But SQL*Loader is much more sophisticated because Import is designed to handle files only from the Export utility.

Import is run by starting the *Data Manager* from the Enterprise Manager console, then selecting *Import* from *Data* on the strip menu. When the import wizard starts, it looks almost identical to the Export wizard we have just seen.

The first window displayed is just like Figure 8.29, except that it asks you to select the file to import. Then Figure 8.30 is displayed, but this time it only lists the objects actually in the backup file and asks you which ones are to be imported. A number of other screens are displayed before the summary window appears, providing the last option to view and confirm what is to be done before it starts. When the *Finish* button is pressed, the import job is run exactly as was described for the export.

The import job will fail if the object already exists inside the database, so verify its nonexistence before the job starts.

Now that you have observed Export and Import, you will agree that although these tools can be run from an SQL command line, using the wizard is much easier. Of course, you don't have the advantage of being able to create a script file and keep it for use again in the future, but since export is unlikely to be used on a regular basis, this shouldn't present a problem.

8.5   SUMMARY

This chapter has given you an insight into how an Oracle database can be backed up and recovered. Described in this chapter are only some of the possible methods that are available. For instance, this chapter has concentrated on using the Recovery Manager because it can automate the whole process for you, by creating scripts for backups and then selecting which files should be used for recovery. If you don't like the idea of the tool selecting the backup, then recovery can be performed manually or via what is known as the Operating System method.

We also took a quick look at the Import and Export utility which although not a backup and recovery tool, does provide a mechanism for extracting and loading parts of the database.

9 Tuning the Database

Anyone who has ever managed a database will at some time have been asked to tune the database. This chapter describes some of the techniques and tools that are available to tune an Oracle8 database. Since this a huge topic on which entire books have been devoted, please do not expect to find everything that you ever wanted to know about tuning a database. However, after reading this chapter the reader should have an appreciation of what is possible.

9.1 TUNING STRATEGY

Before you launch into tuning the database, take a step back for a moment to define your test strategy. This is a very important step, because otherwise you will spend far more time tuning than is necessary, possibly not achieving your goals.

The first step is to write down your tuning objectives. Examples of these could be:

- support a minimum of x transactions a second or minute
- report y must complete in less than z seconds or minutes
- support a specific number of concurrent users

When defining your objectives, it is extremely important to determine the minimum acceptance criteria. For example, suppose a report is currently taking 45 seconds to run and you would like that report to run in 5 seconds. If the first attempts at tuning improved the response time to 9 seconds, and it wasn't obvious how further improvements could be made, is nine seconds acceptable?

Everyone's objectives will vary. For instance, some organizations will know for each report and online transaction how long they should take. Others will say that the system must support a given level of throughput, or a specific quantity of work must complete within a certain window. Therefore, choose objectives that are appropriate for your business needs.

9.1.1   Testing Approach

Another important decision is how the system will be tested. Ideally a test environment should be created that simulates your production environment. Many people throw their hands in the air at this suggestion and say that this is impossible. Before you reject this idea, stop for a moment to consider the impact on your business without it.

The first point to remember is that this test system doesn't have to be identical to the production environment. But obviously the closer it is, the greater confidence you should have that your production system will behave as expected.

Once a test system is in place it can be used for tasks other than database tuning, such as:

- testing new software versions before upgrading
- trying out new features
- testing any database reorganization
- verifying your backup and recovery strategy

For any organization running a mission critical system, a test system should be considered as essential as backups. Without one, you live on a knife edge. Software upgrades are implemented and everyone hopes that there are no problems with the new software that will bring the entire business to a halt. Again, new features would have to be implemented without knowing whether they would benefit the system. Therefore sites without a test system tend to implement new features less frequently.

The problem with presenting a test system to management is that it is often seen as an intangible benefit. When a test system exists, its success can be partially measured by the improvements in performance resulting from database tuning and from smooth upgrades and the other areas where it can be used. Unfortunately, in our world today, areas often only get noticed when they fail, and smooth working areas are taken for granted. A test system is a success when nobody notices it is there!

If your organization doesn't possess some form of test system, and can't see why one is needed, then wait for the failure which costs the company money and management will be asking how much it will cost and when a test system can be available.

One area that causes problems when setting up the test system is how the tests will be run. Depending on the applications to be tested, it may be necessary to purchase additional tools. For example, to simulate 100 users of the system, it is much easier if a software tool creates the users, than to ask 100 users to come to work say on a Saturday and ask them to use the system. By using software, a controlled test is created because you know exactly how the system is being used and it can be repeated many times.

The database used by the test system may be a copy of the production database or most likely it will have evolved from a production database and carry special test cases to stress certain parts of the system. The actual data in the database is an important consideration because it is no good stressing the system only to find that certain types of data cause problems. Therefore, try to evolve your test database so that it tests as much of the system as possible. Once this database exists, don't forget to backup the database on a regular database. The loss of this database could have almost as much effect as losing the actual production database.

A final point to consider is how the system will be tested. Will there be one big test suite that is always run, or will it be modular and specific components selected? When changes are made to the database to improve performance, will only one change be implemented or many? Ideally, implementing one change at a time is the ideal scenario because it allows you to see exactly how the change impacted the system. Unfortunately, if your test system takes many hours to set up, then changes will have to be batched together, otherwise testing would never be completed.

When a database is being tuned, changes will be required to either the database, application code or both. Before the tuning process starts, the DBA should identify whether application changes are allowed and if so, make those groups aware that some of their valuable time may be required implementing changes. It is not uncommon during tuning to identify SQL statements that have been written inefficiently or, even worse, identify a piece of application logic that needs to be rewritten. Hopefully, the only changes required to the database will be those with user-transparent implementation. Therefore the only person affected by this change is the DBA, who has to schedule the time to implement it.

9.1.2   Test Results

During testing it is very important to maintain a record of all the test results. First a base position should be created and the times for this run recorded. Then all subsequent tests can be compared against this one.

Great care should be taken when results are collected to ensure that during the test run, nothing else was running on the machine at the time that could affect the elapsed time and resources used. This is especially important when the development and test environment share the same computers.

The logging of the results can be as sophisticated or simple as is suitable for your business. For example, for each test run you may only record, the elapsed time and the number of records processed. Typically though, far more information is recorded, such as CPU and I/O usage and statistics specific to the Oracle8 server.

All these results could be written on paper or better still, recorded in a spreadsheet so that analysis can be performed on the results. There is nothing more impressive than showing management a stunning graph of how performance has improved as a result of your testing efforts. A picture replaces a thousand words, and when it comes to database tuning, this statement is very true.

9.2   ORACLE8 PERFORMANCE MONITOR

A tool for monitoring the performance of an Oracle8 database that is provided with the product is the *Oracle8 Performance Monitor.* This tool can be started by selecting it from the folder *Oracle for Windows NT*. It requires no setup and is a nice way of graphically displaying Oracle8 performance information. If the tool looks familiar to you, it should, because it is the *NT Performance Monitor* which includes statistics for Oracle8 databases.

Using the Performance Monitor, four types of monitoring are available:

- Chart   monitor specific database resources
- Alerts   send an alert when a specific resource limit is exceeded
- Log   record the performance information into a log file
- Report   produce a report of log information

Anyone familiar with managing NT systems who knows how to use these tools does not require any additional training because this tool has simply been extended to report the Oracle8 specific data which is described here in Table 9.1.

However, when we look at the Performance Pack in this chapter, there is an even more powerful Performance Manager tool which offers extensive drill-down capability and customization and many more data items than we will see with the Performance Monitor. But since not everyone will have the Performance Pack, because it is an extra cost item, we will first see how to monitor database performance using the tools provided.

Table 9.1 Oracle8 Items Available for Monitoring

Oracle8 Item	Description
Buffer Cache	The percentage of time have read from the cache. This is a running value
Data Dictionary Cache	The percentage of time spent reading information from the data dictionary
Data Files	Displays the read or write rate at that moment for any selected datafile in the database
DBWR stats1	Shows the rate at which the buffers are being scanned by the DBWR process and the rate at which LRU scans are being performed
DBWR stats 2	Displays the checkpoint and timeout rates
Dynamic Space Management	Rate of recursive calls
Free List	Shows the data block contention
Library Cache	The percentage of time something is found in the cache where the shared cursors and the shared pool are located
Redo Log Buffer	Number of requests for space in the buffer
Sorts	The number of sorts being performed in memory or on disk

9.2.1   Chart

When the Performance Monitor first starts, the chart usually appears. If it is not visible, it can be displayed by either clicking on the ▣ icon or by selecting *View* from the strip menu and then *Chart*. When the chart is first displayed, two Oracle statistics are already provided, but before you can seriously use this tool, some customization is required.

Begin by specifying which items are to be monitored. This is achieved by selecting *Edit* from the Strip menu and then *Add to Chart* or by pressing the ➕ icon. Selecting either of these approaches will display Figure 9.1.

By default the display is for the computer you have logged onto, but you can select to monitor any computer running NT on the network. The first task is to

Figure 9.1 Add Items to the Chart

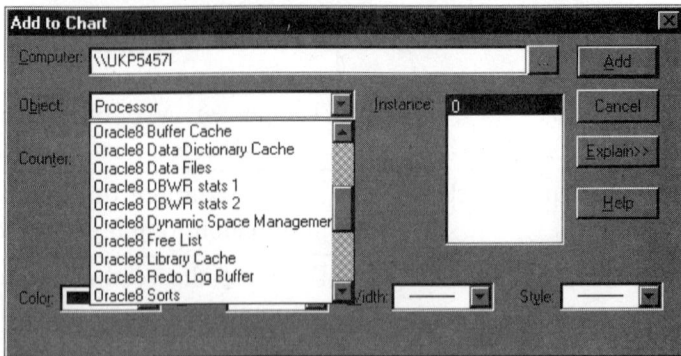

select from the comprehensive list of Oracle8 statistics, which ones are to be monitored by selecting them from the drop down list.

Hint: If the first time you start this tool no Oracle Statistics are available, then the setup in the Registry which tells the tool the username, password and database to query has not been setup. Refer to the Oracle documentation on how to setup the information in the Registry.

Depending on the statistics chosen, some more information has to be supplied. For example, suppose we have decided to monitor some of the datafiles of the Oracle8 databases, then we would select *Oracle8 DataFiles* from the list and Figure 9.2 is displayed. Now we have to say whether we want read or write statistics by clicking on the appropriate item in the *Counter* section. In the *Instance* section, all the datafiles are displayed. Unfortunately an extremely small window displays this information, therefore it will be necessary to scroll this box to find the correct filename.

Figure 9.2 Monitoring Oracle8 Datafiles

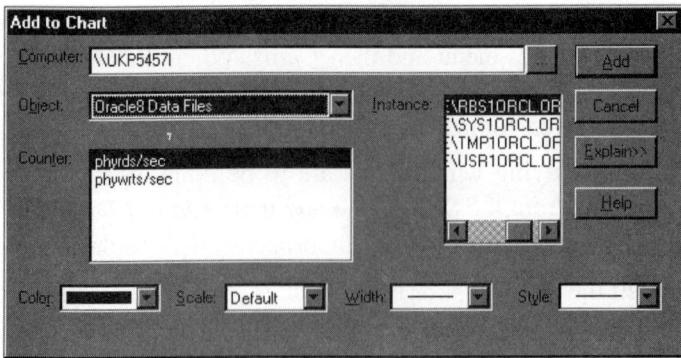

Finally, the attributes of the line displaying the information can be changed, such as its color and width. When the button *Add* is pressed, this data item will appear on the chart. This process is then repeated for every Oracle8 statistic that needs to be monitored.

Hint: Save the chart settings using *File* and then *Save As* so that this setup does not have to be repeated everytime this tool is used.

Figure 9.3 displays a typical chart, after customization, where we can see the database activity being regularly collected. Depending on the information being displayed, the *y* axis may need changing. This is easily achieved by selecting *Options* from the strip menu and then *Chart* and Figure 9.4 appears.

Some very useful customizations are possible, such as whether a graph or a histogram is displayed. A histogram may be preferred because there is one bar on the graph for each item being monitored. Enabling the grids is useful because it facilitates easier reading of the chart. The scale of the *y* axis can be modified by setting a maximum value and the refresh interval for the chart can be modified. Clicking the *OK* button will apply these changes to the graph.

Figure 9.3 Oracle8 Performance Chart

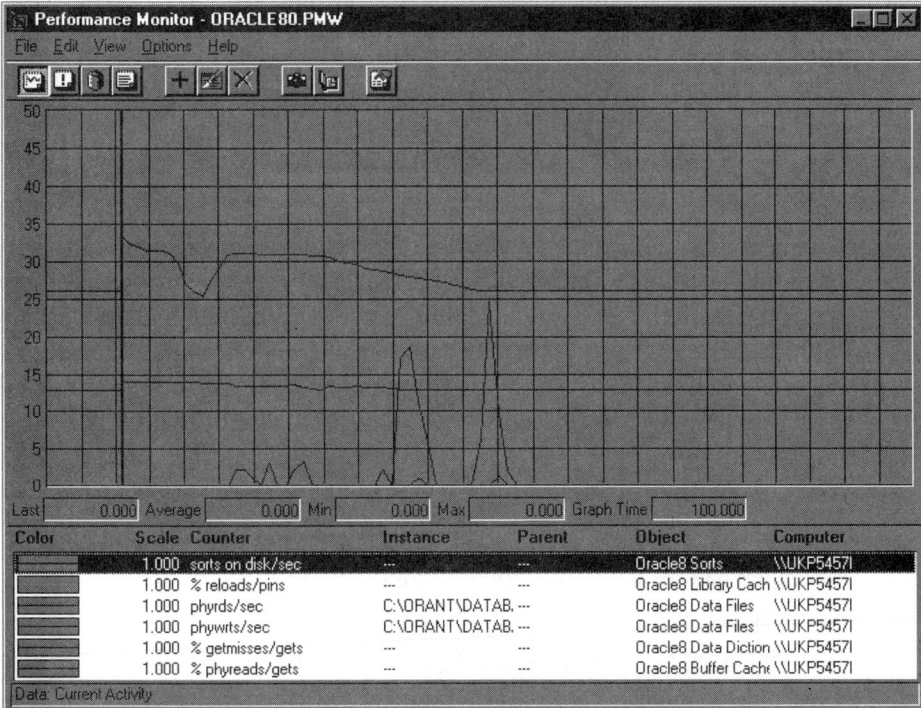

Using the chart to monitor an Oracle8 database should be considered an essential part of database tuning because it allows you to home in on particular troublesome areas.

Anyone who has ever read other books about tuning an Oracle database will see references to querying the Oracle system tables for performance information. The problem with this approach is that many people cannot remember which table to query, and it isn't exactly a friendly approach. By using the Oracle8 Performance Monitor, you don't have to query the tables because it is doing it for you. The other benefit of using this approach is that the data is being regularly updated, otherwise you would have to keep executing the SQL statements and then display the information graphically manually.

Figure 9.4 Customize the Chart

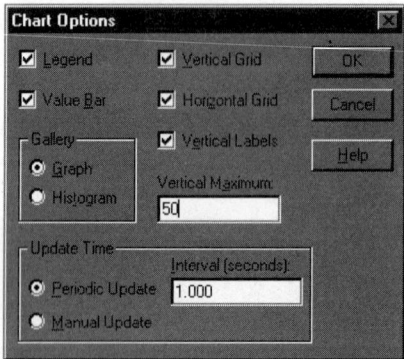

9.2.2 Monitoring the Database

Trying to explain to someone how to tune a database is very difficult because what may seem bad on one system is perfectly okay on another. Therefore, the numbers used to tune a database cannot be found in a book. Instead, you will have to see what is good for your system by monitoring it when performance is good and then using this information when performance degrades. But, if system performance is always bad, then what do you do? Well, one approach is to call in the experts to seek their advice. Alternatively, you can look at system performance to see if the following things are occurring. Some simple guidelines for tuning a database are:

- is the data in the buffer, therefore reduce I/O;
- keep the SQL statements in the cache.

From the Performance monitor we can see whether these events are occuring. If we refer to the chart in Figure 9.5, here we are monitoring when the datafile is being accessed and when the buffer is being used. In the real world, the display is colored, which unfortunately does not display too well in a black and white book. Imagine that the bottom line is blue, representing the datafile I/O, the next line is pink for the buffer cache and the top line is yellow for the data dictionary.

Figure 9.5 Monitor I/O

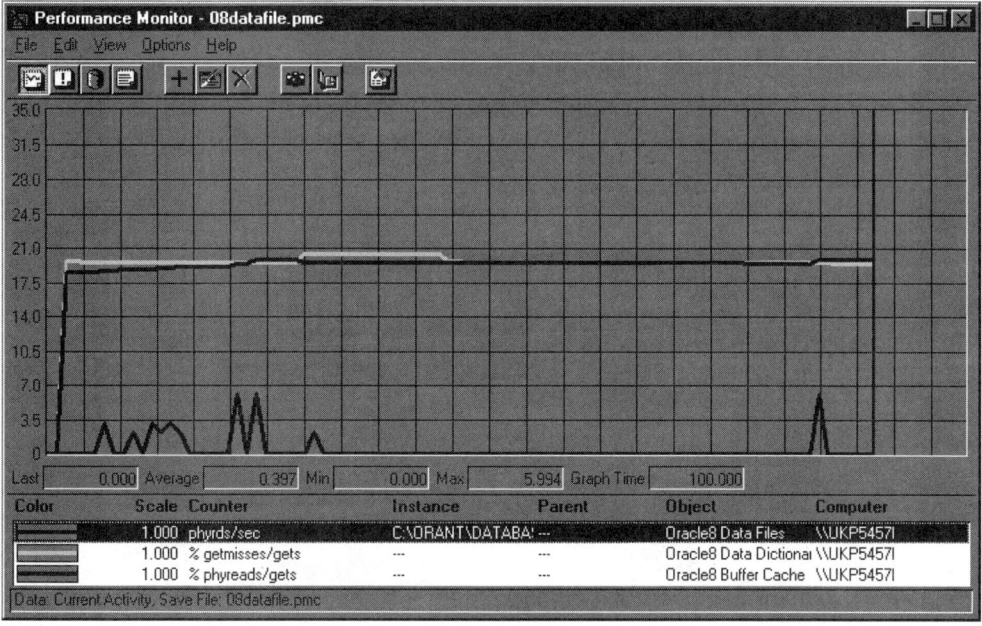

When this chart is analyzed in the context of the queries against the database then we can start to tune it. For example, while this graph was being displayed, three different queries were being continually executed against the database. We can see from the bottom line that initial I/O was incurred to bring the data into the buffer. At the same time the buffer usage line increased. If we look at the bottom line then we can see that there is a period where there is no I/O. We know at this time that we were querying the database, therefore all the information was in the buffer, which is a measure of a well tuned database. Later, we see a spike on the graph where we have incurred the same amount of I/O again, which is an indication that the data was not in the buffer and had to be reread. From this information we can assume that the buffer size needs to be increased to prevent this information from being removed from the buffer.

9.2.3   Alerts

To sit and watch the chart all day could be very boring and time consuming and not exactly a good use of a DBA's time. Therefore, to avoid this situation, the *Alert* facility should be used. This option is similar to the chart facility; that is, you select what you would like to be alerted about, as shown in Figure 9.6 and here you state whether to alert you if the value of this object either exceeds or falls below this value. There is even the option to run a program of your choice when the condition occurs. For example, in Figure 9.6 an alert has been defined that if more than 5 I/Os are read from the Summary datafile then an alert is sent to the alert log. All defined Alerts are viewed from the alert log which is selected by *Alert* from *View* on the strip menu.

Figure 9.6 Create an Alert

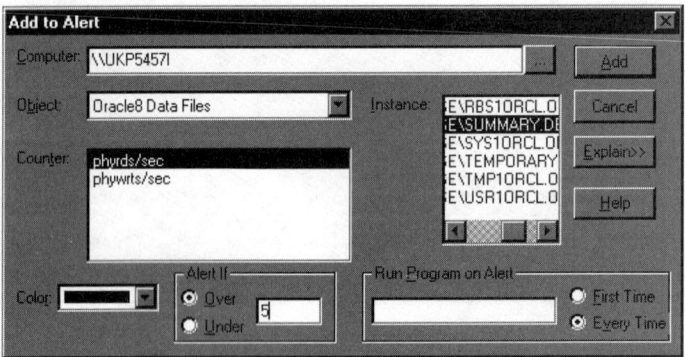

Hint: Don't forget to save your alerts for use next time, otherwise they have to be set up each time the Oracle8 Performance Monitor is started.

A sample alert log is shown in Figure 9.7. Every time an alert condition is met a line is written to the log. In this example we can see that there was some extremely heavy reading of this datafile at 8:30 and 8:32.

Armed with this information, it is then possible to go off in search of the SQL query that generated this heavy I/O to see if it can be improved, or if the database design requires modification. In this case, the heavy I/O is not caused by badly written SQL, but instead is due to the fact that the database buffers are not large enough to hold all the data. We know this because if we look at the chart when this is running, we can see that whenever this query is run I/O is required because it cannot find all the data in the local buffers.

Figure 9.7 Alert Log

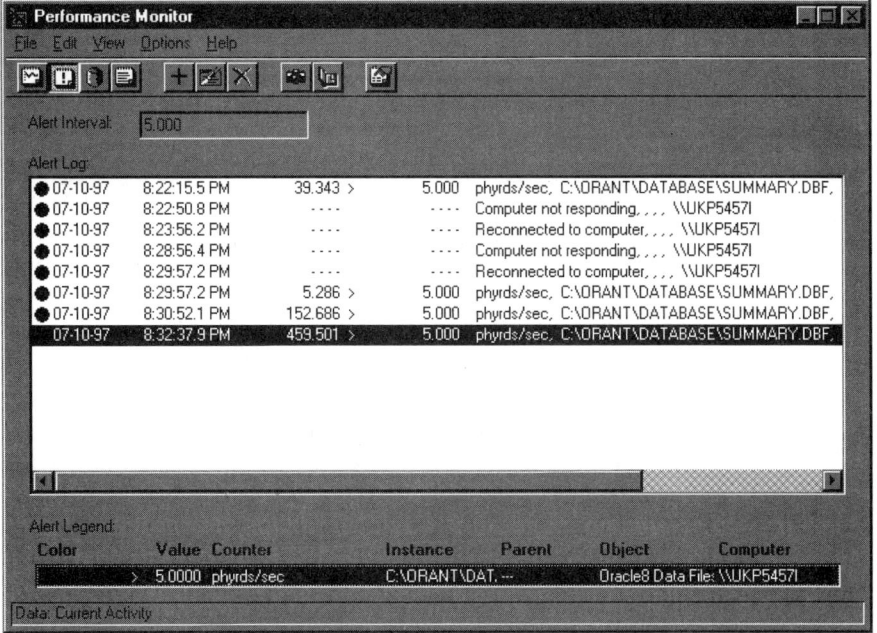

9.2.4   Log

We have already seen that we can set alerts to advise when certain limits are exceeded, but this doesn't allow us to see how the system has behaved over a period of time. Rather than stay glued to our screens, the performance monitor has a *log* option to record specific information into a file which can then be replayed later. This is an extremely useful feature provided the disk space is available to hold all of the log information.

The log facility is not enabled by default, therefore the first step is to create the log file and what it is to contain. This is achieved by selecting *View* from the strip menu and then select *Log*. Logging cannot be started until some data items have been selected for inclusion in the log. All the data items that we have seen previously may be included in the log. To include them, click on the ➕ icon and Figure 9.8 is displayed.

Any number of items can be selected for inclusion in the log by pressing the *Add* button. However, bear in mind that the more items that are selected, the larger the log file will become. When you have finished adding all the items, click on the ✖ icon to return to the log screen.

Figure 9.8 Select the Items to Log

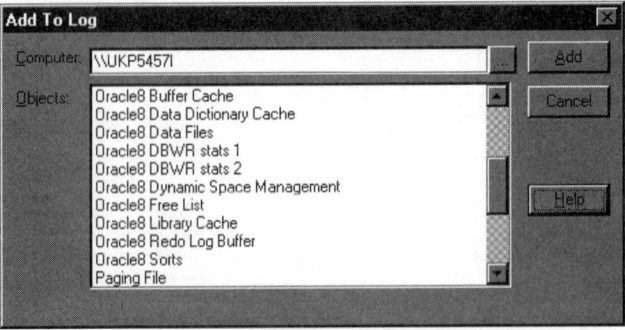

Now logging can be started by selecting *Options* from the strip menu and then *Log* to reveal Figure 9.9. Give the log a name, and if you are monitoring a specific event, then consider naming the file with this event name, such as high_io_on_datafiles. Also, don't forget to include a date in the filename if you plan to collect over a time period.

Figure 9.9 Starting Logging

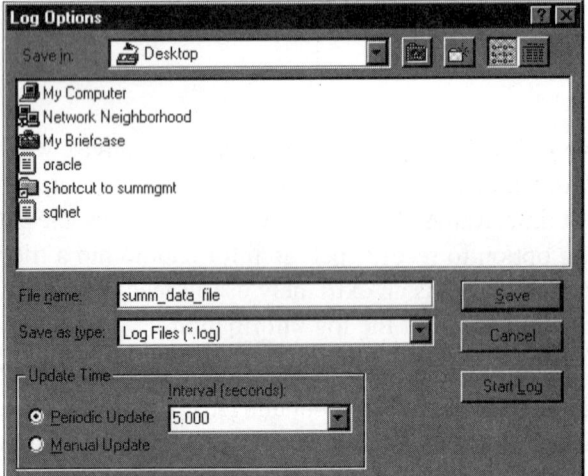

By default, data is collected every fifteen seconds, but this can be changed to any value down to one second. A one second interval may be ideal for trying to detect performance problems, but, it may result in a huge log file and generate its own performance problem. However, if the space is available and it will not impact system performance, then consider using a value less than the default fifteen seconds. Logging will not start until the button *Start Log*, shown in Figure 9.9 is pressed.

The log screen is shown in Figure 9.10 which advises the name of the log file, the status of the collection and the data items being collected.

Figure 9.10 Log

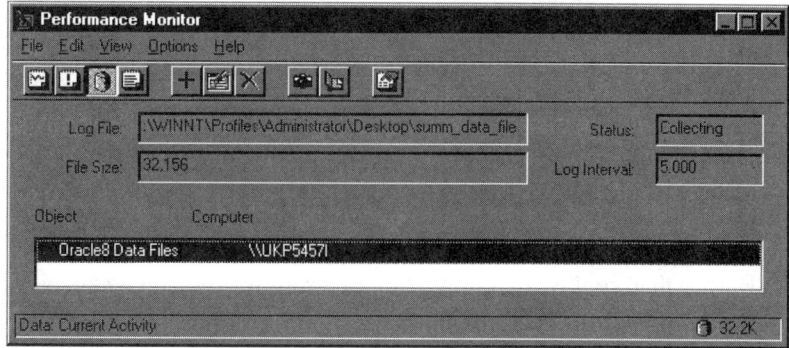

Hint: Keep an eye on the file size by monitoring the number next to the disk icon in the bottom right-hand corner.

At any time while data is being logged, bookmark entries can be added to the log file as illustrated in Figure 9.11. In the example shown below, a comment that a large I/O has just been observed was added to the log. The reason for doing this is that when the log is replayed, these bookmark comments can be used to define a start and end point for replaying the data, thus avoiding the need to replay the entire log when you may be interested in only a portion of the log.

Replaying a log file allows the DBA to monitor specific parts of the system repeatedly by viewing different statistics, provided of course, that these statistics have been included in the log file initially. It may be wise to start by collecting popular items and then reducing them as you discover which ones are not relevant to your system.

Figure 9.11 Bookmark Entries in a Log File

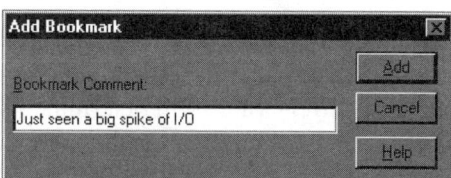

To replay a log file select *Options* from the strip menu and then select *Data From*, which will display Figure 9.12. Clicking on *Log File* will enable you to browse the folders to find the log file to be displayed.

Figure 9.12 Select a Log File

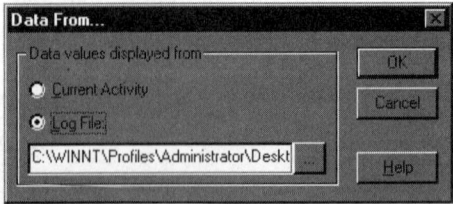

Hint: Don't forget to save your log file configuration for use next time otherwise they have to be set up each time the Oracle8 Performance Monitor is started

---

Rather than replay the entire file, a period of time can be specified by selecting *Edit* from the strip menu and then *Time Window*.

Figure 9.13 is displayed where the bookmarks that we defined previously can be used to mark the start and end time. Don't worry if you haven't defined any bookmarks because you will see the entire contents of the log file by default.

Figure 9.13 Select a Time Period from the Log File

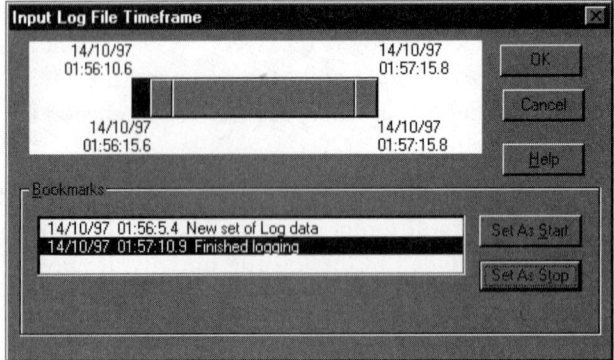

9.2.5   Report

The final option to be discussed is the *Report*, which displays the information from the chart in a textual format. Depending on whether the data being collected is a total or a current value will determine its usefulness. For example, the Oracle8 Buffer Cache value is given as a percentage of the time the cache is hit, therefore it can be considered a running total, whereas the Oracle8 Data File values provide the I/O as a specific point in time.

Figure 9.14 shows a sample report. This report was captured at a time when there was activity upon the database. However, if we had waited a few seconds,

Figure 9.14 Sample Report

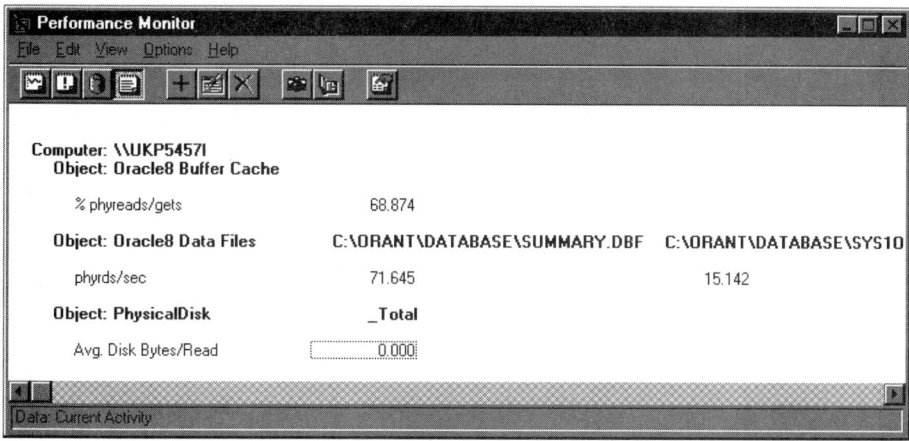

then the data file values would be zero and to the untrained observer it would appear that the reporting process was not working. Also note in Figure 9.14, that the items included in the report are not restricted to the Oracle8 data items; any of the NT items can be included in the report.

The report is displayed by selecting *Report* from *View* on the strip menu. Items are included on the report by pressing the ⊞ icon and then selecting the values as shown in Figure 9.15, as we have done previously for the other display options in this tool.

Figure 9.15 Selecting Items for the Report

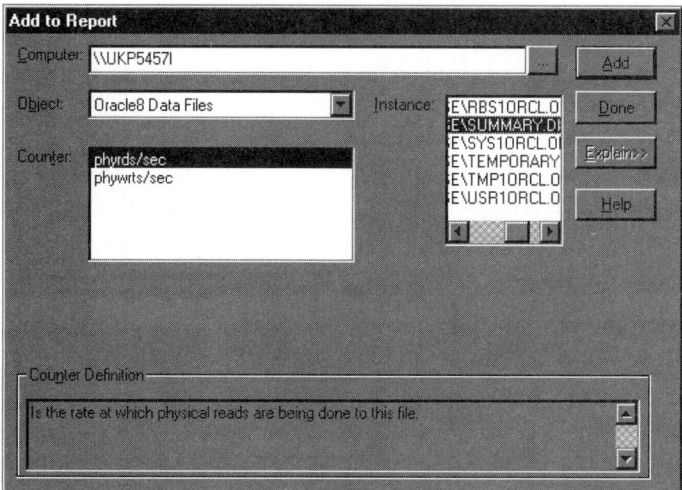

Hint: At any time if you are not sure what the contents of a data item are, then the *Explain* button can be pressed to provide a textual description of the item, as illustrated in Figure 9.15.

Although the report can be useful, especially since its contents can be exported to a spreadsheet by selecting *File* from the strip menu and then *Export Report*. When a database is being tuned, graphical displays, alerts when certain conditions are met and the ability to replay performance information are probably the most valuable tools to the database tuner. Reports can be useful so don't ignore them completely.

9.3   PERFORMANCE PACK

An optional component of Oracle8 is the *Performance Pack*, which is available at additional cost and comprises the tools:

- Performance Manager
- Oracle Trace
- Oracle Expert
- Tablespace Manager
- Lock Manager
- Top Sessions

Once we see the capabilities of these tools, anyone who has to tune a database will probably want to request this pack of tools if they are not already available within your organization.

9.3.1   Performance Manager

The Performance Manager will prove invaluable to anyone who has to tune a database because it provides a wealth of information that can be customized to your own requirements, although this shouldn't be necessary. When the Performance Manager is first started a blank screen appears as shown in Figure 9.16, therefore the first step is to select the data to display.

The best place to start is the *Overview* screen, illustrated in Figure 9.17, which is displayed by selecting *Display* from the strip menu, and then *Overview*. The big advantage of starting with the *Overview* screen is that it shows many of the available displays. Another good reason for starting here is that it is possible to drill down and acquire more information from some of the screens.

Figure 9.16   Performance Manager Screen at Startup

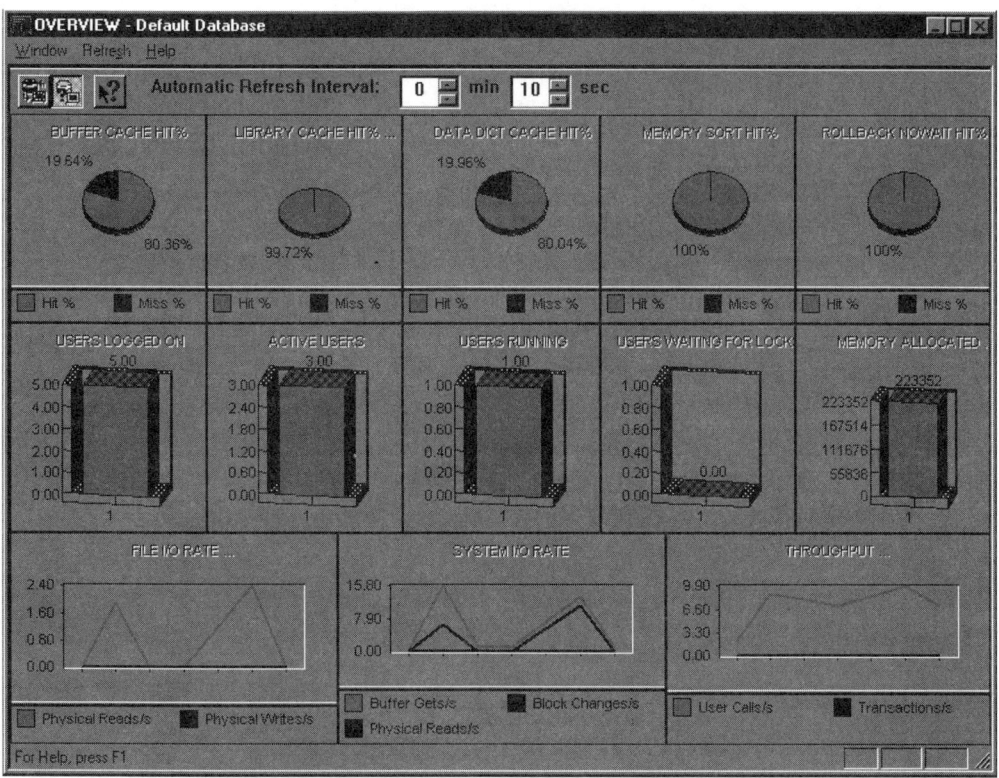

Figure 9.17   Performance Manager Overview

Hint: When any screen is displayed it is not refreshed automatically so always check to see that you are looking at the latest view.

A screen is not refreshed until *Refresh* is selected from the strip menu and either *Update Now* or *Automatic* is chosen. If Automatic is selected, then by default the refresh interval is 30 seconds, but this can be reduced to any value down to 1 second or increased to many minutes. Be careful about choosing a low refresh time because of the resources required to process and display the data.

Anyone who has read anything previously about how to tune an Oracle database, may be wondering why information on how to query the system tables is not provided. It is not described here because the Performance Monitor is doing that job for you, therefore there is no need to know which tables to query, simply select the appropriate graph.

The Performance Manager screens can be divided into seven categories:

- Contention
- Instance
- I/O
- Load
- Memory
- Parallel Server
- User-defined

Within each of these categories there are many screens available. For example, selecting *Memory* leads to all the screens shown in Figure 9.18.

Figure 9.18 Memory Options

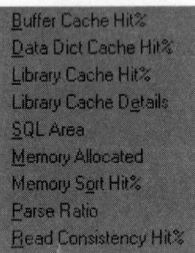

A very useful screen is *SQL Area*, which is shown in Figure 9.19. This screen lists all the SQL statements currently held in the SQL area and their memory requirements. By reviewing which statements are in use, it is then possible to try to size the SQL area to hold all the SQL statements. The SQL Area screen is selected from the memory list shown in Figure 9.18.

Figure 9.19 SQL Area

SQL Text	Version Count	Shareable Memory	Mem/User Persistent	Mem/User Runtime
60	select cols,audit$,textlengt	1	7748	804	1616
61	select con#,obj#,rcon#,ena	1	8002	700	1668
62	select con#,type#,condlen| 1	10745	1116	2180
63	select count(*) from fact	1	5610	472	1424
64	select count(*) from produ	1	5381	472	1360
65	select count(*) from store	1	6387	472	1504
66	select count(*) from time	1	5846	472	1424
67	select count(*) from v$acti	1	11936	484	1232
68	select count(*) from v$ses	1	53210	484	3172
69	select count(*) from v$ses	1	55108	484	3460
70	select count(*) from v$ses	1	27779	500	2172
71	select ctime, mtime, stime f	1	897	0	0
72	select distinct d.p_obj#,d.p	1	9873	564	2616
73	select distinct i.obj# from s	1	9279	504	2172
74	select distinct(privilege#)	1	7089	548	1740

SQL AREA - Default Database — Window Refresh Help — Automatic Refresh Interval: 0 min 30 sec — For Help, press F1

The Performance Monitor offers a drill-down capability on many of the screens. For example, suppose you are monitoring the *Overview* screen and notice that the *File IO Rate* is high. Clicking on the right mouse button displays Figure 9.20. From here not only can you drill down to acquire more detail, but this is also the place to customize the displays. For example, the scale on the graph can be changed, the type of graph changed from, say, a pie chart to a bar graph and the graph can be displayed in two or three dimensions.

Figure 9.20 Display Options

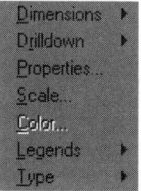

Dimensions ►
Drilldown ►
Properties...
Scale...
Color...
Legends ►
Type ►

Usually a database consists of many datafiles so how do you determine where all the I/O is occurring? Simply click on the right mouse button and select the drill-down option. Figure 9.21 appears, which now displays all the I /O for each datafile as a different color.

Figure 9.21 File IO Details

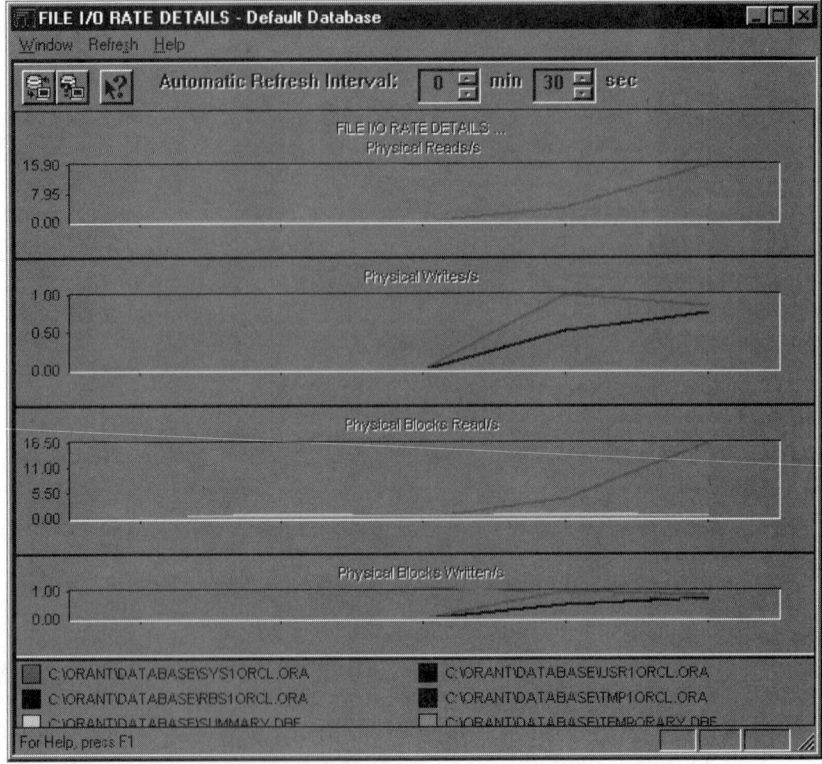

Finally, one should mention that it is possible to create your own displays by selecting *Charts* from the strip menu and then selecting *New SQL Chart*. By completing the boxes the chart is given a name. You must specify the SQL used to generate the chart and then advise on how the information is to be displayed. This is an extremely straightforward process so take advantage of this option.

Hint: Don't forget to save any user-defined graphs.

9.3.2   Oracle Trace

Oracle Trace is a tool for collecting data about a running system. What makes it different from other tools is that it is event based, where an event could be a database transaction or an SQL statement. From within Oracle Trace, it is possible to see exactly the resources being used by a specific event.

At first glance the reader may be wondering why anyone would use Oracle Trace in preference to the Performance Monitor? One very important reason is that the data collected by Oracle Trace can be used as input to the Oracle Expert tool described in the following section and some additional information is provided by this tool. Oracle Trace can only be started from the Enterprise

Manager console by selecting the icon 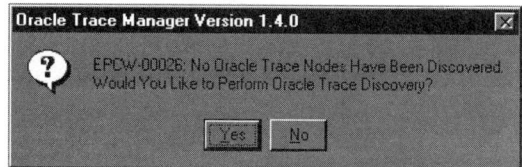.

Before Oracle Trace can be used, some setup is required. First the SQL script *otrcsvr* must be run while connected as user SYS. Then the SQL script *otrcfmtc* must be run while connected as user SYSTEM. Finally, when Oracle Trace is started, it must go through a *discovery process*, as shown in Figure 9.22, just as we did for Enterprise Manager. This discovery process identifies the databases that Oracle Trace may collect about. Although Figure 9.22 may look like an error message, simply confirm to proceed with the discovery process and within a few minutes, Trace is ready for use.

Figure 9.22 Oracle Trace Discovery

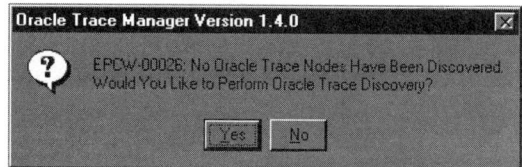

In order to collect performance data using Oracle Trace a *collection* must be defined. This is achieved by pressing the ➕ icon and Figure 9.23 appears, which is the first screen in the wizard. An *event set* defines the data to collect for a product or database. In Figure 9.23, a product called ATM, which is a sample application, has one event set. The node ukp5457i has a database defined, and if we click on *Event Set*, then three events appear called:

- All   collects all data
- Expert   collects data for Oracle Expert
- Default   collects limited data

First select the appropriate event set; if disk space is a problem then try the *All* event set, otherwise use *Default*.

Figure 9.23 Oracle Trace Event Sets

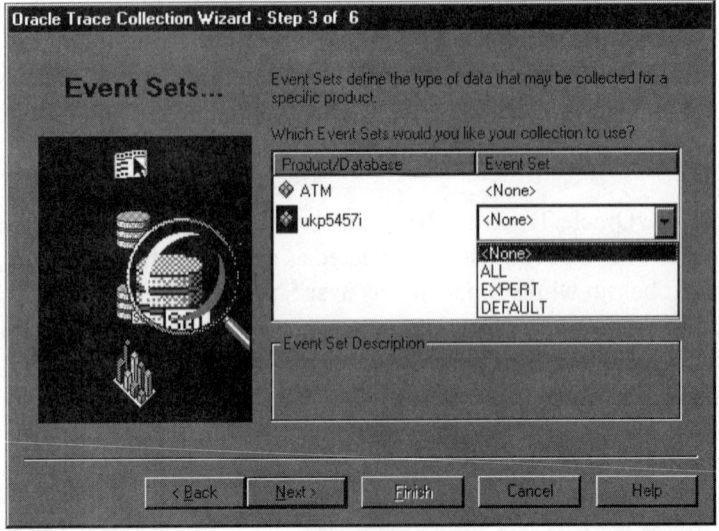

The next step is to give the collection a name as shown in Figure 9.24. Names cannot be very long for the collection file so use the description to help you keep track of what the collection file is supposed to hold.

Other questions will be asked about the collection, such as how large the file may grow to and for how long the collection should run. Avoid defining collections that run for hours, instead schedule several collections over the same period. The advantage of using multiple collections is that you don't have one large file to process and you can start analyzing your data once the first collection has completed.

Hint: Avoid using names with underscores like long_query because the formatting process can't cope with them.

When the collection has finished collecting its data, it must be formatted into a database for analysis. This can either be done manually, by selecting *Collection* from the strip menu and then *Format*, or you can request that the data is automatically formatted after the collection, as shown in Figure 9.25.

Finally, you will be asked to confirm that all the information is correct and the job will be submitted onto the Enterprise Manager console. A collection doesn't have to start immediately, it can be scheduled to run like any other job such as immediately, at a specific time or at a certain time every day or week.

Figure 9.24   Naming a Collection

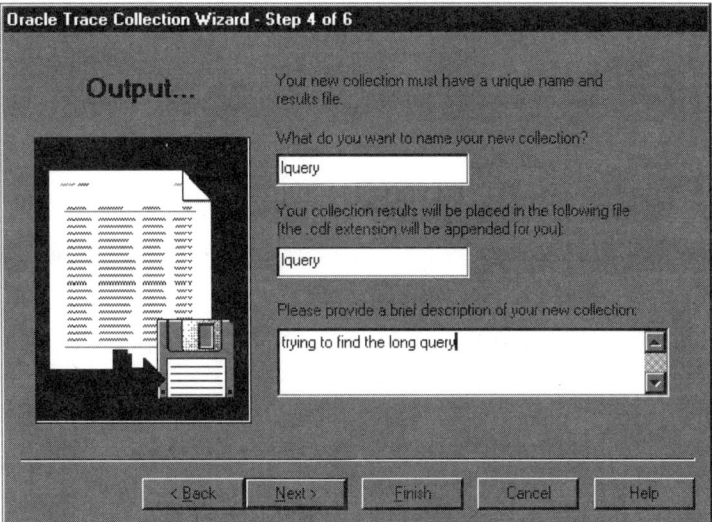

Figure 9.25   Format the Collection

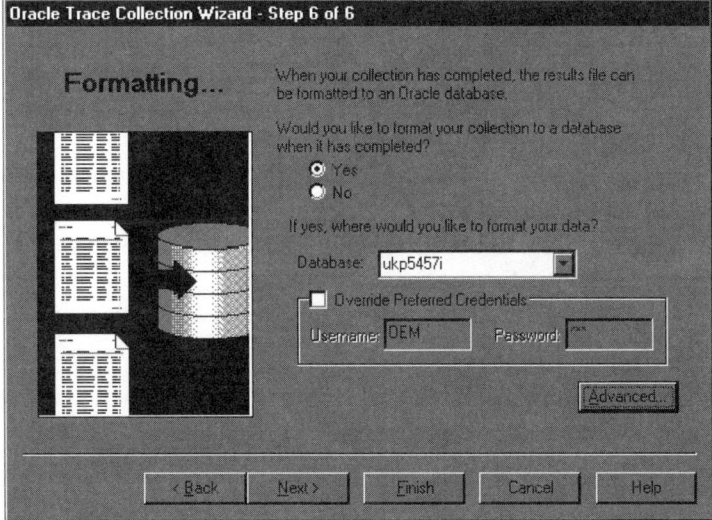

The status of all jobs can be viewed by referring to the main Oracle Trace screen, which is shown in Figure 9.26.

By selecting a specific query, the right window will display all the information about that collection, such as what it is collecting, when it is scheduled to run and the log from when it last ran.

Figure 9.26 Oracle Trace

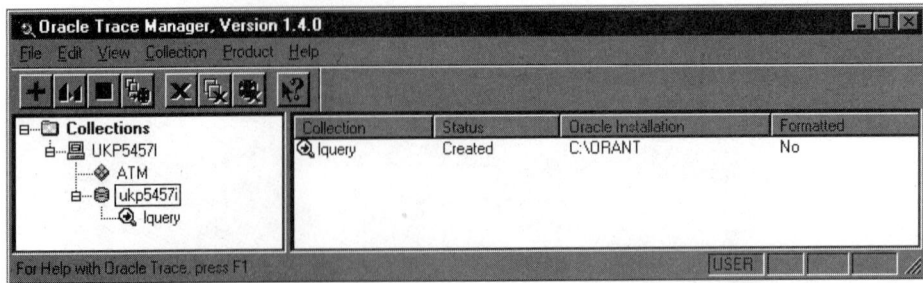

Once the collected information has been formatted into a database it can then be queried. Unfortunately, a little more setup is required because the information is stored in tables with names like v_192216243_f_5_e_1_8_0. Therefore it is strongly recommended that the SQL script *otrcsyn*, which can be found in the Oracle Trace sample folder, is run because then the tables can be queried using friendlier names.

Another very useful script to run is *otrcfunc* which creates a function to calculate the elapsed time for an event. Depending on the number of rows in the Oracle Trace tables, reporting times can also be improved by adding indexes.

Hint: Before running otrcsyn, check that it is using the Oracle8 table names. The script supplied with 8.0.3 contains the Oracle 7.3 table names. Simply change the 7_3 to 8_0.

A standard report can be produced by running the application *otrcrep* against the collection file. However, the best use of the data comes from running your own queries. A number of sample scripts are provided in the sample folder which can be used as the basis for your own queries. Don't forget that often a picture can say a thousand words, therefore consider generating graphs using your favorite reporting tool.

The sample scripts will require editing to reference your collection name and they may also still use the Oracle 7.3 table names.

This is one tool where it is really worthwhile consulting the Oracle8 documentation for detailed information on the contents of the Trace tables and the sample reports.

9.3.3   Oracle Expert

So far, all the tuning methods that we have seen involve deciding for yourself what changes must be made to the database. Have you ever wished that the

Figure 9.27   Oracle Expert

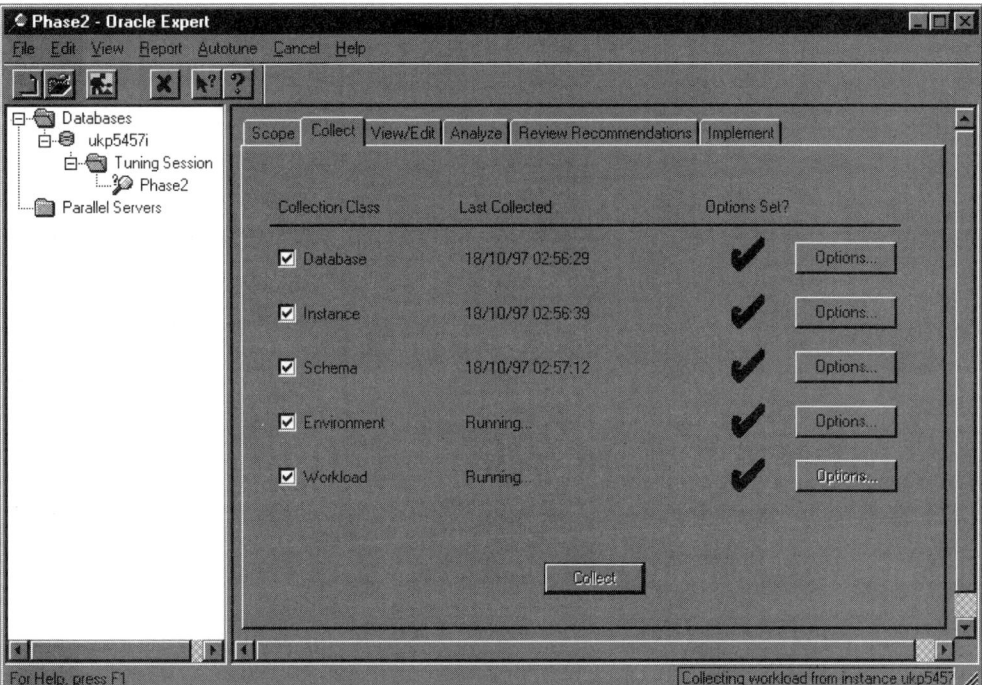

database would design itself? If yes, then maybe Oracle Expert is just the tool that you are looking for.

Oracle Expert examines a currently running system and recommends changes to the database design. It will even provide you with the SQL scripts to change the database. Using this tool requires no expertise and very little training, consequently it is ideal for the novice user who has minimal Oracle database tuning experience. Oracle Expert is started from the Enterprise Manager console by pressing the icon .

It takes a little while to start because it has to collect quite a lot of data in order to suggest changes to the database.

To tune the database five pieces of information are required by Oracle Expert:

- Database; name, users, tablespaces, synonyms
- Instance; parameters
- Schema; tables and analyze information
- Environment; system parameters and device details
- Workload; how database is accessed

The majority of this information is gathered automatically by the tool, but some must be supplied manually. Figure 9.27 shows the *collect* status, but the first tab that should be pressed is *Scope*, which defines the area to be tuned.

Under the *Scope* tab, the user can select which parts of the *instance* are to be tuned, such as SGA, and I/O. Whether the *application* requires tuning for the SQL statements and access methods and if the *structure* needs tuning in terms of placement and sizing.

The *Collect* tab is the one where you will spend the most time. In Figure 9.27, first look at the *collection class* and the *last collected* column. We can see that for the first three classes dates appear, which means that we have collected this information. The other two classes, environment and workload, have a status of running which means that we are currently collecting information for these classes. For each class where you want to collect information, click on the *Options* button to specify what must be collected.

Figure 9.28 Oracle Expert Environment Information

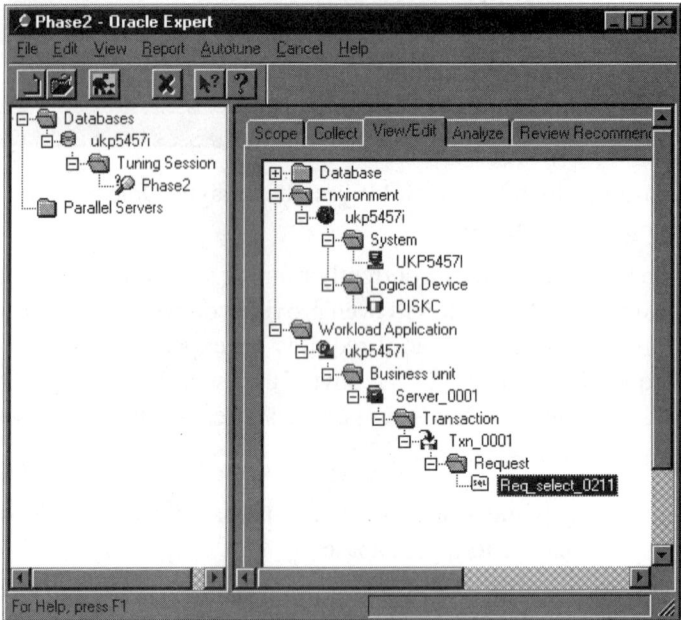

When the *instance* information is collected, it is wise to press the *Options* button and change the collection interval for the instance. One of the really nice features of this tool is the ability to monitor the instance and collect the SQL statements. The monitoring interval will determine how long Oracle Expert spends performing this task. You could leave it running for eight hours to collect a day's worth of data, or if you know that all typical queries are executed within the hour, then the time could be reduced.

When collecting the *Schema* information, if your database comprises many schemas and you only want to tune for a specific part of the database, then press the *Options* button to specify the specific schema to tune.

The *Environment* information must be manually entered. Click on the tab *View/Edit* and click on *Environment* which consists of system and device information. Specify each of the devices that are available and the information will be displayed as in Figure 9.28.

When the *System* area is selected, details such as the available memory and number of CPUs can be supplied.

Figure 9.29 Oracle Expert Rules

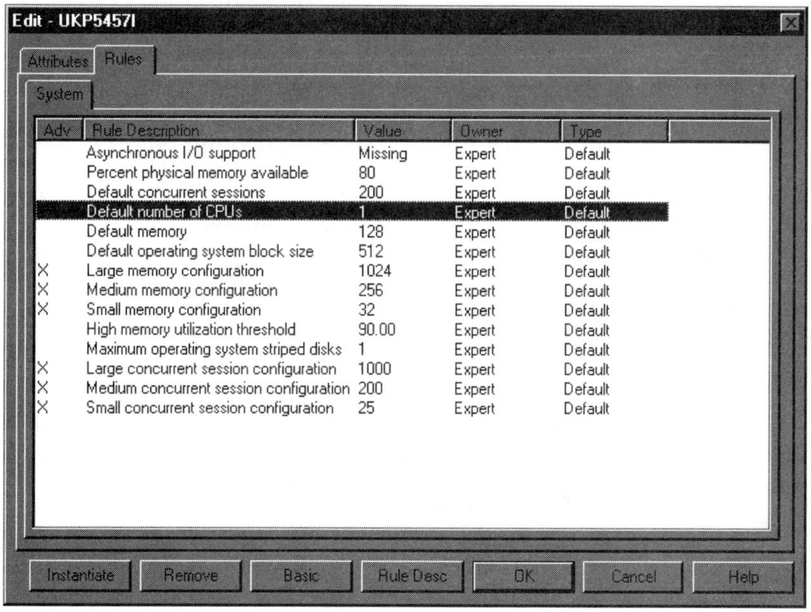

Oracle Expert designs and modifies your database by using a set of supplied rules. These rules may be modified or even removed if they are not appropriate to your system. If rules are available there will be a *Rule* tab; simply click on it and all the rules pertaining to this feature will be shown. In Figure 9.29 we can see the rules for the *System* area in *Environment*. In this example, all the advanced rules have been displayed because the *Advanced* button was pressed. To change any rule simply double click on it and enter the new value. A description for each rule can be obtained by pressing the *Rule Desc* button.

The workload information is crucial to the successful design or redesign of the database because it is this data that is telling the tool how the database is being used. This information can be supplied to Expert either from:

- Oracle Trace collection,
- SQL Cache or
- File containing workload information.

We have already seen how to create Oracle Trace files in the previous section, but one of the really nice features of Expert is the ability to monitor the SQL cache and obtain information on the queries that have been made recently. This is an extremely useful feature with an existing system, because it means that you can obtain useful tuning data without interfering with the day-to-day operations of the database. To the users it is business as usual, you just wait to gather the data. To specify the source of the workload data click on the *Options* button for *Workload* in Figure 9.27 and then click on the *Options* button for *Instance* to specify the time to spend collecting the data.

Hint: Take time to ensure that the workload data accurately represents your system, otherwise the revised design could degrade performance.

Figure 9.30 Oracle Expert Recommendations

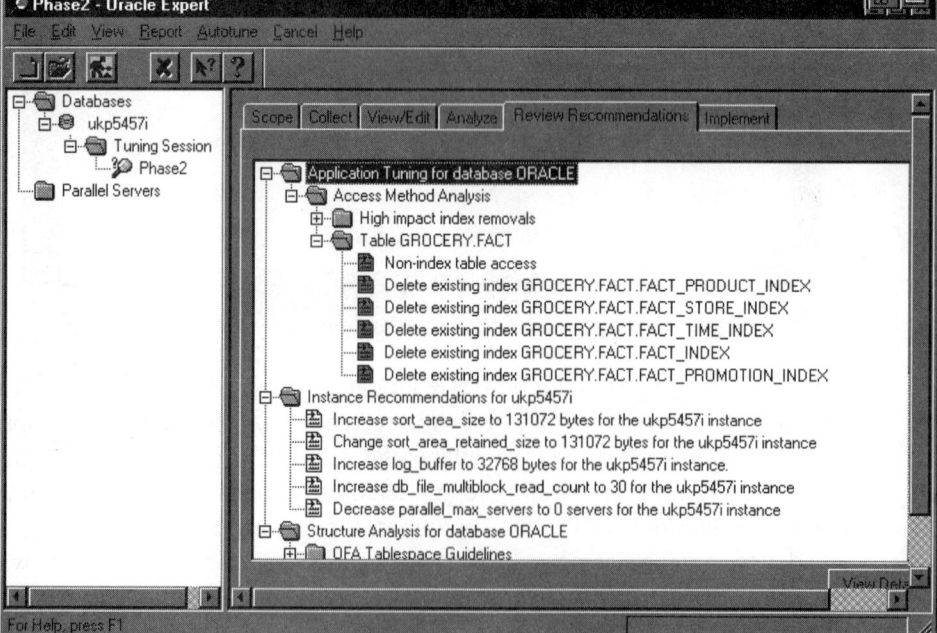

Once all the options have been specified, the data is collected by pressing the *Collect* button shown in Figure 9.27. In this example, the button is grayed out because the collection process is currently running. The collecting of data can take quite some time, especially if the database contains many objects. If you monitor the bottom right-hand window of the main Oracle Expert screen, you can see at what stage it is processing. Therefore, at this time it is a good idea to go away and find another job to do while you are waiting for the database to be analyzed.

Once all of the information has been collected then the design can be analyzed, by pressing the *Analysis* tab and then clicking on the *Perform Analysis* button. When the analysis is complete, click on the *Review Recommendations* tab and Figure 9.30 shows how the recommendations are broken down into three categories: application tuning, instance and structure.

By expanding each category you can see what the suggested changes are to the database. For example, in Figure 9.30 it suggests that in the application section some indexes be removed because they are not being used, and in the instance section it suggests some changes to the database initialization parameters.

The recommendations can then be implemented by pressing the *Implement* tab. The SQL to implement the changes and the parameter changes are created in files that are created when the *Generate Files* button is pressed. Oracle Expert does not actually implement the changes because these files may require some editing and you will want to implement the changes at a convenient time and maybe not all of them at the same time.

Various reports are available from Oracle Expert and are selected from *Report* on the strip menu. The *Session* report provides information on the data collected during this session. The *Analysis* report is very useful because it provides textual description of what and why a change to the database is required. The *Recommendation Summary* is another useful report that tries to explain why the changes are necessary.

Oracle Expert should not be seen as a replacement for an expert database tuner, but it can simplify the process and in some cases make better recommendations on the database design than a DBA, especially one who doesn't know the product very well. The tool is so easy to use and doesn't require much time to gather and recommend data, that everyone who has the performance pack should seriously consider using it when they are database tuning.

9.3.4   Tablespace Manager

We have already met the Tablespace Manager in Chapter 6 when we were discussing administering the database. It is started from the Enterprise Manager console by pressing the icon ▨▨.

When it comes to tuning the database it is extremely useful to use the Tablespace Manager to see which extents are being used and whether they are contiguous. This information is obtained by selecting a datafile and clicking on the *Segments* tab, as shown in Figure 9.31.

Figure 9.31 Tablespace Manager

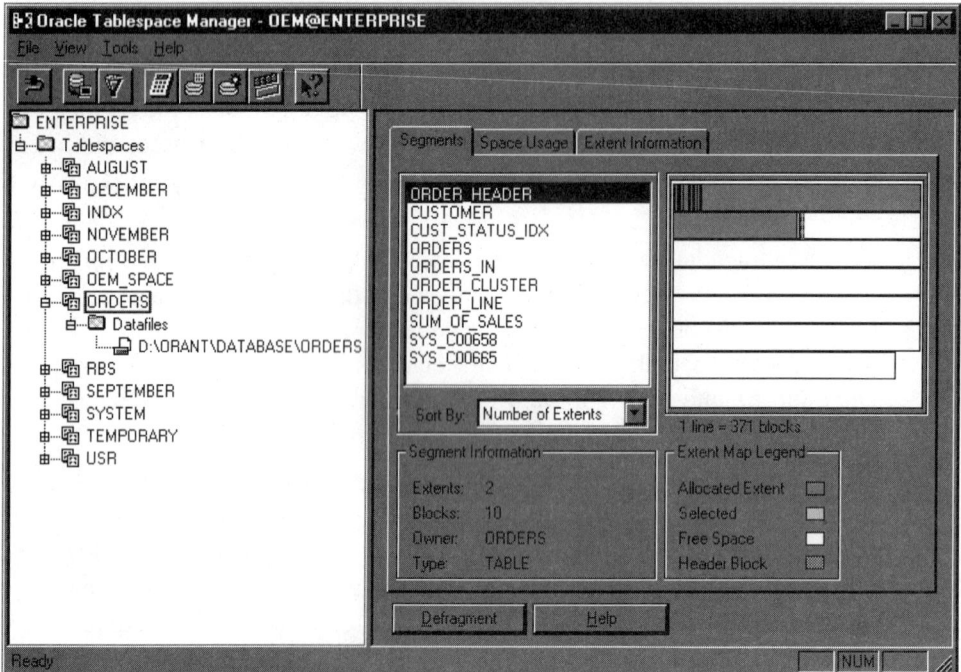

9.3.5   Lock Manager

Usually a big concern for anyone tuning a database is locking within the system. There are several different types of locks held by an Oracle database, but the one that is of most interest to the DBA is the Exclusive lock, which prevents other users from accessing the resource.

To see the locks currently held by the database, start the Lock Manager from the Enterprise Manager console which displays Figure 9.32.

Figure 9.32 Lock Manager

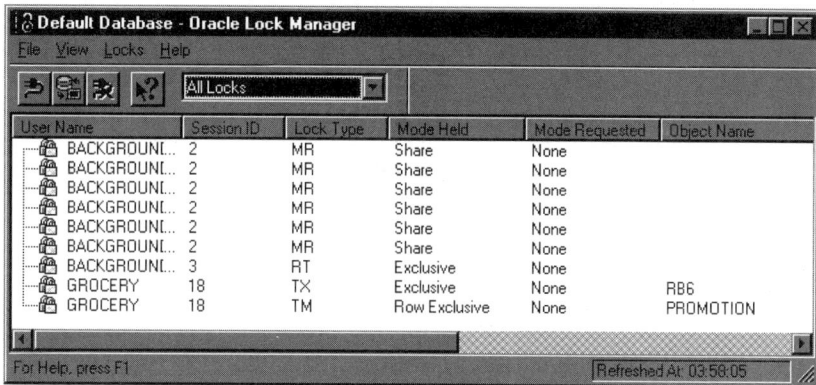

In this example we can see all the locks currently being held, and the one of specific interest to us is the row exclusive lock on the table called Promotion. In a typical production system, this display could be rather unwieldy because there will be a lot of locks being held. Therefore, when locks are causing a performance problem and slowing down the system, the Lock Manager can display only those locks that are *blocking* users by selecting it from the drop down list.

Hint: The display is not automatically updated, so don't forget to select *Locks* from the strip menu and then *Refresh* to display the latest lock status.

9.3.6   Top Sessions

At first glance, you may be wondering why a tool with the name of Top Sessions may be useful for tuning a database. From Figure 9.33 it appears to show only the main users using the database. For each user we can see the username used to attach to the database, whether the user is currently active and what program they are running. This is all useful information, but how does it help us tune the database?

The actual information that is available is determined by the *Options* that are selected. If *Session* is selected from the strip menu, and then *Options*, Figure 9.34 is displayed. The *Statistics Filter* determines the information that is displayed, and there are ten filters which include Redo, Enque, Cache, Operating System, Parallel Server and SQL.

Figure 9.33 Top Sessions

USERNAME	SID	OSUSER	DB BLOCK GETS	COMMAND	STATUS	MACHINE	PROGRAM
BACKGROUND ...	5	UNKNOWN	226	UNKNOWN	ACTIVE	UKP5457I	ORACLE80.EXE
GROCERY	18	Administrator	224	UNKNOWN	INACTIVE	RDBUK\UK...	C:\WINNT\Profiles\All Users...
OEM	9	Administrator	163	UNKNOWN	INACTIVE	RDBUK\UK...	C:\ORANT\BIN\VOD.EXE
OEM	15	Administrator	143	UNKNOWN	INACTIVE	RDBUK\UK...	C:\WINNT\Profiles\All Users...
BACKGROUND ...	6	UNKNOWN	10	UNKNOWN	ACTIVE	UKP5457I	ORACLE80.EXE
DBSNMP	14	SYSTEM	7	UNKNOWN	INACTIVE	RDBUK\UK...	C:\ORANT\agentbin\DBSN...
OEM	19	Administrator	5	UNKNOWN	ACTIVE	RDBUK\UK...	C:\ORANT\BIN\VMS.EXE
BACKGROUND ...	2	UNKNOWN	0	UNKNOWN	ACTIVE	UKP5457I	ORACLE80.EXE

For Help, press F1 — Refreshed At: 04:18:21

Figure 9.34 Top Sessions Options

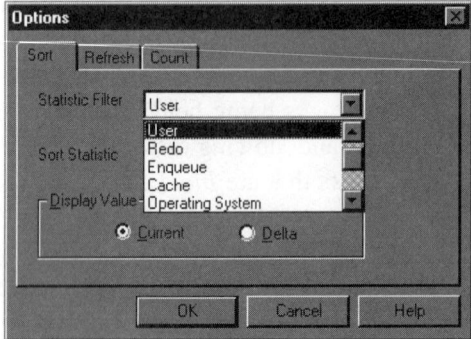

From the Options you can also specify how frequently the data should be refreshed and how many sessions should be displayed.

By double clicking on any user, detailed information is available on general information, statistics, cursors and locks. The *General* tab contains basic information about the session, such as username, program running and some internals. The really useful data can be found by pressing the *Statistics* tab which is shown in Figure 9.35.

Once again the information here can be filtered by selecting the appropriate statistic from the drop down list. In Figure 9.35 we can see how much memory we are using and how often we have issued a commit and rollback statement. If we were to select *Cache* then we could see data such as how many database blocks we have read and accesses to the buffer.

Another useful option to display is the *SQL* where we can see how many times we have fetched data by rowid or different types of table scans. If you need to know whether a process is accessing the database efficiently then always check the SQL statistics.

Figure 9.35 Top Sessions – Statistics

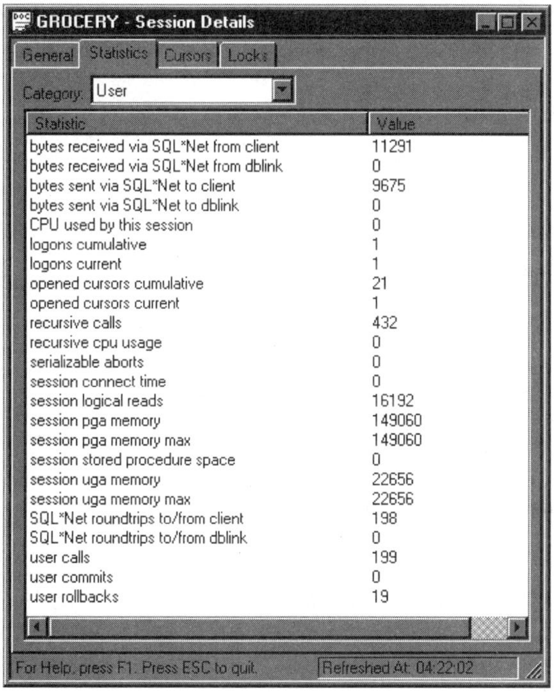

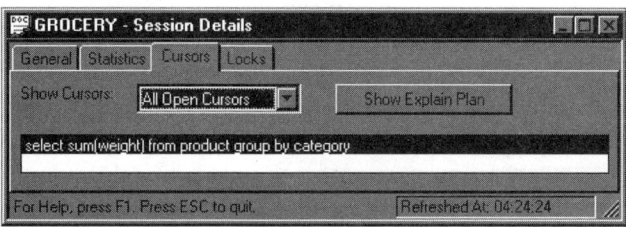

If you click on the *Cursor* tab and then select *All Open Cursors* Figure 9.36 will appear, which shows you the SQL statement just executed by this session. Clicking on the *Show Explain Plan* button will then show the strategy used by this query. Therefore if you suspect poorly performing queries, this is one place to look if you are lucky enough to catch the SQL statement while the job is running.

Figure 9.36 Top Sessions – SQL

If you click on the *Locks* tab you can see the locks held by this user as shown in Figure 9.37. For example, this user has a row level lock on a table called Store and there is also a lock on a rollback segment.

Figure 9.37 Top Sessions – Locks

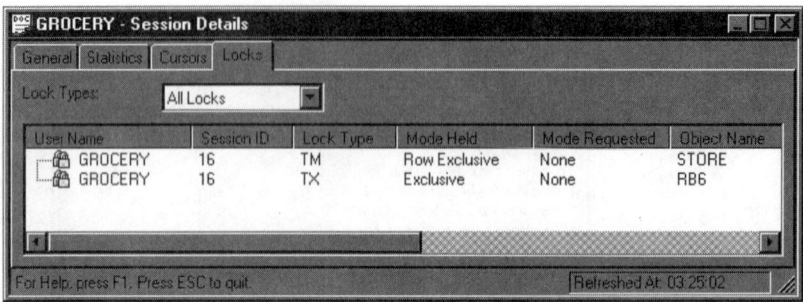

It is also worth mentioning at this point that from Top Sessions you can also select the user from Figure 9.33 and then select *Session* and then *Kill* to remove that session.

9.4   OTHER TUNING

So far we have seen tools that can help us tune the database, but these are not the only techniques available to the DBA. Here is a look at some of the other approaches that can help improve the performance of our database.

9.4.1   Alert Log

The DBA should check the Alert log regularly to see if anything unusual has taken place against the database. It is usually found in *ORANT\RDBMS80\ TRACE* in a file called *<instance>alrt.* It contains the parameters used to start the database instance and advises recovery information and the when the processes used by the instance were started.

9.4.2   Querying the Data Dictionary

Within the Oracle database there are a number of tables within the data dictionary that can be queried to obtain performance information. Many of these tables we have already queried using the graphical tools we have seen earlier. However, you may prefer to query the tables yourself to create your own graphical displays. The tables that are useful can be divided into two categories:

- Instance
- Session level

At the *Instance* level some useful tables to query are:

V$FIXED_TABLE	lists all the tables that can be queried
V$INSTANCE	instance status information
V$LIBRARYCACHE	see how the cache is being used (e.g., how many hits to tables and indexes)
V$SGA	size of the SGA
V$SGASTAT	breakdown of size of each part of the SGA
V$SQL	textt of the SQL statements
V$SQLAREA	SQL statements currently held in the shared SQL area
V$SYSSTAT	more instance data
V$SYSTEM_EVENT	time spent waiting on specific events

At the *Session* level the following tables are useful:

V$LOCK	all the locks held by the Oracle8 server
V$PROCESS	process details
V$SESSION	session details
VS$SESSTAT	more session statistics

9.4.3   SQL Statements

Ideally when an SQL statement is executed it should be in the SQL shared area so that no parsing of the statement is required. However, SQL statements must be identical to reuse a previous SQL statement. Therefore

```
SELECT sum(order_value) FROM orders;
```

is not the same as

```
SELECT sum(order_value) FROM ORDERS;
```

Consequently, to improve performance, make sure that all SQL statements are identical, space for space and that the cases are the same.

To tune the SQL cache take a look at the following value

```
SELECT namespace, pins,reloads FROM v$librarycache;
```

Pins refers to the number of times that an SQL statement was found in the shared area and *reloads* refers to the number of times that one wasn't found in the cache. The goal is to get reloads to zero or at least less than 1% of the *pins* value.

If the shared SQL area is not large enough it can be increased by changing the initialization parameter SHARED_SQL_AREA.

Missing Indexes

The other very important check is to verify that every SQL statement uses the most efficient path to retrieve information from the database, which usually means using an index. We already saw in Section 5.6 how to determine the execution strategy for an SQL statement and using the Top Sessions tool we can extract the plan for a specific user by pressing the *Explain Plan* button shown in Figure 9.36.

We should be on the lookout for queries that don't use an index and instead search the table sequentially. Omitting an index from the database design can very seriously damage the performance of your database and is one of the commonest reasons for poor performance. Creating the index can result in query times improving from minutes to even subseconds when a query is against a very large table. Users will be impressed at the improved response, but it is best to not forget to create the index in the first place.

Optimizer Execution Strategy

Another reason why an SQL statement may take a long time to complete is that the optimizer chooses an inappropriate execution strategy. We can see this from the Explain Plan, but to influence the optimizer we must use a Hint as described in Section 5.6.

Hints can be very useful to improve performance, but use them with care because they have to be hard-coded into the SQL statement and therefore remain a permanent feature.

9.4.4   Initialization Parameters

Throughout this book we have met a number of initialization parameters that affect the performance of the database. Therefore, don't forget to check that each parameter has the appropriate value. The ones to especially check, and this is by no means a definitive list, are:

- DB_BLOCK_SIZE   as a guideline the default value of 8k works well, use 4k for heavy writing and 16k for heavy reading

- DB_BLOCK_BUFFERS
- SHARED_POOL_SIZE
- LOG_BUFFER
- DB_FILE_MULTIBLOCK_READ_COUNT

When selecting a size for DB_FILE_MULTIBLOCK_READ_COUNT do ensure that you don't choose a value that is larger than the I/O subsystem can support.

9.5   NT PERFORMANCE

Very often the DBA becomes so involved in tuning the database that he or she forgets to tune the Operating System that is running the database. One of the nice aspects to using NT is that it is a fairly self-contained system which generally runs well with minimal user intervention. Nevertheless, it is very important that you provide NT with sufficient resources to allow it to do its job.

That means ensuring that your system has:

- sufficient memory,
- adequate disk space and disk drives,
- spare processor speed.

9.5.1   Task Manager

NT provides a tool called the *Performance Monitor*, which can be found in the *Administrative Tools* folder, which graphically shows how your system is performing. When it is started, Figure 9.38 appears. The first graph shows the CPU usage of the system and you have spare processor capacity if the value stays below 100%, although ideally you are looking for a value well under 100%. If the CPU is constantly running at 100% then no matter what database tuning is applied, the system physically cannot run any faster. In Figure 9.38 we can see that we have plenty of spare CPU capacity at this time.

The second graph displays the memory usage of your NT system. The value shown is a combination of the physical memory in the computer plus the Virtual Memory file that is defined from the system icon in the control panel.

The page file is a file that is created on disk and used by NT when the physical memory on the machine has been filled and needs extra memory to perform its work. Every time the system has to swap memory between the physical memory and the virtual memory file on disk, the performance of the system is affected. Ideally, you want to keep virtual memory usage to a minimum and try to use the physical memory of the system.

Figure 9.38 NT Task Manager

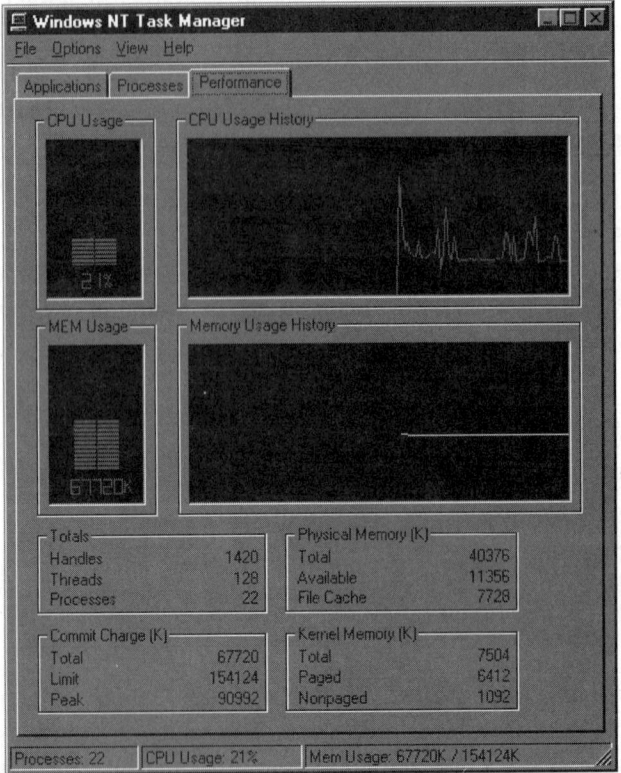

In Figure 9.38 we can see that we are using over 67mb of memory, but this computer only has physical memory of 40mb. When we add in the virtual memory, we have plenty of memory to spare, provided we swap between physical and disk memory. Now if we changed the available physical memory to say 128mb, then virtually all the memory usage would remain in memory and not go to disk, thus resulting in a faster system. Further performance information is available by clicking on the *Processes* tab, which results in Figure 9.39 being displayed. Now we can see the resources being used by each process. Figure 9.39 does not show all the possible information that can be displayed about a process. It can be modified by clicking on *View* in the strip menu and then *Select Columns*.

From this display we can try to fine-tune our system. For example, suppose we want to know which processes are using all of the CPU. If we click on the CPU column then it will sort the data by highest CPU value. This technique can be applied to any of the columns.

Figure 9.39 NT Task Manager – Processes

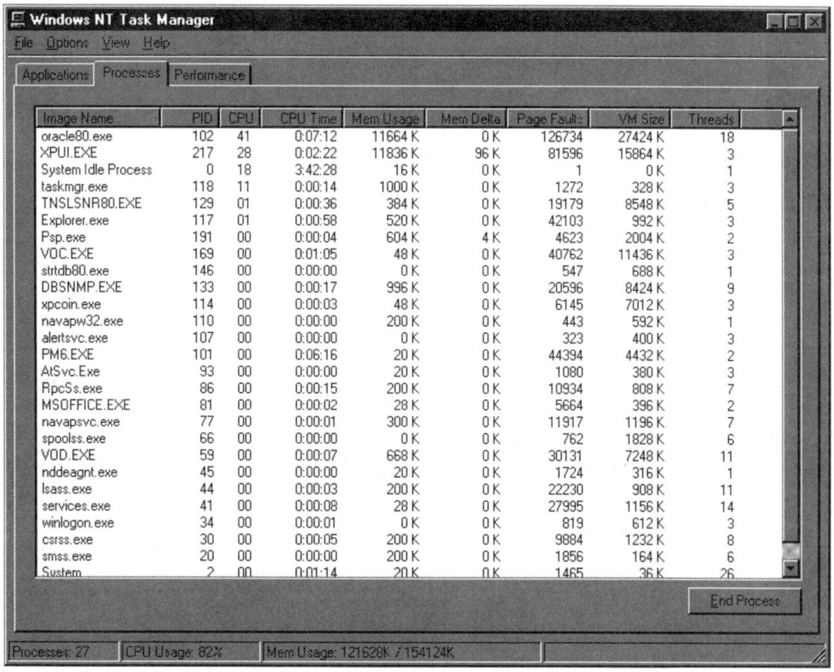

Image Name	PID	CPU	CPU Time	Mem Usage	Mem Delta	Page Faults	VM Size	Threads
oracle80.exe	102	41	0:07:12	11664 K	0 K	126734	27424 K	18
XPUI.EXE	217	28	0:02:22	11836 K	96 K	81596	15864 K	3
System Idle Process	0	18	3:42:28	16 K	0 K	1	0 K	1
taskmgr.exe	118	11	0:00:14	1000 K	0 K	1272	328 K	3
TNSLSNR80.EXE	129	01	0:00:36	384 K	0 K	19179	8548 K	5
Explorer.exe	117	01	0:00:58	520 K	0 K	42103	992 K	3
Psp.exe	191	00	0:00:04	604 K	4 K	4623	2004 K	2
VOC.EXE	169	00	0:01:05	48 K	0 K	40762	11436 K	3
strtdb80.exe	146	00	0:00:00	0 K	0 K	547	688 K	1
DBSNMP.EXE	133	00	0:00:17	996 K	0 K	20596	8424 K	9
xpcoin.exe	114	00	0:00:03	48 K	0 K	6145	7012 K	3
navapw32.exe	110	00	0:00:00	200 K	0 K	443	592 K	1
alertsvc.exe	107	00	0:00:00	0 K	0 K	323	400 K	3
PM6.EXE	101	00	0:06:16	20 K	0 K	44394	4432 K	2
AtSvc.Exe	93	00	0:00:00	20 K	0 K	1080	380 K	3
RpcSs.exe	86	00	0:00:15	200 K	0 K	10934	808 K	7
MSOFFICE.EXE	81	00	0:00:02	28 K	0 K	5664	396 K	2
navapsvc.exe	77	00	0:00:01	300 K	0 K	11917	1196 K	7
spoolss.exe	66	00	0:00:00	0 K	0 K	762	1828 K	6
VOD.EXE	59	00	0:00:07	668 K	0 K	30131	7248 K	11
nddeagnt.exe	45	00	0:00:00	20 K	0 K	1724	316 K	1
lsass.exe	44	00	0:00:03	200 K	0 K	22230	908 K	11
services.exe	41	00	0:00:08	28 K	0 K	27995	1156 K	14
winlogon.exe	34	00	0:00:01	0 K	0 K	819	612 K	3
csrss.exe	30	00	0:00:05	200 K	0 K	9884	1232 K	8
smss.exe	20	00	0:00:00	200 K	0 K	1856	164 K	6
System	2	00	0:01:14	20 K	0 K	1465	36 K	26

Once the process has been identified then you can decide whether to leave it alone, tune it or remove it by clicking on the *End Process* button. Take extreme care when stopping processes because you could make your system unstable if you destroy a process used by NT.

Each Oracle instance that has been started will show as a process called oracle80.exe. You cannot easily see from here which process belongs to an instance unless you can work out from the memory usage which instance has the largest SGA. Other useful information provided is the virtual memory used by each process and how many page faults this process has incurred.

9.5.2 NT Performance Monitor

In Section 9.2 we met the Oracle8 Performance Monitor, which was extremely useful for monitoring the resources used by an Oracle8 database. When we learned how to use this tool, we were in fact learning how to use the NT Performance Monitor, because the Oracle8 version of the tool has simply extended it to report specific Oracle8 information. However, you can use it to report a wealth of specific NT information.

The NT Performance Monitor is started by selecting it from the *Administrative*

Tools folder and by default it starts in *Chart* mode which can then be changed to any of the other display options, such as alerts, reports or log. By clicking on the ▣ icon, data items can be selected by an Object area, such as Processor, Memory, Server and Cache. Then for the object you choose, select the counters to be displayed on the graph. In Figure 9.40, we can see some of the counters available for the Processor object.

Figure 9.40 NT Performance Monitor

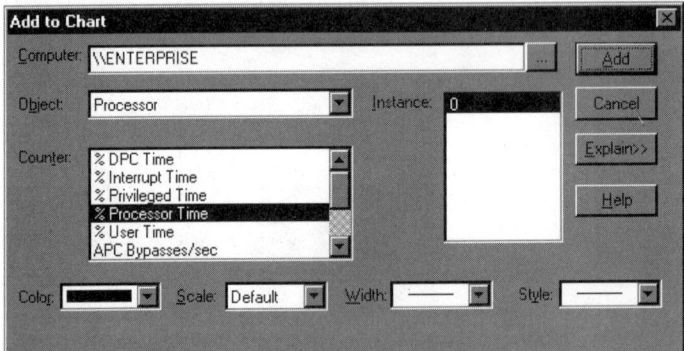

Once the counters have been selected the data is presented and analyzed just as we described for tuning an Oracle8 system.

Hint: If you don't feel qualified to tune your NT system, collect the data as described earlier and then replay it to an NT expert.

9.6   **SUMMARY**

As we stated at the beginning of this chapter, we have just scratched the surface here on how to tune an Oracle database. But we hope, you now have an appreciation for some of the areas such as SQL statements, optimizer strategy, missing indexes, and poor buffer usage that can seriously impact your system performance.

Using the tools and methods described here, you should be in a position to discover and resolve these types of problems. We have also seen how to use tools like Oracle Expert which help automate the process of database tuning. It is not easy to tune a database, but now you should be able to make a start and have the ability to remove basic flaws from your design. Once you have tuned the database to the best of your knowledge, then don't be afraid to ask for help from another expert. This is how you can learn to tune the database better the next time.

10   Distributed Data

So far all the databases we have seen have been on the local computer. Today systems are usually quite complex, involving many databases scattered around an organization. In this chapter, we will see how easy it is to set up a distributed database environment.

10.1   NET8

All network access is done using software supplied with the Oracle database called Net8. Users of the Oracle7 database will know this software as SQL*Net. It is no longer called SQL*Net because now it does a lot more than send SQL statements around the network. Net8 is responsible for enabling clients to access any Oracle database anywhere on the network. It includes a comprehensive set of services which provide security, authentication, naming services and the ability to easily configure the network.

Net8 is very easy to install and set up. It creates a number of files, which are managed using *Oracle Net8 Easy Config*, found in the *Oracle for Windows NT* folder, which we will see how to use shortly. There are four essential components used by Net8:

- Net8 client
- Net8 server process service called TNSListener80
- Oracle Protocol Adaptors
- Network Protocol (e.g., TCP/IP)

8
Oracle

The Net8 client software is responsible for establishing the connection to the Oracle server and exchanging the messages between the client and the server. The Net8 server process, which is also known as the TNS listener, is the program that allows an Oracle8 database to accept a connection from a client. The Oracle protocol adaptors translate function calls from a network protocol such as TCP/IP into the equivalent function call for the TNS listener.

251

Every computer in the network is assigned a unique identification; in a TCP/IP network this is an IP address such as 138.3.8.20. Since numbers are not easy to remember, for each IP address there is also a unique name such as ENTERPRISE. This name is also known as the *host name*, which is much easier to remember than a complex number.

We will see shortly how we can use Oracle Names, but if you are using a naming system like DNS then you can use the *native hostname adaptor* part of Net8 to resolve a name like *enterprise.uk.oracle.com* to identify the appropriate computer.

There are four methods for resolving names in Net8:

8

Oracle

- local naming
- host naming (Oracle8 only)
- external naming (Oracle8 only)
- central naming using Oracle Names

So which naming method should you use?

Local naming is fine to use if the network is small and the number of services that are defined is unlikely to change. The names are held in a local file called TNSNAMES.ORA. The only problem with this approach is that the names must be defined on every machine, which is why it is not recommended for large networks.

Host naming is ideal for TCP/IP networks that contain up to twenty databases. It requires no additional setup, because it relies on existing IP address translation mechanisms such as DNS or a TCP/IP hosts file. Therefore, there is no need to maintain a local names configuration file. A disadvantage of this approach is that it can only be used if the TCP/IP network protocol is used and you cannot specify which Oracle SID to connect to on the remote database. Shown below is an example of how to connect using a host name.

```
CONNECT   system/manager@enterprise
```

Centralized naming is the one to use for large, complex networks that are frequently changing. It means that the network names and addresses are held in one central place and a change has to be made only once. This is also known as *Oracle Names*.

Finally, *external* naming can be used on a network that is already using a naming service. It means that Oracle service names can be added to their existing network.

Net8 has been designed to provide a scalable environment. There is a Connection Manager, which takes requests from many clients and multiplexes them to a server. But this isn't the only task it performs; it can also maintain a list of the clients who are allowed to access the database and act as a firewall to check whether a client is authorized to use it.

10.1.1   Services

Before you can access a database, a service must be defined which advises where the database is located and which SID to use. The service is defined using the *Oracle8 Net Assistant*, which can be found in the *Oracle for Windows NT folder.* First click on *Service Name* and then click on the ⊞ icon, and the *Oracle Service Name* wizard appears as illustrated in Figure 10.1.

Figure 10.1 Service Name Wizard

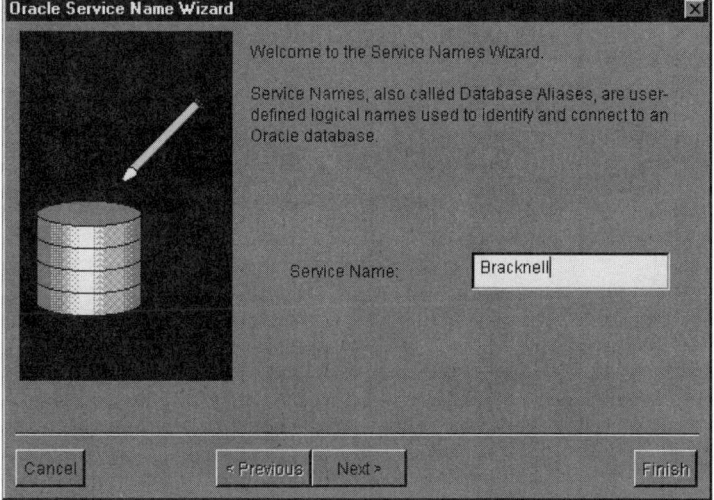

The first step is to give the service a name. This is a very important decision because this unique name will be used by everyone to access the database. Therefore choose a name that will be meaningful to people. In this example, we have called the service Bracknell to denote the database that is held at the Bracknell office.

Click on the *Next* button and Figure 10.2 appears where you must select the network protocol. Here we have selected TCP/IP, but if the database is local then use the Bequeath protocol.

Figure 10.2 Service Network Protocol

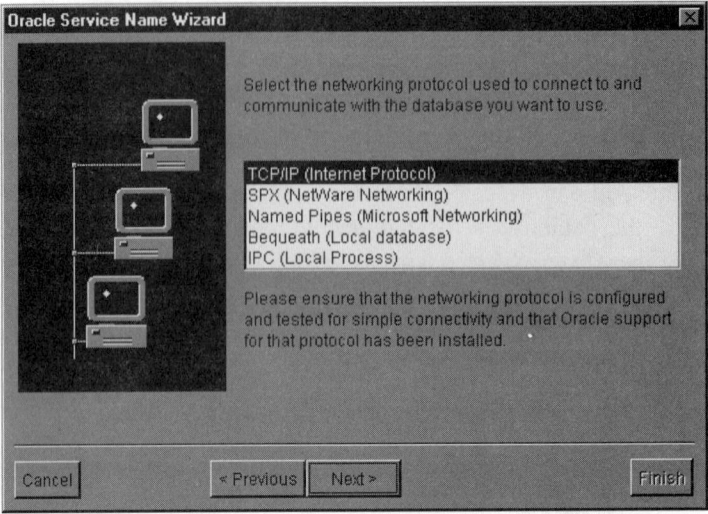

Then Figure 10.3 is displayed, where you have to specify the name of the computer and the port number to use. Usually the port number doesn't have to be changed, so all that is needed is the name of the computer. Do double check that you have spelled it correctly, otherwise when you test the service later it will fail.

Figure 10.3 Service Location

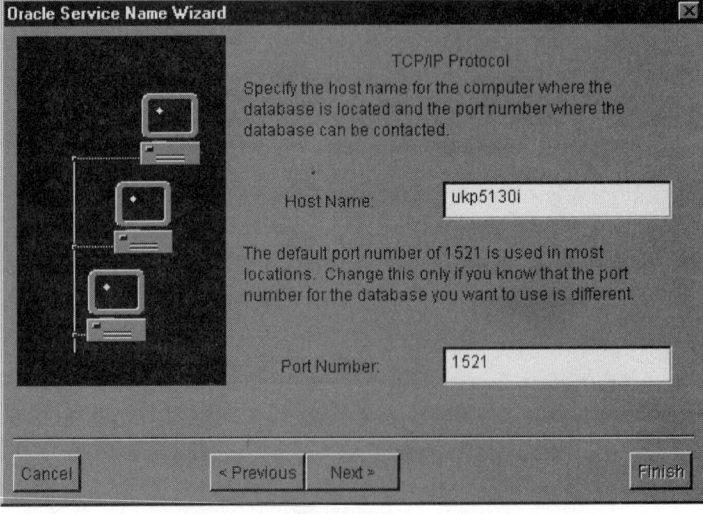

The next screen, Figure 10.4, is where you specify which database is to be used on the host computer. In this example we have specified the default instance called ORCL, but it could be any SID on that computer.

Figure 10.4   Service SID

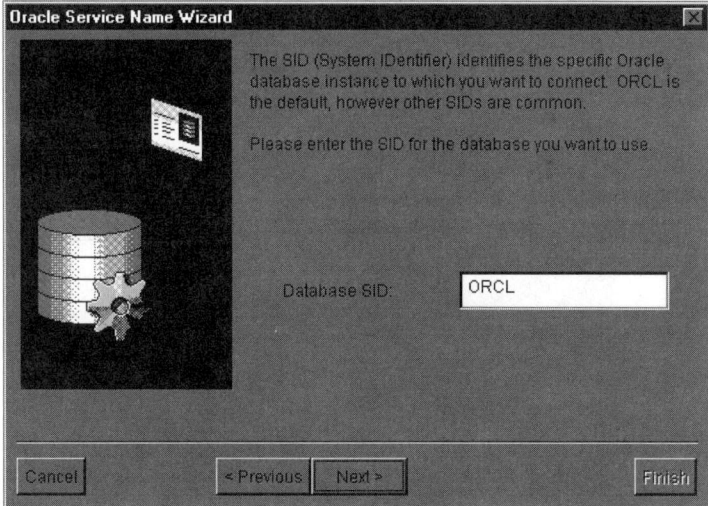

One very important step is the testing of the service. After you have specified the SID, click on the button *Test Service* and Figure 10.5 appears, where you specify a username and password to logon to the database. Clicking on the *Test* button, it will try and connect to the database. If it is successful, then the message "connection test was successful" will appear, otherwise an error will be reported.

In the unlikely event that it does fail, an error message is displayed. Click on the *Done* button and then you can click on the *Previous* button to return to the previous screens and amend the information that was entered.

Once the testing of the service is successful, click on the *Finish* button to finish the definition of the service.

The ability to create services makes managing and accessing databases easy. These service names are used every time we see a database logon screen. Since a service name can refer to any database on the network, we can use this name to connect to any database on the network. Therefore service names provide a very easy mechanism for connecting to a remote database. For example, suppose we wish to query a remote database, we can logon using SQL Worksheet and specify the service name. Net8 makes a connection to the remote database and the client tool, SQL Worksheet, runs on the local machine.

Figure 10.5 Test the Service

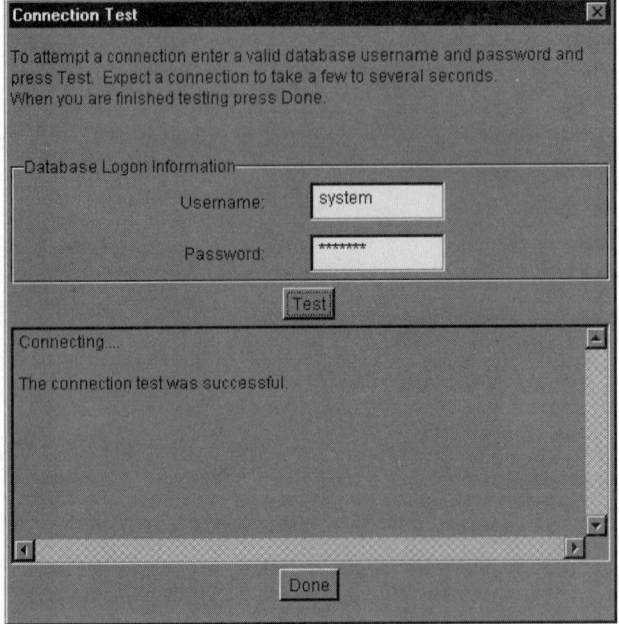

10.1.2　Oracle8 Net Assistant

So far we have seen how to define service names, but Net8 is a very sophisticated piece of software with many options. The *Oracle8 Net Assistant* found in the *Oracle for Windows NT* folder is used to define all the parameters.

There are three components that can be configured in Net8. The first is the *Profile*. Referring to Figure 10.6, simply select the item to configure from the drop down list. Under *Profile* there are a number of components which can be configured, which is the same for all the sites in the list. Net8 requires very little configuration unless you are using some of its special features.

8

Oracle

Hint: Save the network configuration before it is changed.

The list of available services can be displayed in Oracle Net8 Assistant as illustrated in Figure 10.7.

Figure 10.6 Oracle8 Net Assistant Profiles

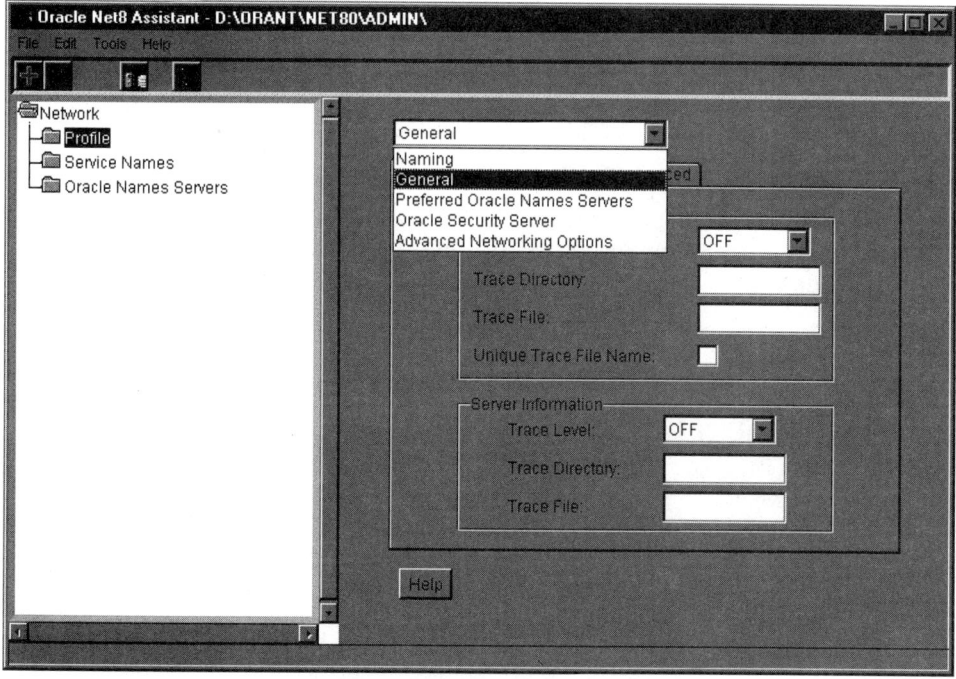

Figure 10.7 Oracle8 Net Assistant Service Names

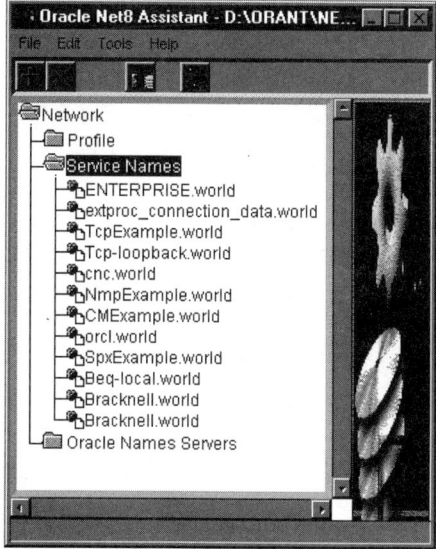

Hint: To see the list of services you must double click on Service Names.

10.2   DISTRIBUTED PROCESSING

Not every time a distributed database is called for, is it needed; often distributed processing or remote access is all that is required. The Oracle database incorporates a client/server architecture, which means that the client and the server do not have to reside on the same computer.

Taking advantage of distributed processing, where the client and the server reside on different computers, is an extremely efficient method to use to take advantage of all the resources that are available. With an Oracle database it couldn't be easier to use distributed processing and therefore access remote data.

10.3   DISTRIBUTED DATABASES

Many organizations have multiple databases located around their network and it is not uncommon to need to access data from many databases at the same time. In Oracle it is very easy to query remote databases as if they were local.

Before any queries can take place some setup is required. A *Database Link* must be created for each remote database that is to be queried. In Figure 10.8, we see how this is achieved using Schema Manager.

Figure 10.8 Creating a Database Link

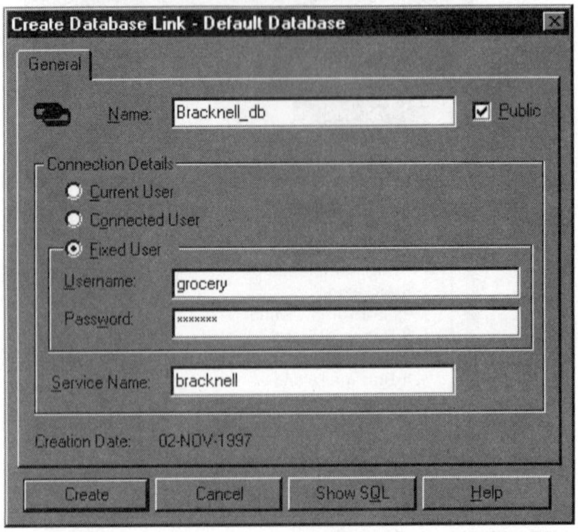

First the link must be given a name. Choose something that is easy to remember and recognize, because it will very likely be used in queries. Then you must define the username and password that must be used to connect to the remote database. In Figure 10.8 we have defined a specific username that will be used every time a connection is made. Alternatively, you could specify that the username and password used to connect to the current database is used to connect to the remote database; this is known as *connected user.*

8

Oracle

A new feature in Oracle8 is *Current User*, which allows you to connect to the database without any checks being made.

The actual database to which you connect is determined by specifying one of the database service names that we defined previously.

Hint: The database link is a schema object and is created in the database that you are currently connected to.

To explain how the database link is used, suppose our company has two telephone centers, each with its own database which is used to take telephone orders. During the day, each site likes to know how many orders the other site has taken. Therefore they periodically query each other's databases to see how business is progressing. By creating a database link, we hide the location details of the actual database which is known as *location transparency.*

A typical query to find out the number of orders at the Bracknell order centre would be:

```
SELECT count(*) FROM orders@bracknell_db
```

However, this approach still requires the developer to include the @<link_name> in the SQL statement. If you prefer to write a normal SQL statement, then a view can be created to hide the detail from the user, as shown below.

```
CREATE VIEW remote_orders   AS
   SELECT count(*) AS no_of_orders
     FROM   orders@bracknell_db;
```

Now the query would look like any other, and it would not be immediately obvious to anyone that this was accessing a remote database, especially if the view was called something like *Orders_Today* instead of *remote_orders*.

Another very useful technique to create location transparency is to create a synonym which points to the object in a remote database. A synonym can be created using the Schema Manager.

In Figure 10.9 a synonym is defined called *orders_b*, which points to the *orders* table in the *order* schema in the remote database, accessed via the link called *bracknell_db*. Now the query would be like:

```
SELECT count(*) FROM orders_b;
```

Figure 10.9 Synonym for a Remote Object

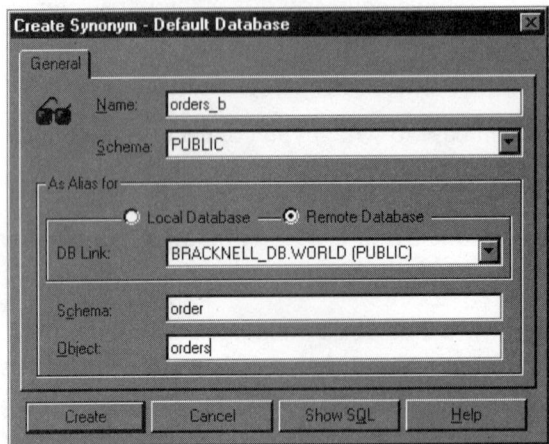

Once again, the actual location of the object is completely hidden from the user. This technique can be extremely useful if access to your data is given to non-computer staff who need to interrogate the database to extract certain information using popular end-user query tools.

Don't forget that stored procedures can be used to contain procedures for managing objects in remote databases. All the examples that we have seen show us querying the database but we can also use the SQL insert, update and delete statements to manipulate our data.

A query can refer to as many remote databases as you like. Just remember that each database you refer too, will require time for the data to be retrieved.

Whenever two or more databases are being updated, Oracle automatically uses a *Two-Phase Commit* mechanism to ensure that both databases are updated. If one update were to succeed and the other failed then the databases would be inconsistent. Since Oracle automatically uses a Two-Phase commit protocol, this is one concern that the user need not have.

The state of all 2PC transactions can be found by querying the table DBA_2PC_PENDING.

10.4 REPLICATION AND SNAPSHOTS

Another type of distributed access that is often required is the ability to copy the contents of a table from one database to another, which is known as *replication*. Oracle8 offers a number of different replication methods.

Before replication can be applied to a database, the following scripts must be run against the database while connected as user SYS or internal: *catsnap.sql*, *dbmssnap.sql* and *catrep.sql*

Hint: Don't use SQL Worksheet to run the script catrep.sql because it will take a long time. Use a tool like Server Manager instead.

Throughout this book we have always used the GUI interfaces to manage our database, but this is the one time when you may prefer to use the SQL interface instead, because even in Schema Manger you have to write some SQL.

Before defining replication, first identify the *master site* from which the information is retrieved and then define a *snapshot* in the *destination* database. The snapshot can either be a copy or a subset of the table that is described by the SQL query. In order to keep the data up to date, for every snapshot that is defined a refresh period is also required. Then at the appropriate time, the data is updated with the latest version from the master site.

10.4.1 Database Link

Before the snapshot can be defined, first a database link must be created to point to the source of the data (as shown in Figure 10.8) or using SQL, as that shown below.

```
CREATE DATABASE LINK head_office.WORLD
  CONNECT TO system IDENTIFIED BY manager
    USING 'head_office';
```

The database link is required to advise where the data is located. Now the snapshot can be created, but make sure that you connect to the database where the snapshot is to reside and don't accidentally connect to the master database. This is a very easy mistake to make and you will wonder why the snapshot can't be created.

If you are using SQL to create the snapshot consider issuing a connect statement just before the snapshot statement. If you are using Schema Manager, then check the top of the window box to see which database you are connected to. This is the main Schema Manager window and not the Create Snapshot window that is shown in Figure 10.10.

10.4.2   Read-Only Snapshot

The first type of replication that we can define is known as *basic replication* or a *read-only snapshot*. Imagine a company that has a master price list for all the goods that it sells. They have 100 outlets around the country and they charge the same price for their goods no matter where in the country you purchase them. To ensure that every store, which has its own local database, is using the correct price, they maintain the price list at the head office, which is known as the master site. Then they create a snapshot at each outlet based on the master price list held at the head office. A refresh period of once a day is specified, and at the end of every day the latest prices are automatically sent to all the outlets.

The SQL to create this snapshot would be:

```
CONNECT  SYSTEM/MANAGER@Chandlers_Ford;

CREATE  SNAPSHOT  all_the_stores
   TABLESPACE  store_details
     STORAGE  (INITIAL 64k NEXT 8k)
   REFRESH COMPLETE
     START WITH sysdate
       NEXT sysdate + 1
   AS SELECT * FROM grocery.store@head_office;
```

Note that when the snapshot is created, we can also specify the storage parameters for this object. Alternatively, a snapshot can be created using Schema Manager. Select *Object* from the strip menu, then click on *Create* and select *Create Snapshot* from the list and Figure 10.10 will appear. Clicking on the Storage tab in Figure 10.10 will enable you to specify the storage options for the snapshot.

In this example we have copied the entire table from head office to our local site, however, we could have selected specific columns or a subset of the data.

Hint: Test the SQL SELECT statement for the snapshot using SQL Worksheet or similar before it is specified in the actual snapshot.

A snapshot can be quite complicated. For example, in Figure 10.11 a selection criterion can be specified. It could specify which columns are to be included or contain a join between a number of tables. No matter which one you choose, the bad news is that you have to enter the SQL for the snapshot.

Figure 10.10 Create a Snapshot

10.4.3   Fast Refresh

There is a problem with the snapshot that we have just defined and that is what happens if we add a new store to the organization? If we retransmit the entire table, then this is not a problem if the table is small, but for large tables this could cause an unnecessary delay. The solution to this problem is to define a refresh interval of *Fast*.

Using the *fast* refresh method, once the table has been replicated, then only the changes made to the table at the master site are sent to the snapshot at refresh time. However, before the snapshot can be defined, a *snapshot log* must be created at the master site. The purpose of the snapshot log is to hold the changes that are made to the master table. Then when it is time to refresh the snapshot, the process is very quick because the changes to the table are easily identified.

The snapshot log can be created in Schema Manager, as shown in Figure 10.12, by selecting *Object* from the strip menu, then *Create* and then select *Snapshot Log* from the list.

Figure 10.11 Create a Snapshot with a Selection

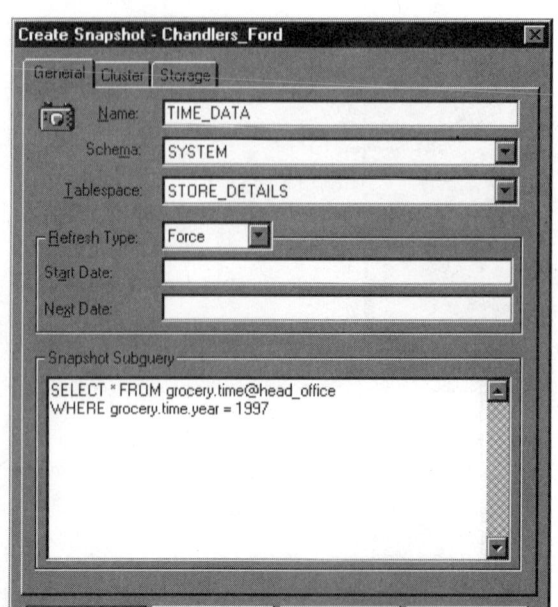

Alternatively, the snapshot log can be created using SQL as shown below.

```
CONNECT  SYSTEM/MANAGER@head_office;

CREATE SNAPSHOT LOG ON grocery.store
  PCTFREE 0  PCTUSED 80
    TABLESPACE system ;
```

Since the snapshot log will hold details of the changes to the master table, if there are likely to be many changes, then take care with how you size the snapshot log. In Schema Manager, click on the Storage tab shown in Figure 10.12.

Once the snapshot log has been defined, the snapshot can then be created. However, don't forget to change your database connection from the master site where you defined the snapshot log to the destination for the snapshot. In the SQL example shown below, we change our connection to the Chandlers_Ford location, then create the snapshot.

Figure 10.12 Create a Snapshot Log

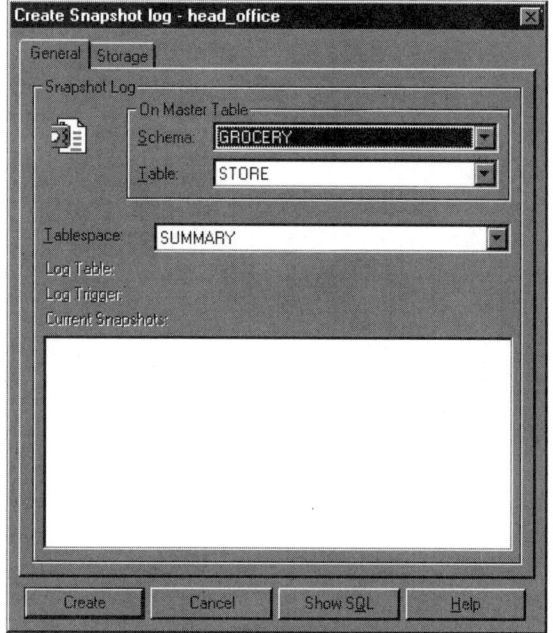

```
CONNECT  SYSTEM/MANAGER@Chandlers_Ford;

CREATE  SNAPSHOT  all_the_stores
   PCTFREE  0   PCTUSED 80
   TABLESPACE  store_details
      STORAGE  (INITIAL  64k  NEXT  8k)
   REFRESH  FAST
      START  WITH  sysdate
         NEXT  sysdate+1
AS  SELECT  *  FROM  grocery.store@head_office;
```

If you were using Schema Manager, the database connection would be changed by selecting *File* from the strip menu, then *Change Database Connection.* The standard *Login Information* screen is supplied so you can connect to a new database.

At first glance you are probably thinking that the only type of snapshot to create is one that uses the fast refresh method, especially if your data is continually changing. Unfortunately, this approach has a catch – it can only be used against simple snapshots, which means that this method may be used only if your snapshot definition doesn't contain a GROUP BY or CONNECT BY clause, have a subquery or a join or any set operations.

10.4.4   Managing Snapshots

You can define as many snapshots and snapshot logs as you like. The Schema Manager is then a very useful tool for presenting an overview of what has been created in your system. In Figure 10.13 we can see that two snapshots have been defined, whether they have been refreshed and what type of snapshot they are.

Figure 10.13 Schema Manager and Snapshots

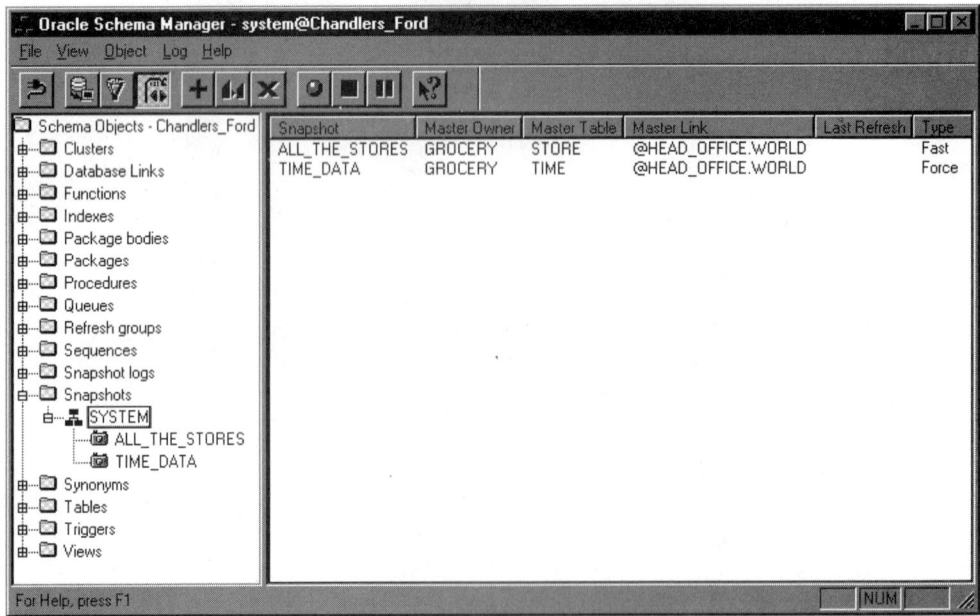

For more specific information, clicking on any snapshot shown in the navigator panel will reveal Figure 10.14 where we can find out everything we need to know such as the type of snapshot, when it was created, where the table is that it is based on and when it was last refreshed.

Do take care when reading the last refreshed date because it displays a date even when the snapshot has never been refreshed. In Figure 10.14, the date is 01-JAN-1950, which is the clue that it has never been refreshed. Should it be necessary to change any of the storage parameters for the snapshot, click on the *Storage* tab.

Figure 10.14 Status of a Snapshot

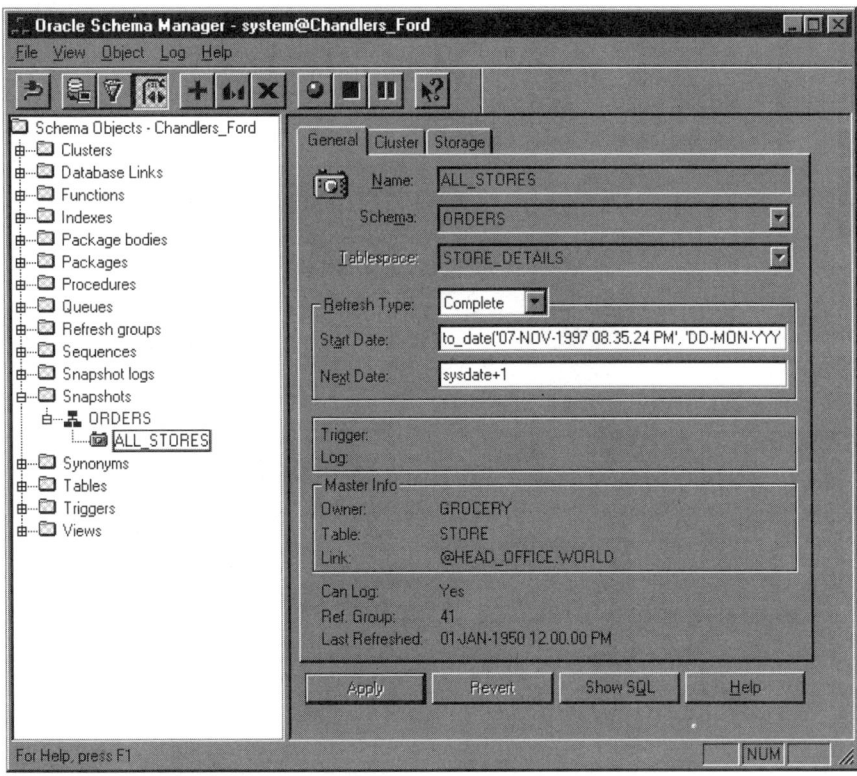

10.4.5 Refreshing the Snapshot

The refresh interval for the snapshot is specified when it is created. In these examples we have asked for it to be refreshed every day, but you can specify any interval, which can include a complex expression that would resolve to every second Tuesday, for example.

A snapshot can be manually refreshed by calling the package DBMS_SNAPSHOT, passing in the name of the snapshot and the type of refresh required. In this example we have specified "f" for a fast refresh.

```
EXECUTE
dbms_snapshot.refresh ('all_store_details','f');
```

Using this approach is okay, but it is time-consuming and error prone. A special job has to be scheduled and you must check that every snapshot has been refreshed. The recommended approach is to create a snapshot *Refresh Group*. This can be achieved through the Schema Manager by selecting this object type from the Create list.

Figure 10.15 illustrates how to create the refresh group. First give it a sensible name and specify the schema in which this object will reside. Then specify the refresh interval, but don't forget that this will apply to all the snapshots in this group.

Figure 10.15 Refresh Group

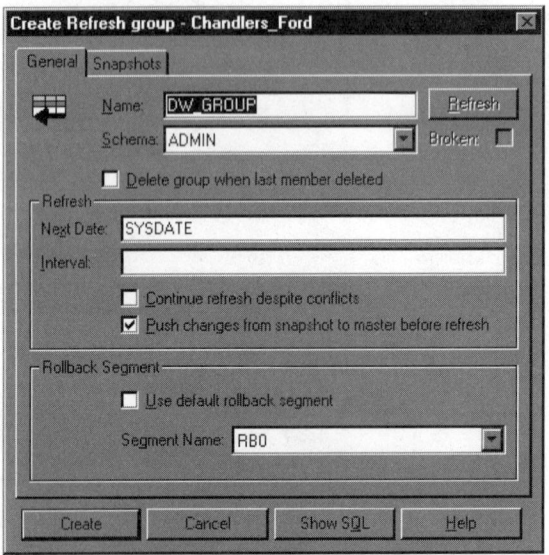

Figure 10.16 Specify Snapshots in a Refresh Group

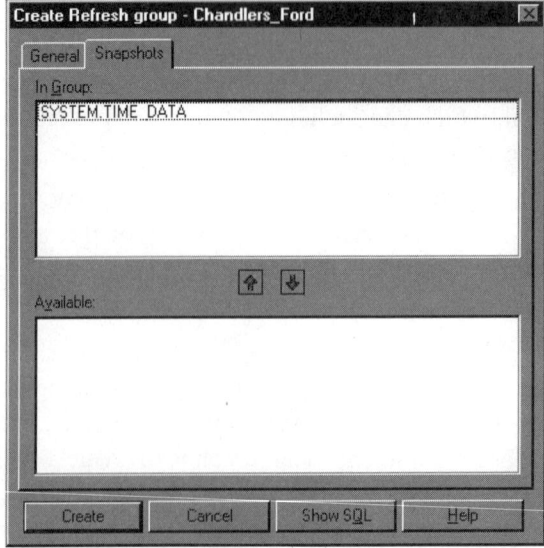

To specify the snapshots that are to be included in this refresh group click on the *Snapshots* tab and Figure 10.16 appears. Now select the snapshots from the bottom box and use the up arrow to move them to the *InGroup* box. When you are finished selecting the snapshots, click on the *Create* button to create the group.

Once the refresh group has been defined, all the snapshots in the group can be refreshed together, by clicking on the *Refresh* button shown in Figure 10.17.

Figure 10.17 Refresh via Schema Manager

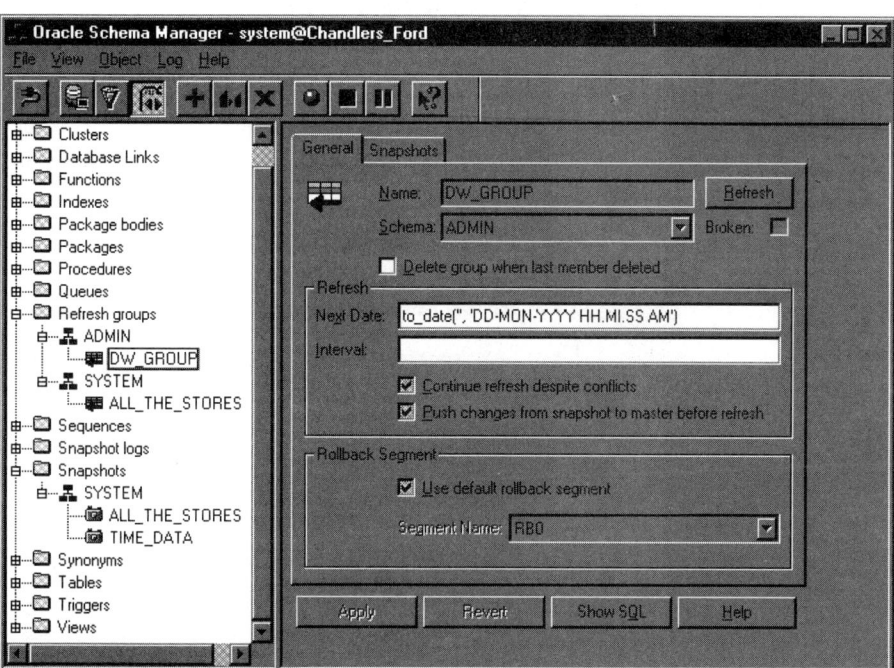

10.4.6 Advanced Replication

We have seen examples only of simple snapshots here but you can also create *complex snapshots* that involve joining many tables, or including clauses like GROUP BY.

Another type of replication is a rollup, where many sites push all their data to one location. Using our outlets as the example again, suppose head office wants to know how many of each product the outlet sells in a day. A snapshot is created in reverse, where the outlet is the master site and the head office database becomes the receiving snapshot.

Another common requirement is the ability to have two-way replication. This is when the master replicates to the slave site and the slave site replicates back to the master site. This is known as symmetric replication and it can be set up using the tools described here. Whenever, symmetric replication is used, you must be extremely careful to ensure that no inaccuracies can occur in your data to avoid replicating bad data.

10.4.7   Oracle Replication Manager

There is another tool that can be used to manage the replication environment and that is the *Oracle Replication Manager* which can be found in the Oracle Replication Manager folder.

From within this tool you can define database connections and see the snapshots, snapshot logs and refresh groups that have been previously defined, even if they were created using SQL or the Schema Manager.

There is a wizard that will take you step by step through the tasks that have to be completed to create a snapshot or set up the master site which can be found by clicking on *File* in the strip menu and then *Setup Wizard*.

Figure 10.18 shows the main screen with the navigator pane on the left, where the hierarchy has been expanded. Here we are looking at the master site and the destination map.

Figure 10.18 Oracle Replication Manager

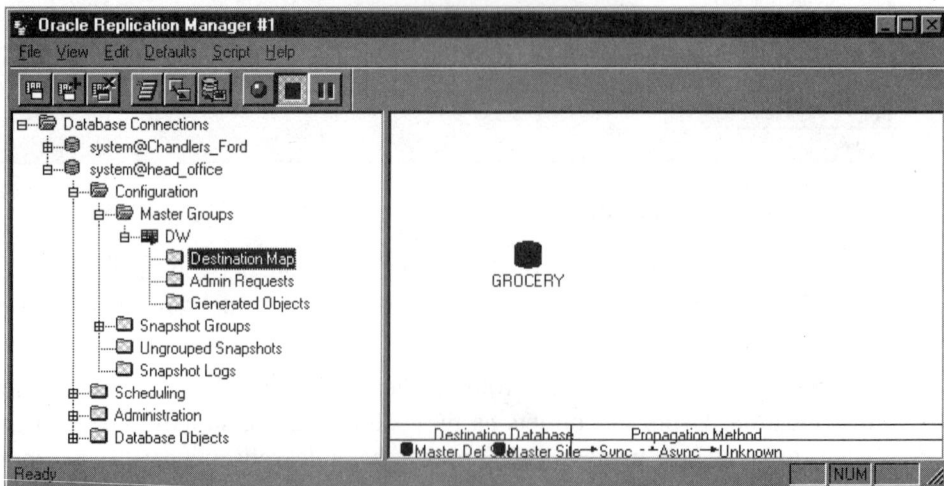

One of the nice aspects of using this tool is that you can drag and drop the objects. For example, you can create a snapshot and then drag it onto the refresh group.

In Figure 10.19 we can see the refresh groups that have been defined at the Chandlers Ford site. There are numerous screens of information available with this tool, so it is wise to explore its full potential.

Figure 10.19 Replication Manager Refresh groups

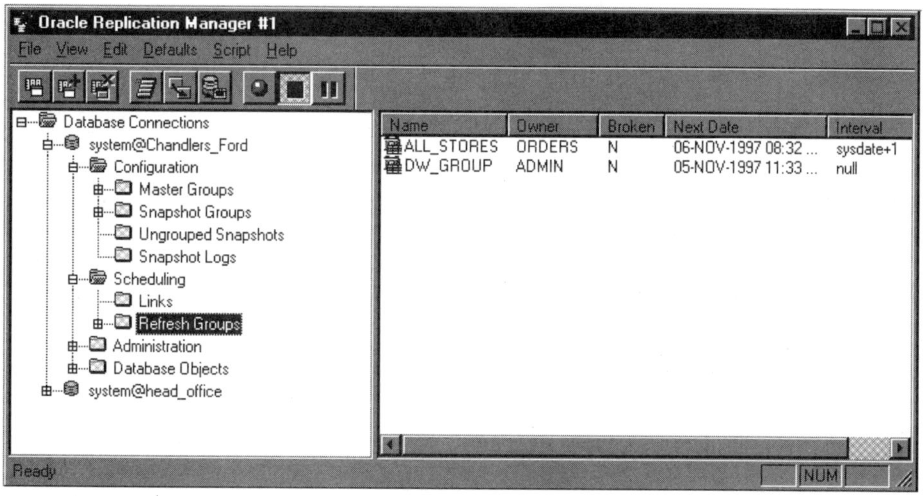

10.5   SUMMARY

This chapter has provided a very brief introduction to the world of replication available in an Oracle server and how you can create distributed queries and databases. The Oracle server has so much to offer in this area any reader planning to create a distributed database should consult the Oracle documentation. There is one book devoted to replication and another for the distributed environment.

Distributed databases can be a nightmare to manage and people often worry about the network. In Oracle8, it is very easy to set up Net8 and the technique of defining a service for a remote or local database is an easy-to-use concept.

Accessing remote data is easy using the Oracle server and through the use of synonyms it is possible to create location transparency. There are many sites around the world using distributed databases and replication, so the good news is that you are not venturing into an unknown world.

11   The Web and Oracle

One of the hottest topics in the computer industry at the moment is the explosion of the Internet. In this chapter we will see how we can make the data in our Oracle database available to the world.

11.1   THE INTERNET

If you haven't heard of the Internet, then all this author can ask is have you been living at the North Pole? Even my elderly mom knows about the Internet and sometimes asks me to locate information for her. The Internet has exploded today in the information it has to offer, and provides a range of services which includes:

- Electronic Mail
- World Wide Web
- Newsgroups
- File Transfer

The one area on the Internet that is exploding is the World Wide Web, which is sometimes called the Web or shortened to WWW. In the beginning a Web site was a collection of pages of information and a few graphics. For example, a company may have some pages describing who they are and what they sell. But now all that has changed, and the World Wide Web has become a new selling mechanism for many companies. With so many homes having access to the Internet, people can now buy your products anytime or anywhere. Although we have concentrated on buying and selling on the Internet, that isn't the only use it can be put to. For example, another extremely useful feature is the ability to provide the latest information to your customers, such as aircraft arrival times, lottery results and press releases. Today when you look at a Web site, such as the one shown in Figure 11.1, the typical features that you might see include:

- Company Product Information (e.g., catalog with pictures)
- Purchase Products
- Obtain a Quote
- Feedback by Electronic Mail
- Video and Sound
- Download Files

Figure 11.1   Typical Web Page

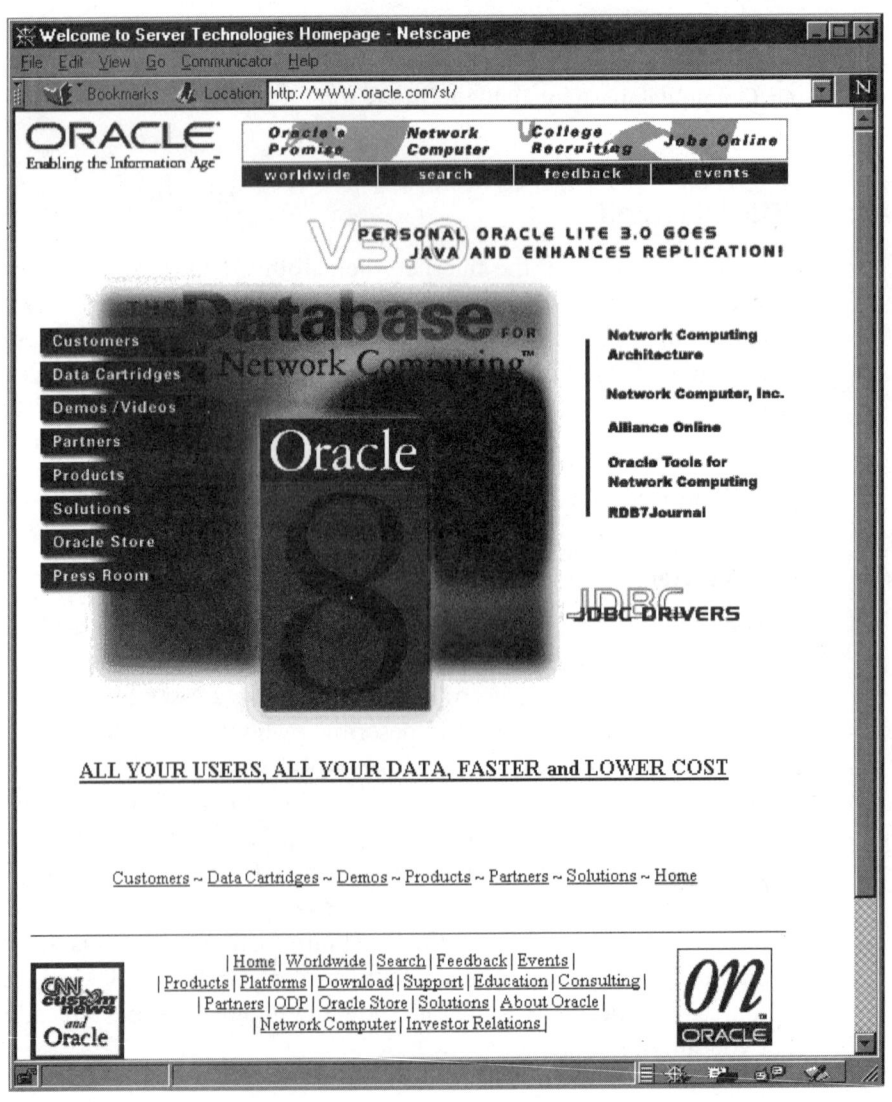

So what does all this have to do with your Oracle database? Well, the information that you need and the order that you are about to take will most likely involve using an Oracle database. Therefore all you have to do is replace your client application with a Web browser-based application. At this point your reaction is probably one of scepticism; it can't possibly be that easy.

First let us see how a Web-based application communicates with the Oracle database. In Figure 11.2, our user requests information which is passed from their browser to the Web server. No Web site can operate without a Web server and the Oracle database will work with a number of servers, although all the examples shown here have used Oracle Web Application Server V3.

Figure 11.2 How a Browser Uses the Oracle Database

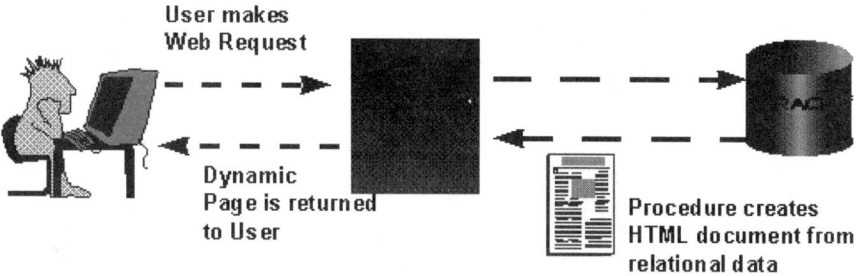

The Web server takes the request and then using the Web cartridge or Web agent it makes a call to the database using a stored procedure. Within the stored procedure, the database is queried and then the it formulates a response in HTML. This is passed back to the Web server via the cartridge or agent, who then returns it to the user's browser. HTML, which is described in Section 11.2, is the language used by the browser to display this information.

Therefore, a Web application is written as a stored procedure and held inside the database. Another useful aspect of this approach is that a database is only accessible from the Web if the appropriate stored procedures have been installed, which is a great security feature, because otherwise DBAs would be extremely concerned about unauthorized access to their data.

Before we see how to Web enable our database, let us take a moment to see how using this feature can benefit our business. There are many sites on the Internet that provide you with information, allowing the visitor to query a production database. For example, visit some of the airlines' Web sites and you can check seat availability and even book a seat. It is entirely transparent to the users that they are querying a database.

We mentioned previously that companies use their Web sites to sell goods to customers. In Figure 11.3 we see an example of a company selling bicycle components over the Internet.

Figure 11.3 Catalogue on the Web

Whenever the subject of buying goods over the Internet is discussed, the question is asked, how safe is this? This problem is addressed by features that are incorporated into the browser and Web server. Therefore, anyone designing this type of system does not have to make any changes to the database to prevent unauthorized access to their data. Many people distrust the Internet because they fear people will obtain their credit card details. However, if we stopped to think about all the other types of credit card fraud, we would probably never use a credit card again.

Providing access to your database from the Web should be viewed just like any other project and planned and implemented accordingly. Now that we have some ideas of what to put on our Web site, lets us look at how we can achieve this.

Hint: If you are stuck for ideas on how to design your Web site, surf the Web yourself to get ideas or ask a professional Web design company to do the job.

11.2   HTML

Web browsers use a language called HTML, which stands for HyperText Markup Language, to describe what a page should contain. Until recently, all applications were written in HTML, but the introduction of the Java language is revolutionizing the world of Web pages. If you have visited a Web site that has moving animations, or a ticker tape display rolling across the screen, then you have seen a Java application.

Java is considered by many to be the language of the future. In this chapter we will concentrate on how to use HTML, since Java applications or applets are often embedded inside HTML.

HTML is a language that describes how a document should be formatted. There is a comprehensive list of tags, such as <TITLE>, which result in input or output on a document. In order to create an application which queries your Oracle database, you need to have a basic understanding of tags because in your stored procedure you have to call functions that are the equivalent of an HTML tag. For example, in HTML you would say <TITLE> and the equivalent Oracle function would be HTP_TITLE. Therefore, if you know the name of the HTML tag, you should be able to easily locate the equivalent Oracle function to call.

At this point the reader is probably saying, oh no, not another language to learn. It is understandable that you would have this concern, but do not worry. If you do not feel like writing a Web application, there are tools available to help you complete the task, like the Developer tools from Oracle.

Fortunately, to create a Web page it is not necessary to learn many HTML commands. Figure 11.4 is an example of a simple HTML document and Figure 11.5 shows us how it appears in the browser.

Figure 11.4 Simple HTML Example

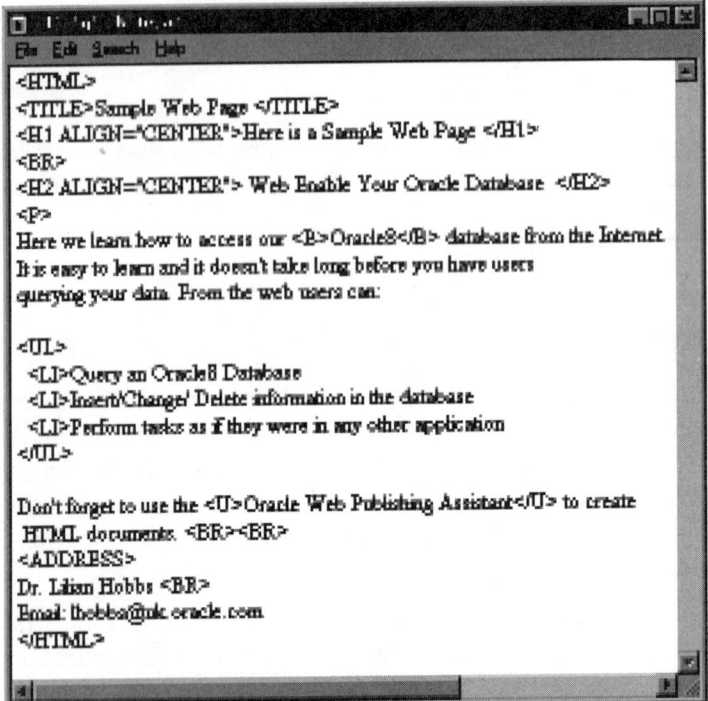

All HTML tags are enclosed within < > and as a general rule, every tag must be terminated with a </ >. Referring to Figure 11.4, the first tag we see is <HTML> which is the first line in any document. The end of the document is declared with a </HTML> tag. The other tags which we have used in this simple examples are:

<TITLE>   Place a title in the Browser box window

<H1>   Top level heading

<H2>   Next level heading

      Line feed

<UL>   Bulleted list

<LI>   Entry in a list

There are many other tags available that enable you to create a table, display a form where data can be entered and various formatting options such as bolding and including an image. If you are not familiar with HTML, many good books are available on this subject.

Figure 11.5 Our HTML as Displayed by the Browser

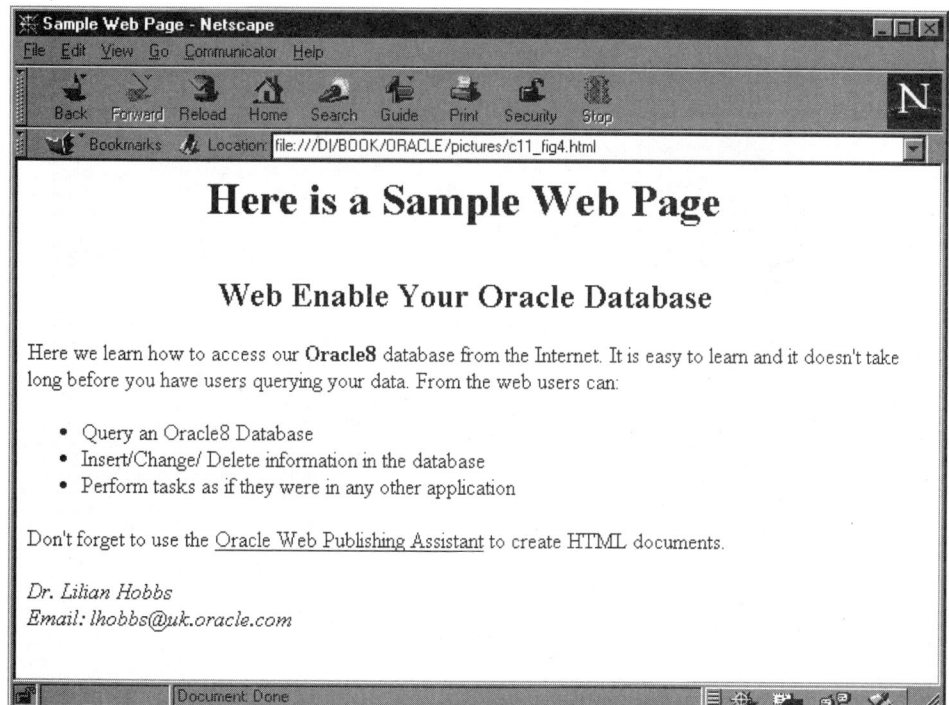

11.3 ENABLING THE DATABASE FOR WEB ACCESS

When we understand what the Internet is and have a grasp of HTML, we are ready to query our database from the Internet. With Oracle8 there are two methods we can use:

- Oracle Web Publishing Assistant;
- A Web Server and the Developers Kit.

11.3.1 Oracle Web Publishing Assistant

Although HTML is an easy language to learn, the first time you have to write any language it is always a daunting task that takes far longer than one anticipates. If you use the Web Publishing Assistant, then within a matter of minutes, there will be HTML documents available to query the database.

Figure 11.6 Oracle Web Publishing Assistant

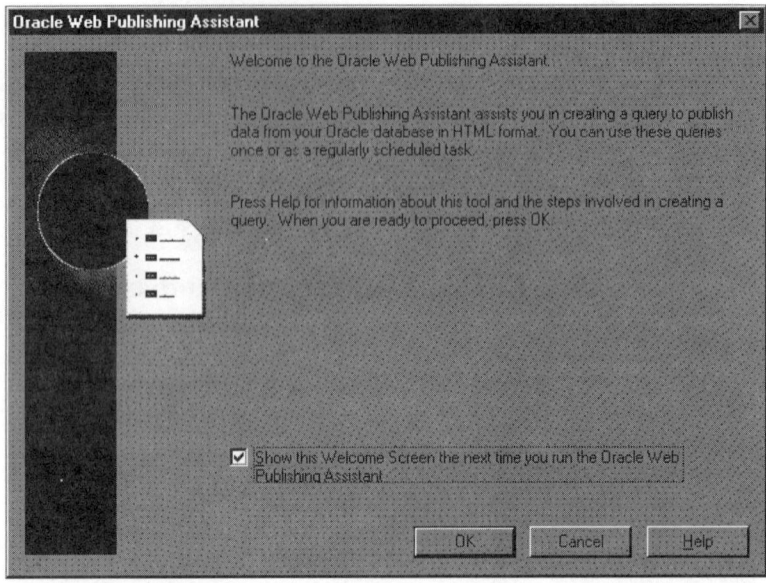

Figure 11.7 Specify Database Details

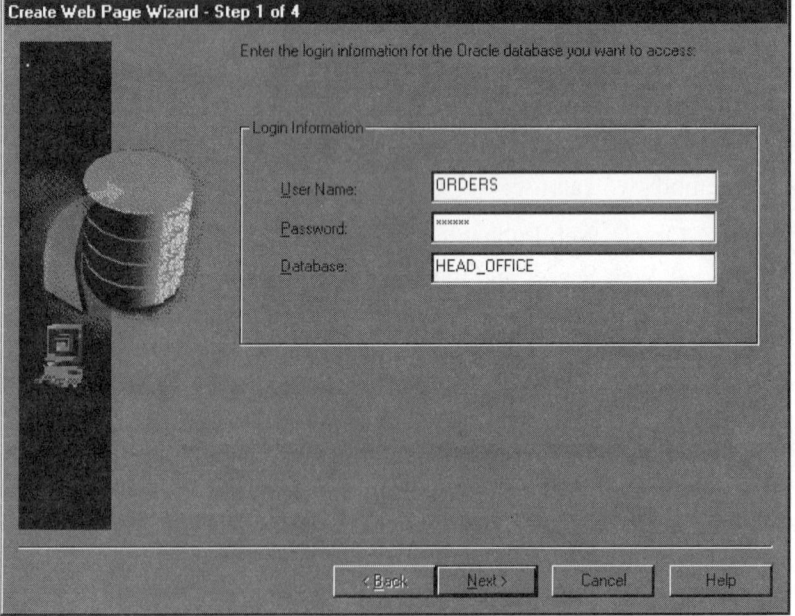

Before using this tool, make sure that *OracleWebAssistant* NT service has been started by checking in the Control Panel that it is running. By default, it does not start automatically. Oracle Web Publishing Assistant can be found in the *Oracle for Windows NT* folder. To create an HTML page click on the ⊕ New icon, which will start the Assistant who will ask you a number of questions. The first page of the wizard is shown in Figure 11.7, which requests the user-name, password and database service to be used. This is a standard Oracle database logon screen which we have met many times before.

The next screen, shown in Figure 11.8, is where you select the table and columns to be shown on the document. All you have to do is expand the hierarchy, selecting either a table or a view and then click on the columns to be shown. If a mistake is made, clicking on the column again will remove it. All columns that have been selected will have a checkmark against them. In Figure 11.8 we have selected three columns from the ORDERS_TAKEN table.

Figure 11.8 Select the Table and Columns

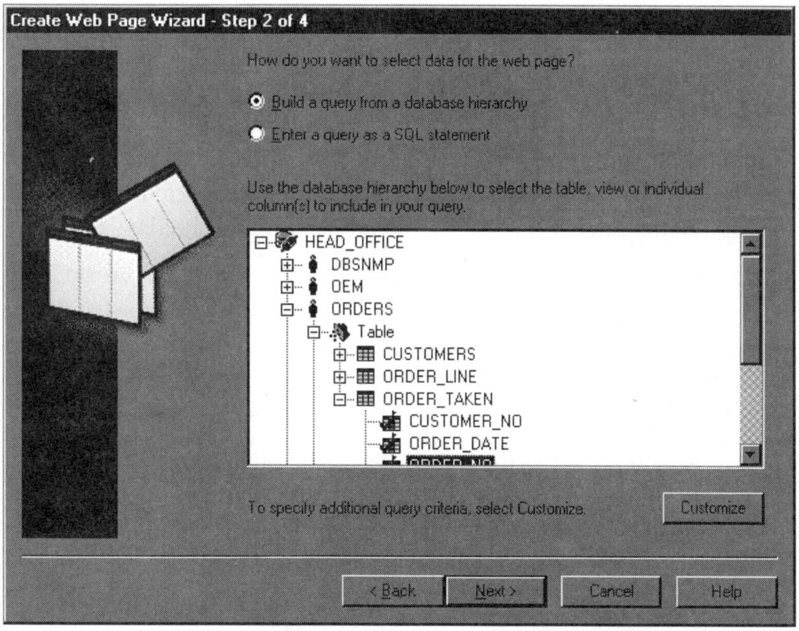

In the example shown here we have created a very simple SQL query. In reality, you will probably want to write more complex SQL statements and this is achieved by clicking on the *"Enter a query as a SQL statement"* option in Figure 11.8. Then Figure 11.9 is displayed, which is a blank box into which the SQL statement is written.

Figure 11.9 Specify a Complex SQL Statement

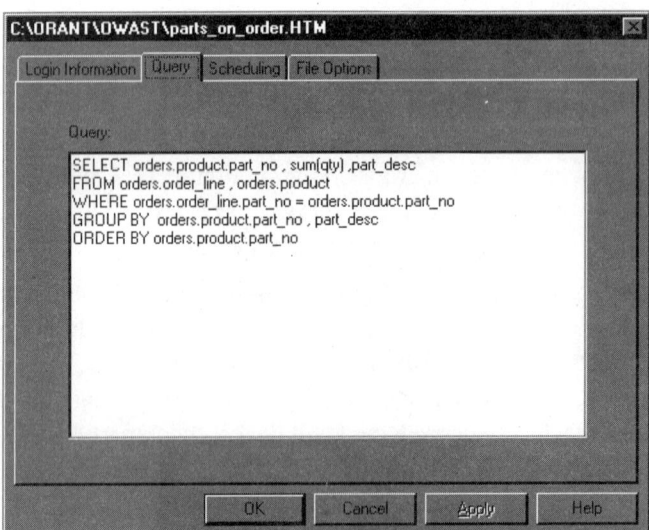

One of the major headaches for anyone responsible for managing a Web site is keeping the data accurate. How many times have you visited a Web site to see old information? This is an important issue, because one has to balance the time spent updating the Web pages with the return to your business of spending your time performing this task, rather than another. Fortunately, the Oracle Web Publishing Assistant solves this problem by automatically updating the document with the latest information in the database.

One important point to remember is that the document created here is considered a static document. That is, the results of querying the database are actually stored in the document. Therefore, you see the state of the database as it was at the time the document was created. Depending on the type of information you are displaying this shouldn't be a problem.

The next screen, Figure 11.10, is where you specify how often the document should be updated, so you need never worry about this again. At the appropriate time, the Web Publishing Assistant queries the database and automatically updates the document with the latest information. The refresh interval can be anything from once a minute to once a month or at a specific time and date.

Figure 11.11 is an example of the screen where you specify the name of the Web document. By default it is called WEB.HTM, therefore you should change it to something appropriate. Since this is the name that is displayed on the main screen shown in Figure 11.12 which lists all the Web documents, it is best to choose a sensible name.

Figure 11.10 Schedule When Document Is Refreshed

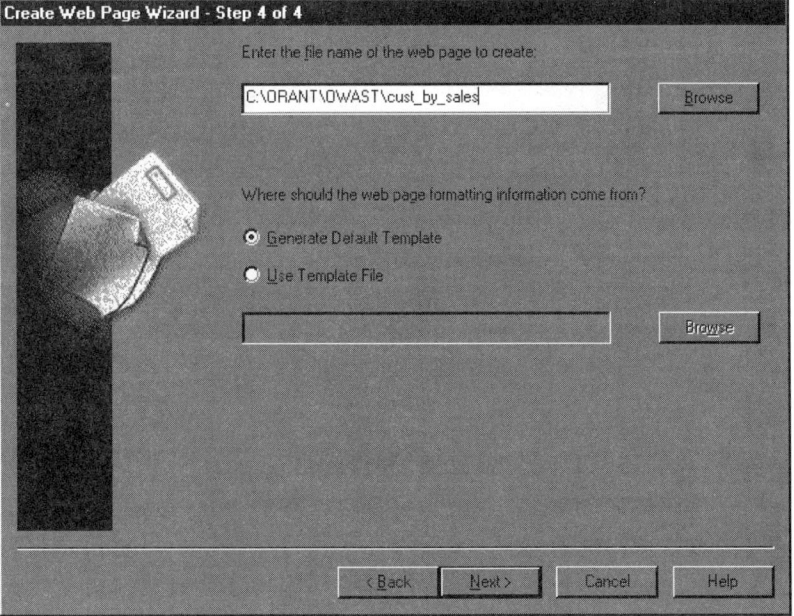

Figure 11.11 Location of the Web Document

The Web Assistant is extremely useful for creating documents quickly, but it does create something that is not very exciting and probably has a layout that you will hate. To overcome this problem, you can specify your own template HTML document into which the data is inserted. The attraction of using this feature is that it enables you to specify a page that may include company logos, graphics and anything else that you want to include on your Web site. It means that you can create a page that would look exactly like all the other pages on your corporate Web site.

In Figure 11.11 you will see two boxes, one which says *"Generate Default Template"* and another which says *"Use Template."* If you don't feel capable of creating your own document, then ask it to create the default template. This will create a file in a folder called *<document name>.htx*. This file contains all the HTML tags plus some special ones to retrieve the data from the Oracle database. Simply customize this template to your own requirements and then this will determine how your data looks.

Clicking on the *Finish* button, the Web page is created and by default it is located in ORACLE_HOME\OWAST along with its template. Every time the document is updated, the new version is placed here.

In Figure 11.12 we see the main screen from the Oracle Web Assistant which lists all of the documents that have been created. From here we can manage these documents, such as creating new ones, deleting ones that are not required and modifying existing ones.

Figure 11.12 Web Documents

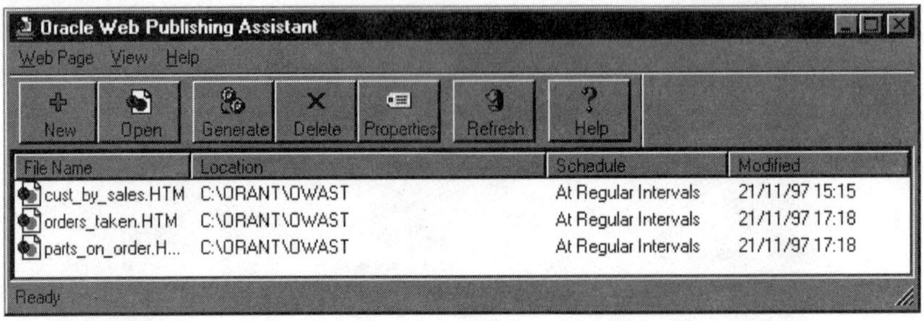

One cautionary note is that the date displayed in Figure 11.12 is the date the document was created or last modified. To see the date when the document was last refreshed, you will have to use the Windows NT Explorer tool on the folder to view this date.

If you double click on the document listed in Figure 11.12 or click on the *Open* icon, the document is displayed in your default browser. Clicking on the *Properties* icon, the attributes of the document are displayed, such as its refresh interval and SQL query statement. If you click on the *File Options* tab, Figure 11.13 appears.

Figure 11.13 Edit the Template

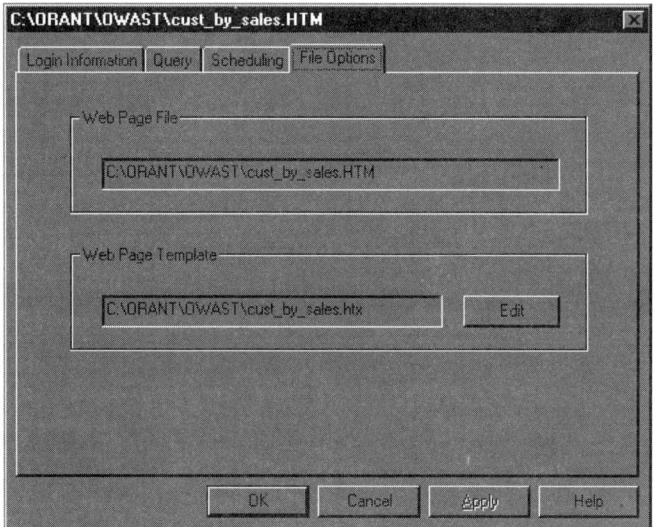

An extremely useful option is seen when you click on the *Edit* button; the contents of the template are displayed in an editor, which allows you to modify how the document is to appear. When you have finished changing it, save the file as usual, then click the *OK* button. When Figure 11.12 appears, click on the *Generate* icon, followed by the *Refresh* icon to create a document with the new format.

Hopefully, you will now agree that this tool is so easy to use that it will encourage you to Web-enable your database. If you are thinking that these static Web pages are unsuitable for your business, think again, because you will probably find that there are many pages that you can generate using this tool, such as a list of this week's special offers or static data that rarely changes, like a list of all your branches and their telephone numbers. There are probably more static documents in your Web system than you may first realize. Therefore, don't disregard this tool until you know how much interaction is required with the reader on your Web site. We will see in the next section how we can interact with our reader.

11.3.2   Oracle Web Server

In the previous section, we saw the format of our documents because our browser translated the HTML into its display format. However, this approach only works if you are viewing a static Web page on your local machine. If you know the address of anything on the Web, such as Oracle Corporation's Home Page at *www.oracle.com* and your computer is connected to the Internet, then you can retrieve that page. However, to see that page, a *Web server* must be present on the host machine to accept your request for information, find the appropriate document and return it to you. Referring to Figure 11.2, we saw that a request from the browser is passed to the Web server which then gets the information from the database.

Figure 11.14 Web Server Administration

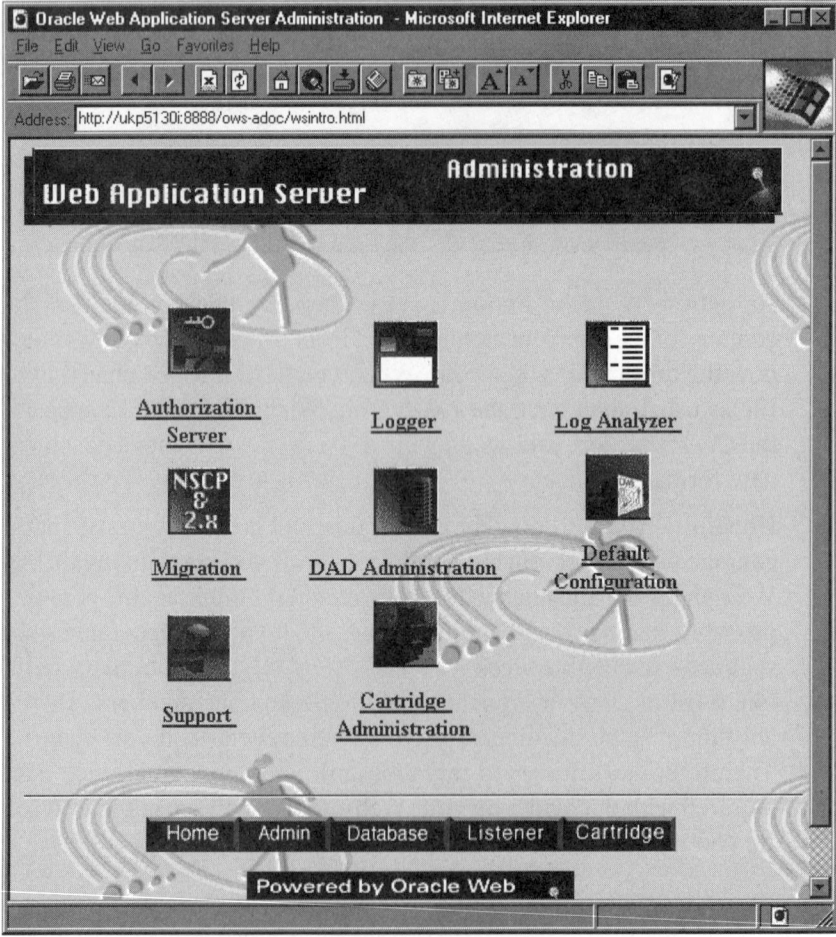

There are quite a few Web servers available on the market. Without one, your site is not visible to the Internet or Intranet, but when used with a Web agent or Web cartridge, the power of your database can be really unleashed. Here we will describe how to use the Oracle Web Application Server, but the techniques described here will work equally well with other Web servers.

Before a database can be accessed by a Web browser some preparatory work is required. First check that your Web site has been correctly configured and will display ordinary Web pages. Setting up a Web server is not too difficult. They come with easy-to-follow instructions and some, like the Oracle Server, use a dialog via the browser to configure themselves as shown in Figure 11.14.

Figure 11.15 Create a DAD

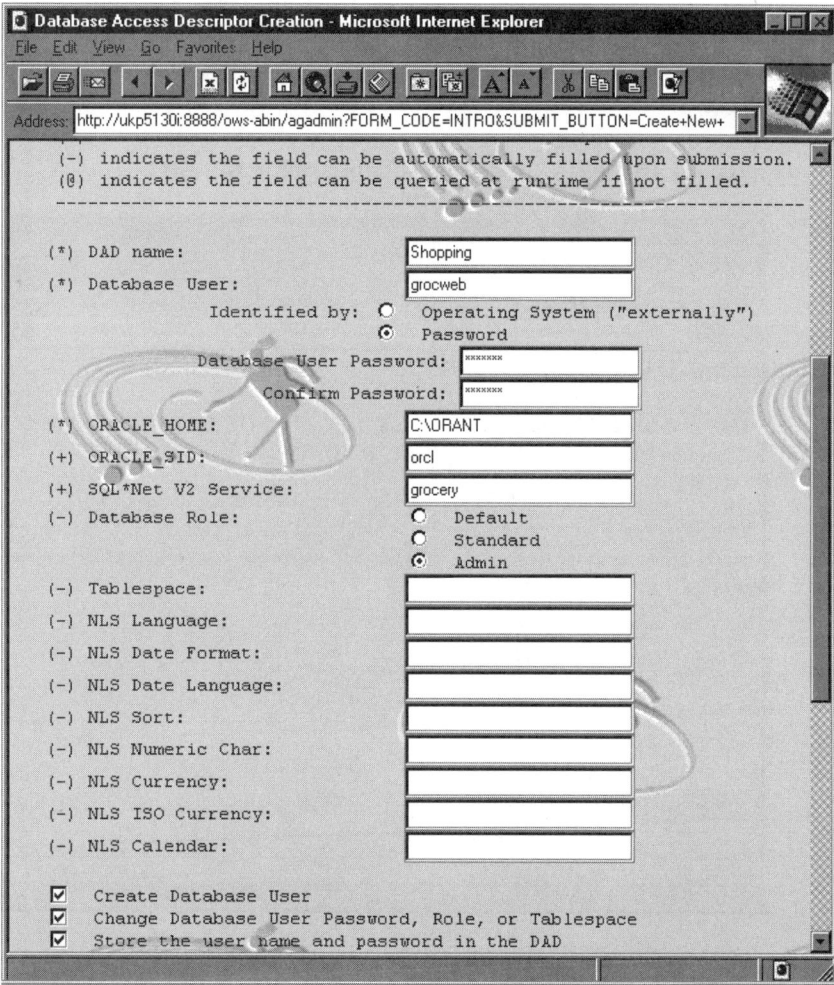

To access the database from the Web using the Oracle Web Server, a Database Connection Descriptor (DAD) must first be created. This is done by clicking on the *DAD Administration* icon in Figure 11.14. Then select *Create New DAD* and Figure 11.15 appears.

A DAD is created for every database that is to be accessed. Since you are accessing the database a username and password must be supplied and this procedure will automatically create the user in the database, if requested. Then advise where the database resides and its Oracle SID. One word of warning: the Oracle Web server needs to connect to the database using an SQL*Net V2 service name, rather than a Net8 service name.

At the bottom of the Create DAD screen is a section for remote databases which is shown in Figure 11.16. Currently an Oracle8 database is considered a remote database so this section must be completed. When all the information has been entered, submit the form by clicking on the *Submit New DAD* button.

Figure 11.16 Define a Remote Database for the DAD

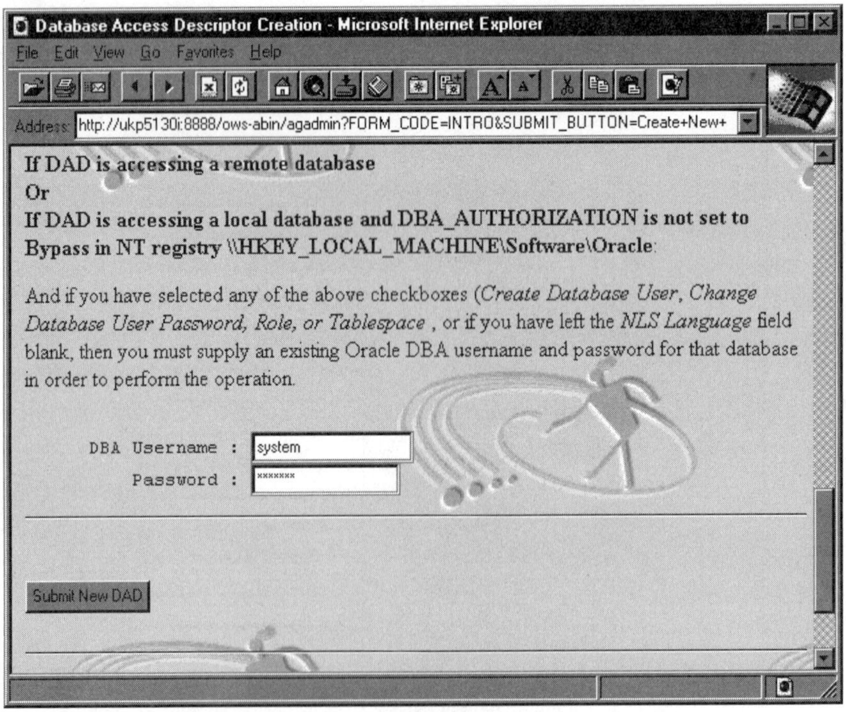

Hint: If the page is resubmitted, you will need to re-enter all the password information because it is not retained when the document is redisplayed.

Once the DAD has been created, the next step is configuring the PL/SQL cartridge to access the database. This is achieved by clicking on the *Cartridge Administration* icon in Figure 11.14 which displays the list of cartridges currently available, as illustrated in Figure 11.17.

Figure 11.17 Cartridge Administration

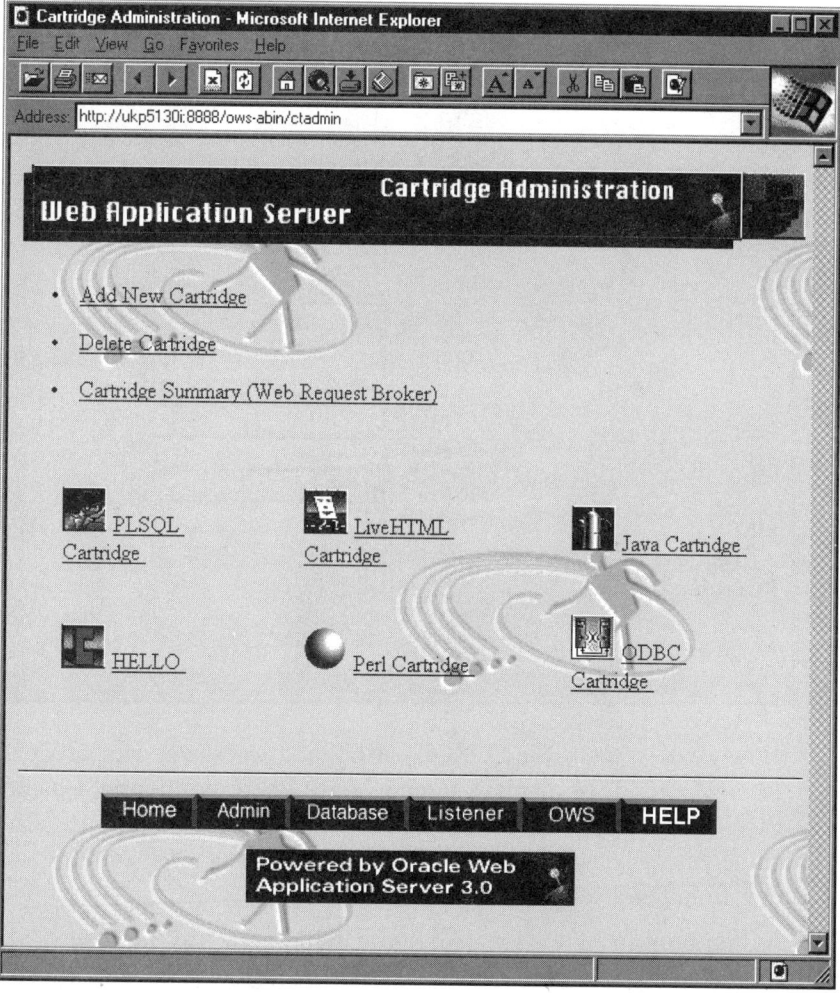

Figure 11.18 Set up the PL/SQL Cartridge

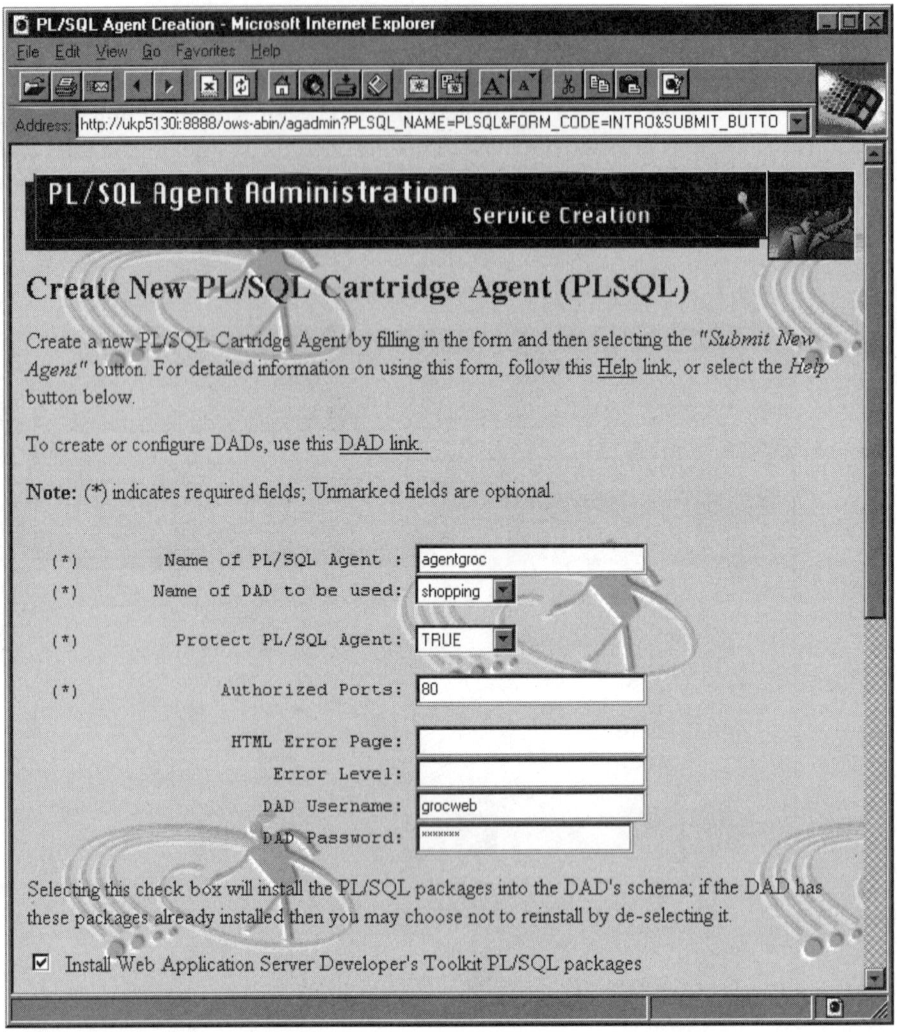

Now we must set up the PL/SQL cartridge to access our database. Clicking on *PL/SQL Cartridge* displays Figure 11.18 where we define a name for our PL/SQL agent and the database username and password to use. Choose this name wisely because it will be used as part of our URL to retrieve information from the database.

At the bottom of Figure 11.18 you will see a box marked *"Install Web Application Server Developer's Toolkit PL/SQL Packages,"* which must be clicked to install the developer's kit. It is the Web server developer's kit that

Figure 11.19 Progress of PL/SQL Catridge

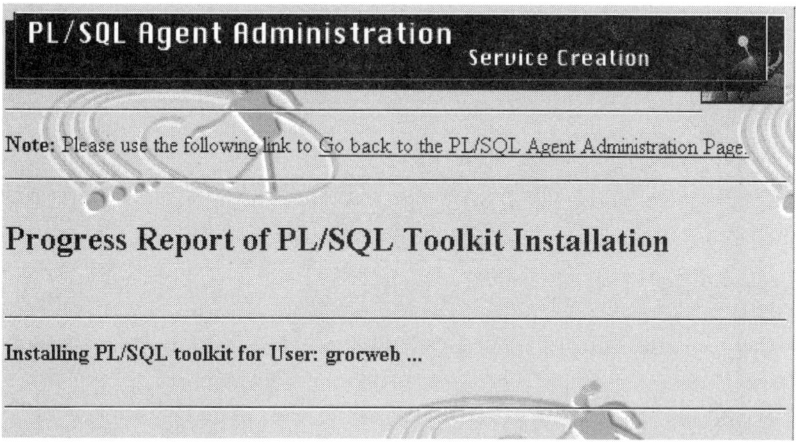

will allow you to write applications that access the database. It achieves this by creating a number of packages. Inside these packages are procedures and functions that will enable you to construct a procedure that will generate a document in HTML format which can be sent to a browser.

The installation of the procedures can take a few minutes so please be patient. It is easy to think that nothing is happening and be tempted to press the stop icon on the browser. Please don't do that. If the computer is close by then you may hear the disk drive working, alternatively start the NT Task Manager to check that the computer is working. None of this should be necessary because eventually the browser will return with either a Success or Failure message.

You can monitor the progress of the creation of the packages in the database by following the display shown in Figure 11.19. Each package will be listed and whether or not it was successfully installed in the database.

Once the PL/SQL cartridge has been configured there is a little more setup which must be done before we are ready to start writing our Web application. If you are curious as to the packages that were installed during the PL/SQL cartridge setup, start the *Schema Manager* and click on *Packages*. In Figure 11.21 we can see a package called HTF and HTP which are ones we will use to create our Web-based application.

Before we can write our application the Listener must be restarted to pick up the changes we have just made. This is not a difficult task to perform, when the PL/SQL catridge is setup, click on the *Listener* button shown in Figure 11.20 and Figure 11.22 appears.

Figure 11.20 Configuring the PL/SQL Cartridge

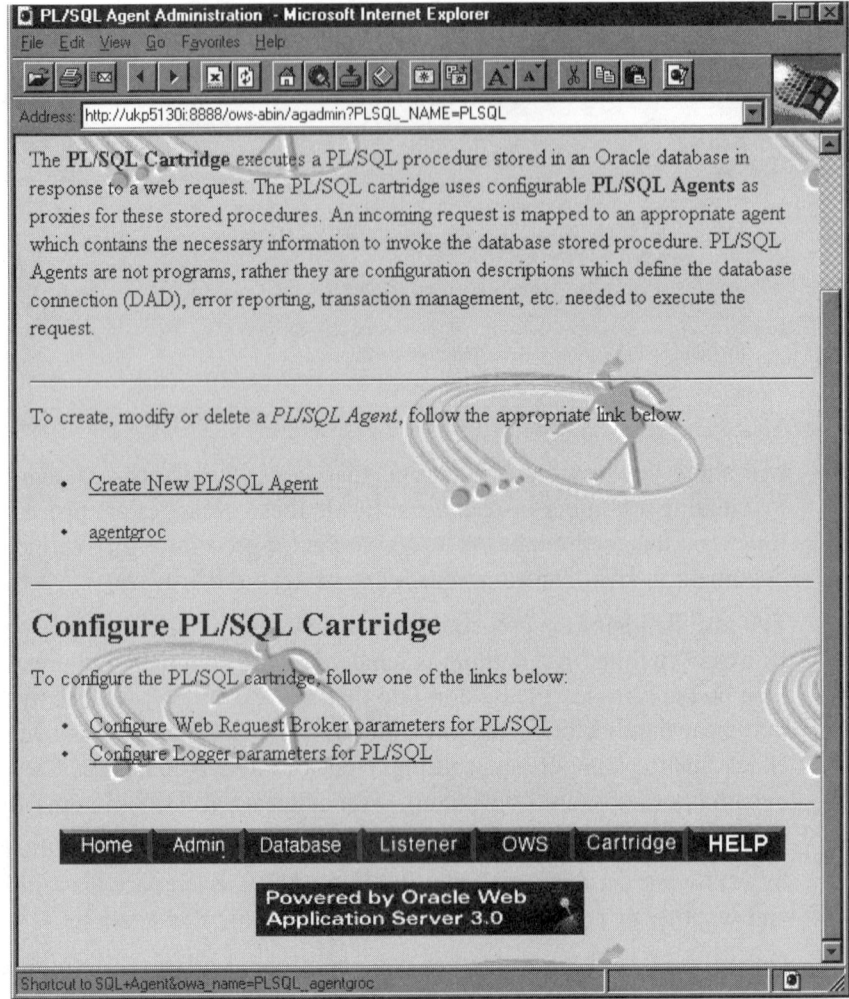

Figure 11.22 is typical of how a Web server is managed. A browser is used to configure and manage the server. The screens show you the current state of the component, and in Figure 11.22 we can see that the Listener called www is running. To stop the Listener, click on *Stop* and then to restart it click on *Start*. *To* change any of the parameters of the Listener click on *Configure*.

In Figure 11.20, at the bottom of the window there is an option called *Configure Web Request Broker parameters for PL/SQL*. This is where we can change the virtual path name that will be used by the browser to invoke the application.

Figure 11.21 Procedures in the Database

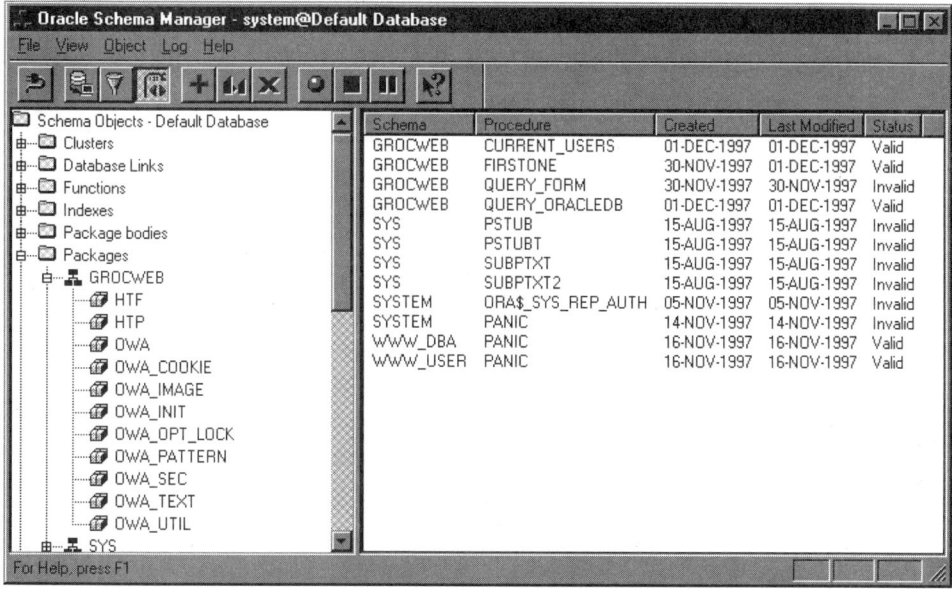

Figure 11.22 Restart the Web Listener

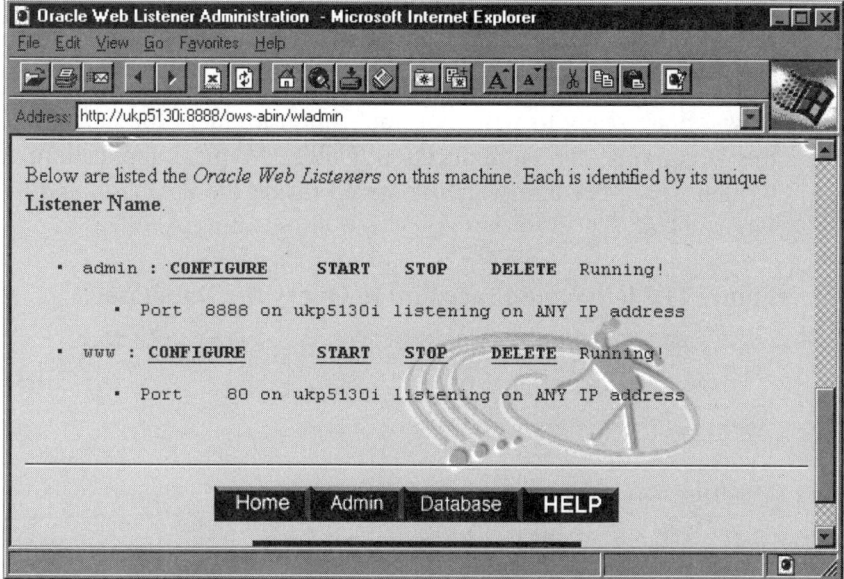

Figure 11.23 Virtual Path Names

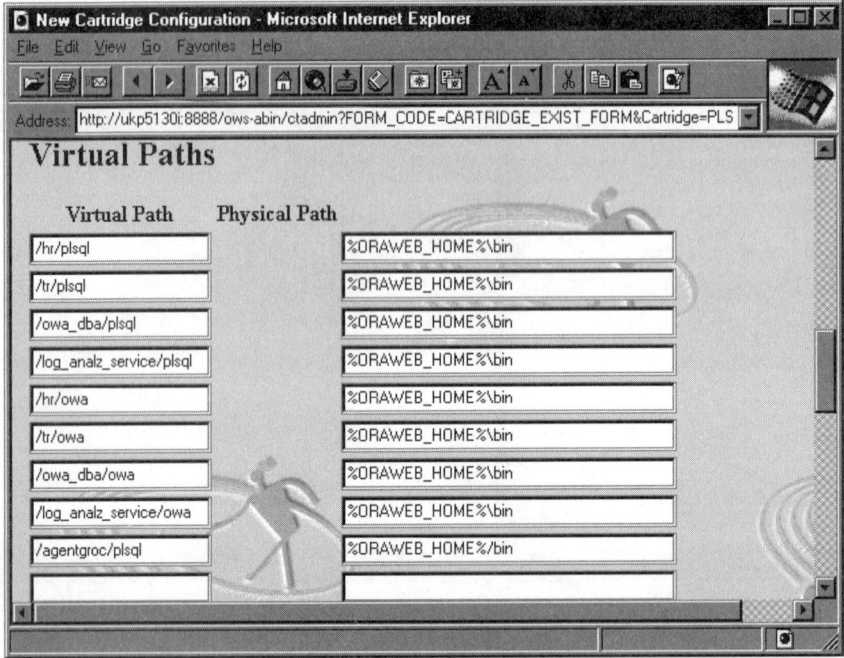

In Figure 11.23 the virtual path used is *plsql agent name/ plsql*, which in this example is *agentgroc/plsql*. If you don't want to use this URL then you can change it for something more suitable.

Now we are ready to write our application to query the database, however, this is not your normal application. Unlike a typical application, this one is written in a procedure which is stored inside the database, as illustrated in Figure 11.24.

Figure 11.24 Sample Procedure to Query the Database

```
CREATE OR REPLACE PROCEDURE query_oracledb
IS
  the_data boolean;
BEGIN
  htp.htmlOpen;
  htp.headOpen;
  htp.htitle('Query an Oracle Database');
  htp.headClose;
  htp.bodyopen('/ows-img/orhmbkgn.jpg',
      'text= "#000088"');
  htp.paragraph;
```

```
htp.print ('This is an extremely simple Web
       application which queries the database. All it
       does is read one of the tables and display some
       data. Now it is time to see what you can do.');
htp.paragraph;
the_data:= owa_util.tablePrint
  ('GROCERY.TIME','BORDER',OWA_UTIL.PRE_TABLE,
  'week - 199700 , year ' , ' ', ' Week, Year');
htp.br;
htp.mailto ('lhobbs@uk.oracle.com',
               'To send email to Lilian' );
htp.bodyclose;
htp.htmlClose;
END;
```

Figure 11.24 is an example of a very simple procedure and we can see how this looks in our Web browser in Figure 11.25. From your browser you call the stored procedure using:

computer name / plsql agent name/ plsql/ procedure name

which is *ukp5130i/agentgroc/plsql/query_oracledb.*

If we had changed the virtual path in Figure 11.23, then we could have replaced */agentgroc/plsql* in the URL with something more suitable like *ordersys.*

Figure 11.25 Query an Oracle Database from the Web

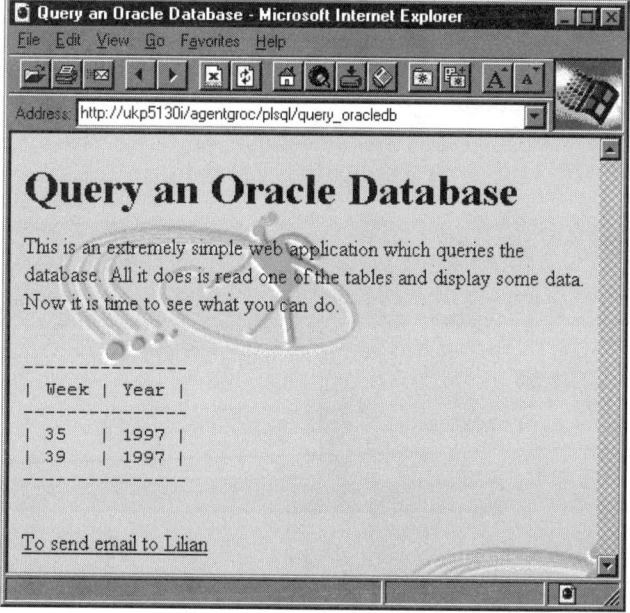

You can now see why it is necessary to have an understanding of HTML. Our procedure in Figure 11.24 looks very similar to the HTML we have written previously in this chapter. For example, to display the heading "Query the Oracle Database" we call *htp.htitle* and pass in the description as a parameter. To start a paragraph, *htp.paragraph* is called. The background image is displayed by passing its name as a parameter into *htp.bodyopen*.

This example actually retrieves information from the database and this can be achieved using various methods. Here we have chosen to use *owa_util.tableprint* where we pass in the table name and the columns we require. We have chosen this procedure because the results are displayed in a table, but it is not the only option.

Figure 11.25 shows a static Web page, but in the application development environment, from the browser, you can ask for input and the information supplied can be passed into the procedure as parameters, which are used to extract information from the database. This is how you build an application that is querying the database for specific information, such as, when did flight 106 leave London, or is part *y* in stock?

Your Web application will result in many procedures being created and we can see these in Schema Manager as illustrated in Figure 11.26, where we can see our procedure *query_oracledb* that is displayed in Figure 11.25.

Anyone who is considering building a Web application should read the documentation thoroughly to understand all the functions, procedures and utilities that are available to make Web development easy. If this approach doesn't appeal to you then Web-based applications can be built using tools like Oracle's Developer/2000.

Figure 11.26 Our Web Application Procedure

11.4 JAVA

Java is an object-oriented programming language which was developed by Sun Microsystems. Its introduction is having a significant impact on the World Wide Web.

The problem with HTML is that it creates a rather static document, some interaction is possible but it is rather limited. A small program can be written in Java, called a Java applet, and these applets are then embedded in a Web page.

When a Java applet is included on a Web page, when you attach to the Web page the Java progam is automatically transferred to your local computer and run there. There is no need to worry about viruses being inside the Java applet because the language has been designed to prevent a virus from infecting your system. Other advantages of using Java programs are that they can run on any computer that has a Java-enabled Web browser and whenever the Java program changes you automatically receive the latest version the next time you attach to the Web page.

When Java applets first started appearing on Web pages, they performed tasks such as animation (e.g., a cartoon character runs across your screen), enabled you to run a game or provided information via ticker-tape style displays; now Java applets enable you to purchase goods from the Internet. Java is helping to revolutionize the Web; therefore, it is recommended that the reader watches for Java developments.

Oracle provides two Java DataBase Connectivity (JDBC) drivers to enable Java programmers to access Oracle databases. One of the drivers is for developers who are writing client/server applications and the other is for Java applet writers. The latest versions of these drivers can be downloaded from Oracle's Web server at www.oracle.com.

11.5 SUMMARY

This is a very brief introduction to developing a Web application. Once again, an entire book could be devoted to this subject, but this has given you an appreciation of what is possible. Today many Web applications are written using the HTML equivalents in their procedures but in a few years they could all be Java based.

Usually a screen layout in an application is designed by an application programmer. The Web is changing that process and now many Web sites are designed by graphic artists who tell the Web developers how the screen should look and some even create the Web pages themselves. The Web is one of the most exciting areas in the IT industry today.

12   NT Clusters

This chapter was written by Ramu V. Sunkara, Director in Oracle System Products Division. He is responsible for Oracle Fail Safe Solutions.

8
Oracle

In this chapter we discuss Oracle Database solutions for the NT Clusters Market (Oracle Fail Safe and Oracle Parallel Server), how to use NT clusters and the type of applications where this would be appropriate. We will also review when it is appropriate to use the Oracle Parallel Server.

12.1   NT CLUSTERS AND ORACLE SOLUTIONS

- How much revenue is lost during downtime because you are unable to serve your customers?
- How many times have you rebooted your Windows NT systems (for example, during a software or hardware upgrade)?
- What happens to your business if the system fails and your database becomes inaccessible?
- Can you add more nodes (machines) to solve your database scalability problems?

No enterprise can afford to risk downtime of their database systems. Oracle database solutions for NT Clusters, *Oracle Fail Safe* and *Oracle Parallel Server,* solve these problems by providing high availability and scalability for Oracle databases. *Oracle Fail Safe* is a highly available single instance database and *Oracle Parallel Server* is a highly available, scalable multi-instance database. Both of these solutions are available for Oracle7 release 7.3.3 onwards and for Oracle8.

Figure 12.1 positions Oracle Database solutions for the NT Clusters market. An Oracle Fail Safe Database offers high availability compared to a standalone Oracle Database. An Oracle Parallel Server Database offers high availability

Figure 12.1 Oracle Fail Safe Data Server and Oracle Parallel Data Server

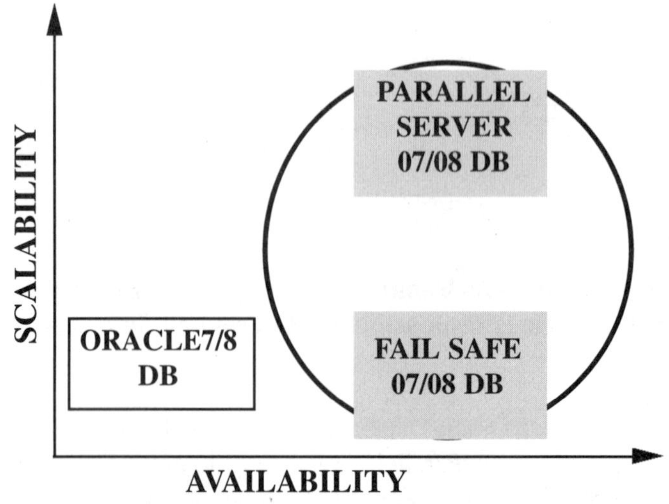

and scalability when compared to standalone and Oracle Fail Safe solutions. Oracle Fail Safe is layered on Microsoft Cluster Server (Shared Nothing Cluster technology) that is part of Windows NT 4.0 Enterprise Edition. Oracle Parallel Server is layered on Shared Disk Clustering Technology provided by Oracle Partners. The following gives a brief comparison of the cluster database solutions.

Oracle Fail Safe Data Server

Targets departmental and workgroup customers using Windows NT clusters for partitioned workloads and data.

Provides highly available single-instance databases.

Tuning and other management operations are the same as for a single-instance Oracle database.

Currently limited to two node clusters until more than two nodes are supported by Microsoft Cluster Server.

Oracle Parallel Data Server

Targets enterprise-level and corporate customers seeking highly-available and scalable Windows NT cluster solutions.

Provides highly available and scalable, multi-instance parallel databases.

Tuning and other management operations require multi-instance Oracle database and cluster-configuration knowledge.

Supports clusters with more than two nodes today provided by Oracle Parallel Server partners.

12.2 ORACLE FAIL SAFE

Oracle Fail Safe is a layered product on Microsoft Cluster Server (MSCS), which is a part of the Windows NT Enterprise Edition 4.0. Oracle Fail Safe Data Server allows a single node in the cluster to serve one or more Oracle databases at any given time. The database fails over to the other cluster node during planned outages (for example, during a software or hardware upgrade) and unplanned outages (for example, a node crashes or a software problem occurs). The database is accessible at all times except for the time it takes to fail over. Oracle Fail Safe Data Server provides five major features for standalone Oracle databases.

High Availability

Oracle Fail Safe ensures fast, automatic database failover during both planned and unplanned outages.

Ease of Use

Oracle Fail Safe Manager extends all Oracle Enterprise Manager operations to databases running in the Microsoft Cluster Server environment and includes wizards to automate complex tasks, extensive online help and a tutorial to get you started.

Active/Active Configuration

Each cluster node serves one or more independent workloads and databases to maximize the overall throughput of the cluster.

Robustness

Oracle Fail Safe ensures that the database fails over, recovers and is available following all kinds of outages. It automatically detects and corrects most database, network and cluster configuration problems that might cause failures in case of problems.

Virtual Server

The database is available at a fixed network address, regardless of which physical cluster node is hosting the database server instance.

12.2.1 Fail Safe Data Server Usage

Workgroup and departmental users who need high availability for their databases and their database workload can be accommodated by one cluster node. For such customers Oracle Fail Safe offers an easy to use solution that automatically handles the cluster configuration and management of single-instance Oracle databases.

It should be used in the following situations.

Planned Failover

Shutting down one cluster node at a time to perform a rolling upgrade of hardware or software.

Unplanned Failover

Quickly and automatically initiating failover in response to a software or hardware failure.

Static Load Balancing

Manually moving a database workload from a heavily used cluster node to a less heavily used one in the cluster.

(Refer to the section on Oracle Fail Safe Data Server Solutions for typical customer configurations.)

12.2.2   Fail Safe Data Server Components

Figure 12.2 shows the various software components for Oracle Fail Safe Data Server, in addition to the basic Oracle database instance. The MSCS cluster is serving an application server on one node and an Oracle Fail Safe database on the other.

Figure 12.2 Oracle Fail Safe Data Server Components

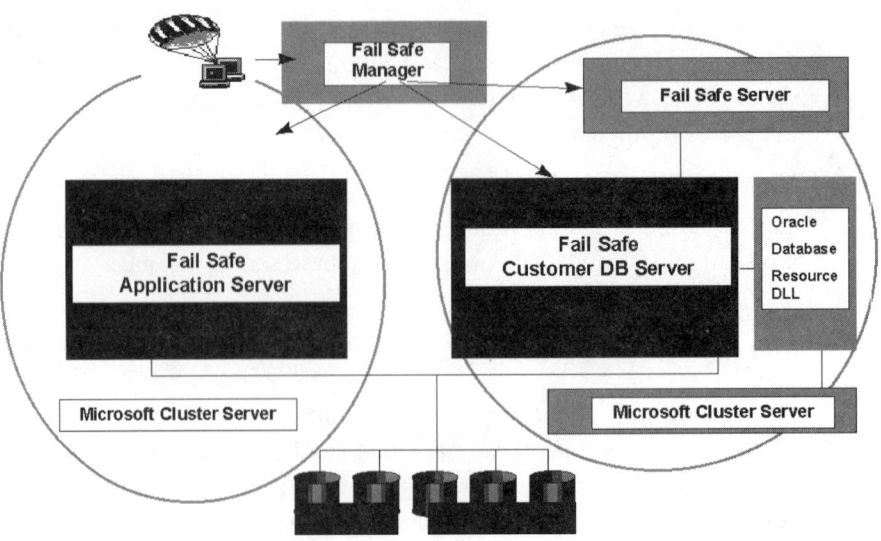

The components in Oracle Fail Safe Data Server are:

- Fail Safe Manager
- Fail Safe Server
- Oracle Resource DLL
- Oracle database instance

The *Fail Safe Server* runs on all the cluster nodes and is layered on Microsoft Cluster Server. The *Fail Safe Manager* is the console for the Fail Safe Server. The server does atomic replication of the Oracle database configuration, populates MSCS with the appropriate information based on the Oracle database resources and dependencies, works with MSCS to ensure that Oracle database instance fails over during all kinds of outages, optimizes the failover timings and performs the management operations.

The *Oracle Resource DLL* is used by MSCS and by Oracle Fail Safe Server to start, stop, and monitor the Oracle database. Oracle Fail Safe Manager automates the configuration and management of Oracle databases on Windows NT clusters from within the Oracle Enterprise Manager Console. It offers wizards, dialog boxes, and property sheets to configure Oracle Fail Safe Data databases and define conditions for failover and failback.

12.2.3   Fail Safe Terminology

The following terms are used by Oracle Fail Safe Data Server.

Fail Safe Group

The unit of failover is defined as a *Fail Safe Group*. Minimally a Fail Safe group includes a virtual server (see below), network name and IP address by which clients access the service provided by the Fail Safe group. Each Fail Safe group runs on only one cluster node at any given time. If the cluster node hosting the Fail Safe group fails, another cluster node hosts the Fail Safe group based on the failover policies for that group. Each Fail Safe group is populated with the appropriate resources based on the service the group is offering to its clients. For example, if a Fail Safe group has a database, all the clients access the database at the virtual server address for the Fail Safe group. The independent workloads on a cluster are partitioned into different Fail Safe groups.

Virtual Server

A node independent address is used by the clients to access the service provided by a Fail Safe group. Clients use the Virtual Server address regardless of the cluster node hosting the Fail Safe group. For example, the database clients accessing a Fail Safe database will always access the database as if it is residing at a given Virtual Network name all the time, irrespective of the cluster node hosting the database. For all practical purposes, on the network a Virtual server looks like a physical network node for clients outside the cluster. In Oracle Enterprise Manager, all Virtual Servers are listed as nodes. The Fail Safe Server and MSCS ensure that all the software components are working together to make certain the Virtual Server feature works correctly.

Fail Safe Database

An Oracle database that is part of a Fail Safe group is called Fail Safe Database. Clients access the Fail Safe Database at the Virtual Server address for the Fail Safe group.

Microsoft Cluster Server (MSCS)

The MSCS environment currently is a "shared nothing" NT cluster environment. That is, each cluster node serves independent workloads and has exclusive access to the disks and other resources used by the application it serves. In a typical two-node NT cluster, each node has a private system disk, is attached to a shared storage interconnect (usually SCSI or fiber channel) between the nodes to which Microsoft NTFS formatted disks are attached and maintains one or more network connections between each cluster node. For each application (e.g., a database server instance) running on the cluster, one node is designated as the preferred node and the other as the backup node. During an outage, the applications and resources "owned" by the failed node are automatically reassigned to the backup node. Because both systems perform useful work (an active/active configuration), this is a major advantage over "standby" availability solutions in which resources on the backup node wait idly to pick up work if the preferred node fails.

12.2.4   Creating a Fail Safe Database

1. Create the standalone Oracle database on any cluster node by placing all the data, log and control files on the clusters disks. Placing the database initialization file on the cluster disk is optional.

2. Create a Fail Safe group using the Fail Safe Manager giving a Virtual Server (Network Name and IP Address) information that would be used by the database clients.

3. Add the standalone Oracle database to the Fail Safe group using Fail Safe Manager. Drag the standalone Oracle database into the Fail Safe group to invoke the Add Database to Group wizard. Answer the questions posed by the wizard.

After the above three steps, the Fail Safe servers on the cluster do the cluster-wide configuration replication of the database. Fail Safe server queries the database to Figure out the disks used for the database files, populates them in the Fail Safe group and uses the Virtual server information to set up Network services (TNS Listener, Agent, etc.). After the configuration is replicated on each cluster node, it confirms that the Fail Safe Database works correctly on all the cluster nodes. The Fail Safe server is fully integrated with Microsoft Cluster Server cluster and is registered as a Windows NT service on all cluster nodes. The Fail Safe server optimizes the failover timings for the database based on the database initialization parameter by limiting the amount of instance recovery time.

12.2.5   Planned Failover

During a planned failover, the Fail Safe server works with the MSCS to efficiently move the database from one node to the other. The specific sequence of events is described below.

Failover Event Sequence for Planned Failover

1. Oracle Fail Safe server initiates a checkpoint and later shuts down the database server.

2. Oracle Fail Safe server notifies the Microsoft Cluster Server software to move the Fail Safe group physical resources to the second cluster node.

3. Microsoft Cluster Server starts the Oracle database instance using the Oracle Resource DLL and other required resources on the second cluster node.

4. Client applications then reconnect to the Oracle Fail Safe database at the same Fail Safe group network name.

12.2.6   Unplanned Failover

An unplanned failover follows a similar sequence. Typical database failover policies usually specify that one or more attempts to restart the database should be made before initiating a failover. Therefore, in some cases, a failure may simply result in automatically restarting the database, rather than in initiating a complete failover.

Failover Event Sequence for Unplanned Failover

1. Microsoft Cluster Server software detects a failure.
2. User-specified failover policy for the Fail Safe group is implemented.
3. If failover is initiated, Microsoft Cluster Server starts the Oracle database instance using the Oracle Resource DLL and other required resources on the second cluster node.
4. Oracle instance performs database recovery.
5. Client applications then reconnect to the Oracle Fail Safe database at the same Fail Safe group network name (virtual server address).

12.2.7   Optimizing Failover Timings

The following factors determine the amount of time it takes to fail over a Fail Safe database:

- Database workload at the time of failover determines the instance recovery time
- Failover policies specified for the Fail Safe group and resources
- Amount of time it takes to reestablish connections post-failover
- Cluster hardware configuration and performance characteristics

Two features help optimize the time it takes for the database to failover.

- Oracle7 and Oracle8 data servers allow users to connect before the instance recovery is complete. Immediately after failover the database instance is up and the users login and begin work and continue while the database is doing recovery. Of course if the user's request runs into a row lock conflict with the recovery of the database, the users are blocked.
- Oracle8 offers an *incremental checkpointing* feature that improves the performance (duration and number of I/Os) of instance recovery, thereby providing higher availability of the database. Recovery performance is roughly proportional to the number of data buffers that were updated but not yet written to disk (dirty buffers) prior to the failure. The user has the

ability to influence the performance of instance recovery by setting an initialization parameter DB_BLOCK_MAX_DIRTY_TARGET. This parameter specifies an upper bound on the number of dirty buffers that can be present in the buffer cache of an instance at any moment in time. Thus, it is possible to influence recovery time for situations where the buffer cache is very large and/or where there are stringent requirements on the duration of instance recovery after failover.

To maintain the number of dirty buffers in the buffer cache below the specified value, the database writer (DBWR) has to perform more writes as the value of the parameter decreases. When the number of dirty buffers exceeds the specified value, DBWR writes out the buffers in "oldest dirty buffer first" order, thus ensuring that the checkpoint advances. On one hand, smaller values of this parameter impose higher overhead during normal processing because more buffers have to be written. On the other hand, the smaller the value of this parameter, the better the recovery performance, because fewer blocks need to be recovered. The default value of the parameter is all the buffers in the cache. Setting the parameter to "0" disables writing buffers for incremental checkpointing.

Fail Safe databases are optimized for high-availability during both planned and unplanned outages.

12.3   SYSTEM MANAGEMENT

Oracle Enterprise Manager has been enhanced to support the configuration and management of Oracle Fail Safe Database solutions. Oracle Fail Safe Manager is the application that is provided in the OEM console. On the cluster, the intelligent agent is made highly available by the Fail Safe Server. For each Fail Safe group there is one Fail Safe Intelligent agent serving the databases in that Fail Safe group. From the OEM console perspective, each Fail Safe group looks like a network node. Figure 12.3 shows the Enterprise Manager System Management console framework for a typical Fail Safe Cluster.

Figure 12.4 shows the Navigator window of the OEM console managing two Fail Safe Clusters: NTCLU-145 and NTCLU-150. A separate folder is provided for Fail Safe Clusters listing all the cluster aliases. The Fail Safe Manager gives more information regarding each of the Fail Safe Clusters. Each Fail Safe group (Virtual Server) looks likes a Network node. For example, in Figure 12.4, the network node NTCLU-148 maps to the Virtual Server address of the Fail Safe group hosting the "tpcc.world" database. The cluster nodes in the

Figure 12.3 System Management Components for Oracle Fail Safe

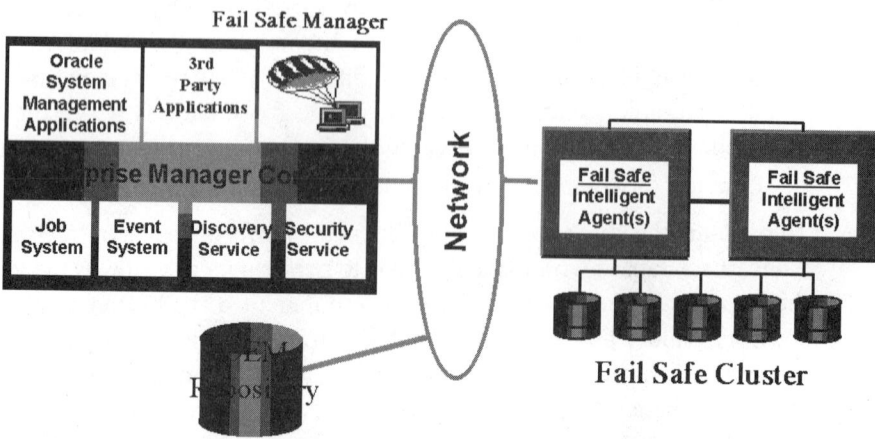

Figure 12.4 Oracle Enterprise Manager for Fail Safe Database Solutions

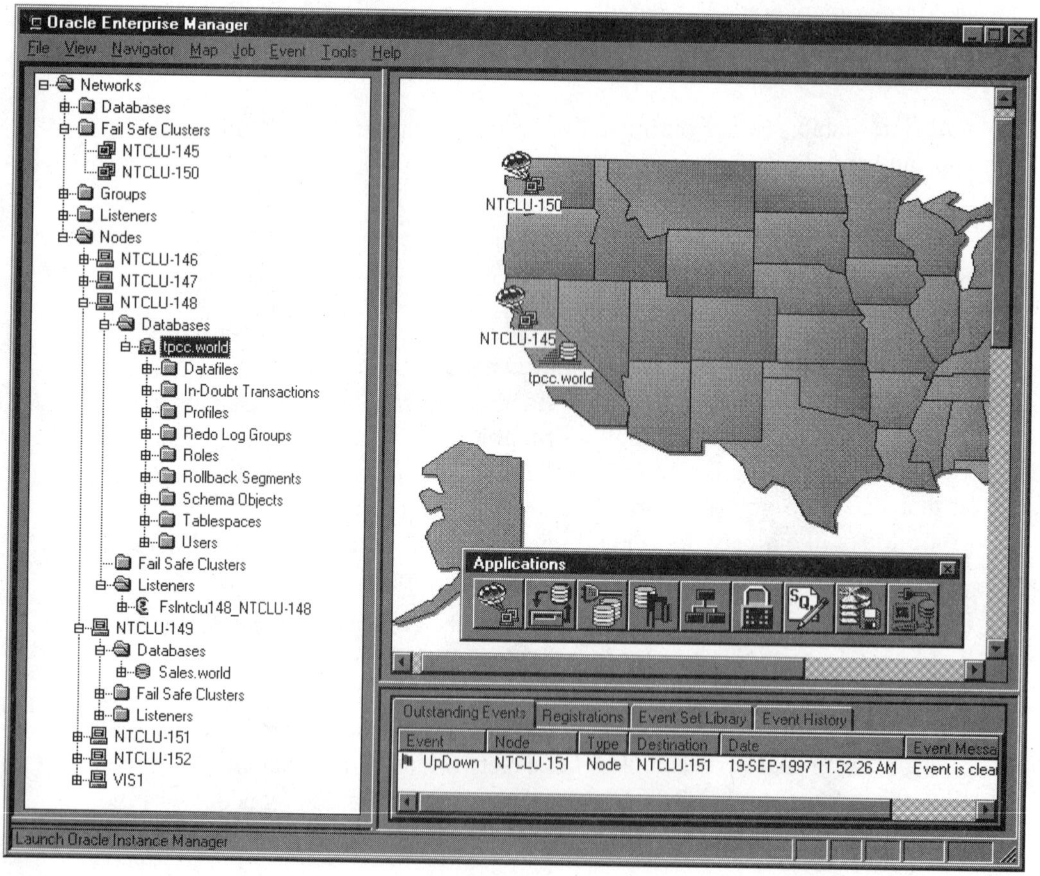

Fail Safe Cluster NTCLU-145 are NTCLU-146 and NTCLU-147. Each Fail Safe database (e.g., Tpcc.world) is displayed as a single instance database with all the standard information like the datafiles, in-doubt transactions, profiles, redo log groups, roles, rollback segments, schema objects, tablespaces and users.

12.3.1   Oracle Fail Safe Manager

Oracle Fail Safe Manager is the graphical user interface providing access to the Oracle Fail Safe server on the cluster. It allows configuration, managing, trouble shooting and load balancing of Oracle Fail Safe databases. The Oracle Fail Safe Manager tree view shown in Figure 12.5 shows ckuster nodes, Fail Safe groups, standalone databases and Fail Safe databases, and cluster disks that reside on the shared interconnect. NTCLU-145 is the cluster alias with two cluster nodes: NTCLU-146, NTCLU-147.

Figure 12.5 Oracle Fail Safe Manager

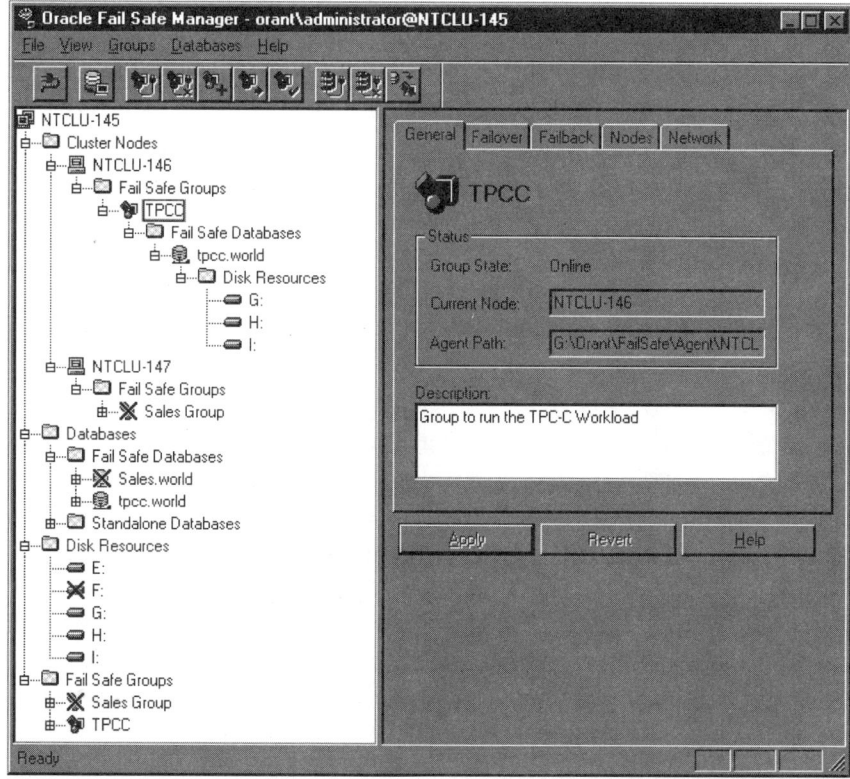

Figure 12.5 shows two Fail Safe groups: TPCC and Sales Group. Currently the TPCC Fail Safe group is being hosted by NTCLU-146 and the Sales Group is offline on NTCLU-147. The Virtual Server information for each of the Fail Safe groups is listed under the *Network* tab in the property pages on the right window.

The basic Oracle Fail Safe administrative tasks include:

- creating a Fail Safe group
- creating a Fail Safe Database
- specifying failover and failback policies for a Fail Safe database
- initiating a planned failover

Fortunately, Oracle Fail Safe Manager provides the wizards and dialog boxes to make performing these common system management operations easy.

Creating a Fail Safe Group

From the *Fail Safe Manager Groups* menu, click *Create Fail Safe Group* to open a wizard to help you create a Fail Safe group. A Fail Safe group is a collection of resources that fail over as a unit if the failover policy of any member resource triggers a group failover. An important step in the Create Fail Safe Group wizard is the one that helps you associate the virtual server network address with the group.

Creating a Fail Safe Database

Assuming a standalone Oracle database has been created on the cluster disks, you can use the tree view in Fail Safe Manager to drag the database into the appropriate Fail Safe group. When you do so, Oracle Fail Safe Manager opens a wizard. This Fail Safe database will always be accessible at the virtual server address for the Fail Safe group to which you have added it..

Moving Fail Safe Groups and Databases

Over time, you will probably want to move groups and databases in order to perform load balancing or routine maintenance such as software upgrades on the server nodes. To move a Fail Safe group from one node to another, simply drag the Fail Safe group icon that holds the database (for example, TPCC GROUP in Figure 12.5) and drop it onto the icon for the new node (for example, NTCLU-147). Oracle Fail Safe Server then ensures minimum interruption of service by performing an orderly shutdown and startup of each database in the Fail Safe group on the respective cluster nodes.

Operations such as configuring a Fail Safe database (adding a standalone database to a Fail Safe group) or moving a Fail Safe group to another node involve numerous steps that take place cluster-wide and can require several minutes to complete. For such operations, Oracle Fail Safe Manager displays the progress of the operation in a summary window similar to the one in Figure 12.6.

In Figure 12.6, the standalone database "tpcc" is configured to be a Fail Safe database by adding it to the Fail Safe group "TPCC." The standalone database configuration is replicated by the Fail Safe server on all the cluster nodes. Later the Fail Safe server confirms that the Fail Safe database can fail over. If the Fail Safe database cannot fail over for some reason (for example, one of the database disks is not a clustered disk), then the entire operation is rolled back by the Fail Safe servers on all cluster nodes.

Figure 12.6 Cluster-wide Configuration of a Fail Safe Database

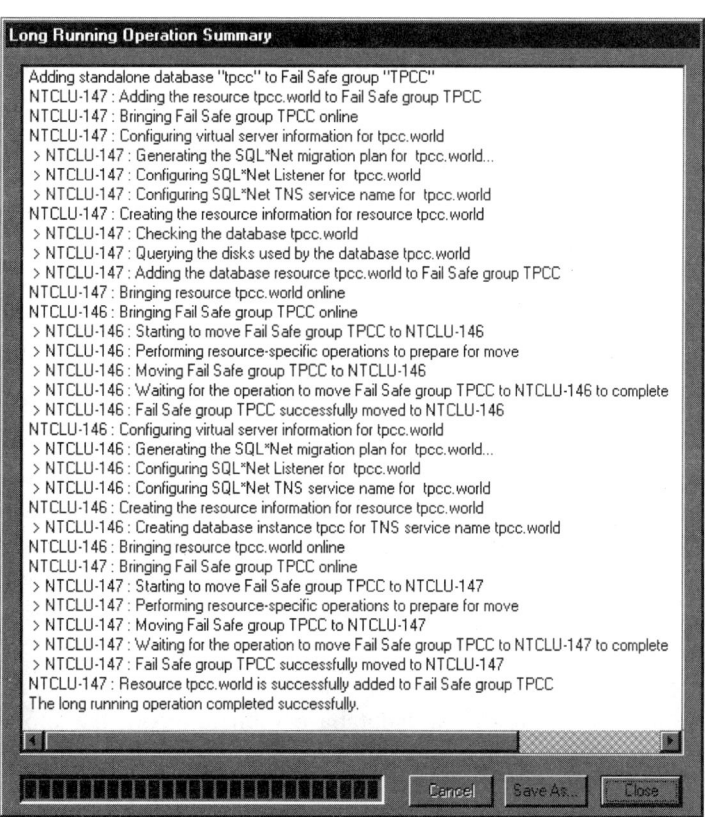

As your system becomes more complex and hardware and software configurations change, if the Fail Safe group does not failover or the clients are unable to access the service provided by the Fail Safe group, administrators can verify the configuration and failover of each Fail Safe group. Under normal operations, the verify commands rarely need to be used. However, when recovering from disasters or when migrating databases from standalone systems onto a cluster, they can save considerable time and will automatically take care of many steps that would otherwise need to be performed manually.

Starting and Stopping of Fail Safe Databases

Fail Safe databases startup and shutdown should be done using the Oracle Fail Safe Manager.

Job Scheduling, Performance Management and other DBA tasks

Because each Fail Safe group is represented as a network node in the Oracle Enterprise Manager Console, to submit a job for a Fail Safe group, you submit the job to the virtual server address (network node) of the Fail Safe group. The Oracle Intelligent agent that is part of the Fail Safe group processes all the jobs for the Fail Safe group.

12.4 DATABASE APPLICATIONS

For all the database applications, failover of a Fail Safe database looks like a network outage. Applications need to consider two issues:

1. How to reestablish the connection to the database
2. How to reestablish the state of the application after the failover occurs.

The extent to which applications handle the above two issues depends on error-handling logic in the application software when they lose the connection to the Oracle Fail Safe Data server. For example, SAP R/3 Release 3.1H reestablishes the connection to the database, and to a large extent, reestablishes the state of the application prior to failover. This make the failover transparent to the application end-users as show in Figure 7. After the initial results for a query are returned (step #1), the application software reconnects if it encounters errors (step #2), replays the query, and returns the rest of the data tuples to the client (step #3). How errors are handled (performing steps 1, 2, and 3) depends on the sophistication of the database applications. If the application software does not handle the errors appropriately, the client applications have to reconnect manually to the Fail Safe database.

8

Oracle

Oracle8 offers a new OCI feature called "*Transparent Application Failover for High Availability*." After a failover, this feature first reestablishes the connection to the database and also partially restores the state of the OCI application.

Upon failover, OCI libraries automatically reconnect (steps #2, #3) and resume work without having to manually reconnect. The client is connected to the virtual server for the Fail Safe database running on one of the nodes after failover. as shown in Figure 12.7.

Figure 12.7 Autoreconnect after Failover

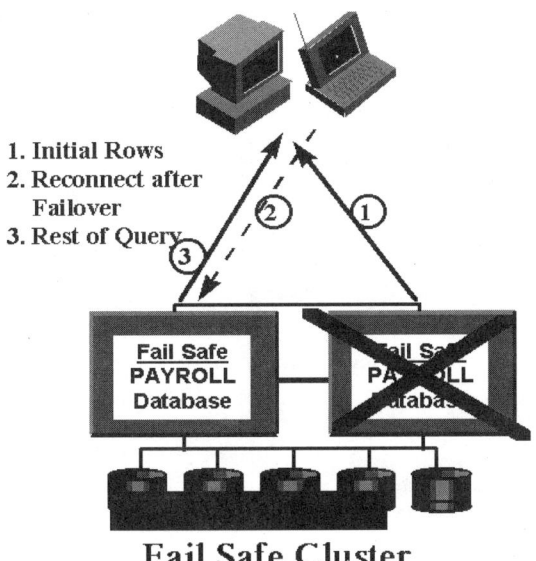

1. **Initial Rows**
2. **Reconnect after Failover**
3. **Rest of Query**

Fail Safe Cluster

Following the failover of the PAYROLL Fail Safe database to the other node, the OCI library in the client application reconnects to the same virtual server and replays the query that was in flight at the time of failover. A query running at the time of the failure is automatically restarted after reconnect based on the state of the query. Any update activity occurring at the time of the failure will be aborted and rolled back automatically, the enduser of the OCI application will receive an abort message, but will be able to reissue the update and have it run after being automatically reconnected. The new session after the failover has all the properties of the previous session.

12.5   FAIL SAFE SOLUTIONS

Sites are deploying Oracle Fail Safe in a number of configurations based on the high-availability problem they are solving. Three Fail Safe customer configurations are described below.

Partitioned Workload

Figure 12.8 illustrates a partitioned workload situation. The total workload on the cluster is partitioned into two Fail Safe groups. The Fail Safe group which has the Fail Safe Database "HR" is served by one node, and an associated Fail Safe group comprising the Human Resources Application Server is served on the second. The application server is processing the application client requests by accessing the data in the Fail Safe Database "HR."

Figure 12.8 Partitioned Workload Fail Safe Solution

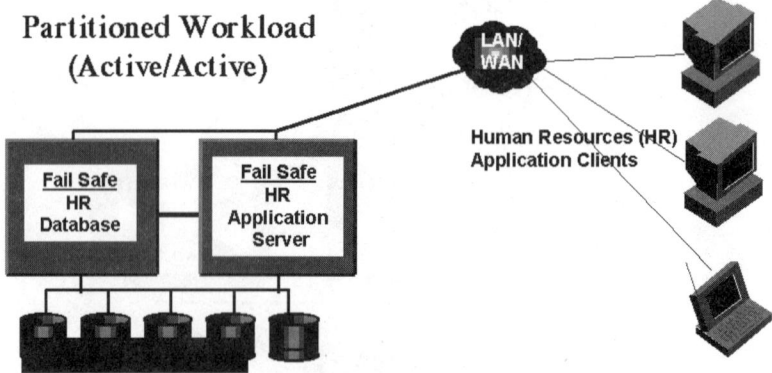

This configuration is used by most of the Enterprise Resource Planning software solutions like SAP, BAAN, PeopleSoft and Oracle Applications. Application clients always access the Application Server at the Virtual Server address associated with that Fail Safe group. The Application Server in turn accesses the Fail Safe database at the Virtual Server address of the Fail Safe group hosting the database. This configuration gives high availability for the database and the application server. The Fail Safe cluster will be providing less throughput and exhibiting slower response time when only one of the cluster nodes is serving both the application and database.

Partitioned Databases

Figure 12.9 illustrates a partitioned databases solution. In this configuration (like that for the partitioned workload), the workload on the cluster is split among two

Fail Safe groups. The Fail Safe group containing the Fail Safe database "Marketing"is served from one node and the Fail Safe group containing the Fail Safe Database "Sales" is served from the other. If one of the nodes goes down, the other node in the cluster will serve both of the Fail Safe databases.

Figure 12.9 Partitioned Databases Fail Safe Solution

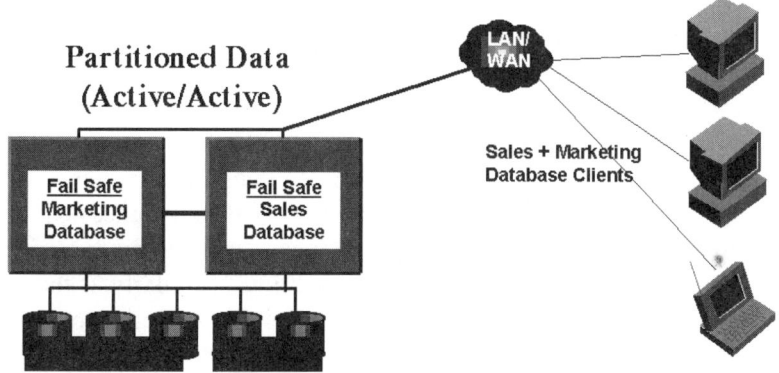

Partitioned Data
(Active/Active)

Fail Safe Cluster

Standby Database

Figure 12.10 illustrates a standby database solution. There is only one Fail Safe group on the cluster and it contains the Fail Safe database "Corporate". The other cluster node is passive; it is used as a standby for the Fail Safe database "Corporate". If the node running the Fail Safe database "Corporate" is taken offline for software upgrades or because of an unplanned outage, then the standby server hosts the Fail Safe database "Corporate".

Figure 12.10 Standby Database Fail Safe Solution

Stand-by Solution
(Active/ Passive)

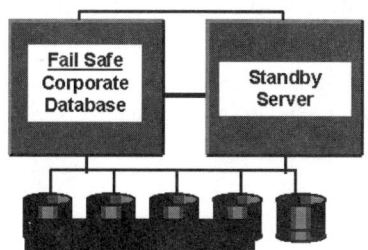

Fail Safe Cluster

The costs associated with customer downtime determine the optimal Oracle Fail Safe solution for any business situation. The cost of the overall solution must be balanced against the business costs of prolonged downtime. The goal is to eliminate as many single points of failure as possible and minimize the potential for downtime, all within a "reasonable" budget. Redundant network connections and RAID or mirrored disk storage systems are basic elements for most systems of this kind.

More subtle are tradeoffs concerning the size of the normal workload on each system. If both nodes of the cluster run at 100 percent capacity, then minimal resources are available to handle the load of the second system in the event of an outage, which means client systems will experience significantly slower response during and after a failover. Running both systems at slightly less than 50 percent capacity ensures that clients will experience no loss of response time after a failover. However, this means that the equivalent of an entire system remains idle under normal conditions. Similarly, if the customer has the resources to quickly repair or replace failed systems, then the temporary period during which one cluster node serves both workloads will be small. In the future, when Microsoft Cluster Server supports more than two nodes, the workload from a failed system can be spread over many nodes, and all nodes can safely operate at much closer to 100 percent capacity.

12.6   ORACLE PARALLEL SERVER

Oracle Parallel Server allows multiple cluster nodes to access the same database simultaneously. Users benefit from the increased transaction processing power and higher availability of multiple computer systems. Through the use of parallel cache management, Oracle Parallel Server takes advantage of high availability, high performance, and incremental growth made possible by loosely coupled systems. Parallel Database technology can make it possible to overcome the memory and CPU limitations of a particular node, enabling a single clustered configuration to support a much larger user base. The Oracle Parallel Server on Windows NT is designed to take full advantage of all the benefits offered by loosely coupled systems. In today's parallel database market, there are two basic architectural approaches: shared nothing and shared disk.

Shared Nothing Model

In a shared nothing database architecture, the database is divided into partitions. Each node has exclusive access to a single partition. On a failure, another node takes ownership of the partition. Informix XPS, IBM DB2/6000 PE, TANDEM Nonstop SQL and Terradata use this architecture. On one hand, if the data is partitioned well, a shared nothing environment might be very scalable. On the other hand, a shared nothing environment reduces the flexibility and increases the complexity of management. Furthermore, in shared nothing environment, if the query patterns do not match the partitioning schema then the performance deteriorates.

Shared Disk Model

A shared disk architecture used by Oracle Parallel Server allows all the nodes to access all the data in the database. There is logically and physically only one database which allows adding nodes and disks to increase system performance without having to reconfigure the database. Since every node has access to the entire database, there is communication overhead to maintain database consistency across nodes. The issue of strengths and weaknesses of a particular architecture is secondary to the most important issue, which is, *"How well does the database product serve the requirements of a given application?"*

OLTP Environments

In an OLTP environment, a shared disk environment allows for flexible load balancing. On one hand, because all the nodes have access to all the data, incoming connections and tasks can be evenly spread across nodes. On the other hand, global coherency control is required to maintain data consistency.

By contrast, in a shared nothing environment, coherency control is purely local, because each partition of data can only be accessed by one node. Load balancing is somewhat inflexible here because the data can only be accessed by the node directly attached to that data. If all the users access the same portion of the data, one node might be overloaded while the others remain idle. Also, if a transaction updates more than one partition, an expensive and operationally undesirable distributed commit protocol becomes necessary to ensure consistency across nodes. None of the currently available open shared nothing architectures support OLTP applications.

A shared disk architecture is currently the only choice to implement OTLP applications on clusters. Another important feature of the shared disk architecture is high availability. Because, in a shared disk environment, all the nodes have access to all the data, they possess an inherent fault tolerance. If one node fails, another node can simply take over. Also the workload can be flexibly adjusted, so that other nodes can participate in taking over the workload. This avoids one node becoming a performance bottleneck for the whole system.

Data Warehousing

In data warehousing, a shared disk database makes it possible to dynamically change the degree of CPU parallelism. This environment also allows the advantage of flexible load balancing. The data shipping used in this approach benefits from high interconnect bandwidth. In a shared nothing environment, functions are shipped to nodes for queries, processed locally, and only the results are shipped back to the coordinator. Therefore, this approach may require less interconnect bandwidth. On the other hand, queries on nonpartitioned keys involve all the nodes in the system. If one partition is significantly larger than the others it still can be worked on by only one node. Therefore, the response time for the query is limited by the processing time for the largest partition, while the other nodes cannot be used to speed up the process.

The best database architecture to suit your needs will depend on the applications you are going to run. If the type of queries is hard to predict, a shared disk architecture is certainly more flexible. If the type of queries to be run is fairly predictable, or if a lot is known in advance about what queries will be run, a well-partitioned shared nothing environment can be more scalable. The trend in parallel software points to the appearance of *hybrid* shared disk/shared nothing architectures. Where appropriate, OPS takes advantage of shared nothing optimizations in a shared disk configuration to offer the best of both worlds.

The following sections describe the various components of Oracle Parallel Server, how they work, system management and some key applications using Oracle Parallel Server.

12.6.1   Parallel Server Components

Figure 12.11 shows all the software components of Oracle Parallel Server for a 2-node Windows NT cluster. Each cluster node has an Oracle Instance that can access the shared database simultaneously. Each of the Parallel Server Instances has integrated Distributed Lock Manager (DLM) and uses the Parallel Server API for the underlying cluster services. Cluster Manager (CM), I/O

Figure 12.11 Oracle Parallel Server Components

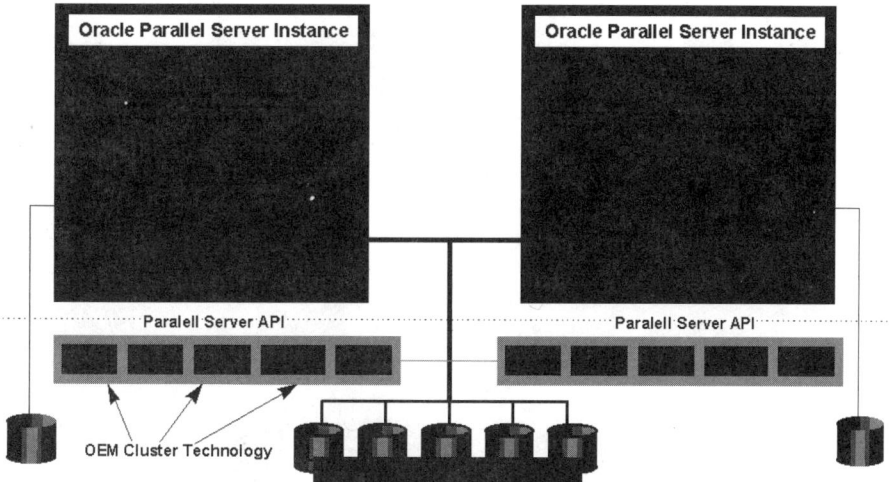

Services (IO), Interprocess Communication (IPC) and Performance and Management (P&M) and Start services (Start) together make up the clustering technology under the Parallel Server System. All the cluster components are part of the Operating System Dependent layer (OSD) and the Parallel Server could run on top of any set of OSD components that comply to the Parallel Server API, which will be described shortly.

The following sections briefly describe the Distributed Lock Manager, Parallel Cache Management, Transaction isolation and concurrency control, and what happens when a cluster node crashes.

The Integrated Distributed Lock Manager (DLM)

Oracle Parallel Server is a shared disk environment, an essential part of which is the Integrated Distributed Lock Manager (DLM) software, which is shown in Figure 12.12. DLM allows multiple resources to be shared by multiple nodes. The Integrated DLM synchronizes modifications made to the Oracle database files so that no changes are lost. The Oracle Parallel Server uses the Integrated DLM to synchronize disk block access between multiple nodes. Suppose node 1 in a cluster needs to modify block number "n" from the database file. At the same time, node 2 needs to update the same block "n" to complete a transaction. Without the Integrated DLM, nodes 1 and 2 could update the same block at the same time. In this case, only the changes written to the disk by the second node would be saved and the changes by the first node would be lost.

Figure 12.12 Distributed Lock Manager coordinates access to shared data

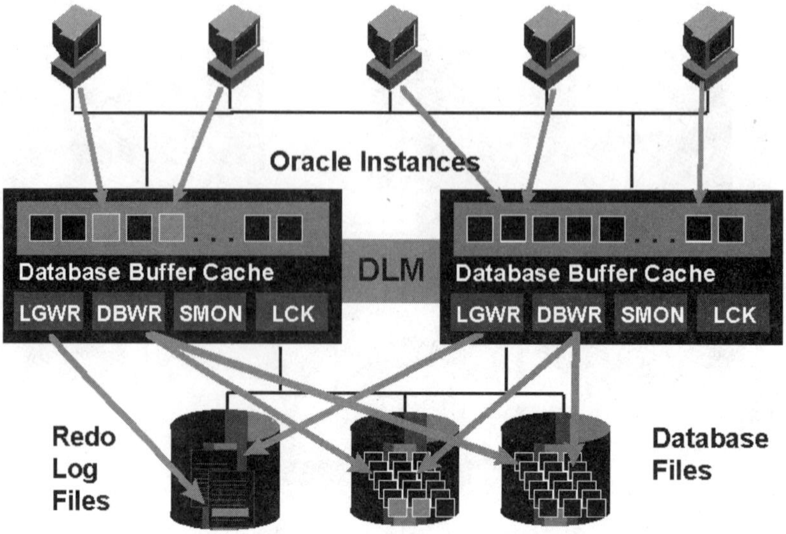

The Integrated DLM assures that only one instance has the right to update a block at any one time. This provides data integrity by assuring that all changes are saved in a consistent manner. The Integrated DLM itself uses redundant, fault tolerant and scalable algorithms in its implementation to ensure high scalability, high availability, high throughput and speedy internal recovery from node failures. Now let us look at the key features of the Integrated Distributed Lock Manager.

Distributed Architecture

To provide superior fault tolerance and enhanced runtime performance, the Integrated DLM maintains a lock database in memory, to keep track of database resources and locks held on those resources in varying modes. The lock database is distributed among all the instances.

Fault Tolerance

For highest availability, the Integrated Distributed Lock Manager provides uninterrupted service and maintains the integrity of the lock database in the event of multiple node or instance failures. The database is accessible almost continuously as long as there is at least one Oracle instance active on that parallel server database. This also enables instances to be started and stopped at any time, in any order.

Lock Mastering

This determines which Oracle Instance will manage all relevant information about a given resource and its locks. The master node is the node that maintains information about the locks on all nodes that are interested in that resource.

Deadlock Detection

The Integrated DLM handles deadlock detection, using either a distributed or centralized detection methodology. Distributed deadlock detection is more expensive, since all nodes must be scanned for deadlocks. In centralized detection, all lock requests go to one particular node. Some users' locks could then take longer to acquire if the user session does not happen to reside on the centralized deadlock node.

Lamport SCN Generation

Generates SCNs in parallel on all instances.

Parallel Cache Management

Oracle Parallel Server achieves high performance by using parallel cache management (PCM). Each node in a cluster has a local cache containing data that has been recently accessed by transactions running on that node. For example, in Figure 12.13, if instance 1 running on node 1 is updating block *n*, a copy of block *n* is in the local cache of node 1. Once instance 1 commits the transaction, it will still hold a DLM lock on block *n*, and that block will remain in the local cache of node 1 instead of being written to disk.. If node 2 needs access to data that is currently in node 1's buffer cache, node 2 will submit a request to the DLM. This is called a "ping." Node 1 will then write the needed blocks to disk, and only then will node 2 be notified by the DLM to read updated and consistent data from the disk. Parallel cache management ensures that each shared buffer cache in a node remains consistent with the shared buffer caches in other nodes with minimal use of the Integrated DLM.

The Oracle Parallel Server parallel cache management maximizes concurrent data access and minimizes I/O activity. One way the Oracle Parallel Server improves performance and reduces overhead is by not releasing the DLM locks until another instance on the cluster requests to have a DLM lock on the same block. In real-world applications, especially with disjointed sets of data, the probability of an instance reusing a block that it just accessed is much higher than that of another instance using the same block. Parallel cache management improves the speed and efficiency of Oracle Parallel Server.

Figure 12.13 Optimized parallel cache management

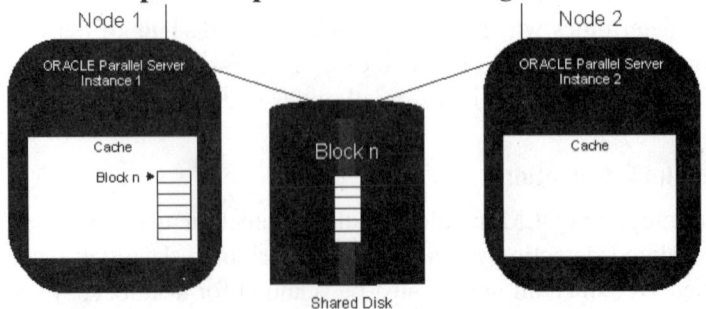

Transaction Isolation and Concurrency Control

Transaction isolation ensures that modifications to data made by one transaction are not visible to other transactions until modifications are committed. The mechanism used by database systems to ensure transaction isolation is called *concurrency control*. Concurrency control mechanisms lock the data being modified by a transaction to prevent access by other transactions. These locks are released when the transaction commits. Oracle Parallel Data Server uses internal locking mechanisms for concurrency control to provide maximum concurrent access to data for all transactions. Other databases for loosely coupled systems do not make a distinction between cache management and transaction isolation. They use an external lock manager for both. The result is that neither is done optimally; the lock manager can become overloaded, and a much larger number of I/O operations may be required.

The Oracle Parallel Data Server uses the highly efficient concurrency control technique to achieve higher performance. The Integrated DLM is used only for parallel cache management. The highly efficient internal row-level locking technique, described earlier, is used for concurrency control. This reduces the load on the Integrated DLM and thereby minimizes CPU and internode network overhead.

For example, consider two instances of the Oracle Parallel Server running on two Windows NT cluster nodes in the cluster shown in Figure 12.4. Suppose instance 1, running on node 1, is performing an update on row *i*. Instance 1 will hold one row lock that only locks row *i*, and one DLM lock that locks block *n* containing row *i*. Suppose instance 2, running on node 2, initiates an update to a row that is in block *n*. Instance 2 submits a request for block *n* to the DLM. Instance 1 will release the DLM lock on block *n* without having to wait for the first transaction to commit. Note that instance 1 still holds the row lock on row *i*. Now instance 2 can obtain the DLM lock on block *n*. If instance 2 needs to update a different row than row *i*, the update will be done right away. Only if instance 2 needs to update the same row *i* will it wait until instance 1 commits that transaction. This technique is extremely fast and efficient. The DLM lock on block *n* is released by Instance 1, and block *n* is written to disk as illustrated in Figure 12.15.

In Figure 12.16 instance 2 obtains a DLM lock on block *n*, and can obtain a row lock on row *j* different from row *i* without having to wait.

Figure 12.14 Instance 1 Updating Row *i* holds a DLM Lock on Block *n* and a Row Lock on Row *j*

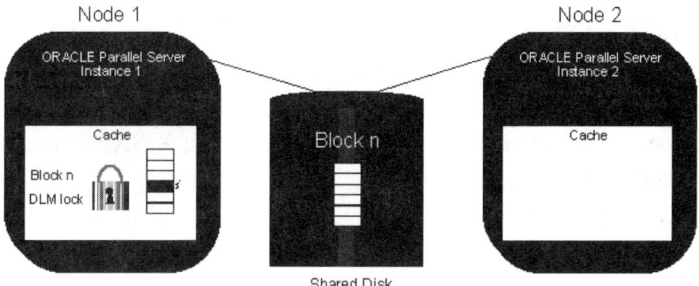

Figure 12.15 Instance 2 Requests to Update Block *n*

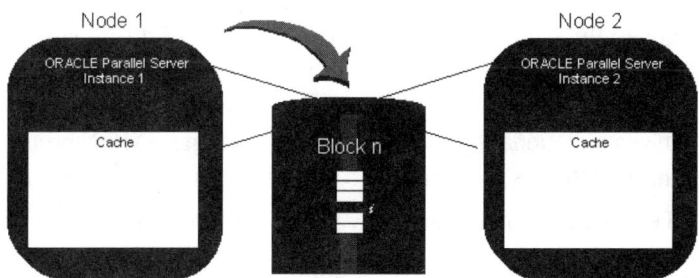

Figure 12.16 Instance 2 Reads Block *n* from Disk

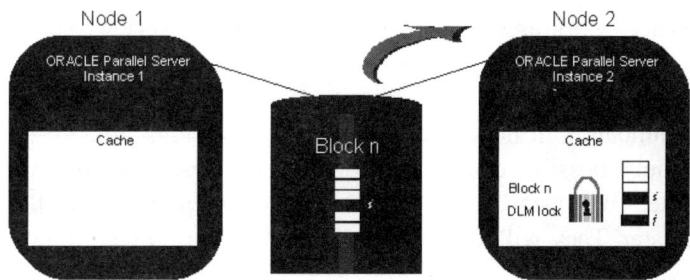

Node Failures and Joining the Cluster

If a node goes down (either from network failure, cluster interconnect failure, CPU failure, etc.) or an Oracle instance fails or the Windows NT operating system crashes, the surviving instances on other members of the cluster take over and perform instance recovery for the lost node. The following is the sequence of events during a node failure, shown in Figure 12.17.

- Node failure is detected by Cluster Manager after receiving no heartbeats from the dead node.
- Lock activity is suspended while Cluster Manager reconfigures the cluster.
- The distributed lock database is remastered by DLM. Each surviving instance releases locks owned by remote instances and local resources locks are resubmitted to DLM; resources in X/SX are marked as invalid. Lock activity is suspended.
- One of the surviving instances completes a stable list of failed instances and invalid resources. These remain blocked until completion of cache recovery. Surviving buffer caches are accessible but no IO or lock activity is permitted.
- Redo is applied one thread at a time, starting with the lowest successful thread checkpoint by one of the surviving instances. The database is generally available at the end of recovery for all threads. At end of each thread, the thread is checkpointed, closed and archiving is initiated. SMON of the instance doing instance recovery for the failed instances updates the data dictionary for distributed transactions. SMON processes then cycle through the system, partially recovering dead transactions in each rollback.
- TP manager completes recovery of indoubt transactions.

Oracle Parallel Server takeover is complete, and the clients connected to failed instances reconnect to the other surviving instances.

An instance failure on your Oracle Parallel Server will not affect other instances working with the same database. Recovery will be almost transparent to user applications. Any node can also be brought back online without affecting the OPS in any way. On most vendors' implementations, there is also built in redundancy in node internode communications links to provide protection against possible communications layer failures. When a new node is added, other OPS instances are informed of the intent of a new OPS node to join the cluster. They will then establish communication with the new OPS instance.

Figure 12.17 Steps in Parallel Data Server Recovery

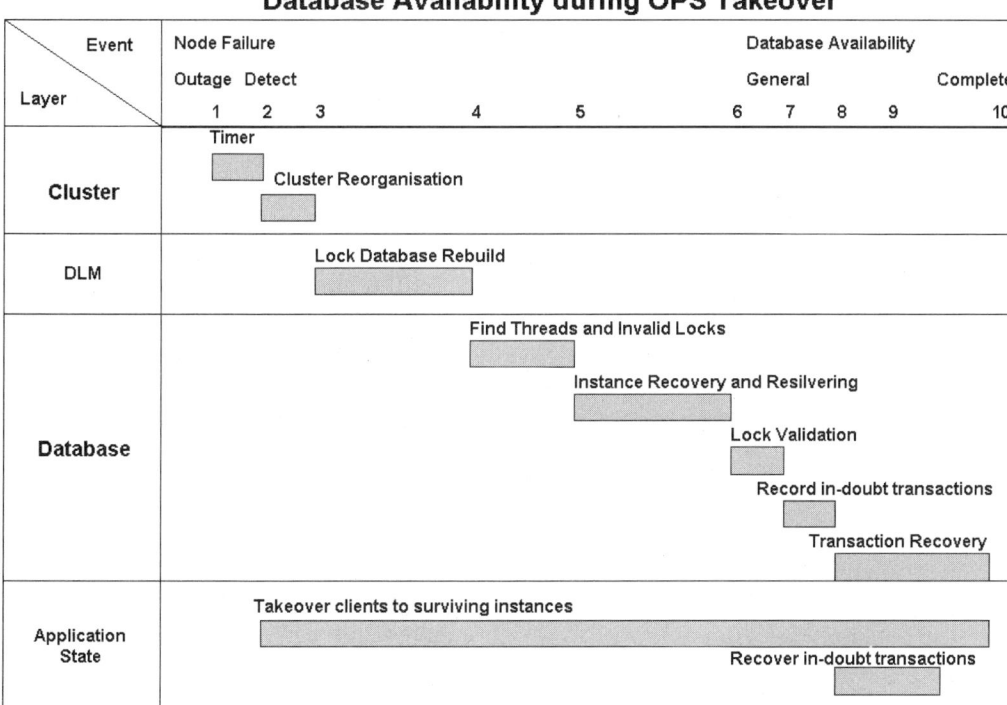

Database Availability during OPS Takeover

Event / Layer	Node Failure					Database Availability				
	Outage Detect					General			Complete	
	1	2	3	4	5	6	7	8	9	10

Cluster — Timer, Cluster Reorganisation

DLM — Lock Database Rebuild

Database — Find Threads and Invalid Locks, Instance Recovery and Resilvering, Lock Validation, Record in-doubt transactions, Transaction Recovery

Application State — Takeover clients to surviving instances, Recover in-doubt transactions

12.6.2 Shared Disk Cluster Technology

Oracle Parallel Server application programming interfaces (APIs) shown in Figure 12.11 define the requirements and interfaces for several Operating System Dependent (OSD) components for NT Systems, some of which are mandatory and some optional for Oracle Parallel Data Server. Oracle is working closely with all the major vendors to integrate and qualify OSD implementations. The list includes Compaq, Data General, DEC, SNI, HP, IBM, and NEC, and is growing. Many of these vendors also support Microsoft Cluster Server used by the Oracle Fail Safe Data Server.

The Operating System Dependent (OSD) layer consists of several software components distinct from the Oracle Parallel Server. These components provide key services required for a proper operation of the OPS options. Typically, these components are implemented as a set of separate but coordinated hardware and software modules supplied by VAR partners. In total, the OSD components provide what can be viewed as the Oracle Parallel Data Server interface to the cluster and its distributed services. In the Windows

NT clustering environment, all OSD modules work with Oracle Parallel Data Server through a well-defined set of APIs. Each required or optional OSD module interacts with the OPS runtime environment as a single DLL. The OSD layer's most important components are the Cluster Manager (CM), the Inter-Process Communication (IPC), and the IO (Input/Output) and Performance and Management (PM).

The Cluster Manager (CM)

In a clustered environment, it is essential that all active cluster nodes communicate and maintain a consistent agreement on the cluster membership set, even in the presence of multiple failures. The CM is a software component that manages the cluster resources, hardware entities such as network cards and disk drives, or logical items such as logical disk volumes and the Oracle database. The CM provides a common consistent view of cluster membership across the cluster. It runs on all nodes and monitors the topology of the cluster. On each node of the cluster, the CM module maintains information on cluster membership. It also sends periodic messages, called heartbeats, to its counterparts on the other systems of the cluster to detect system failures. It is responsible for defining the *potential* members of a cluster, and coordinating the common consistent view as to which members are active and which are not. The active subset of nodes is known as the *real* cluster – an OPS cluster is always a real cluster: no instance is allowed to operate on a nonactive member. The CM layer periodically queries all nodes for their current node membership. It is responsible for detecting changes in the state of active members, for diagnosing changes, coordinating a new common consistent state among remaining active nodes and notifying OPS of the actual changes in membership. It is critical that all OPS instances receive the same membership information; notification of node changes will thus cause relevant OPS recovery operations to be initiated. If any node is determined to be nonresponsive or otherwise not a properly functioning part of the system, the CM will take care of stopping the parallel server instance on that node.

On a node or instance failure, CM will automatically reconfigure the system to isolate the failed node and notify the DLM about the status change. The Integrated DLM will subsequently recover any of the locks from the failed node (a process called remastering of the locks). Oracle can then recover the database to a valid state, as shown in Figure 12.17 Any node can also be brought back on-line without affecting the OPS in any way. CM handles cluster membership and watches the health of other nodes on the cluster. It provides cluster membership interface support and drives the cluster membership state model for all Parallel Server nodes.

Inter-Process Communication (IPC)

This module defines the protocols and interfaces required for the OPS environment to transfer reliable messages between instances. Messages are the fundamental logical units of communication in this interface. The core IPC functionality is built around an asynchronous queued messaging model. This layer is designed to send/receive discrete messages as fast as the hardware allows. With an optimized communication layer, various services can be implemented above it. This is how Oracle's Integrated Distributed Lock Manager carries out all of its communications. Inter-Process Communication between nodes in a homogeneous cluster machine is an important issue for Oracle because of the increasing number of machines requiring processes to communicate without a common shared memory segment. IPC is becoming more and more critical from a performance standpoint, and numerous hardware vendors are optimizing their protocols for their next generation hardware. Here is where the cluster interconnect comes in. These interconnects are capable of transferring data directly to and from the application data buffers and eliminate the need for and overhead associated with traditional network stacks. Very high performance shared nothing clusters require a form of I/O shipping, where I/O requests are sent by the cluster communication service to the system physically hosting the disk drive. There are two kinds of Oracle OSD IPC Reference components: Connection based components such as Windows NT Named Pipes, Winsock 2.0 TCP/IP, and Datagram based components such as simple UDP and reliable UDP.

IPC component for Windows NT has been designed to make use of the latest low latency, high bandwidth cluster interconnects such as Tandem's ServerNet, the VIA Architecture (from Compaq, Intel and Microsoft) and Digital's Memory Channel.

Input/Output

The IO module provides the cluster with simultaneous access to shared devices from all OPS nodes to the cluster disk farm. This is needed for proper operation of the OPS environment. The ability of the underlying OS/Cluster implementation to support simultaneous disk sharing across all nodes that run coordinated OPS instances is vital in an OPS environment. Unlike failover based technologies like the Microsoft Cluster Server, all OPS instances are active and can operate on any database entity in the shared physical database simultaneously. It is the role of the *Distributed Lock Manager* component to coordinate the simultaneous access to shared databases in a way that maintains both consistency and data integrity. At a high level, the OPS shared IO model can be described as a distributed disk cache implemented across nodes that define the OPS cluster. The core of OPS can be viewed as a major client of the cache. Disk blocks from the shared devices are read into a particular node instance cache only after mediation by the Integrated DLM. Other node instances may read the same blocks into their caches and operate on them simultaneously. Updates to those blocks are carefully coordinated. In general all shared disk based IO operations are mediated by the Integrated DLM.

The IO OSD component also defines basic shared disk requirements and related IO *Fence-off* functionality. There are two kinds of cluster fence-off:

- *Implicit Fence-off* requires NT System level support to shut down a device. CM should be able to detect cluster instability and call NT system shutdown procedures to fence off IO. CM uses NT system calls hidden from OPS.

- The *Explicit Fence-off* mechanism suspends and resumes IO to the devices from a given node. This is used by the parallel server when the cluster is being reorganized by the CM.

The OPS environment utilizes normal WIN32 and NT IO calls, via the NT raw file system, to access shared devices. Furthermore, very high disk IO performance will be achieved by using high speed storage arrays which will be connected to each node in the cluster via fiber-channel links.

Performance and Management (PM)

The PM component helps Oracle tools access the performance data for OPS. It defines DLM lock statistics, dump and management interfaces.

Oracle Parallel Server Certification

The Oracle Parallel Server Certification Process is a process whereby Oracle assists VARs through final Parallel Server OSD's test/qualification. VAR Partners are companies providing technology and service, high speed inter-connects, clustering software, shared file systems, shared storage subsystems or integration and consulting services in the Windows NT clustering space. These partners will be using OSD modules (as defined in the Cluster Interface Specification) for OPS to enable OPS to run on their platforms. They may develop the OSDs themselves or license them from a technology provider, or use a combination of the two to arrive at a solution appropriate for their platform. These platforms will have to be certified by Oracle before Oracle supports OPS on the said platforms.

12.6.3   System Management

Oracle Parallel Server Management (OPSM) extends Oracle Enterprise Manager functionality to manage Oracle Parallel Server. The OPSM extensions to OEM consist of a set of applications which allows a DBA to:

- Proactively manage an Oracle Parallel Server located anywhere in the enterprise. This enables them to have more control over the system and significantly reduces downtime.

- Schedule jobs against the Oracle Parallel Server database and individual instances. This feature makes *lights out* management a reality.

- Monitor performance of the Oracle Parallel Server through charts and graphs. Drill-down operations can be performed on the key metrics to view performance statistics at an instance or an object level.

Figure 12.18   Parallel Server Management Architecture

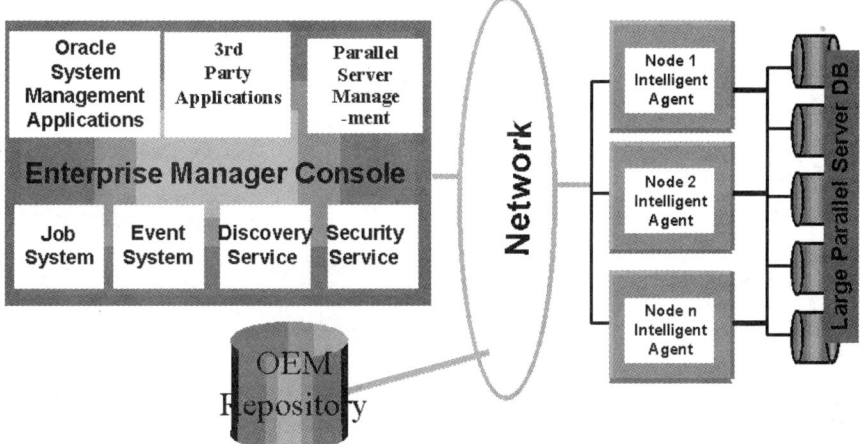

As shown in Figure 12.18, there is one Oracle Intelligent agent per node in the cluster. The Intelligent agent receives the request, schedules the request and then transmits the results back to the console. Every node which has an instance of the parallel database has an Intelligent agent running on it.

This section deals with the following Oracle Enterprise Manager Console functions that have Oracle Parallel Data Server support.:

- Parallel Data Server databases in the Navigator Window
- Parallel Data Server Start Up and Shut Down
- Performance Monitoring of Oracle Parallel Data Server

Figure 12.19   Oracle Enterprise Manager for Parallel Server Database

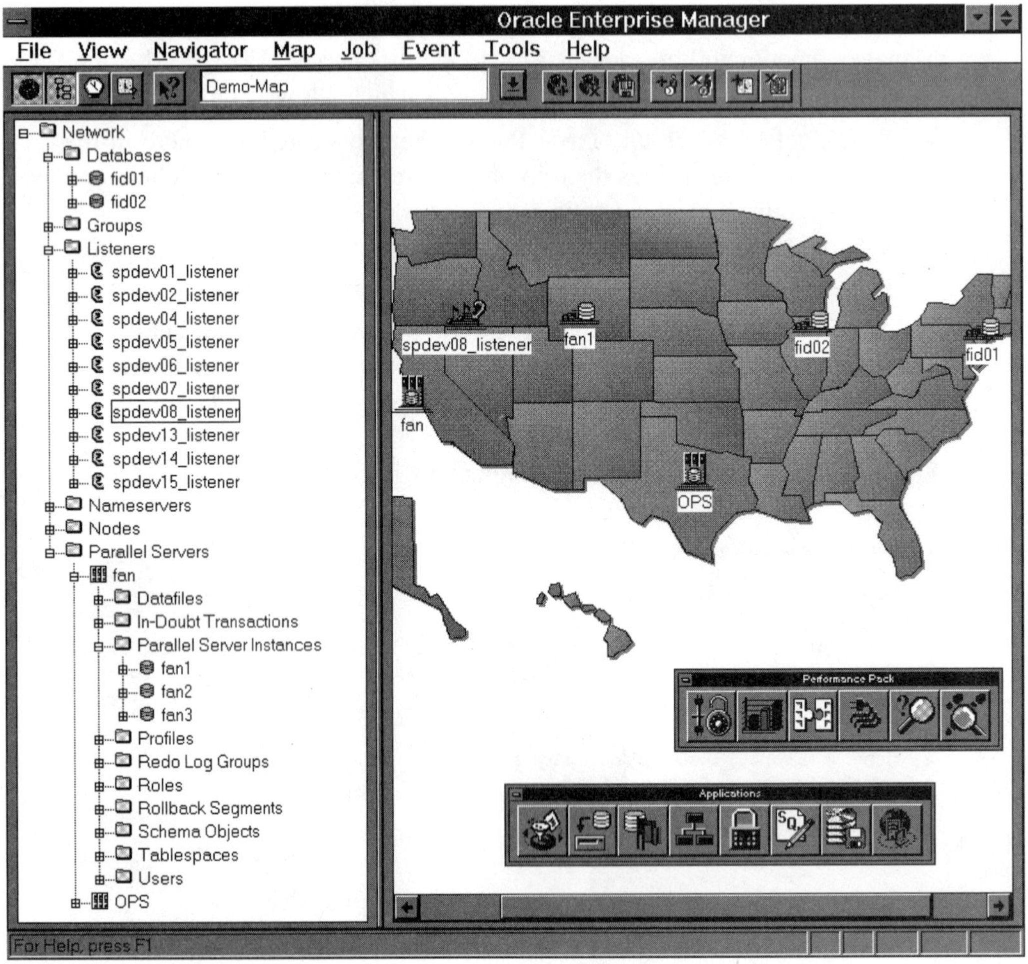

In the Navigator window of the OEM console, illustrated in Figure 12.19, a separate folder is provided for Oracle Parallel Data Server. This folder displays information about the datafiles, in-doubt transactions, profiles, redo log groups, roles, rollback segments, schema objects, tablespaces and users. This is the same information which is available for single-instance databases through the Navigator. In addition, the parallel server folder displays instance information. Further drill downs can be performed on the instance node to track instance-specific information.

Parallel Server Startup and Shutdown

Starting up the Oracle Cluster services, listeners and instances on every single node of the parallel server has traditionally been a time-consuming and tedious task. This task has now been vastly simplified by Oracle Parallel Server Management utilities which let the DBAs start and shut down the Oracle Parallel Data Server from a single node. In addition, these tasks can be performed from the OEM console as shown in Figure 12.20.

Figure 12.20 Parallel Server Management: Startup and Shutdown

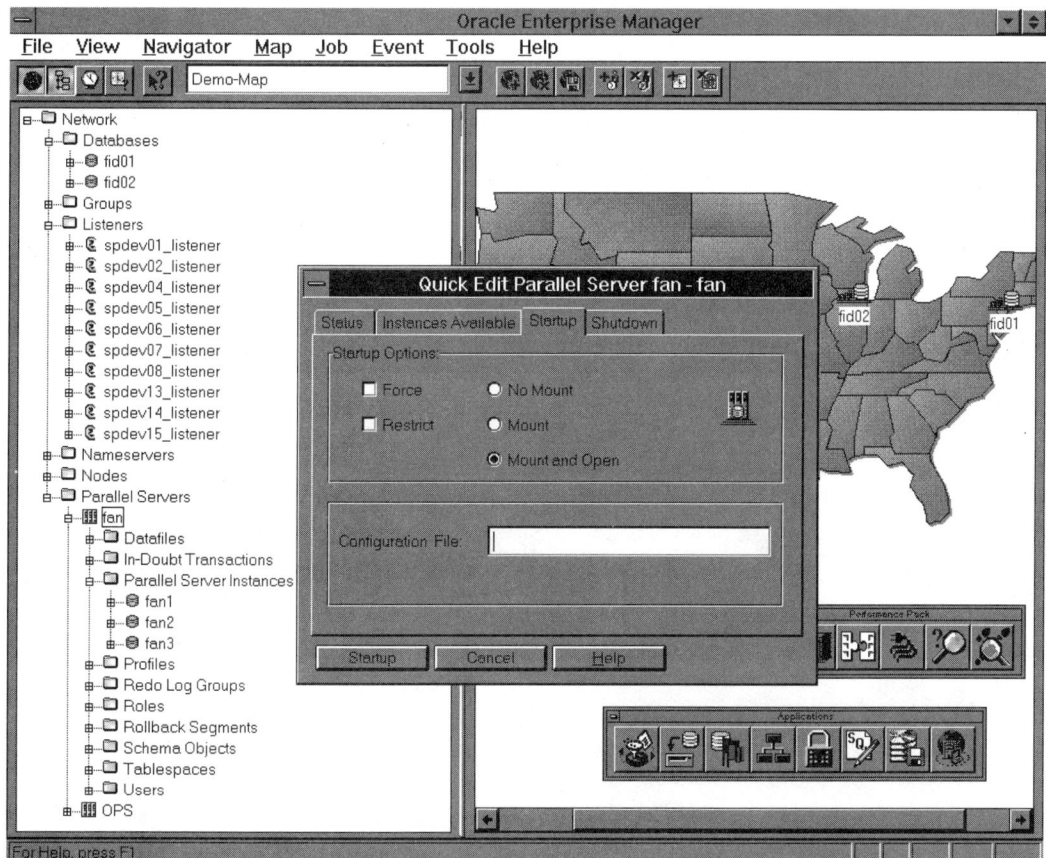

From the Oracle Enterprise Manager console, the DBAs can start up and shut down all instances of Oracle Parallel Server, or selected instances of the parallel server. Starting the instances also initiates all of the required services, such as listener and Oracle cluster services. A result box displays the progress of the instance startup or shutdown operation. In addition, the status of the various instances of the Oracle Parallel Server can be monitored from the OEM console.

Oracle Performance Monitor

The Performance Monitor, available as an applet within Oracle Enterprise Manager, is an application designed to capture, compute and present performance data that help DBAs focus on key performance metrics. There are six Oracle Parallel Server performance metrics which can be monitored by Oracle Parallel Server:

- Data block pinging displays the total block pings on the Oracle Parallel Data Server. Block pings on the individual instances or tablespaces can be obtained by drilling down further.

- Sessions Chart displays the sessions attached to the Oracle Parallel Data Server and related information such as the instance name, session id, session serial number, process ID, status, username, and lockwait.

- File IO Rate Chart shows the rate of physical reads and writes for all files in the parallel server database. Further drill downs can be performed to obtain the same information either at the instance level or file level.

Figure 12.21   Parallel Server Management: Performance Monitoring

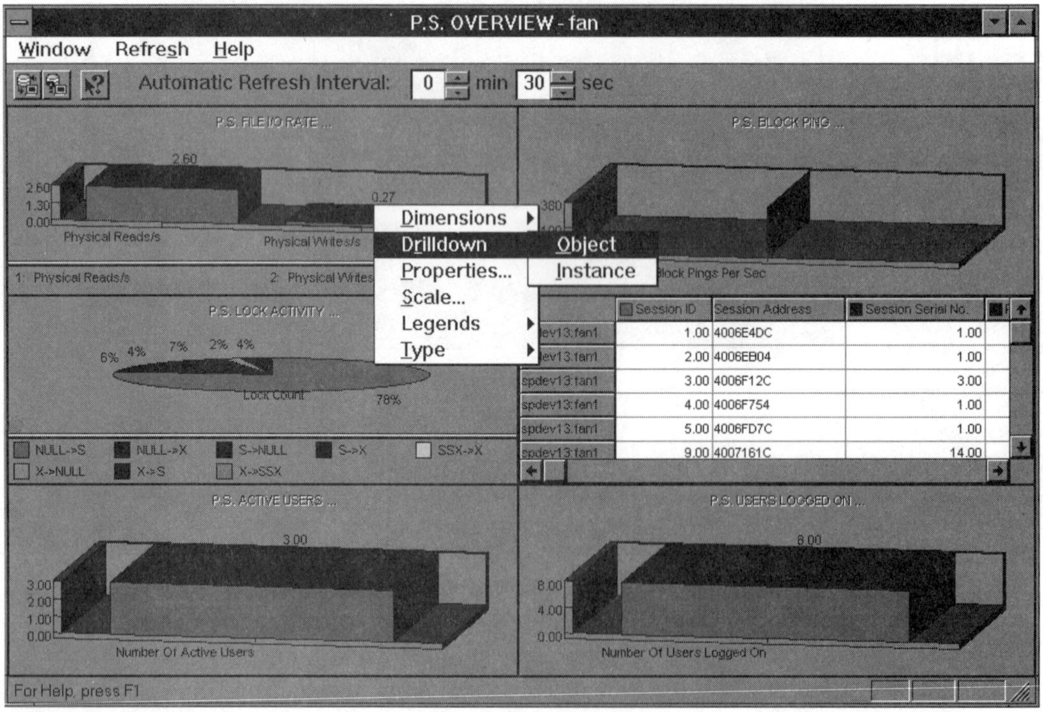

- The Lock Activity Chart displays the statistics on the lock activity rate for all of the different lock types parallel server-wide. Lock activity information for a particular lock type at the instance level can be obtained by drilling down.

- The Users Logged On Chart displays the total number of user sessions logged on to the Oracle Parallel Data Server, regardless of whether activity is generated or not. This information is also available for each instance.

- The Active Users Chart displays the total number of active users on the parallel server.

Examples of some of these charts are illustrated in Figure 12.21.

Oracle8 has two new features that make it easier to manage the Parallel Server Databases.

Global Dynamic Performance Views

Global fixed views (GV$ views) are a new Oracle8 feature designed to ease administration and monitoring in an Oracle Parallel Server environment. The database administrator can look at most statistics on the Oracle Parallel Server system centrally, from a single instance session. These views extend the current administration and tuning mechanism provided with the V$ fixed views. With the addition of GV$ fixed views in Oracle8, a database administrator can monitor dynamic performance kernel information for all the instances in the Parallel Server configuration. It is unnecessary to logon and query each node for status separately. This is particularly useful for clusters with more than two nodes. In addition, the views can be used in conjunction with the new Oracle8 feature, Instance Groups. Global fixed views are accessed using the Parallel Query feature of Oracle. Upon execution of a query against a global fixed view, Oracle allocates a single parallel query slave per instance referenced to process the query. Additional control over query processing is provided.

Instance Groups

For ease of administration in large cluster environments, different instances in a Parallel Server environment can be logically grouped together, so parallel operations can be performed upon all of the grouped instances at once. An instance group is defined as a set of instances and can be referenced as a single unit. An instance group then can be used for a specific purpose, such as one group for OLTP activity. To avoid interfering with online transactional processing (OLTP) performance, a different group could be used for large parallel tasks.

8
Oracle

In addition, instance groups give a much greater degree of control over *where* a parallel operation consumes resources. Using the dynamic parameter PARALLEL_INSTANCE_GROUP, a specific group can be used for a particular operation. Once this parameter has been set to group A, for example, all parallel operations initiated from that instance will spawn query slave processes only within the named group. For example, an administrator wants to ensure that a long-running query does not consume resources on instances dedicated to OLTP throughput. The parallel query slaves can be forced to run on a designated set of instances, instead of on the set of instances serving OLTP users.

12.6.4   Future Directions

Oracle is committed to making Oracle Parallel Server a more manageable and easy-to-use product. With this in mind, Oracle plans to address the following five areas of Oracle Parallel Server Manager.

Ease of Installation

In order to make the Oracle Parallel Server install across multiple nodes faster and error-free, OPSM will use Oracle Software Manager to distribute the Oracle Parallel Server binaries to these nodes.

Ease of Configuration

A GUI tool will be available to help the DBAs configure the Oracle Parallel Server and create the database. This tool would have a knowledge base to make recommendations for configuration based on application type, number of nodes, workload size and other parameters. Tools to provide configuration support of the disks and other hardware components are also planned.

Ease of Operation and Management

Event monitoring support for Oracle Parallel Server, a richer job menu for both Oracle Parallel Server database and instances, kernel-bound parallelized backup and restore features, and tighter integration of load balancing tools are a few of the upcoming enhancements due from Oracle.

Ease of Monitoring and Tuning

Oracle Parallel Server tuning and monitoring will be taken to the next level by providing a single-system image of Oracle Parallel Server. This will be accomplished by providing global view tables which maintain statistics pertaining to all instances of the Oracle Parallel Server. Oracle Parallel Server will be instrumented so that data can be collected and analyzed by Oracle TRACE. Similarly, Oracle Expert will contain more Oracle Parallel Server specific rules so that it is able to provide recommendations for improving Oracle Parallel Server performance.

Ease of Analysis

A slew of tools are being planned to address Capacity and Resource Planning, Performance Prediction, Resource Utilization and Accounting, and Trend Analysis and Reporting needs.

12.7   PARALLEL SERVER SOLUTIONS

12.7.1   Applications Well Suited for Using this Technology

Oracle Parallel Server works best for applications that have elements of one or more of the characteristics described below. Even if an application only partially fits into one of these categories, you can take advantage of the performance, high availability, incremental growth, ease of database administration, and ease of application development on a Windows NT cluster running the Oracle Parallel Server. Applications developed on single nodes can easily be migrated to the Windows NT cluster.

OLTP with Random Access to a Large Database

These are applications with mostly random patterns of access to a database that is significantly larger than the memory caches of the instances accessing the data. An example is a department of motor vehicles information system where individual records accessed by one node are not likely to be accessed from other nodes in the same period of time. Another example is a branch banking system where each branch usually accesses its own accounts and only occasionally accesses accounts from other branches.

In mission critical OLTP deployments in clustered environments, XA API compliance will be significant. Because the Oracle lock manager is session based, the XA interface can be integrated with the OPS environment. Today this is the case with UNIX cluster systems in many large customer OLTP deployments around the world. At these sites, TP monitors play an important role with OPS. On those platforms, TP monitors such as Tuxedo (from BEA Systems) or Encina (from IBM) can access Oracle Parallel Server databases through the XA interface. The XA interface has been enabled for the Oracle Server on Windows NT since the March 1997 release of v7.3.3.0.

Departmentalized

These are applications that primarily modify different tables in the same database. An example is a system where one node is dedicated to inventory processing, another is dedicated to personnel processing and a third is dedicated to sales processing. In this system data sharing between nodes exists, but is limited. Note that there is only one database to administer.

Collaborative Applications

The collaborative services of Oracle InterOffice – messaging, directory services, calendar maintenance/scheduling, workflow and document management – are based on scalable, reliable relational database technology which enables you to share, exchange, and manage information productively. In the near future, Oracle InterOffice will take full advantage of the scalability and high availability features of Oracle Parallel Server on Windows NT and ensure business-critical transaction processing in a clustered environment.

Data Warehousing Systems

These are applications with low data update contention and make up a rapidly growing market for Windows NT. An example is a database of financial transactions that is queried throughout the day, and has new data added to it but once a day. In this area, scalability is the key factor. Oracle Parallel Server with Windows NT clustering is ideal for data warehousing environments.

12.7.2   Oracle8 Transparent Application Failover for High Availability

Oracle8 provides additional capability for application failover support which is transparent to the users on the system. Oracle8 allows reconnection to a surviving node, minimizing loss of application work and providing higher availability of the data. Previously, a loss of a node or the instance running on that node caused all the user connections to fail. But the Oracle8 failover feature connects the user to the same session on the surviving node, allowing him or her to continue working without having to reconnect.

Significant processing time and costs can be saved on queries using the failover feature. A query running at the time of the failure is automatically restarted on the new node, *at the point where it failed.* The query does not need to be restarted from the beginning. Any update activity occurring at the time of the failure will be aborted and rolled back automatically, using normal Oracle process failure mechanisms. The user will receive an abort message, but then will be able to reissue the update and have it run on the reconnected node. The new session on the surviving node has all the appearances of the previous session and maintains the same state. These unplanned failures are handled automatically with minimal impact on the users.

12.8 PERFORMANCE HINTS

The following are some hints for DBAs trying to optimize Oracle8 Parallel Data Server installations.

12.8.1 Reverse Key Indexes Minimize Pinging

8
Oracle

Reverse key indexes are another new feature of Oracle8 that dramatically improves performance in Parallel Server configurations. When inserting records on an ascending key, IO bottlenecks can occur on the index block update because all index updates occur at the same place in the index tree. Also, performance can be adversely affected by block "pinging", when two instances encounter contention while repeatedly trying to update the same index block. Reverse key indexes in Oracle8 spread the distribution of index updates across the index tree by reversing the data value of the index key. For example, on insert of order 123, the index is updated for order number 321 in a reverse key index. The system still knows to get index key 123 when requested, but the actual update to the index block is for the entry 321. As the next order 124 comes in, the index entry then goes into the entry for 421, thereby spreading the work load across multiple index blocks.

12.8.2 Performance Gains with Disk Affinity

Disk affinity is further enhanced in Oracle8, providing performance improvements. Partition-to-node affinity information determines slave allocation and work assignments, creating a deterministic assignment of partitions to Oracle instances. For parallel Data Manipulation Language (DML), this assignment of partitions results in an increased likelihood of buffer cache hits. For shared nothing Massively Parallel Processing (MPP) systems, the Oracle Parallel Server assigns slave processes to partitions by instance, taking the disk affinity into account. Affinity information that persists across transaction statements improves buffer cache hit ratios and reduces block pings between instances.

12.8.3   Dynamic Control of DML Locking

To improve performance in the Oracle Parallel Server environment, DML locking on selected tables can be turned off with the command

```
ALTER TABLE DISABLE TABLE LOCK
```

This command disables both table and partition-level DML locks, and bypasses extra traffic away from the Integrated DML, which provides a performance benefit. DDL statements are not allowed on the selected tables when DML locking is disabled.

12.8.4   Load Balancing

Load balancing also can be accomplished by disconnecting users from an overloaded node and allowing the failover mechanism to migrate the sessions to another node with more capacity. Therefore, the administrator can maintain 100 percent availability across instances. If one instance is overloaded, the administrator can manually disconnect sessions using the command

```
ALTER SYSTEM DISCONNECT SESSION "SID,SERIAL#"
POST_TRANSACTION
```

This command allows users to complete their transactions before disconnecting and migrating the session to the failover node. This mode guarantees there is no transaction running at the time of the failover, so there is no loss of transactional activity or service. The database administrator controls which node to send the failover to, and in what manner.

12.8.5   Planned Maintenance

The failover feature is also useful for planned maintenance activities. When the database administrator is planning an instance shutdown for maintenance purposes, users can be moved to other nodes in an orderly and nondisruptive manner. The users experience no interruption in service.

8
Oracle

Oracle8 provides a Shutdown Transactional command when the instance needs to be taken down for scheduled maintenance. For example, an administrator needs to take down one instance of a four-node Oracle Parallel Server configuration for maintenance purposes. The administrator would issue shutdown transactions [time-out], which gives clients a specified length of time to finish transactions. Subsequent transaction activity will be executed on the failover node. By automatically reconnecting to a failover instance, the clients continue to operate with no loss of work while their original instance is shut down.

When the last transaction is complete on the primary instance, a SHUTDOWN IMMEDIATE is performed.

12.8.6 Improved Availability with Incremental Checkpoints

Incremental checkpointing is a new feature available in Oracle8 that improves the performance (duration and number of IOs) of instance recovery, thereby providing higher availability of the data for both Oracle Fail Safe and Oracle Parallel Server. Recovery performance is roughly proportional to the number of data buffers that were updated but not yet written to disk (dirty buffers) prior to the failure. The user has the ability to influence the performance of instance recovery by setting the initialization parameter DB_BLOCK_MAX_ DIRTY_TARGET. This parameter specifies an upper bound on the number of dirty buffers that can be present in the buffer cache of an instance at any moment in time. Thus, it is possible to influence recovery time for situations where the buffer cache is very large and/or where there are stringent requirements on the duration of instance recovery.

12.9 SUMMARY

Oracle's leadership database solutions, Oracle Fail Safe Data Server and Oracle Parallel Data Server, for clustered computing architectures have evolved since 1987 and are now available for the NT clustered computing environments. Oracle Parallel Server was first introduced for Digital OpenVMS platforms in 1987 and Oracle Fail Safe for the UNIX platforms in 1992. NT customers could chose Oracle Fail Safe if they need high availability for their single-node database used in a partitioned workload or partitioned database scenarios. If the customer needs scalability for a single database beyond one cluster node, Oracle Parallel Server is recommended. Oracle recommends either RAID or disk mirroring solutions to minimize the effect of a disk failure for the clustered database solutions.

Oracle Fail Safe

Oracle Fail Safe Data Server is a highly available single-instance database, is easy to use and a robust database solution layered on Microsoft Cluster Server. Oracle Fail Safe Data Server works with Oracle7 and Oracle8 data servers. Oracle system management framework, Oracle Enterprise Manager, is augmented by Oracle Fail Safe Manager on the client side and by Oracle Fail Safe Data Server and Fail Safe Intelligent agents on the cluster nodes. Oracle

Fail Safe Manager has built-in wizards, dialog boxes, default setting to help you configure, manager, load-balance and trouble-shoot Fail Safe database solutions. Oracle Fail Safe Data Server works with Microsoft Cluster Server (MSCS) to atomically replicate the configuration of Oracle databases, ensure that the database fails over during all outages and that failover time is optimized based on the database workload.

Sites are using Oracle Fail Safe solutions in three configurations:

- partitioned workload
- partitioned databases
- standby

Most of the Enterprise Resource Planning (ERP) solution vendors, SAP, BAAN, PeopleSoft, Oracle Applications, etc. are deploying Fail Safe solutions using the partitioned workload model. The cluster configuration these customers are deploying is based on the customer needs and the budget.

Oracle Fail Safe database solution is part of the Fail Safe solutions products Oracle is developing for various customer needs where high availability, ease of use and robustness are key requirements.

Oracle Parallel Server

Oracle Parallel Server is a highly available multi-instance, scalable and mature database solution for the NT Clusters. It is layered on the "Shared Disk" clustering technology provided by VAR partners. All the cluster nodes in the Parallel Server solution are connected to the shared pool of database disks and have concurrent read and write access to the data located on these shared disks. For system management, the Oracle Enterprise Manager framework is augmented for managing and tuning of Parallel Server database solutions.

Oracle Parallel Server has a robust integrated Distributed Lock Manager (DLM), Parallel Cache Management (PCM) technology. DLM allows all the parallel server instances across the cluster to access the same database. If one instance needs to update data modified in another instance's buffer cache, the DLM instructs the second instance to write the data to disk so that the first instance may access the same data buffer. Oracle Parallel Data Server optimizes parallel cache management and internal concurrency control features to minimize the communication overhead between the cluster nodes and maximize the performance of each cluster node.

Oracle Fail Safe Data Server and Oracle Parallel Data Server for Oracle8 continue to expand Oracle's proven lead in the NT Clusters market. Many

OCI client applications, for example, will find that the transparent application failover feature (automatic reconnection feature) now makes errors during failover transparent to end-users. Similarly , the incremental checkpointing feature optimizes the failover timings. The new features add dramatic improvements to ease of use, availability, performance, and scalability.

13   Using Objects

8

Oracle

In this chapter we will learn how we can use and create objects in an Oracle8 database. The objects option is new for Oracle8 and in coming years this is a technology that is going to grow in popularity and usage.

13.1   WHY USE OBJECTS?

For anyone who has been in this industry for some time, it will come as no surprise that databases have evolved just like many other technologies in our industry. Back in the 1970s it was all the rage to use a network or hierarchical database. Then in the 1980s, databases based on the relational model became very popular. Today, many users of databases can probably be excused for thinking that the only type of database is relational, because this is the one that is receiving all the attention.

Followers of database technology will know that for some time, a new type of database, based on the object model has been purported to be the basis for the next generation of database systems. The uptake on object databases is very slow, probably because most people don't understand what they offer and since relational databases are tried and trusted technology, they prefer to use a technology that will support their business.

With the release of Oracle8, Oracle has provided an attractive solution to this problem by offering an *Object Option* to the Oracle8 server. By adding this option, a relational database is turned into an Object-Relational Database, thus providing the best of both worlds. The user retains all the benefits of a relational system and enhances it with object extensions.

The attraction of using objects is that the database can be extended to support new datatypes that describe not only the structure of the data, but also the actions that may be performed on this data. In the object world, these actions are called methods, therefore an *object datatype* will consist of:

- attributes and
- methods.

343

Another advantage for the application developer is that by defining an object, the complexities involved in managing that object can be hidden inside the object definition. This is very useful in the business world where some complex operations are often required to complete certain tasks. When objects are used with an object-oriented programming language, improved application development time is possible.

Finally, another factor to consider is that as we move into the information age, information is no longer numbers and text. Today, we expect to see what is known as complex data such as video, audio and images. Relational databases were never designed to hold and manage this types of information, whereas object databases are ideally suited for managing this data.

Take a look at any web site today. It includes pictures that one would normally see in a catalog, video of an interview or product being used and audio welcome messages or company announcements. Wouldn't it be nice to hold all this information in the corporate database?

In order to extend the Oracle8 database into an object relational database, the following functionality has been provided:

- Object Types   create your own object types

- Object Views   create a view that comprises existing relational data and use the object extensions against relational data

- Object Extensions both SQL and PL/SQL have been modified to support objects

- Program Interfaces object support is provided in Pro*C, Pro*COBOL, PL/SQL and Oracle's OCI.

We will now look at the various types of objects we can create using the Objects option in the Oracle8 server.

13.2   OBJECT TYPES

There are many definitions of what an object is, but this is how it is defined for the Oracle server. An *object type* is a schema object that consists of:

- a *name*   which identifies the object;

- *attributes*   such as those defined for a table. One can think of an object attribute exactly the same way as you do for a column in a relational table;

- *methods* which are functions or procedures written in PL/SQL and stored in the database or they can be written in languages like C and held externally.

The first step in using an object in Oracle8 is to create an *object type*. The attributes which comprise the object are defined using either the built-in datatypes or the user-defined ones. The built-in datatypes provided include all the Oracle7 datatypes plus the following new ones:

- BLOB   binary large object
- CLOB   character large object
- BFILE   binary large file object
- NCLOB   fixed-width multibyte character large object
- VARRAY   varying array
- TABLE   nested table
- REF   reference

Object types are created and managed using the SQL extensions, CREATE TYPE, DROP TYPE, ALTER TYPE and GRANK/REVOKE TYPE. In Oracle 8.0.3 they cannot be created and managed using Oracle Schema Manager, but SQL Worksheet does accept this new syntax.

Hint: Maintain script files which define these object types.

13.2.1   Create an Object Type

Below we can see how to create a very simple object type called *client_name*. This object type has three attributes, title, first_name and surname, and its purpose is to describe how a client is named.

```
CREATE TYPE client_name AS OBJECT
  ( title         VARCHAR2(4),
    first_name    VARCHAR2(20),
    surname       VARCHAR2(20) ) ;
```

When we look at this definition, it looks almost identical to a table definition except for the AS OBJECT clause.

13.2.2   Create a Table Using an Object Type

We can now use this object type in the definition of a relational table. Suppose we want to create a table called PERSON that contains only a person's name and their unique id.

```
CREATE TABLE person
  ( person_id   CHAR(8) PRIMARY KEY,
    person_name client_name );
```

The definition of the person's name is based on the client_name object type, but looking at the definition this is not immediately apparent. Therefore one should consider using a naming convention to denote object types, such as _t.

Data is inserted into the table using the SQL INSERT clause, but when it comes to the object, its name must be defined and the values enclosed within brackets. This is illustrated below, where the object type client_name is populated with the value of Dr. Lilian Hobbs.

```
INSERT INTO person VALUES
('Lilian', client_name('Dr.','Lilian','Hobbs') );
```

13.2.3   Retrieving Data Held Within an Object

To retrieve data that is inside an object, using the following SQL statement will result in an error because one of the items to be retrieved is an object type.

```
SQLWKS> SELECT * FROM person;
ORA-00932: inconsistent datatypes
```

Object types have their own naming convention and must be referenced using the format:

```
alias.column name.object attribute
```

to retrieve the title of a person in our table. If we use the alias *p* on the table, then to return the title column we must specify:

```
p.person_name.title
```

The following SQL statements retrieve the persons id, title and surname.

```
SELECT person_id,
p.person_name.title, p.person_name.surname
  FROM person p;

PERSON_ID PERS PERSON_NAME.SURNAME
--------- ---- -------------------
Lilian    Dr   Hobbs
1 row selected.
```

13.2.4   Create an Object Type Based on Another Object

Object types can also be created using other objects that have been defined. Suppose we want to identify vice presidents from our list of people. This can be achieved by creating a VP object type that uses the CLIENT_NAME object type as shown below.

```
CREATE TYPE vp AS OBJECT
   ( company          VARCHAR2(30),
     vp_of_group      VARCHAR2(25),
     vp_name          REF client_name );
```

This is the first time we have seen the REF datatype in use. This clause defines the relationship between objects, which currently must be one-to-one. In this example we have created a relationship between the object *vp_name* and the object *client_name*.

13.2.5   Create an Object Table

An object table is a special type of table that allows objects to be viewed like a relational table. In the example below, a table called PERSON_TAB has been created based on the object type CLIENT_NAME which we defined in 13.2.1.

```
CREATE TABLE person_tab OF client_name;
```

Values are inserted into the table as usual as shown below.

```
INSERT INTO person_tab VALUES
('Mr','Mark','Large');
```

They can then be selected either requesting the entire contents of the row as shown here:

```
SELECT * FROM person_tab;

TITLE FIRST_NAME               SURNAME
----- -------------------      -------
Mr    Mark                     Large
1 row selected.
```

or individual columns can be displayed such as title and surname:

```
SELECT p.title, p.surname FROM person_tab p ;
TITLE SURNAME
----- -------
Mr    Large
1 row selected.
```

13.2.6   Using a Varying-Length Array

One datatype that doesn't exist in a relational database is the array. It is a commonly used datatype in application programs, but when it comes to the database, DBA's have devised elaborate techniques to overcome this missing datatype. Anyone who understands the relational model, realises that to include an array is heretic, but unfortunately, in the real world, there are some very useful data structures, and the array is one of them.

One of the datatypes supplied with the Objects option is the VARRAY which is defined as an ordered set of elements that comprises:

- a count of the number of elements in the array, and
- the maximum number of elements the array may contain.

By storing information using a VARRAY, the position of the information in the array is guaranteed and you can refer to explicit positions in the array. In the following example of a customer's telephone numbers, we always store the mobile number in position 2 in the array and the land line number in position 1.

To create the array, the first step is to define the attributes of the array. Here we have chosen two, a phone number and an indicator denoting the type of phone number, although we could omit the phone type if we guarantee to always use the correct location.

```
CREATE TYPE phone_number AS OBJECT
  ( phone_no    VARCHAR2(12),
    phone_type  CHAR(1) );
```

Next we define the object type as a VARRAY and here we must specify the exact size of the array, which in this example is 6 elements. Therefore we can store up to 6 telephone numbers for any one customer.

```
CREATE TYPE all_phones AS VARRAY(6) OF phone_number;
```

Now we can define the object type where we include the VARRAY in the definition of the object. Here we have added the customers reference number and name.

```
CREATE TYPE cust_phones AS OBJECT
  ( customer_no   VARCHAR2(8),
    cust_name     VARCHAR2(20),
    phone_nos     all_phones);
```

Creating the table is the next step.

```
CREATE TABLE customer_phone_numbers OF cust_phones;
```

With the table created we can insert data into the table. Note how we have to reference each of the pieces in the array. The format is

varray object name (object name of the object type in the array)

which in this example is *all_phones(phone_number)*

```
INSERT INTO customer_phone_numbers VALUES
  ('LILIAN','Lilian Hobbs',
    all_phones(phone_number ('441344123456','L'),
        phone_number ('44385123456','M')
      )
  );
```

In figure 13.1 we see how the data in the array can be displayed using PL/SQL. Note that each element in the array is referenced before the individual column, that is *phone_details(1).phone_no.* In this example we retrieve the entire array into the structure called phone_details. Then we extract the individual components of each element from the array.

Figure 13.1 Display Data in VARRAY

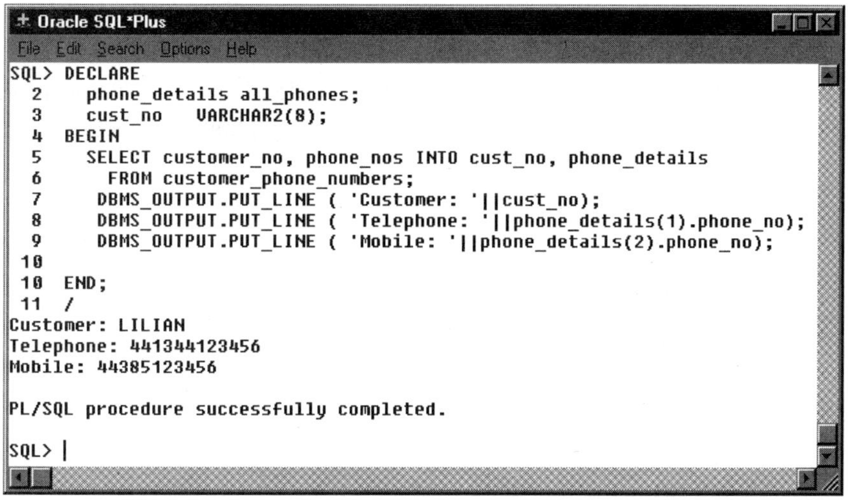

```
± Oracle SQL*Plus                                              _ □ ×
 File  Edit  Search  Options  Help
SQL> DECLARE
  2      phone_details all_phones;
  3      cust_no    VARCHAR2(8);
  4  BEGIN
  5    SELECT customer_no, phone_nos INTO cust_no, phone_details
  6      FROM customer_phone_numbers;
  7      DBMS_OUTPUT.PUT_LINE ( 'Customer: '||cust_no);
  8      DBMS_OUTPUT.PUT_LINE ( 'Telephone: '||phone_details(1).phone_no);
  9      DBMS_OUTPUT.PUT_LINE ( 'Mobile: '||phone_details(2).phone_no);
 10
 10  END;
 11  /
Customer: LILIAN
Telephone: 441344123456
Mobile: 44385123456

PL/SQL procedure successfully completed.

SQL> |
```

13.2.7   Nested Tables

The VARRAY datatype can be extremely useful, but it does impose the restriction that only a finite number of elements can be stored. As we all know, the real world is not like that; for example, an order could consist of one line or twenty lines. Therefore nested tables are ideal to use when:

- mapping a one-to-many relationship,
- an unordered list is needed,

- there is no maximum upper limit on the number of entries,
- access to line items rather than the entire structure is required,
- support for indexes is required.

Now we will see how to create the list of customer phone numbers using a nested table rather than a **VARRAY** datatype.

First create the object type which describes a single line in the nested table.

```
CREATE TYPE phone_number AS OBJECT
  ( phone_no    VARCHAR2(12),
    phone_type  CHAR(1) );
```

Now create an object type that defines a table based on the previous object type.

```
CREATE TYPE all_phones AS TABLE OF phone_number;
```

Create the table using the clause **NESTED TABLE**.

```
CREATE TABLE cust_phones
  ( customer_no    VARCHAR2(8),
    cust_name      VARCHAR2(20),
    phone_nos      all_phones)
    NESTED TABLE phone_nos
      STORE AS all_phones_nst;
```

Insert data into the table. The first example places null values in the nested table and the second example inserts two telephone numbers.

```
INSERT INTO cust_phones VALUES
('LILIAN','Lilian Hobbs',
   all_phones ());

INSERT INTO cust_phones VALUES
('LILIAN','Lilian Hobbs',
   all_phones(phone_number ('441344123456','L') ,
       phone_number ('44385123456','M')
));
```

13.2.8   Object Views

Anyone who has ever built a relational database will know that views are extremely useful because they allow you to view complex data simply, and see only a subset of data rather than the entire table.

Therefore it should come as no surprise that we can also create views in the object world, and here they are called *object views*. In the relational world we talk about a view being a virtual table, that is, a view of one or more tables that don't physically exist. An object view is another virtual object, which allows you to view relational and object data together. The benefits of using object views are:

- you can try object-oriented techniques without converting tables,
- they provide a mechanism for slowly converting data from relational to object,
- they provide the ability to use a relational database with an object-oriented application.

Creating an object view is not very difficult. First define a table (normally this would already exist).

```
CREATE TABLE order_header
  (order_number    CHAR(10),
   order_date      DATE,
   order_value     NUMBER(8,2),
   order_location  VARCHAR2(4) );
```

Next create a TYPE that matches the layout of the table.

```
CREATE TYPE   order_header_t AS OBJECT
  (order_number    CHAR(10),
   order_date      DATE,
   order_value     NUMBER(8,2),
   order_location  VARCHAR2(4) );
```

Now create the actual view using the type definition defined previously. Every row returned by the view must have a unique identifier selected from the available columns. Here we have chosen *order_number* because we know it will be unique.

```
CREATE VIEW order_view OF order_header_t
  WITH OBJECT OID(order_number)   AS
    SELECT o.order_number, o.order_date,
       o.order_value, o.order_location
    FROM order_header o;
```

The information can now be retrieved from the database as if it were an ordinary view using an SQL SELECT statement, or modified, deleted or data inserted into using the SQL statements UPDATE, INSERT and DELETE.

Since we are working with views, the rule that the data in a view cannot be updated if the view contains a join still applies. However, this problem can be overcome by using an INSTEAD OF trigger.

The first example was a simple one referencing only one table, but object views can involve many tables provided the object type matches the layout of the view. In the following example, information is extracted from two tables and included in a type definition called *customer_order_t*.

```
CREATE TYPE   customer_order_t AS OBJECT
   (order_number     CHAR(10),
    order_date       DATE,
    order_value      NUMBER(8,2),
    cust_no          CHAR(10),
    cust_name        varchar2(30)   );
```

Now define the view referring to the two tables. Note how the unique object id is defined using the unique identifier from each of the tables.

```
CREATE VIEW cust_order_view OF customer_order_t
   WITH OBJECT OID (order_number, cust_no) AS
      SELECT o.order_number,   o.order_date,
         o.value, c.customer_no, c.cust_name
      FROM   orders_in o, customer c
      WHERE c.customer_no = o.customer_no;
```

13.3   METHODS

Although not a mandatory component when an object type is created, defining methods for an object is when the real benefits of using objects start to be realized. A method is defined using the MEMBER clause in a CREATE TYPE definition, where a method can be a function or a procedure and it must return a value.

To define a method, first the CREATE TYPE statement defines the object type and names the methods. In the example shown below we are going to create a method called *get_name*.

```
CREATE TYPE client_name2 AS OBJECT
   ( title           VARCHAR2(4),
     first_name      VARCHAR2(20),
     surname         VARCHAR2(20),
     MEMBER PROCEDURE get_name ) ;
```

Next the body of the object type is defined using the CREATE TYPE BODY clause, and this is where the methods are actually described. In the example shown here, the procedure GET_NAME performs the task of joining the title, first name and surname together into a single string.

```
CREATE TYPE BODY client_name2
   AS
      MEMBER PROCEDURE get_name   IS
         full_name   VARCHAR2(47);
BEGIN
   full_name := title||' '||first_name||' '||surname;
```

```
END get_name;
END;
```

Next a table is created using this object type, here we have created a name called PERSONS.

```
CREATE TABLE persons OF client_name2;
```

Now data can be inserted into the table, as we have seen previously.

```
INSERT INTO persons VALUES ('Mr','Mark','Large');
```

Finally, we can invoke the method GET_NAME by calling it inside a PL/SQL block as shown in figure 13.2. We begin by using the DECLARE clause to define two variables, *which_person* establishes which object we are looking at and *your_name* is used to return the result from the method. The actual procedure commences with the BEGIN clause where we establish which row in the table we require. In this example there is only one row, but normally we would require a WHERE clause to restrict the selection. We then use the variable *which_person* as part of the method invocation. The method is invoked as *which_person.get_name*. The package DBMS_OUTPUT.PUT_LINE is used so that we can see the results of the method.

Hint: Don't forget to SET SERVEROUTPUT ON; to see the output from DBMS_OUTPUT.PUT_LINE.

Hopefully, now you can start to appreciate the benefits of using methods with object types.

Figure 13.2 Calling a Method

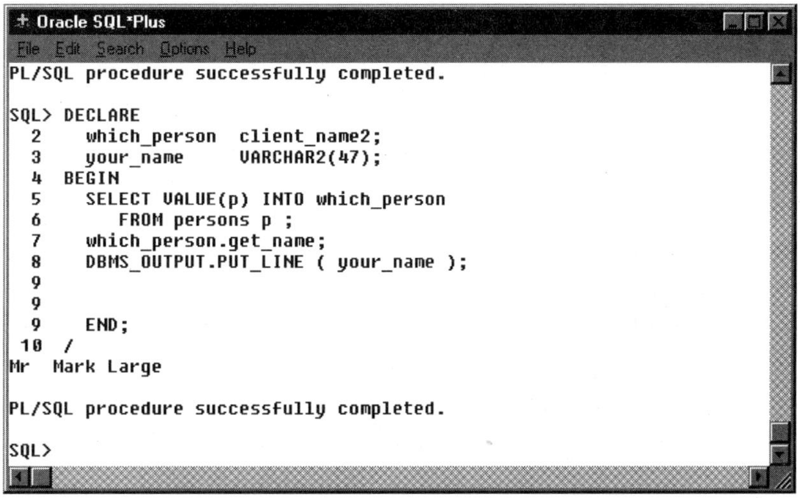

Since these methods are updating the database, there is an optional clause PRAGMA RESTRICT_REFERENCES, which states how you can access the database. The qualifiers are:

- WNDS   does not modify database tables
- RNDS   does not query database tables
- WNPS   does not modify variables in the package
- RNPS   does not reference package variables

In the example here we state that the method get_name may not write to any database tables.

```
CREATE TYPE client_name2 AS OBJECT
      ( title          VARCHAR2(4),
        first_name     VARCHAR2(20),
        surname      VARCHAR2(20),
        MEMBER PROCEDURE get_name,
   PRAGMA RESTRICT_REFERENCES (get_name, WNDS ) ) ;
```

13.4   OTHER DATABASE DESIGN ISSUES

Just because a table is defined using object types doesn't mean that you can't apply normal database design techniques to it, therefore you can create indexes and constraints.

For example, in the previous section we defined a table called *persons* from the object type client_name2. To improve performance we can create an index on table persons, on the data item surname, as shown below.

```
CREATE INDEX person_idx ON persons
   (surname);
```

13.5   LARGE OBJECTS

At the beginning of this chapter one of the reasons we gave for using an object-oriented database was to store and manipulate unusual datatypes such as video and sound. Prior to Oracle8, this type of information could be stored in the LONG and LONG RAW datatype, but this datatype imposed a number of restrictions.

Defining a large object, which is called a LOB, means that you can store and manipulate LOBs up to 4gb, which is a 100% improvement on the 2gb limit of the RAW datatype. Another significant difference is that a LOB can be:

- internal, that is stored in the database, or
- external, stored outside of the database.

13.5.1   Internal LOBs

Three different types of LOBs can be stored inside the database:

- BLOB is used for unstructured data such as image and video.
- CLOB is used for single-byte character data such as a recipe.
- NCLOB is a fixed-width multibyte character using the national character set that has been defined for the database.

Creating a table that uses a LOB requires no new syntax because you simply specify this datatype as shown below. Here we have defined a table where we store our welcome messages for our system for each week.

```
CREATE TABLE welcome
   ( message      VARCHAR2(50),
     for_week     INTEGER,
     mess_video   BLOB );
```

However, due to the size of these files, we probably don't want to store them with the other data in the table. We can store the LOB separately from the data by using a storage clause such as the one shown here.

```
CREATE TABLE welcome
   ( message      VARCHAR2(50),
     for_week     INTEGER,
     mess_video   BLOB )
     LOB (mess_video)
        STORE AS (TABLESPACE videos
           STORAGE   (INITIAL 1M NEXT 64K) ) ;
```

It is not uncommon to store the data in a separate tablespace and note how we can define the storage options for the individual LOB.

13.5.2   External LOBs

Including LOBs in a database can suddenly cause the size of your database to increase significantly. While it may seem attractive to store all the data in one place, there are some management problems associated with this approach. A major one to consider is the time required to backup and restore the database. Without the LOBs the database may be backed up in a matter of minutes, but include the LOBs and we could be looking at an hour or more.

A very useful feature is the ability to define an external LOB as a BFILE datatype, where the actual contents of the LOB are held outside of the database. All that is held in the database is the location of the LOB in the Operating System.

Before any external LOB can be stored, an alias must be created that points to the directory on disk where the file is held. This is achieved by using the **CREATE DIRECTORY** command.

In the example below we create a directory called web_video which points to a location on the NT system where we store all our video files.

```
CREATE DIRECTORY web_video AS
  'd:\web_page';
```

Now we create a table that includes a BFILE datatype

```
CREATE TABLE web_pictures
   ( description    VARCHAR2(30),
     date_used      DATE,
     web_pict       BFILE);
```

Information is inserted into the table using the normal INSERT clause, the only difference is we have to use the BFILENAME clause to pass in the directory location and the name of the file.

```
INSERT INTO web_pictures VALUES
   ( 'China Holiday','23-NOV-1996',
     BFILENAME('web_video','gt_wall.jpg') );
```

In the example above, BFILENAME requires two parameters. The first is *web_video* which is the name of the directory we have created that advises where the external file is located. The second parameter is *gt_wall.jpg*, which is the name of the external file.

13.5.3   Manipulating LOBs

One of the major benefits of using LOBs is the ease with which they can be managed and various methods are available:

- a package called DBMS_LOB
- PL/SQL
- OCI

The DBMS_LOB package contains a very extensive range of routines to facilitate easy management, such as COPY and APPEND, and then there are routines like GETLENGTH (shown in the following example) where we can extract the size of the object.

```
DECLARE
   image          BFILE;
   image_no       INTEGER := 101;

BEGIN
   SELECT web_pict INTO image FROM web_pictures
     WHERE description = 'China Holiday';
   DBMS_OUTPUT.PUT_LINE('Size of the Image is: ' ||
     DBMS_LOB.GETLENGTH(image));
END;
```

Some very useful functions are also provided, including EMPTY_BLOB and EMPTY_CLOB which enable you to define an object as currently being empty. For example, here we are inserting data into the table called welcome but saying that the blob data is empty so that we can return later to store it.

```
INSERT INTO welcome VALUES
   ('Sign On', 1, EMPTY_BLOB() );
```

There is also an extensive range of calls available from within OCI to manipulate these LOBs. It is recommended that the Oracle documentation be consulted for more information on using this approach.

13.6   SUMMARY

This short introduction to objects in Oracle8 is intended to provide the reader with an appreciation of how this new feature can be used. Once fully understood, there are endless possibilities as to how this new technology can be used within your business. As with anything new, take it slowly and understand how to use it using a simple example and then try something more ambitious. This is one occasion where you do not want to jump in at the deep end. Start at the shallow end and then you will wonder why it has taken so long for objects to be added to relational databases.

14 The Future

Anyone working in the IT industry cannot say they have a profession where nothing new happens. We work in an industry where what is popular today is either even more popular in a few years, gone forever or remembered as one of those passing fads.

There was a time when COBOL programming was all the rage and no one had ever thought of writing a Web-based application, but that was yesterday. Today, there are some exciting new developments taking place that are changing the way we work and do business.

The Windows NT Operating System from Microsoft is one of those very interesting new areas. It is not often that an operating system captivates the industry, but NT has everyone looking at it. Many organizations are deploying some of their new systems on NT to see its suitability for production and critical applications. It is one of the most rapidly growing sectors in the industry, so anyone deploying NT systems is definitely moving in the popular, cutting-edge world.

To be successful, these applications need a good development environment and usually a database. The number of players in the database market has changed considerably in recent years, leaving only a few well known products to choose from.

The Oracle Corporation has taken its very popular and sophisticated database product and released it on NT. Hopefully, this book has illustrated how powerful this product is, offering an extremely comprehensive range of features to support your business.

When you choose to base your system around the Oracle database you are already using a sophisticated tool. The good news is that although the Oracle database has only recently become available on NT, the Oracle database is continually evolving and when new features are introduced they are usually available on NT.

Throughout this book we have never really discussed the types of applications suitable for the Oracle database on NT. This topic has been deliberately omitted because you will probably be quite surprised at how capable an NT system can be, especially when we include features like Oracle Fail Safe.

An Oracle database on NT can be used for online ordering, it is ideal for Web-based applications and, using the Oracle Data Mart suite, it would feel quite at home managing a data mart or data warehouse.

Building a data warehouse or data mart on NT is proving a popular choice with many organizations and many of the features in the Oracle database are ideally suited to solving and managing data warehouses. The Data Mart Suite from Oracle which uses the Oracle database provides all the tools you need to create, manage and query a data mart.

Most NT systems are part of a network and we have seen the distributed capabilities of the Oracle database which facilitate easy distribution of data around the organization. It is quite likely that there will be many NT servers in the system, all holding their own copies of data, so let the Oracle server manage that data.

Relational technology has been with us since the 80s and the introduction of object-oriented programming tools means that developers would like to use those concepts in a database. The objects option in the Oracle database now means that we can create an object-relational database. Since this is a new feature in Oracle8, this is definitely an area to watch for new developments.

So what does the future hold for the Oracle database on NT? Well, the future looks very bright indeed. The number of NT systems around the world is growing rapidly. There is a wide selection of tools available to develop your application. The Oracle database is a sophisticated product with rich functionality and this book is based on version 8.0.3, the first release of many for the Oracle database on NT.

Index

Other Books from Digital-Press

A Complete Guide to Lotus Notes 4.5 by Simon Collin
1997   450pp   pb   1-55558-175-7

Local Area Networks, Second Edition by John McNamara
1996   200pp   pb   1-55558-149-8

Microsoft Exchange Server V5.0: Planning, Design, and Implementation
by Tony Redmond
1997   728pp   pb   1-55558-189-7

Migrating to the Intranet and Microsoft Exchange by Randall J. Covill
1997 250pp   pb   1-55558-172-2

The SQL Server 6.5: Performance Optimization and Tuning Handbook
by Ken England
1997   250pp   pb   1-55558-180-3

TCP/IP Explained by Philip Miller
1996   450pp   pb   1-55558-166-8

Visual Basic for Network Applications by Simon Collin
1997   250pp   pb   1-55558-173-0

. . . .

Feel free to visit our web site at: http://www.bh.com/digitalpress

These books are available from all good bookstores or in case of difficulty call:
1-800-366-2665 in the U.S. or +44-1865-310366 in Europe.

E-Mail Mailing List

An e-mail mailing list giving information on latest releases, special promotions, offers and other news relating to Digital Press titles is available. To subscribe, send an e-mail message to majordomo@world.std.com.
Include in message body (not in subject line): subscribe digital-press